continued from the front flap

the future in an implicit plea for improved
social justice in and through education. It is
not a book to make readers angry: it is a
book to make them *think*, and by thinking
to develop moral attitudes and values that
might lead to the will to moral action–
action that is controlled, clear in understanding of purposes, constructive and
responsible.

As a book of ideas it provides much material
for discussion both by students and by their
teachers. Far from any presumption of
finality, it is a challenge to others to
demonstrate and defend ethical views in
education or elsewhere which may conflict
with the author's own.

———————

Les Brown was Professor of Education at
the University of New South Wales and
Head of School until his retirement in 1978.
He began his career as a high school teacher
(1935–39) and then from 1940 served in the
Australian Imperial Forces in the Middle
East and Pacific campaigns before returning
to High School teaching (1946–57). After
obtaining 2 master's degrees in education
and English literature he was awarded his
Ph.D. from London University (1959). He
became a Senior Lecturer at Teachers'
Colleges in 1959, and later, in 1966, at the
University of New South Wales. He became
Associate Professor in 1966 and in 1971 was
appointed to a Chair of Education. He was
co-founder and first president of the
Philosophy of Education Society of
Australasia in 1970 and is a Fellow of the
Royal Society of Arts. His books include
General Philosophy in Education and *Aims
of Education*. In 1969 he was the founding
editor of the journal *Educational
Philosophy and Theory*, of which, since
retirement, he has been a joint editor.

JUSTICE, MORALITY AND EDUCATION

Also by Les Brown

GENERAL PHILOSOPHY IN EDUCATION

AIMS OF EDUCATION

JUSTICE, MORALITY AND EDUCATION

A New Focus in Ethics in Education

Les Brown

St. Martin's Press   New York

All rights reserved. For information, write:
St. Martin's Press, Inc., 175 Fifth Avenue, New York, NY 10010
Printed in Hong Kong
Published in the United Kingdom by the Macmillan Press Ltd.
First published in the United States of America in 1985

ISBN 0-312-44948-8

Library of Congress Cataloging in Publication Data
Brown, Les, 1914–
Justice, morality, and education.
Bibliography: p.
Includes index.
1. Educational equalization—United States.
2. Right to education—United States.   3. Education—
United States—Moral and ethical aspects.   I. Title
LC213.2.B76   1985   370.19′0973   85–2457
ISBN   0-312-44948-8

Especially to my wife. And also, with affection
and compassion,
to our grandchildren – Andrew, John and Penny –
and to all other children the world over:
that in their respective life prospects
fundamental justice may prevail.

Contents

Preface

The general purpose of this book is to offer an ethical basis for making independent moral judgements. For teachers and students of education these may relate frequently to educational problems and situations, but moral judgements have, and need to have, a much wider application than to any particular professional area. The *specific* purpose is to provide rational grounds for explaining injustices and immorality in education, such as inequalities in educational opportunity, to counter bland and unsupported value assertions. When we come to reflect on it, many of us for much of our lives are apt to make summary value judgements without clear supporting reasons – though taking for granted that such clear reasons are never difficult to summon up when needed. Some engaged in scholarly or pseudo-scholarly pursuits are apt to do the same, declaring their points of view in value statements without explaining them. Why do we claim so confidently that inequality of educational opportunity is wrong? Basically what we seem to have in mind is that all should have equal opportunities because all of us are equal, but this justification is inadequate as it stands – as we shall see – requiring us to examine, among other things, what we mean by 'equal'. Before we can give a satisfactory answer to this question we need to come to grips with what we mean in a fundamental sense by justice, morality and education, and when we do, we find that the three are interrelated in such a way as to make the answer surprisingly simple. As for the larger purpose, we establish a basis of understanding of some of the major ethical issues that arise as we consider what we mean by morality, insisting on the need for a rational justification of any ethical position we may take, and illustrating with one such possible position.

Returning to the specific purpose, we show that justice, morality and education can each be reduced to elemental meanings, and that no substantive variations of these elemental meanings can alter cases of injustice in education in their conspicuous social manifestations. This method allows us to establish firmer justifications for alleged injustices in education than any which rely solely on value declarations, such as may arise spontaneously from sociological evidence of social disadvantage, or in the assertions of ideologues who may hold their values to be axiomatic or self-justifying.

Although the conjunction of justice, morality and education in their elemental meanings may indicate that it is wrong that some children should begin life's competition at a relative disadvantage, and that this disadvantage should be compounded, in some cases, throughout the years of formal schooling and beyond, it would be an error to interpret our standpoint as egalitarian. Any tendency toward a doctrinaire egalitarianism which assumes that all can be made equal – or approximately so – by some means such as a common curriculum, challenges the significant achievements in intellectual and aesthetic culture of civilized societies which have depended upon the pursuit of excellence by a few. Any implication of the practicability of a general levelling would be as well a simple misunderstanding of the nature of education, which cannot ignore the needs of each *individual* as a developing person.

We have no wish to use conceptual analysis as an end in itself. Analysis is used only to bring to the surface the irreducible, non-contradictory meanings of the three major terms of our title, so that if we may not presume to steer a course by them from the beginning, at least we may use them and test them as fixed and stable references whenever we need to. In contrast to these constants or fixed points as we perceive them to be in our conceptual firmament, there are many substantive expressions which revolve in planetary variations around the fundamental notions. The Socratic injunction to examine our words is thus profitable, at times, in the development of an entire structure of thought. Education, justice and morality are not as self-evident as we may have thought prior to examining them.

Confidence in the particular interpretation of the elemental notions we have offered comes from their use in many different circumstances throughout the book, and their retrospective examination in the final chapter. This does not put them beyond the need for critical appraisal by others: criticism is indeed invited, and it is possible that some may have grounds for rather different fixed references. If they do they have to justify them, as we have justified ours, with reasons, and in a way that takes account of fundamental ethical understandings. Any position which offers reasons for holding views about injustices in educational situations must be taken as superior to any *ex cathedra* stance of unjustified value declarations. But the quality of the reasons have themselves to be evaluated, and it is always the strongest case – not any case for any position – which demands acceptance. The giving of reasons for an alternative viewpoint on the fixed references is not in itself, that is, sufficient justification for varying our own.

As always in explanations of complex relationships, it would help to be able to say everything at once. In some circumstances, as in mathematics, we become aware of serious limitations on our understanding which, if we could free ourselves of them, would allow us to make mercurial moves rather than to take slower and more deliberate steps. We cannot communicate at once all the things we need to say on our topic, and we shall not understand some things, such as the complexity of the field, until we have reached the end. In the organization of chapters, therefore, the plan is for a progressive development of understanding, with the core of preceding thought brought forward to the new, and the new generally dependent on the preceding. Consistent with the principle of progressing from the relatively simple to the relatively complex, we explain and attempt to justify the three formal notions, testing them in subsequent discussions, and re-evaluating them at the end. The formal notions are themselves abstract, calling for some initial demands on the reader. After that their significance is likely to become clearer as we move to more practical perspectives.

It is important to note that a special sense of 'formal notion' is used which departs from the extreme structural formality of some interpretations and uses of it. This variation is used so that each formal notion will be given sufficient foundational meaning to be directional throughout the discussion. It focuses on what is *necessary* for each of the notions to be translated into its relevant activity. In one of its various senses, 'definition' might be used to convey our particular sense of 'formal notion', but there is advantage in contrasting substantive notions with the formal in order to distinguish between what is primary and fundamental for each notion, and what are no more than secondary and substantive variations of it. That distinction enables us to make quick references in subsequent discussion without the need for repetition of explanation – keeping a questioning eye, at the same time, on whether the formal notion is as fundamental as we claim it to be.

After education and justice in the first chapter, the second is devoted to the formal notion of morality, but because of the central importance of a moral point of view the discussion then widens to substantive considerations on morality and the defence of a coherent moral standpoint. The distinction between moral justice and legal justice links the second chapter to the third. Special attention is given to children's rights and animal rights as a basis for subsequent attention in Chapter 5.

At the end of Chapter 3 much of the fundamental theoretical work is completed to provide a stance for understanding certain practical perspectives. However before moving to these practical considerations, especially in Chapters 5, 7 and 8, a further basis of understanding is required: that is, a clearer understanding of the relationship between reason and certain dispositions with which it interacts. Chapter 4 then is a bridging chapter between the first three chapters and Chapter 5 on practical considerations. It is concerned not with logically necessary relationships, but with contingent psychological possibilities, as well as with certain conceptual distinctions to aid in an understanding of these relationships. In the following chapter it is shown to have ethical implications for practice, such as in moral education.

As a practical chapter, Chapter 5 deals with selected areas where ethical perspectives are relevant both to everyday affairs and to some of the distinctions and points of view developed in the preceding chapters. Chapter 6 fulfils an important function of developing a set of contrasting ideas as a background for reflection on our contemporary social situation. These ideas are not inert, embedded in historical epochs to which they have a peculiar relevance, but everyday practical ideas which suggest rather a universal relevance. Traditions of thought on individual–state relations provide a background of ideas for the practical considerations in Chapter 7 which culminate in the problem of equality of educational opportunity. Chapter 8 is both a review and an evaluative chapter, especially with reference to the formal notions. In particular it leads to the significance of the complex perspective to which we have referred, conjoining education. justice and morality in their elemental meanings, and showing both the simplicity and the starkness of the moral problem of equality of educational opportunity as it is brought into contact with these fundamental notions.

There can be no apologies for providing a relevant background of others' thoughts on morality, justice and education, including social justice, both as a resource of ideas with which to compare and stimulate one's own, and as an antidote to the influences of those who function – like Orwell's carthorses in *Animal Farm* – merely as competent and conscientious followers of their chosen masters.

It would be hazardous to infer political intention from our criticism of injustices in either traditional capitalist or traditional socialist systems of government. In the recognition of injustice or immorality according to the formal notion of justice or morality the questions of underlying political values and political intentions have no relevance. An act is just or unjust, that is, whatever the motives or intentions of an author may be in commenting on it. There is, in fact, no political intention behind the criticisms offered. In practice it is difficult to see that rational preferences for either capitalist or socialist systems of government can be made from moral principles alone, for such principles may themselves conflict (liberty and equity for instance). An aggravating factor in practical political deliberations is human imperfection, so that in the last resort ideal social theory based on defensible moral principles finds itself in interaction with a pragmatic inclination which asks, Which system – given both moral convictions and an appreciation of human imperfections – is preferable in practice? The dangers of misunderstanding the pragmatic, or of yielding to pressures for quick solutions, as well as the possibilities of social improvement, must nonetheless point the compass clearly toward moral principles in most circumstances, unless the direction is also utopian. Denial of political purpose in the present work is justified by the complexity of these considerations.

The general structure of the book, with its increasing complexity, is illustrated in the division into Parts. The first three chapters are concerned with Basic Conceptions and Underlying Principles. Further theoretical explanation is necessary on the nature of practical deliberations, but this has a practical orientation and so is united with practical applications to form Part II, which has been called a Practical Interlude. It is in fact much more than merely digressionary and illustrative, since the explanations of the relationships between dispositions and reason in practice have on-going significance as we consider Social Justice in State-Individual Relations constituting Part III.

Although the pronoun 'we' has been used consistently instead of the singular form more common in philosophical discussions, there would be no point in attempting thereby to delude the reader into *agreeing* with every point of the argument. The stylistic preference has been prompted rather by conventions adopted in some formal discussion groups, thereby underlying the common purpose of members without encouraging conformity of viewpoint. The constant challenge to the reader must be to see if he has the better reason in justifying a contrary point of view, realising, with Bacon, how difficult it is to claim that in practical situations we have attained truth in moral matters – able entirely to expunge 'vain opinions, flattering hopes, false valuations, imaginations', and the like (Of Truth). Applying his instruction to our present circumstances, 'Read not to contradict and confute, nor to believe and take for granted; nor to find talk and discourse; but to weigh and consider' (*Of Studies*),* we therefore add, to make our own purpose clearer:

> *Read not for ultimate solutions to moral problems, but to under-stand others' views and to discuss them*, the reasons for which will be unfolded at various points as we proceed.

---

* The reference to *Of Truth* is p.3 of *Essays*, and to *Of Studies* p.150 of the same, Everyman edition, J.M. Dent, London.

Acknowledgements

Despite an attempt to pick out the main threads of relevant philosophical traditions from Plato to Aristotle, through to Hobbes and Locke, Hume and Kant, then to Mill, it is impossible to dismiss from the mind many contemporary influences, both in philosophy and in jurisprudence. An indication of these is reflected in the bibliography, as in references to Bernard Williams, John Mackie and Joel Feinberg in general ethics, and to Peter Singer in the specific area of animal interests; to John Rawls in social theory; to Lord Lloyd of Hampstead and Ronald Dworkin in jurisprudence, particularly on aspects of the philosophy of law. To all of these, and to many others whose influence at present has been dimmed through processes of assimilation, I acknowledge in humility a significant debt.

L.M.B.

PART I
Education, Justice and
Morality: Basic Conceptions
and Underlying
Principles

1 Education and Justice

EDUCATION

In this chapter we shall begin with the meaning of 'education', and then move to the meaning of 'justice', for it is the relationship between these two basic concepts which will develop as crucial to some of the most outstanding of our moral and social problems, in particular equality of educational opportunity to which we lead in the closing chapters. For this purpose 'meaning' will be given a specific reference. We shall attempt to find for each of 'education' and 'justice' its *formal idea*, and by 'formal idea' we shall mean the most fundamental, abstract, and irreducible idea which will still be meaningful to us. Each will be a bedrock notion with which all the substantive notions people have of 'education' or 'justice' will be consistent, but which will at the same time allow meaningfulness to these wide-ranging substantive variations. And each will serve as a fixed reference or touchstone throughout the book.

We shall declare without hesitation what we hold to be the formal notion of each, and the common plan will be this : first, we shall measure each against the relevant views of philosophers, since these might be expected to be held from a reflective or contemplative stance; second, we shall keep each in mind throughout the book, and in this way measure it against other relevant views in subsequent chapters; and third, in the final chapter we shall review and evaluate each of the formal notions for suitability and consistency of application.

The Formal Notion of Education

We hold that the formal notion of education is *a developing of individual potentialities consistent with social values*, stressing the gerundial form rather than the finite suggestion of 'development'. 'Social values' applies both to moral and other values relevant to the individual's needs for life in a particular society. This does not mean

3

that the only values he holds, or ought to hold, are those endorsed by society, but that his potentialities ought *not* be developed toward a capacity for *conflict* with social values. Conversely, there are normally some social values that he ought to be encouraged to accept.

In this formal notion of education we set no criteria for what are to count as social values. We merely accept that the developing of individual potentialities necessarily occurs within a social context. We have yet to clarify our views on what *moral* values are, but before we do this, our linking of moral values with social values anticipates that there is somehow a morality involved in living together with a degree of harmony. Without that minimum, societies could not exist. If education were widened to the developing of potentialities, without restriction, it could refer to potentialities for anti-intellectualism, for intellectual and moral retrogression rather than advancement. That would leave us with a formal notion capable of admitting opposites. Further, if 'individual' were not included, the developing could refer to totalitarian conceptions of a patterned education for all, in disregard of individual bents or propensities.

What is referred to in the 'developing' of the formal notion of education are the latent powers of the individual. Education then refers to the verb 'educe' which conveys exactly this sense, without any substantive considerations of how the powers are to be educed or in what direction. Education is a process, a developing. As such it refers to no object to be won, however frequently it may be described as a metaphorical *stage of development*, with the implication of something beyond it which is education's ultimate point of fruition. There are literally no such things as 'levels' or 'stages' of education.

In the formal notion of education the 'developing' has no end, no absolute. (It may be given a purpose, but that at once makes it a substantive notion.) To that extent biographical expressions are misleading, such as that someone 'received his education' at Oxford or Cambridge, or at Eton or Harrow, or at some unknown Secondary Modern. The most learned dons never gain an education in a final sense, never acquire an ultimate education so that they can say that the long task is at last accomplished. It is in conflict too with our formal notion of education to state that education is the development of every individual's potentialities, or that it is the all-round development of a person – intellectually, morally and physically. Each of these statements implies a finiteness which education does not have, although the second is vaguely more moderate in its demands, not reaching for the highest pitch of fulfilment but satisfied rather with a balanced attention to *every* aspect of development and a neglect of none. It is unrealistic to consider developing all potentialities, since they compete for time, interest and effort; and especially with children at school it is often difficult to know when potentialities have been developed as far as possible. These are substantive considerations which are expressed in many statements of the purposes of state education, as in the recent Constitution of the People's Republic of China (Article 44).[1] If education is to be reduced to three specific areas of potential development on a criterion of compatability with social values, additional criteria are needed to justify the exclusion of potentialities for such things as parenthood (not covered entirely by moral development), sporting prowess (not covered entirely by physical development), fine craftsmanship (not covered entirely by intellectual and physical development). Potentialities capable of development even in socially approved ways are not finite: all-round development is not finite in its reduction to the intellectual, the moral and the physical. However full we fill the bag of human potentialities or of needs for human development, it is never *completely* full. Yet these substantive considerations draw attention to one important aspect of the formal notion of education. The qualification 'consistent with social values' has a positive as well as a negative significance. The positive sense implies that there *are* values which society wishes its young to learn, so that education is not merely a question of directing certain tendencies away from social conflict. Social values are themselves substantive, but to the extent that all civilized societies promote, through schooling, a developing of *intellectual* powers at least, which will be in the interests of children themselves as well as of society, the positive aspect of considering others' interests as 'consistent with social values' will be seen to give to the formal notion of education a moral significance, while at the same time linking the formal with the substantive. The formal notion of education has both social and moral significance.

The assumptions of determinacy with respect to potentialities and all-round development are carried through to the notion of development itself. Development in education implies improvement, not regression and not stagnation, but it is not always obvious what is to count as improvement. We shall not concern ourselves with specific learning objectives which are susceptible to measurement, but rather with educational activities which are much more difficult to evaluate, not merely empirically, but also, and particularly, for want of an appropriate scale by which to measure them. These are areas of values, and we shall illustrate by reference to moral education. We shall begin, for purposes of contrast, with the simple, and move to the complex. The question of what is to count as improvement in moral education is not difficult to answer with respect to children before they are able to reason, for then their moral education is concerned with a knowledge of substantive rules governing what ought to be done, according to parents or teachers, and a little later according to social expectations, such as in learning the rule that private property is to be respected. The knowledge of substantive rules is readily measurable. When the ability to reason becomes evident, it is again not difficult to assess children's understanding of rules in the answers they give to questions such as why we should respect other people's property, or why we should keep promises. But when we advance to the stage where moral values are independently chosen, though external influences on moral conduct are not entirely removed, how can we then determine what is to count as moral *improvement*? If the accepted values are stable there is no change, and without change there can be no improvement. If there *is* change, by what standards is it to be judged as a morally improving change, or a change for the better in a moral sense? By his own standards a tax evader may improve, not merely in method or results, but in his resolution to defraud the government, or to let others bear the tax burden, as well as in his disregard for others' interests, and in his contempt for the law and for those who follow it. His values may be judged good or bad, but they may not be judged true or false. Value criteria are needed to judge them, and these themselves have to be justified. We can proceed no further with the problem of value improvement in moral education until we have discussed the question of morality in Chapter 2. But it is clear that we have begun to cross the border between the formal and the substantive.

We shall end our initial statement of the formal notion of education by showing that by taking a finite view of education as development, rather than a continuous *developing* of (selected) individual potentialities, we are led to a reification of education which becomes self-stultifying. For we come to realise that as long as we think of education as an object to be attained we realise too that it is not apprehendable at any moment of time. There is simply no moment when we may be said to *have* education. If there is no moment of time when we may be said to have education, then we never do in fact have it. There is no object, education, which can be attained in experience, no such thing as *education*, it seems, in itself. Therefore a search for education in itself appears to be a futile search, abandoned historically by many such as Socrates in Plato's *Republic*. Education as a non-finite individual developing leads to no such sterile conclusion.

The formal notion of education which we have proposed is a considered judgement reached largely by reflective deliberation. Though partly intuitive, it has not come in any single flash of intuition, but rather by paring substantive notions, while still leaving sufficient covering to be meaningful. Yet it cannot claim to have been reached by any systematic deductive procedure. Like all such judgements it is fallible, but examinable by reason and therefore discussable. We shall now illustrate further some substantive ideas of education to throw the formal, fundamental, irreducible notion of education into bolder relief. At the same time we shall show that substantive ideas of education, however widely they may vary, are consistent with the formal notion of education.

Selected Substantive Ideas of Education

Educational Activities

Our understanding of education is clearer in reference to activities than to abstract ideas, if for no other reason than that concreteness is easier to grasp than abstraction. Children usually have no intuitive ideas of education, though they may have intuitions of many things *relating to* education: with respect to older children, for instance, that they have suddenly reached understanding independently of reasoning. When sufficiently advanced intellectually, some children may have intuitive understandings not of education taking place, but of it *not* taking place, by which they refer not so much to intellectual stagnation (or to a temporary cessation of the *developing* of intellectual potentialities), as to a break in their *learning* programmes or activities. In other words their thoughts are substantive, directed toward learning activities which are loosely referred to as 'educational' activities. These activities thus form one area of substantive ideas of education, with great variety, and consistent in their contribution to developing certain individual potentialities (whether realised or not either by learner or observer) with the formal notion of education. The substantive link with the formal is through *learning*. Parents know that teaching consists of a range of activities including informing, demonstrating, persuading, encouraging, repeating, and so forth. Learning is recognized as the process whereby some of the objectives of parents for their children, or teachers for their pupils, are achieved, or whereby adolescents or adults achieve certain objectives set by themselves. Then education is commonly applied to the achievements of learners, to the results of the teaching–learning process, even when some learners are self-taught, self-directed, pursuing objectives of their own making. Educational objectives may be career-oriented, referring to various levels of achievement set as graded vocational goals, with little or no thought of a developing of individual potentialities. These substantive notions of so-called educational activities are distinct from the formal notion of education which we have proposed, though consistent with it whenever a developing of potentialities is occurring. There are other learning activities involving progress, improvement, or a developing of a kind which we would positively wish to exclude from the category of educational activities. We would not want to say, for instance, that education includes progress, improvement or development in facial appearance or bodily conformation; or development of skills in mugging or thuggery; or progress in a blasphemous vocabulary; or improvement in marbles or hop-scotch; or discovery of a source of pleasure in drugs; or progress in self-control under alcohol. In order to distinguish between progress, improvement or development which might be included in *educational activities*, and that which might not, we require judgemental criteria, such as the criterion included in the formal notion of education, that the activities in question conform with social values – both moral and non-moral – or at least not be so inconsistent with them as to prepare youth for headlong social conflict as a preparation for emergent citizenship. This criterion would then exclude, as educational activities, those regarded as anti-social or immoral by a particular society, as well as those regarded as trivial: that is, scarcely valued at all. (There is much more to be said on moral values and morality, which we shall defer to the next chapter.) Substantive education will therefore vary from society to society, so that there are no *absolute* standards by which to judge activities as 'educational'. At the same time, and in this connection, it needs to be stressed that the criterion included in the formal notion of education does not impose any classification of 'socially approved' on proposed educational activities before they may be implemented. What is intended in the formal notion is simply that the criterion needs to be subject to an onus of justification condition; namely, that the onus is on the proposer of any educational activity which is in tension with social values, norms or expectations to justify it. In other words, the formal notion of education states no imperative governing educational activities: it is simply a reduction from them in so far as they are substantive interpretations of education, with many possible forms or expressions. It is what education *means* in its most elemental sense. Substantive educational activities do not convey that meaning.

Purposive Ideas on Education

In addition to a variety of substantive notions of education which refer in the main to *learning* activities, there is another class of such notions which is characterized by *directiveness*, since they are associated with individual ideals, or with purposes or goals which individuals allege either are, or ought to be, universal. Again the possibilities are wide and far-reaching. Generally education's direction, and the activities which give it that direction, are influenced not so much by those representing the mean of social opinion, or by mere conformism with social tradition, but by individuals with high personal standards in education, and equally high standards for the development of other individuals. They have learnt to appreciate such things as rationality, human sympathies and artistic sensibilities, as well as high standards of performance in a range of human accomplishments. Not only is education an *individual* activity in the sense that it is individuals who are being educated, even when the *means* may be in terms of social interaction: it is also individual in the major influences bearing on it, which comprise the personal values of many different thinkers on the subject, including philosophers, educationists, teachers and parents. But as soon as education's direction is linked with personal ideals, or with individual values or preferences, we reach at once the perplexing situation faced by Aristotle in his *Politics*, in which he complained of the absence of any common principle for proceeding in education, since some favoured the useful in life, some virtue, some the higher knowledge, as the aim to be pursued (Book VIII, ch. 2, 1137^b)[2]. Ideas on the direction education should take thus constitute varieties of *substantive* notions of education, each consistent with- if they are to be educational at all – the formal notion. Even if education were interpreted in terms of the useful in life, or vocational training, there is implied some developing of potentialities in most circumstances, though a case would need to be made for it before specific job-training were declared educational. More often the substantive notion of education has been directed toward a developing of the intellect, or of the mind, as it is sometimes stated, in a particular way. For some, as we shall see, this has been of such an overriding concern as to exclude as educationally irrelevant, or unimportant, the developing of other potentialities such as for certain physical skills, or for particular aesthetic or moral values (though among philosophers the linking of intellect and moral values has not been unusual). If ever we could expect educational thinkers to reduce substantive considerations to formal notions it is philosophers of whom we might have the highest hopes. We shall therefore turn selectively to them, partly to measure our formal notion against theirs, and if that expectation is not fulfilled, again to illustrate substantive notions of education which contrast in their individual emphases and preferences with the elemental formal notion. In this we should keep in mind that the formal notion of education is itself directional.

Philosophers on Education

Aristotle

It is Aristotle who, most of all among philosophers interested in education, offers some initial prospect of a standard against which to measure our formal notion. That is because he considered that the highest activity of which some men are capable – and *only* some men, as Plato too had believed – is intellectual contemplation. Inasmuch as it reaches toward universal truth it is 'divine in comparison with human life', (*Nicomachean Ethics*, Book x, ch. 7, 1177^b).[3] It is intuitive reason which grasps first principles (Book vi, ch. 6, 1141^a, and Book vi, ch. 8, 1142^a). This is the highest wisdom. In contrast with contemplation with its intrinsic satisfaction there are activities which are called the *practical* and *productive*, both of which are directed at extrinsic ends. While contemplative wisdom leads to enjoyment in pure theory, as in the arts of metaphysics, mathematics and physics, practical wisdom achieves happiness from rational deliberation and the recognition of particulars, and excellence in deliberation lies in finding the truth about what is the best thing to do. This is not merely a *rational* best, but also a *moral* best. 'The man who is without qualification good at deliberating is the man who is capable of aiming in accordance with calculation at the best for man of things attainable by action' (Book VI, ch. 7, 1141ᵇ). Moral goodness requires practical wisdom, and practical wisdom requires moral virtue (Book VI, ch. 13, 1144ᵇ).

What could be more promising? Would not the *contemplative* wisdom with its command of first principles slough off all substantive questions on education – important as these might be in some situations, especially in considering how to act in practical morality? For the most part we are disappointed, certainly in the *Nico-machean Ethics*. It is only in the *Politics*, and then only in the closing statement, that he expresses the view that the three basic principles of education are the 'mean, the possible, the becoming' (Book VIII, ch. 7, 1342ᵇ). It is his intuitive glimpse of education as concerned, not with finite ends, but with the *possible*, the *becoming*, which fits so well with our own formal notion of education as a *developing* of potentialities. Even his notion of the mean as a virtue which avoids the evils of *excess* and *deficiency* has some relevance to our qualification 'consistent with social values', especially in the context of his emphasis on education for all, and on everyone belonging to the state (*Politics*, Book VIII, ch. 1, 1137ᵃ). But that correspondence is not to be pressed too far. All we need note is his acknowledgement of social values, norms or expectations with which, presumably, the education of the young in their preparation for citizenship should not conflict, and which should be used constructively in their upbringing.

For the rest, nothing could be further from Aristotle's thoughts on education than universal truths of the elemental kind we have been seeking in the formal notion of education. For in the *Nicomachean Ethics* Aristotle stepped boldly into substantive questions to which his views on education were related. It was characteristic of him to seek answers to questions of *ends*, or *purposes*: the ultimate question of his *Nicomachean Ethics* was what is the purpose of man's existence, what is his end, or what is the 'good' for man. To the ultimacy of this question his views on education were directed. The end of man, in his view, is *happiness*, but it is not happiness in any hedonistic or pleasure-seeking sense; it is happiness of the reason, or intellect. To him happiness was a moral concept. *Eudaimonia* was anything but a state of passive contentment. Much less was it to be sought in such things as wealth or honour. As a spirit or activity of good, *eudaimonia* was simply a compound of *eu*, or good, and *daimon*, spirit. 'Happiness is an activity of soul in accordance with perfect virtue', he says (*Nicomachean Ethics*, Book I, ch. 12, 1102ᵃ), but while every soul has a rational principle, there are individual differences among men, so there are different excellences or virtues to be recognized. Even if it takes a lifetime, 'for one swallow does not make a summer, nor does one day', the man who achieves happiness is the one whose activity of soul achieves an appropriate excellence (Book I, ch. 7, 1098ᵃ).

In his falling back on *purposes* or *ends* Aristotle at once opened the way for many substantive variations from his own, since each depended on personal ideals, but at the same time set the stage for one particular substantive notion of education which still has many adherents. That is the notion of a *liberal education* to which we shall now turn.

To Aristotle, as we have noted, it was the pure intellect that stood supreme, contemplative wisdom above practical wisdom, and that in turn higher than productive wisdom. The notion of leisure provides a conceptual link with the Greek idea of a liberal education, for the Greek word 'skhole' which has given us 'school' meant *leisure* (as well as other things) and education for Aristotle and Plato before him was for freemen. It was these who had the time to cultivate the intellect. Slaves can be trained merely in routine or repetitive operations, for they are differently constituted by nature from freemen, and have 'no deliberate faculty at all'. (Book I, ch. 13, 1260ᵃ) The slave is but 'a living tool' (*Nicomachean Ethics*, Book VIII, ch. 11, 1161ᵇ). As for the education of children, some of the things they will be taught are of a useful kind, but care is to be taken lest some of the useful things they learn should vulgarize them. Anything is vulgar if it makes the body or soul or mind 'less fit for the practice or exercise of virtue'. Even with respect to those of the liberal arts which it is proper for freemen to acquire, they should not be attended to with the attitude of a perfectionist, for that too might impair the development of the liberal mind (*Politics*, Book VIII, ch. 2, 1337ᵇ).

Our contemporary distinctions between liberal and vocational studies, and between 'pure' mathematics and 'applied' mathematics, are reflections of this belief in the pre-eminence of the intellect, and on its exalted, metaphysical character[4] which put it within reach of the few rather than the many (as Plato too had believed in his attribution of a quality of divinity to his philosopher–rulers). (*Republic*, VII, 540.)

These are all substantive notions of education founded on an intellectual ideal. An extension of this substantive ideal was to link the intellect with moral virtue, reminding us of a contemporary concern that development of the intellect alone can readily take us to the brink of human annihilation. In the *Nicomachean Ethics* moral virtue is introduced as the product of *habit*, and Aristotle notes that the Greek word *ethike* is formed by a slight variation of *ethos*, or habit (Book II, 1, 1103ª). The *kind* of habits which we form from our youth are crucial to moral development (1103ᵇ). Because moral virtue aims at what is intermediate in passions and in actions, it is itself a *mean* between – as we have seen – excess and deficiency. Appropriate moral virtues formed by habit are courage, temperance, those concerned with money such as liberality, those concerned with honour such as humility, those relating to control of anger such as good temper, virtues of social intercourse such as friendliness and truthfulness, shamelessness and justice. As an habitual disposition, each of these inclines an individual to choose a morally right action, which in his view will be a mean. In this substantive development from the liberal ideal of the intellect searching for first principles, Aristotle has himself moved from the contemplative stance to the substantive stance of 'practical wisdom', as he called it.

Mill and Others

In the Nineteenth Century the espousal of a liberal education by Mill and others, particularly by means of a university education, again serves to contrast the substantive with the formal. When in 1867 Mill delivered his Inaugural Address as rector of the university of St. Andrews, the first task he assumed was to 'dispose of the notion of professional, or vocational, education, as proper for universities'.[5] Skilful lawyers, physicians or engineers had first to be 'made men' through an appropriate education. The university leaves its mark, he explained, through mental exercise and habits, so that a man becomes in consequence a better lawyer, or even a better shoemaker, by grasping principles instead of relying on a memory crammed with details (*Inaugural Address*, pp.4–5).

The transition from knowledge for its own sake to the development of intellectual attitudes and skills leads to the second traditional emphasis in the theory of a liberal education. A critical attitude develops to human affairs, exposing false beliefs and assumptions, dogmas and prejudices, challenging even the conventional knowledge toward which it turns. In attitude the mind becomes open, flexible, tolerant. It acquires skills of reasoning, habits of logical thought, as Mill explained with reference to science in particular. Though not strictly a philosopher, Newman also wrote under a strong Aristotelian influence, describing the function of 'a Liberal or Universal Education' as 'intellectual culture' stressing knowledge as its own end, and the development of the rational mind in a way which showed how close his liberal ideal was to Aristotle's contemplative wisdom. The business of universities was to raise the intellectual tone of society, to cultivate the public mind and purify the national taste. For the individual it was to cultivate the intellect, teaching him to 'see things as they are, to go right to the point, to disentangle a skein of thought, to detect what is sophistical and to discard what is irrelevant' (*Discourses on University Education*).[6] Ideally the attitudes and skills of the liberal intellect become a way of life, a life-long pursuit of knowledge in a spirit of free enquiry. The contemporary ideal of liberal education has not changed in these main features, yet in many respects it has become assimilated to the principles of all rational discourse.

In these substantive notions of a liberal education a concealed purpose was not difficult to find, even though it supposedly represented the spirit of education itself, and so might otherwise have led us to a formal notion. Ironically while Mill emphasized the liberal ideal in his *Inaugural Address*, he became increasingly instrumental in his view of a liberal education, especially in his notion of preparing the youth of a nation for intelligent and moral citizenship (p.35–6). In giving liberal education a social purpose Mill was firmly in the Greek tradition. But in giving it also something of a personal stamp he showed how readily the notion of a liberal education can be turned to the service of an ideal, or of a philosophical preference. Then the disinterested pursuit of knowledge is apt to be so broadened as to encompass whatever are held as desirable educational objectives. Those who include the education of the emotions, of the aesthetic sensibilities, or of moral values, or who wish to designate as 'liberal' the diverse components of curricular plans or policies commonly called 'personal development', have lost touch with the liberal tradition that has come to us from the Greeks.[7] Inasmuch as the pursuit of knowledge is truth-seeking, and truth-seeking is a moral activity, a liberal education has a moral inclination. Yet in principle it is its own end. It has no moral purpose; it is not instrumental to anything. We are not able to assert that an educational activity is one that promotes intellectual and moral development, for if it is a liberal education that we have in mind, though intellectual development is expected to ensue, it aims to promote nothing; and in principle it is an error to include the wide implications of moral development in its ambit, though integrity and respect for truth are both entailed in the pursuit of knowledge for its own sake.

There are two related explanations why concepts of a liberal education fail to cross the substantive barrier into the formal. First, it is itself an ideal, a philosophical preference, and as such one of many possible ideals all leading in different directions and some of them conflicting. Second, and because of this, it cannot stand as a reduction from all substantive notions of education to a single fundamental formulation with which they are all consistent. Both the liberal ideal and its corresponding vocational prejudice were conveyed in the *Republic*, when Plato referred to the elegance of calculation 'if it is pursued not for commercial ends but for the sake of knowledge (VII, 525).[8]

Next to the idea of a liberal education as a contender for a formal notion of education – but one which we must now also dismiss as substantive – is the notion that education is the development of individuality. In its liberal sense of promoting the individual character of every person, this idea has its source in various traditions such as the naturalism of Rousseau: typifying all children, Émile was to be free to grow according to his nature, unconstrained to the beginning of adolescence, and away from the corrupting influences of society.[9] And in ways which Rousseau could not have envisaged, geneticists in particular and biologists generally have given empirical support to the notion of individuals developing uniquely, distinct from all others. In his essays *On Liberty* Mill expressed the spirit of individuality in his prefatory quotation from Humboldt's *Sphere and Duties of Government*, in which the 'grand, leading principle' was to be 'the absolute and essential importance of human development in its richest diversity' (p.57).[10] Individuality was to be the object of everyone's ceaseless efforts, and especially of those, such as teachers, who have influence over others. The ideal of individuality gave rise to lyrical expressions, even by Mill himself, who argued that it was only 'by cultivating it and calling it forth ... that human beings become a noble and beautiful object of contemplation ... (p. 127). Fifty years later a prominent educationist, writing from a biological perspective, expressed a similar view, again in the Humboldt tradition, stating the purpose of education to be the creation of a richly variegated society of *different* individuals. In this he reacted sharply to educational purposes which subordinated the individual to the state, or bent

education to a democratic ideal of interacting individuals prepared
for willing and efficient social participation. The original notion of
natural development, or development according to an individual's
nature, is thus extended to the notion of education to *advance* this
growth, and the growth metaphor is further extended to the notion of
the necessary *cultivation* of the plant as a whole, which then becomes
designated as *individuality*. Individuality is the whole, but what is the
nature of this whole? Since the emphasis in Humboldt, Mill and
others is toward the utmost fruition of *differences*, in a composite
development toward individual uniqueness, the richest possible
variegation might include trivialities such as facial appearance and
length of legs, or temperamental excesses such as propensities for
tantrums or petulance, or complacency, or bland good humour and
profound ignorance and indolence. These are not intended in the
Humboldt tradition, but their exclusion requires criteria for the
purpose. Mill himself objected to the 'wearing down into uniformity
all that is individuals ...' and the development of individuality was a
process of bringing individuals... 'nearer to the best thing they can be'
(p.128). What the best would be was not clearly conveyed. So
individuality is not to be identified with personality, presumably,
which would include everything distinctive about a person including
any mannerisms of speech or of gait, but is frequently so unspecific as
to be bounded merely by vague moral limitations. When individuality
is specified as the development of the individual intellectually,
morally, and physically, as it sometimes is, it falls under the
limitations already discussed.

Education as the development of individuality – as Mill, Humboldt
and others conceived it – was after all a distinctly substantive,
purpose-oriented notion, aimed at bringing out all that was unique in
an individual, and at the same time resisting pressures from the state
toward the kind of conformity and patterning that a universal public
education might bring. There was inevitably a multiplication of
substantiveness as soon as consideration was given to the significant
question of how 'natural' or 'different' an individual was permitted to
be: that is, which of his natural or unique tendencies would need to
be modified toward the acceptable because they conflicted with
social values, norms or expectations. In this there was at least an
acknowledgement that the proviso we have included in our formal
notion of education ('consistent with social values') is inescapable.
But if the formal notion of education were then stated as 'the
development of individuality, consistent with social values' there

would remain two difficulties: first, 'development' – as we have already noted – implies a finiteness of end to be achieved, as though education would be able to complete the process of individuality-making with respect to each person; second, 'individuality' can only be given meaning in substantive ways, with many possible interpretations such as personality (itself subject to substantive variations), moral character, uniqueness in comparison with others, and so forth.

Review of Formal Notion of Education

The first observation to be made is that the selective study of philosophers' views on education has not been generally fruitful in providing a formal notion of education with which we might compare our own. The promise offered by Aristotle in his notion of contemplation as the pursuit of first principles or universal truths has yielded the only defensible formal notion in its account of education as 'the mean, the possible, the becoming', and it is this which lends support to our own formal notion. Apart from that there has been recognition of the need for our qualification of 'consistent with social values', in so far as education is accepted as a social responsibility, and any educational activity of developing the potentialities of those who are to become citizens must not permit the growth of tendencies likely to be consistently or radically in conflict with these values, regardless of any preference for 'naturalness' or 'differences'. Philosophers' views of education are generally purpose-oriented, even in the more attractive notions of education for the development of the intellect for its own sake (or the pursuit of knowledge for its own sake), and of education as the development of (unique) individuality. With the exception of Aristotle's brief intuitive observation at the end of his *Politics*, philosophers' notions of education, as we have examined them, are substantive notions, not formal notions.

A second observation to be made is that in reaching the formal notion of education it has been necessary to resist any reifying tendencies, for to think of education as an object to be attained leads to contradictions. From a reifying stance, if education refers to becoming, there is nothing to isolate, there is literally no such object as education.

A third observation is that the *becoming* cannot be *any* becoming, the possibilities to be pursued cannot be *any* possibilities. Therefore the becoming, or in terms of our own statement of the formal notion, the *developing*, cannot refer to any potentialities at all. It has two important characteristics which show that substantive considerations in education are highly significant in practice. First, it is not aimless or contingent, but directional, and directiveness presupposes the giving of direction by someone, either by the self or by others. But direction can be given capriciously, or perversely, and an assumption in this idea of education is that the direction given to the becoming is toward *improvement*. Intuitively we could never accept that any change in any direction would qualify as educational becoming. So the second characteristic of this formal idea of education is that of improvement, which itself implies a purpose, though not an end to be attained, and if the becoming is to be given direction by an educational purpose, the purpose itself must dictate criteria for choosing an appropriate direction for educational activities to take. We are here on the edge of substantive considerations, for as soon as purposes are allowed, many different interpretations of education become possible.

The fourth observation to be made is a conclusion that we may now be reasonably confident that the formal notion we have advanced is defensible as the irreducible, fundamental, most abstract (but still meaningful and non-contradictory) expression of education. But we have yet to see how it stands up in discussion of substantive matters in subsequent chapters.

JUSTICE

The Formal Notion of Justice

We shall now state what we hold to be the formal idea of *justice*, and then give our reasons for holding it. We shall measure it against first, commonly held intuitive ideas of justice; second, the views of selected philosophers on justice; and third, some of the views held in jurisprudence. The formal notion of justice is *fairness in the treatment of persons*. Like formal notions generally, this requires some explanation. The sense of equality is lurking here in 'fairness', but '*equality* in the treatment of persons' would be misleading because of individual differences, and such an expression is suggestive of egalitarianism, not of justice. Our notion of *fairness in the treatment of persons* includes first, consistency with rules; second, a sense of balance and proportion; third, the idea of equality of treatment in relevant respects; fourth, a special connotation of *person* which will be developed in Chapter 2. We have reached this judgement without any Aristotelian presumption of a capacity to see universal truths or first principles, although we have used a reflective or contemplative stance, influenced by experience as well as by already formed impressions and viewpoints. We cannot escape a fundamental impression that the idea of justice is *fairness*, but fairness is a composite notion, including fairness as consistency in the application of rules or standards, as well as fairness as *equity* in its adjectival sense of 'equitable', for that gives to fairness the dimension of evenness or a proper balance between or among people according to circumstances and relevant criteria. Fairness in the application of rules is in itself not wide enough for *justice*. Being fair in a system of taxation is being even in establishing a proper balance between and among persons according to income and capacity to pay. Colour of skin, race, or religion are irrelevant, so is occupation, whether a recent migrant or not, and so forth. In the formal notion of justice as fairness it is significant that the words 'equity', 'equitable' and 'equal' are all related to fairness. (The Latin word *aequus* has various possible meanings, namely, *equal, fair*, and *even*.[11]) Yet if we are to make use of a formal notion of justice in subsequent discussion we shall need a simpler form of expression than one which refers to fairness as consistency in the application of rules, and as equity in establishing a proper balance or proportion among persons. Apart from its unwieldiness there is the added difficulty in the ambiguity of 'equity', which is used not only in the sense which we have given it, but also in a legal sense of justice departing from the rigidity of statute law toward 'justice without law' as it is sometimes called; that is toward justice which avoids excessive inequalities of treatment when persons are alike in relevant respects. 'Fairness' may apply separately to consistency in the application of rules, to equity as balance or proportion among persons, or to equality of treatment for equals. These are related but not identical notions.

Since in some circumstances *equity* is intuitively so close to the heart of justice (notably in cases of *social justice* as we shall see in the concluding chapters) a note on its ambiguity will assist to justify the formal expression of justice which we have chosen. The general sense of equity is a fair balance or proportion among people in a relevant situation, such as one involving the distribution of goods and services. Impartiality is central to it. The legal sense of equity gave rise historically to this general sense, but had a special flavour of its own. Historically the older courts in England, called 'common law courts', had part of their functions handled subsequently by 'equity courts', which received petitions (originally to the king) complaining about alleged injustices in common law. Since these were often referred to the Lord Chancellor, who until Tudor times was a leading church-man, the common expectation was that such petitions would receive fair treatment according to what were called principles of 'equity and good conscience'. In this was a clear implication that moral justice transcended legal justice in some circumstances. The Lord Chancel-lor thus had powers to supplement and even to correct common law. While this spirit of equity implied the highest degree of impartiality and fair-mindedness, it is clear that each judgement was limited by human imperfection, so that even in the case of the Lord Chancellor there could scarcely have been an expectation of *perfect* justice in equity. Indeed, it seems to have approximated rather to rough justice in the early days of English equity, varying, it was said, with the length of the Chancellor's foot.[12] Excesses apart, equity at its best is seen as the product of a humane mind always in tension with ideals of objectivity and impartiality, but on that very account recognizably human, understanding, balancing as best it can a complexity of personal, social and legal considerations. In equity there is something of Shakespeare's humanity as expressed by his Portia, if we can make allowances both for her partiality and for her typically Elizabethan racial prejudices. The partiality of judges in equity might have sometimes approached Portia's, but at least she conveyed something of the spirit of equity. Equity at its best – and equity in intention – were needed not only to fill the gaps in common law but also to temper it with a humane concern for the individual whenever the common law would be harsh in its application. Against that was a limited capacity for striking the best possible balance between a wide-ranging and contending number of issues or considerations in law, tradition, social values and the conflicting claims of a particular case. For two reasons then, *equity* is not included in the formal notion of justice: first, it is ambiguous, trailing clouds of doubt or even derogation from its legal origins; second, it has common or non-legal application to particular situations of distribution of goods and services rather than a universal application. Justice is wider than equity, though in some situations equity expresses justice as fairness in the treatment of persons. For universal application neither 'equity' nor 'fairness' is sufficiently unequivocal on its own. We do not merely treat 'others': we are concerned with treating *persons*, which at once widens our perceptions of the boundaries of justice, as we shall explain in the next chapter. It is sufficient to note at present that the species description of 'human beings' is inadequate to convey the moral depth of fairness which we require in the formal notion of justice. We need a formal notion which will take account of human passions at their most excited and most bestial, as in extending fair treatment without malice or retribution to prisoners of war who have inflicted casualities on our comrades, to convicted criminals who might have caused us personal loss, even to children in the classroom who have exacerbated our endurance and lacerated our egos. In equity a balance or proper proportion might be established by considering a separate category of prisoners of war, or of convicted criminals, or of intractable pupils; but to treat them as persons is to treat them in a moral way which accepts no such separate categories or sub-classifications.

Our formal notion of justice is as comprehensive as it needs to be to take account of all cases, without at the same time erring on the side of substantiveness. This is recognized – as it is in the need for the inclusion of *persons* – when we consider limited statements of justice, such as that justice is observance of rules, or protection of individual rights, or impartiality, or observance of social values, norms or expectations. There are two obvious objections to the identification of moral justice with the keeping of rules: first, the rules themselves may be unjust, and often have been and are – even in the law; second, the category of justice is wider than the category of rules. Justice is more than fairness in following rules, though it figures prominently as such in childhood, as well as later. There are rules not only for games, but also for associations of people in a wide range of honourable and dishonourable activities: rules for cricket, rules for clubs, rules of secrecy for illegal organizations, and so forth. To declare that justice is protection of rights is again too restrictive. It is clear that there are legal rights, such as for blacks, or other groups of persons, which are discriminatory and difficult to defend as just. There are many other rights outside the law, such as rights claimed by students at school, which are not obviously rights of individual justice. Reduction of justice to a concept of rights protection thus has two flaws: first, rights that are asserted or claimed may not be relevant to questions of justice; second, those rights which *are* demonstrably relevant to justice do not constitute the *whole* of justice. Impartiality is a procedural principle, itself falling short of perfection, and at most one element only of justice, though it is not difficult to defend it as a necessary element in a *prima facie* sense.

The need for the *prima facie* qualification is evident when we reflect that in some circumstances impartiality may be less just than partiality: to be strictly impartial in the allocation of resources, for instance, would mean that those in desperate poverty would receive no more than others already provided with basic necessities. To provide according to need would be to act partially to the specially needy. Justice must be wider then, than the idea of impartiality. Justice as observance of social values is similar to the expectation that all should follow the rules. It conceals first, the fallacious assumption that values as standards or expectations are necessarily moral; second, the fact that the category of justice is much wider than the category of social values, norms or expectations. None of these four – referring to rules, rights, impartiality and social values – can stand as the formal notion of justice.

Intuitive Ideas of Justice

Having defended the formal notion of justice as *fairness in the treatment of persons* as adequately as we can at this stage (further dimensions will be added in the next two chapters on morality and rights respectively) we now attempt to measure it against other formulations, beginning with our intuitive ideas of justice. This we do, not because we are able to claim reliability generally from our intuitions, but because a sense of *injustice* lies so close to common experience as to leave the possibility that significant components of justice may well be embedded in it. From early childhood almost to the end of our lives, at least within the limits of our ability to communicate with others, we have certain intuitive, unanalysed notions of what justice is, although our attitude is frequently negative. We think and speak of *injustice*, that is, more than of justice. In childhood the commonest source of family disaffection is children's supposition of unequal treatment. Then injustice is seen as unfairness – unfairness as unequal treatment: favours in the form of kindness and gifts, basic provisions of food and clothing, and even consideration of wants or desires, are expected to be distributed as evenly as possible. A second facet of justice emerges in playing games. As soon as we are old enough to understand rules we insist that they be followed. Intentional breaking of rules is usually for personal advantage, and children's perception of this as unfair is not so much out of respect for intrinsic fairness, but – as with unequal treatment – rather for self-protection. Thus even in childhood we detect injustice in anything savouring of arbitrariness, and we feel safe when our relations with others are governed by *rules*. A third facet of injustice in childhood is psychological. We have our developing self-images, our incipient individualities and with other children in the family, and with other children in the class-room, we frequently measure ourselves against others. For this reason we tend to develop a hypersensitivity to favouritism toward others and to personal slights toward ourselves. The envy that some develop in competition with others may stay with them throughout life. Injustice is given a cutting edge by our self-protective relations with others.

It is much the same at the other end of our life-span, as well as in between. Some of the elderly feel that they have been poorly treated by the society to which they have contributed all their working lives. There are perceived inequalities as the young and the old are compared, a suggestion of arbitrariness, envy and a sense of personal slight. In the competitiveness of mature adulthood many are swayed by convictions of equality, strongly motivated by self-protection and self-interest, offended whenever they suffer in comparison with others, insisting that if there were only firm rules to govern social organizations they would have fared better. Sensitivity to perceived injustice is never more poignantly exhibited than in the contesting of wills. Then an assumption is usually made that all surviving children should receive equal shares, and the bitterness of alleged unfairness is apt to be transferred from the deceased to the major beneficiaries, with the minor beneficiaries harbouring grievances and a sense of alienation. Still the strands of intuitive injustice are to be seen: equality, fairness based on rules (or otherwise a suspicion of arbitrariness), envy, protection of self-interest. Vaguely too in these intuitive notions of injustice is the belief that all of us, as equals, have equal rights: that children of the one family have equal rights, that citizens of the one society have equal rights, that inequalities in treatment are violations of rights. In all of these intuitive ideas there is much to be unravelled, and certainly there are misconceptions, particularly of equality, and often too of rights. Rules, equality, equity and impartiality, protection of rights are all there, so that intuitively we have some of the ingredients of justice in some situations, without any formulation of a formal notion that will fit all cases. Our intuitive ideas of injustices are generally egocentric and defensive, and therefore allow many substantive variations in the interpretation of justice, some of which would certainly conflict for the very reason of a biased and dominant self-interest.

Philosophers on Justice

Intuitive ideas of *injustice* have indeed shown how widespread in
ordinary experience are substantive notions of justice, and how much
a disciplined approach to the formal notion is needed to give us the
confidence of a fixed and stable reference point. Can we expect from
philosophers a stronger concern for the irreducible idea with which
we might measure our own formal notion of justice? We shall begin
with Aristotle in view of his judgement of education in a formal
rather than a substantive sense when referring to education as a
becoming.

Aristotle

On one thing Aristotle (like Plato earlier) made no mistake: people
simply are *not* equal. They are not equal in ability, for instance, in
work capacity, in knowledge, in self-mastery, in leadership potential,
in dependability, in dedication to the service of others. Therefore in
this Greek view it was just to treat individuals accordingly – not as
equals, but as *unequals*. In his *Nicomachean Ethics*, Aristotle
observed a general supposition about justice: '... the unjust is
unequal, the just is equal, as all men suppose it to be, even apart from
any argument' (Book v, 1131^a). An act is unjust when a person is so
treated that he has too little, while a person who takes too much for
himself in a similar way acts unjustly (1134^a). If Aristotle had left it at
that we would have been given the impression that justice is no more
than calculating how to restore a proper mathematical balance
between and among individuals, some of whom have too little and
others have too much. Indeed *equality* was conceived very much, at
times, in those terms. Aristotle was interested in the kinds of cases
that would be called *legal* justice, governed by rules embodied in law,
or by rules that *ought* to be embodied in law, so his interpretations
were attempts to give order to a disordered judicial system. He
suggested that there were two distinct areas where a regulatory
justice was called for: first, with respect to such things as punishments
and compensations; second, with respect to distribution of benefits.
The first constituted Rectificatory, Corrective, or Commutative
Justice, and in such cases he believed that arithmetical proportion
would be adequate to restore the balance of right and wrong. The
second constituted Distributive Justice, and to that he believed that

geometrical proportion was appropriate. Whatever is just is proportional: it was clear to Aristotle that the man acting unjustly has too little of what is good (ibid., 1131^b). In the first case, to be governed by arithmetical proportion, an assumption is to be made by the courts, according to Aristotle, that the parties in dispute are morally equal in that the civil courts are not to be called upon to decide on whether acts are morally right or wrong. A wrongful act is an equal loss to the one who has been deprived of something as it is a gain to the other. Rectification of the situation involves the judge taking from the gainer something equivalent to what he has wrongfully appropriated, and allotting it to the loser (1132^a). The second case is rather more difficult: the goods that are to be distributed are to be related to the respective merits of the recipients. With the goods divided into portions, the portions are to be in the same ratios, one to the other, as are the merits of the recipients. Thus geometrical proportion, like arithmetical proportion in the first case, achieves equality of ratios (1131^b) and justice is vindicated as equality.

But such a calculating approach was not to be his final word on justice. Justice is not merely a way of acting, but of acting in a certain way under the influence of one's character or dispositions. However much he extolled reason in the perception of justice as a proportion, in rectificatory or distributive justice, or in justice as reciprocity, Aristotle's deliberations led him to acknowledge the force of dispositions in justice. For justice 'is essentially something human'. To perform an unjust deed, or a just deed, is to act 'as the result of a certain state of character' (1137^a). Thus he distinguished between the equitable and the legally just. While the equitable is just, it is superior to legal justice in so far as it corrects it. The difficulty about the law was that it sought to make universal statements – statements applicable to all men – but in some circumstances it was not able to do so correctly. It is of the nature of practical affairs, Aristotle noted, for some cases to arise which are not covered by the universal statement, and then the deficiency of the current law needs to be corrected by a decree, one that is 'adapted to the facts' and is not merely a rigid application of the law (1137^b).

It was Aristotle who in this way provided the precedent for the English equity system with its flexible, human adjustment of the law, especially in times when the common law was often confused, outmoded, and in its application likely to create injustice rather than justice. But despite this promising perceptiveness, Aristotle's thoughts were fundamentally on the practical world of everyday affairs, on *substantive* considerations, that is, not on the formal notion of justice in any irreducible or elemental sense. If his thoughts on justice as an idea were to be expressed as a general principle, it would be appropriate in part, but only in part, to say that *justice is equality*. About that he had much more to say than about any other single principle, but it would only partly express his idea of justice, because he also held, through his observation of the inadequacies of the law as he knew it in particular, and through his appreciation of the complexities of practical human affairs which would always prove intractable to the law in special circumstances, that *justice is equity*. That was his most significant insight on justice in the formal sense.

Plato

The only justification for exploring Aristotle's antecedents in Greek philosophy is that in the *Republic* Plato asks at the very outset, What is justice? and there is some hope there that his recollections of Socrates (as Plato is believed to convey them in Book I) might have reached a fundamental concept. That hope too is in vain, for Socrates was illustrating a method of enquiry, and concluded – with typical irony– that the search for a definition of justice left him ignorant (354). As for Plato, his primary concern in the *Republic* was for the characteristics of the good society: justice had meaning only in the context of society. It was an attribute not merely of an individual, but first and foremost of a whole city-state (Book II, 368). His idea of justice is as difficult to reduce to simple terms as Aristotle's. It is primarily that justice is a function of a just society, and a just society is organized on natural endowments. In that sense justice is social harmony. Inasmuch as justice is an individual activity, it is the unison of virtue and intellect in those who have command of their minds and their dispositions, and can therefore rule or judge with knowledge, self-discipline, self-denial and fairness for all. For the rest it is no more than doing what they as citizens are best suited by nature to do. If there was ever a substantive idea of justice it was this. Following Socrates' early appearance, he seemed all too eager to give up the search for any formal notion of justice, with relevance to any of the many substantive forms justice might take, directed by his own political ideal and preconceptions. To search for this formal notion was not his aim. Had it been so it would have been a perfect instance of value preferences controlling reason.

Hume

Like Plato, Hume in the Eighteenth Century was preoccupied with justice as a moral concept. In this he was worlds apart from Kant, who a little later in the same century drew a sharp contrast between legal justice and moral justice, and gave to *moral* justice the binding quality of a moral law.[13] By contrast Hume's thoughts were sociological and psychological, descriptive of the social situation as he found it. Would this down to earth approach produce a fundamental notion of justice?

Hume held that justice is a contrived notion, one that is the combined result of a psychological condition of 'selfishness and limited generosity', characteristic of mankind, and a sociological condition of limited resources, 'the scanty provision nature has made' for men's wants[14] (*A Treatise of Human Nature*, Book III, Part ii, pp.494–7). In that sense it is artificial, not natural, although in another sense justice *is* natural, for a sense of virtue is indeed natural, and 'no virtue is more natural than justice' (p.484). Justice is simply an adjustment which man makes, given his own limitations, to the limitations of the world as he finds it. If man's nature and natural resources were both generous, the very concept of justice would be destroyed, because man would have no use for it. Men would find no need to restrain each other by rules if they were mutually benevolent in pursuing the public interest. Both property rights and promises are found to be matters of convention. If we imagine a *state of nature* preceding any societies, there would simply be no place in it for either property or promises, and no such thing as justice or injustice. As for the 'natural' virtue of justice, it is no more than a pleasing sentiment (p.501, 517). Hume's idea of justice is that it is an accommodation of human nature to natural resources, each of them something less than desirable. It is contrived, certainly, to suit particular social circumstances: justice is relative, not absolute, and will be contrived in different ways by different societies.

Such a conclusion on justice was simply another preoccupation with substantive matters. Hume had penetrated no closer to justice than had Plato. A sentiment of justice – pleasing or otherwise – is not a concept of justice. Justice as a utility for social regulation is descriptive of its purpose, not of its fundamental character.

Mill

After Hume, and in the next century, Mill developed his ideas on justice in his *Utilitarianism*.[15] He noted first that we have subjective feelings of justice, sometimes of a peculiar strength, but these are akin to our other moral sentiments in that they provide no criteria for conduct, and indeed, give a false impression of objectivity. Yet like Socrates, he sought eagerly to find what justice itself is, what its distinguishing characteristics are. First he instanced various objects of injustice (or of justice): depriving someone of personal liberty, property or other legal entitlement; taking or withholding from a person something to which he has a moral right; giving a person what he *deserves* (as a case of justice), or what he does not deserve (as a case of injustice); breaking faith with someone (though as with other obligations of justice, not absolute in the sense of excluding possible exceptions); being partial. As for equality, Mill saw it as close to impartiality, and often as forming part of the conception of justice. But here he was thinking of the variability of individual conceptions of equality, and commented on the ease with which people's convictions of equality as justice gave way to expediency when it suited them. This might have suggested that Mill was being merely descriptive, giving the 'is' but still holding fast to an ethical 'ought' about equality as central to justice. He seems rather to have become despairing of finding any order in the notion of justice amid the welter of its different applications. He observes that the ideas of justice and its obligations are not always subject to legal determination or regulation: justice is a moral concept, as well as a legal one. He is strongly attracted to the relationship between *justice, morality and desert*, believing that at the bottom of our notions of right and wrong is the thought of whether a person ought or ought not to be punished for his conduct.

The sentiment of justice is a 'natural feeling of retaliation or vengeance' (*Utilitarianism*, p.325); it is a desire that those who break a rule of conduct should be punished for it. The brute feeling of vengeance becomes moral when it is completely subordinated to social sympathies, or thoughts of human well-being. The rule itself we universalize, supposing it to apply to all, and to be for their good (p.326). As for individual rights, they invariably invoke questions of justice. Whenever we think of justice we refer to some conduct which is right or wrong, and at the same time to something, in some circumstances, which a person can claim (against another or against the state) as his moral right (p.323–4). These individual rights should be protected by any society which is concerned with our well-being. What Mill calls 'the highest standard of social and distributive justice' is justice according to *desert*: 'we should treat all equally well (when no higher duty forbids) who have deserved equally well of *us*, and ... society should treat all equally well who have deserved equally well of it ...' (p.335). This leads him, without his having offered any clear guidance as to how desert is to be individually evaluated, to his principle of utility, the notion that an act is good in so far as it contributes to the greatest happiness of the greatest number. He follows Bentham's principle as he says (p.336), of 'everyone to count for one, nobody to count for more than one': one person's happiness is supposed equal in degree to that of any other.[16] In the first analysis, the highest justice is to be seen in social terms: justice is the name for whatever moral influences contribute to the greatest happiness principle and so to the social good. Justice as equality is still perceptible in this notion of utility: beyond equality of treatment corresponding to equality of desert, is the equality of everyone's right to happiness.

Review of Philosophers on Justice

Plato was preoccupied with the ideal society, Hume with the actual society according to his perceptions of it. Mill was preoccupied with an overriding principle of happiness, in the interests of every member of every society. In all three cases the preconception so dominated the respective views of justice that external and substantive notions ruled out any possibility of discovering the fundamental or formal notion of justice.

   In some respects the thoughts of selected philosophers on justice have not been markedly different from common intuitions of justice, at least superficially: the importance of rules, impartiality in the application of rules leading to an equality of consideration, though not necessarily to equality of treatment, the rights of individuals within the one social group, and the underlying importance – associated with a structure of rules and their impartial application – of the social group itself having the capacity to impart justice to individual members. In other respects substantive differences among them may be explained in part by the social circumstances of their times: Plato and Aristotle with respect to their emphasis on inequality among citizens, despite their acceptance of the formal principle of equality of treatment; Mill for his Victorian attitude to wrong-doing and to desert in his so-called 'sentiment of justice'. The major contribution of the philosophers as a group to our understanding of justice has come from Aristotle: it was he who noted that the practical affairs of men are so complex that is inconceivable that all situations of human conflict should be covered by positive law. Therefore, though he distinguished justice from equity, it was equity which he saw as a necessary supplement to the law, and since his time the notion of equity has become an important consideration in our general idea of justice. Philosophers have not provided us with a formal notion of justice by which we might measure our own; substantive considerations have led them in other directions.

Justice in Jurisprudence

The extent to which thinkers of all kinds are influenced substantively by their times is illustrated in the now ironic view of a jurist writing in the United States in 1915, when social values had their own flavour. Justice, he asserted, is the repression by the state of individual interests which conflict with its own.[17] If philosophers' primary views were not bent toward formal notions of justice, what of the interests of jurists? Might we not expect some interest from them in the conceptual foundations of justice? This is an expectation likely to be fulfilled only if they are prepared to distinguish, as Aristotle and Kant had done, between legal justice and moral justice, acknowledging the possibility of conflict between them.

Among jurists, the formal recognition of rules, equality of treatment by reference to the same rules for all whether rich or poor, and without arbitrary discriminations in other respects, and recognition of individual rights, are still of central importance as they were to the philosophers. But jurists, sociologists and others have not been slow in observing the contrast in some countries between formal principles of justice on the one hand, and on the other hand substantive justice, or the content of the law, and its application to cases. Formal principles on their own are insufficient to ensure that justice is done.

It is one thing to show the propriety of bringing different cases under the same general rule; it is another thing to establish the propriety of the rules themselves. Aristotle's formal principle of treating unequals unequally is similarly inadequate unless there are substantive principles added to it which show on what relevant grounds inequalities are to be determined: those who on a formal principle of equality are to be treated equally are necessarily different in many separate respects. The task in the activity of justice is to treat equally all those who may be classified equals in relevant respects, and to achieve that calls for much more than the abstraction of formal justice. (Social criticism in Victorian and Twentieth Century literature has made one law for the rich and one for the poor something of a by-word). In South Africa, with some laws applying specifically to the black population, the formal principle of unequal treatment of unequals requires to be justified by reference to additional principles which explain the relevant categories of unequals. Jurists have been concerned primarily with such aspects as these in the administration of legal justice, or with the activity of justice, or with broad questions of the relationship between legal justice and social values, rather than with the abstract or formal notion of justice. An instance of the impact of social values on legal justice is the extension of jurists' interests from issues of traditional importance, such as rights, to matters of relatively new social concern such as the environment.[18] Another instance of the strong orientation of jurisprudence toward the *activity* of justice rather than toward its formal idea is in various attempts to explain the nature of this activity. Thus in the activity of legal justice the picture presented by jurists is of the intellect in command, but it is intellect welded with moral values of impartiality and integrity. There is generally a supposed conformity to rationality: a determination to elicit the facts, to distinguish between false evidence and true, to view every party in dispute with respect, to make allowance for human limitations, to be guided by whatever rules are relevant to the case, to hold in subjection one's own prejudices or preconceptions, to preserve self-mastery so that determinations are, as far as humanly possible, influenced by reason and never by caprice. This is to state a substantive ideal.

When jurists link justice with particular judicial determinations the substantiveness is compounded. Inasmuch as justice is the product of one man's deliberations, or even of the deliberations of a judicial panel, it is recognized by some as entailing a degree of subjectivity. Inasmuch as it is influenced by legal tradition, as well as by social values, it is not without rules or criteria to which to refer, but whatever the influences bearing on it, the judgement is seen ultimately as a personal one. It is sometimes claimed that in its most constructive and imaginative forms it may do more to influence both tradition and social values than to be influenced by them.[19] Thus some jurists acknowledge that every judge takes something of himself to his judgements, something of his own attitudes and values which he cannot always suppress, however much the ideal of impartiality would benefit by their exclusion, and something of himself too with respect to intellect or perspicacity. Some jurists remind us that when a panel of judges – with a presumed equal comprehension of matters discussed in common among them – find themselves unable to agree, it becomes evident that intellect is necessary but not sufficient for consensus on justice. By showing that judges may be influenced by both social and personal values, jurists thus draw attention to the limits of rationality in activities of justice, including impartiality and objectivity. Accounts of activities of justice such as these accord with both intuitive and philosophical views of justice in substantive senses. On other matters such as creativity they explain possibilities of justice in activities of judicial determinations, when imaginative constructiveness is accompanied by perspectives of equity in its humane insights.

Reflections on the activity of justice show the extent to which justice is seen by jurists as a substantive, not a formal notion. Of those who *do* attempt to reach a formal notion the formulation of most interest is Perelman's, that justice 'consists in observing a rule which lays down the obligation to treat in a certain way all persons who belong to a given category'.[20] How does this notion compare with our own? We have to note that the 'certain way' could be just or unjust, as long as it is consistent, so in this expression justice or its opposite would equally fit the formal notion; and the treatment could be fair or unfair, as long as it is consistent. Similarly in Hayek's notion that justice is 'the principle of treating all under the same rules', there is no indication in the statement of the quality of the rules, so that opposites again might be admitted. For these reasons we have confidence again in the formal notion of justice which we have proposed, as being a reduction beyond which it is not practicable to proceed if we are to retain meaningfulness through non-contradictoriness in subsequent discussion.

The formal idea of justice may find expression in many different practical situations, both inside and outside the law. It may be reflected in a humane concern for fairmindedness and equity in appropriate situations when the rules of law or administration are inadequate. It would not be evident in a contrary case of a judge or administrator cutting loose from laws and other rules, on the pretext that these are irrelevant to a particular situation, and acting capriciously or arbitrarily, without any concern for treating persons fairly. Justice may be expressed whenever some individuals have power over other individuals, and so are in a position to deliver fair treatment to them. The formal idea of justice may be detected as central to many social situations in family, school or community, to government resource allocation, to umpires' or referees' decisions, as well as to non-discriminatory acts or procedures. Hearing evidence, becoming familiar with all aspects of a case, briefing jury in criminal cases, are not activities of moral justice, as such, but delivering a judgement in court which satisfies the formal principles of justice which we have suggested, *is* an activity of moral justice. So too is giving a decision in a game, recommending someone for promotion in a competitive staffing situation, and so forth, in so far as these too satisfy our formal principle of justice. We cannot merely achieve justice, we can also conceptualize it: we can form a notion of what it is.

We shall end this chapter with two explanations. First the formal notion of justice is an *idea*, not an ideal, though there are substantive ideals of justice as there are of education, and each may offer a motivational support to principles of action derived from the formal notion. Second, the foreshadowed distinction between moral justice and legal justice signifies both that some laws are contrary to morality, and that some administration of justice, in the courts or elsewhere, is contrary to morality. Conversely, some activities of legal justice are moral inasmuch as they satisfy the formal notion of justice which is also a moral notion. This is something we have yet to explain in the next chapter when we consider morality both as a formal notion and in particular substantive senses.

2   Morality

In the previous chapter we arrived at a formal notion of education whose qualification – 'consistent with social values' – has both positive and negative aspects, the former considering the interests of children (as well as the interests of society). It is in the interests of children, for instance, to be guided by teachers and parents into an understanding of social values which may pertain to their particular society, such as respect for property – public and private, community co-operation, respect for heritage, compassion for the ill, the elderly the intellectually and physically handicapped, and for the socially underprivileged. We suggested that such a consideration implies that education is a moral notion, along with the consideration that the developing of potentialities contributes to personal satisfaction. Similarly in the formal notion of justice as fairness in the treatment of persons there is implied a particular way of considering others, which in the value words 'fairness' and 'persons' is implied to be a *moral* way. We have now to make good these claims by an examination of the nature of morality. To link specifically with the previous chapter, in the following section we shall state and explain the formal notion of morality. Then, having already included 'persons' in the formal notion of justice, we shall explain the moral significance of this expression which will at the same time enlarge our understanding of justice. In the next section (p. 45) we shall be concerned with substantive matters, all of which will be shown to be consistent with the formal notion of morality and the primary and secondary principles related to it. These substantive considerations will provide a wider perspective on morality, as well as a background of understanding before presenting a coherent statement of an ethical standpoint.

THE FORMAL NOTION OF MORALITY

Statement of Formal Notion

The formal notion of morality – in the sense in which we have used 'formal notion' – is *a practical consideration of others' interests*

34

Nothing short of that will satisfy the fundamental nature of morality for reasons which we shall now state.

First, by the interests of others we imply *individual* others' well-being (not others considered in the mass such as impoverished Third World peoples), those things that are beneficial to them, such as their security, their mental and physical health, their capacity for satisfaction from life's activities. In an educational sense it refers to a special source of satisfaction, which is the developing of certain individual potentialities, such as a potentiality for increasing intellectual command, a potentiality for skilled motor co-ordination, a potentiality for creativity in a variety of artistic expressions, a potentiality for enjoyment of social relationships, a potentiality for leadership, for scholarship and so forth. Though some adult presumption is not in the interests of children, some *is*, such as a teacher's presumption to know – with respect to certain phases of childhood – what is in children's interests, and to know this better than the children do themselves. It is to know, for instance, what children *need* in the developing of potentialities, sometimes in contrast with what the children themselves *want*. Left to their own resources – in the sense of Rousseau's *Emile* – some children would express no want for learning of any kind except what they absorb as they are left to their own resources. Even in adulthood there are ample instances of conflicts between wants and needs, or between wants and interests. If X is advised that it would be in his interests to ring a known criminal Y at 8 p.m., with a guarantee of quick profit, X's wants may blind him to what in fact his best interests are. So morality requires that the interests of *individual* others be considered, sometimes above the individual's personal wants.

What is it though, to 'consider others' interests'? This raises the second point of morality. 'Consider' is, like 'interests', a normative word, for it implies not merely 'giving thought to', but also 'being thoughtful for'. Such a consideration is still not enough on its own for two reasons. First, it may leave the object of the thoughtfulness – a child, a parent, a needy community member – exactly as before, well-being no further advanced by virtue of benevolent *thoughts*. Therefore benevolent thoughts are not enough on their own. We need both 'benevolence' and 'benefaction' in their literal senses: both 'well-wishing', and 'well-doing'. In other words, the thoughtfulness directed toward the interests of another must be converted to a beneficial act. That is the reason for the qualification 'practical' in the formal notion. Second, even if the thoughtfulness directed toward another's interests is of a practical kind, the act may serve the interests primarily of the agent, not of the presumed beneficiary. It is not enough for us to claim that the *consideration* is a kind of *moral* consideration, for that would lead to circularity: we would be exploring the fundamental character of morality by using a component which we have already accepted as 'moral'. Therefore we need a second qualification to 'consideration', namely, 'disinterested'. Then we leave no doubt that 'a practical and disinterested consideration of others' interests' captures the spirit of the elemental notion of morality. The attentive, thoughtful family doctor may be considering the interests of a patient in his practical concern for physical and mental health, and may derive personal satisfaction from the realisation that his patient is recovering under his treatment. But his primary motive may still be a substantial profit from professional services: that is, his practical consideration may not be authentically moral in the sense in which we use 'morality'. Similarly the teacher who gives his time to a group of students after school hours, in the hope that they will perform well in public examinations, may be motivated primarily by a concern for his own professional advancement, even though he derives some satisfaction from a realisation that his services for them are beneficial to their futures. His practical consideration of their interests is not disinterested. 'Consideration' itself, therefore, is in need of a dual qualification. But it is the following expression of 'others' interests' which largely rescues us from this need, indicating that in so acting the element of disinterestedness is already there. Apart from that, we need to question whether a consideration of others' interests can properly be claimed to require *total* disinterestedness, without, that is, any concern at all for one's own interests. This cannot be justified as we reflect on practical situations. The family doctor has interests of his own to consider – his personal health, his own security, his recreational needs for life satisfaction – as well as having thoughts for the well-being of his patients. Similarly when giving charity to the poor we cannot entirely neglect our own circumstances. In Good Samaritanism by to-day's roadside it would be foolish to neglect one's own security in heavy traffic. The proportion of self-regarding to other-regarding considerations is not significant for a formal notion of morality. We shall therefore exclude from it the qualification 'disinterested' before 'consideration'.

In this preliminary justification of the formal notion of morality as we have stated it, it will appear odd – following our statement of the formal notion of justice in the preceding chapter – that we have used the word 'others' rather than the word 'persons', for to this point it is persons rather than any more general form of 'individuals', human beings' or 'others' that we have had in mind. Indeed, to this point 'persons' is precisely what we have in mind. The reason for using the more general form 'others' is that we may have grounds subsequently for extending the boundaries of morality beyond persons, and as we shall see, even beyond human beings. But to further justify the formal notion of justice, specifically to justify it as a *moral* notion, it is to 'persons' that we must now turn. Then having tied up this loose end from the previous chapter, and explained why 'others' is used in the formal notion of morality, we shall return to this formal notion and attempt to give it further justification from intuitive and traditional ideas on morality.

Persons

We interpret 'person' widely to apply to all those who are aware of having interests of their own, with desires, motives and a striving to achieve their goals, thereby developing an individual identity or selfhood as distinct from that of others in their social environment. We have no wish to restrict 'person' to those who are capable of distinctively well-reasoned choices, or who have a high degree of *autonomy* in using individual reason, self-reliance and self-mastery in setting and achieving their goals. To insist on such criteria, indeterminate as they are, would be to give to 'person' a specificity which is little more than an expression of particular ideals or values. Every person is respected, nonetheless, as rational to some degree. A person is simply one who is aware of his own individuality as a thinking, feeling, desiring, striving human being, with a life of his own to lead, and who is aware as well that his interests, plans, goals and actions can be influenced, for good or ill, by others about him.[1] To recognize another as a person is, in this sense, to see him both as a distinct individual and as one similar to ourselves in these very respects. It is to see him from his own perspective as far as this is possible, assuming as closely as possible the standpoint from which he views himself. In this way to have respect for persons is to perceive a commonality of values and reason, regardless of individual variability. An important qualification is that we do not respect those whose desiring, planning, striving activities are immoral, bent plainly toward harming others: respecting persons is a moral concept. Limited sympathy and capacity for empathizing may lead to a misperception of personhood in some, such as prisoners in the dock, children in the classroom, unemployed in queues, peasants in paddy-fields, oppressed serfs, and so forth, especially when perception is of groups rather than of individuals. From the individual perspective of those so misperceived, consciousness of personhood may be expressed in outbursts of indignation. Higgins' contempt for Eliza in Shaw's *Pygmalion* provoked her to assert that she too had feelings, the 'same as anyone else', though to him she was a mere guttersnipe, fit only for laboratory experimentation and manipulable at his will and pleasure.[2]

Thus the formal notion of morality – in so far as it refers to other human beings with normal human capacities – refers to persons, but for the reason given is extended to the more general form 'others'. In the formal notion of *justice* we are concerned solely with fairness in the treatment of human beings by other human beings, and to perceive them as *persons* adds a necessary dimension to any treatment qualifying as justice. We can be fair or even-handed in our treatment of various animals, but 'justice' refers to our treatment of other rational beings like ourselves. Justice is a moral notion: it is, as fairness in the treatment of persons, also a practical consideration of others' interests, with the 'others' referring to persons in the case of justice. We shall now turn to intuitive and traditional ideas on morality.

Intuitive Ideas of Morality

The formal notion of morality has been arrived at in much the same way as the two other formal notions. Again we shall explore intuitive ideas for any possible evidence to support this formal notion. These intuitions relate to things we regard as good or bad, right or wrong, things that ought to be done or ought not to be done, things referred to variously as exemplary, praiseworthy, iniquitous, reprehensible, and so forth. Our earliest moral impressions are of rules, of obedience or disobedience to them, of rewards and punishment. It is wrong to be cruel, we learn in childhood, to hurt family pets; it is wrong to cheat in games, to tell lies, to break promises; it is wrong for parents and teachers to have favourites; it is right to help in the home, to be polite to guests, to respect others' property. Already, without extending the list, we have included some of the intuitive strands of justice: the notion of rules, the importance of fairness and consistency in their application, equality of consideration and equality of treatment. As well there is respect for individual rights and for social values. Morality is seen as wider than justice even in these intuitive notions, for we would not think of children's cruelty to one another as unjust, or adults' cruelty in hunting animals for sport, though some at least would regard them unequivocally as immoral. We would not want to argue that morality is protection of rights, or that it is impartiality, or conformity to social values. Each of these is too narrow a conception of morality as it is of justice, and raises contradictions. To say that morality is helping others in need is too narrow, and is contradictory too unless we specify and in some way justify the needs as warranting support: the need of a traitor for protection from his country's law is not a need we would regard as morally supportable. Morality is not observance of maxims on telling the truth and keeping promises because, apart from our intuitions that morality must be much more than this, even these maxims are not universally applicable. We come close to the formal notion in the idea of benevolence, but this also is too narrow for the formal notion of morality is more than the idea of *giving thought* to others' welfare.

We shall return to these intuitive ideas when we have looked briefly at some of the traditional philosophical views of morality.

Philosophers and Others on Morality

Hume

Naive intuitions of morality would have been justified by some Eighteenth Century moral philosophers as expressions of a *moral sense*, or a 'sentiment of humanity', something that is part of human nature. Hume agreed that distinctions between good and evil cannot be made by reason, because reason alone is incapable of causing action, while our notions of good and evil are (*A Treatise of Human Nature*, Book III, p.462).[3] Although he used reason specifically for the discovery of truth and falsehood (referring either to concepts – 'the *real* relations of ideas', or to empirical facts – 'the *real* existence and matter of fact'), he recognized that moral truths and falsehoods are involved with man's natural psychological condition in which reason plays a part, with respect to action, only by prompting or directing a passion (pp.458, 462). Virtue is a matter of feeling, an impression. Ironically, in this emphasis on morality as a natural sentiment, Hume substituted his own dogma of nature for a dogma of reason. For moral sentiments, he declared, 'are so rooted in our constitution and temper that... 'tis impossible to extirpate and destroy them' (p.474); and virtuous motives, which give rise to virtuous actions, are simply part of our human nature (p.479). The chief source of moral conflict is 'selfishness and limited generosity' (p.494), combined with competition for limited resources. In practical morality it is not only man's nature that is to be understood, but also his social situation – with respect to property for instance – and the various sociological influences that bear on him. Underlying all our moral perceptions is *sympathy*, which is part of human nature (p.618), and in the last resort morality is not so much a matter for the intellect as for taste and sentiment (*An Enquiry Concerning Human Understanding*, Section XII, Part III, p.165).[4]

Yet among those such as Hume who sought an understanding of morality in human nature, observed in experience, it soon became evident that there were conflicting judgements on what that human nature is. In the Seventeenth Century Hobbes had founded a morality on man's self-interest which was also supposedly natural to him. Whatever a man desires he calls good, and whatever he hates is to him evil: nothing is absolutely good or evil (*Leviathan*, p.120).[5] Hobbes saw something artificial or contrived in morality, as Hume did in the next century, inasmuch as it pertained to social organizations, or the system of rules which required general observance so that man's individual desires would have a better chance of being gratified (p.234). Against these rules or laws, the laws of nature were seen as immutable and eternal (p.215).

Eighteenth Century Moralists

Apart from Hume there were others in the Eighteenth Century who believed that some kind of moral sentiment or moral sense is natural to man, in particular noting a general human inclination toward *benevolence*. One of the most influential of these was Shaftesbury, who spoke of benevolence as a unifying principle in social life, directed toward the good of the whole; and this was extended to a 'good and right' impulse to *doing* good ('An Essay on the Freedom of Wit and Humour', Part II, Section III, p.66).[6] Hutcheson saw benevolence as the sole virtue, which gives to man a natural moral sense and inclines him away from self-interest. Butler spoke of the 'natural disposition to kindness and compassion', but above that an overriding conscience which was still part of his nature, and which acted in much the same way as Kant's imperatives to the rational man of good will. Through this rational faculty he became a moral agent, and 'a law to himself' (Sermon II, III, 'Upon Human Nature', pp.23–4). Benevolence he regarded as 'a natural principle'.[7] Gay held that the moral sense is not innate or implanted in us, but 'acquired either from our observation or the initiation of others' (*Concerning the Fundamental Principle of Virtue or Morality*, Section IV, p.785).[8] Hartley argued that benevolence is self-generating: since it leads generally to gratification it continually increases. The moral sense needs to be developed but once it is, the individual finds such pleasure in benevolence that it becomes 'equal to self-interest'. He observed a tendency of self-interest to increase benevolence, and of benevolence to lessen self-interest (*Observations of Man, His Frame, His Duty, and His Expectations*, pp.499–500[9]. A sharp disagreement thus emerged with Hobbes' notion of morality as grounded in self-interest. For those who favoured a moral impulse expressing something in man's nature, it was sympathy, benevolence or social love, or conscience, each of them *opposing* the influence of self-interest, which was an impulse contrary to morality. The moral sentiment so expressed was an *idea* of morality, with understanding as well as emotion, and not merely sentiment in the weaker, affective sense.

What appeared strong among these Eighteenth Century moralists was a sense of *benevolence* toward fellow-men, rather than fundamental selfishness. In this many tended toward moralism – toward advocating how to live better lives, rather than attempting to characterize morality. Compared with our own formal notion of morality, the advocacy of benevolence was one-sided inasmuch as *benefaction* was not always aligned with it. Benevolence is itself caught up with popular senses involving charity or kindness, and these senses are too narrow to stand as a formal notion of morality. Altruism is also close to an irreducible formal notion of morality in its concern for others' well-being as a consistent principle of action, but it too suffers from popular extensions to unselfishness, or selflessness. A lack of concern for one's own well-being does not imply a positive concern for others' well-being. It is the difficulty of translating either 'benevolence with benefaction', or 'altruism' into an unambiguous expression of morality in the formal or fundamental sense that leaves us confident that neither can supplant our own formal notion.

Our earlier intuitive ideas of morality related particularly to practices concerned with social harmony, to ideas of rules and rights and equal treatment, for example, and respect for property. In these ideas, as well as in the notion that cruelty is wrong, there appear to be the elements of a moral sentiment too, a sentiment which is reflected in our more mature, adult intuitions of morality. As we shall see more clearly in the next chaper, our concern in this century has been increasingly with individual rights, with questions of discrimination against individuals or groups of individuals. We have become more sensitive perhaps than ever to questions of arbitrariness in legal and administrative decisions, to personal slights to individuals as though they were in some way inferior, like the Greek slaves in comparison with freemen. We see a moral demand to hold every human being as worthy of equal consideration before the law, so that all discriminatory criteria relating to such things as colour or ethnic background or religion or nationality are irrelevant to the central concern for all individuals as equally human. And in the law, as in administration and other human activities where judgements upon some individuals are made by others, there is an increasing interest in empathising, or attempting to see another's point of view by assuming his own mental perspective, in so far as this is practicable. This is to take a *person* perspective. Sympathy is not a rare quality among us, however variable it may be in depth. The Eighteenth Century sentiment of morality, as concerned centrally with benevolence in our social relationships, appears to come close to one aspect of the formal notion of morality, but on its own benevolence is not enough. If it is authentic it is at the same time disinterested, but it is not necessarily translated to moral acts. We have therefore some reason to be confident at this stage that the formal notion of morality is adequately expressed as a practical consideration of others' interests.

Kant

We shall make brief mention only of Kant, chiefly because his philosophy is difficult to present in readily understandable form without lengthy and complex explanations. But in the mainstream of ethical philosophy he stands pre-eminently for his emphasis on morality as a law from within, and for its indissoluble nexus with reason. Is there in this standpoint a standard of morality with which we might compare our formal notion?

The immediate contrast between Kant's notion of morality and our own is that while ours follows a moral tradition – especially since the Eighteenth Century – of reaching out toward others, Kant's morality is turned inwardly toward the self. Our moral duty is what we must first of all attend to. The very notion of a person is 'that he is able *of himself* to set before him his own end according to his own notions of duty'. There is a contradiction in requiring anyone else to take it as his duty that he should do something which only the individual himself can do. (*Preface to the Metaphysical Elements of Ethics*, IV, p.296).[10] When reason or intellect is in command in practical situations where the individual is called on to decide what he ought to do, there is no need for any external aid from a benevolent person interested in his well-being. The Rational Will leads to moral imperatives directly, as a matter of duty, and this confers 'autonomy shown in the fundamental principle of morality, by which reason determines the will to action' (*The Analytic of Pure Practical Reason*, p.131). In the inner life of morality there is therefore no choice. The good will, which alone is unconditionally good, leads invariably to acts performed out of moral duty, and motivated entirely by a recognition of that duty. We become aware of moral duty as an imperative to obey a law which applies equally to all rational beings, and which demands of us a consistency of conduct. Then we are in a position to universalize it, as we do with promise-keeping, for the very system of promise-keeping within a community of persons is based on the rational requirement that individuals do not break promises at will to serve their own interests. Every moral agent is his own master, obedient to no one but himself as he follows the commands of moral imperatives.

If this inner-directing, law-governing notion of morality can itself be justified, it presents a challenge to our formal notion of morality. But unless there is wide confirmation from others of finding morality in obeying rational commands of duty, Kant's standpoint must be held to be largely intuitive. That indeed is supported by his own attempt to justify the centrality of reason in morality by none other than reason itself. Once pure reason is discovered, he says, it 'contains the standard for the critical examination of every use of it' (Introduction to *The Analytic of Pure Practical Reason*, p.102). His transcendental justification of the Rational Will as directing individual moral duty stands as an expression of a substantive ideal. For that reason it may be taken as presenting no challenge to our formal notion of morality. His emphasis on reason and individual duty still left the individual with moral obligations to others, as he indicated in this categorical imperative:

> So act as to treat humanity, whether in thine own person or in that of any other, in every case as an end withal, never as a means only.
> (*Fundamental Principles of the Metaphysic of Morals*, p.46)

Thus Kant's ethics can still be placed within the framework of a practical consideration of others' interests, so does not contradict the formal notion of morality.

Review of Intuitive and Philosophical Viewpoints on Morality

Intuitive notions of morality in childhood and in adulthood alike are caught up with impressions of justice, equity, discrimination, individual rights, the keeping or breaking of rules or promises. Among philosophers, Kant stands as an exception to a general tendency to contrast benevolence with fundamental egoism, and to see morality as a practical thoughtfulness for others' interests. Certainly a moral sense, or a sentiment of benevolence, is of little value in itself in practical morality. And if it were true – empirically true – that every person has the rational power to obey moral imperatives as a matter of duty to himself, there might be no need for a practical *considera-tion* of others' interests, for it would become as much an inner directed moral imperative as to treat others as ends, never merely as means. The difficulty is that reason does not always speak uniformly to all, even to all with good will toward their fellows.

This survey of intuitive and philosophical viewpoints on morality has given us no grounds to amend our formal notion of morality. Our statement *takes account of* Hume's observation of man's limited generosity, and of Hobbes' emphasis on overriding self-interest. From that base it views morality, consistently with general experience, as an outgoing from ourselves to other selves, a conscious effort to suppress our dominant egocentric impulses in the interests of others' well-being. As Sidgwick observed with respect to general benevolence as a common obligation, 'we owe to all men such sacrifices' considering the effort needed as small in comparison with the service.[11]

SUBSTANTIVE QUESTIONS RELATING TO THE FORMAL NOTION

We shall now enlarge our understanding of morality by showing how various substantive issues arise from the formal notion. First we shall consider moral values and moral principles related to the formal notion of morality, extending the discussion of values to the question of whether they are more clearly justified as objective or as subjective. Then we shall ask whether we may be said to have a *purpose* in morality; that is, in living morally. The third task will be an extension of the second, to consider whether one of the commonest purposes proposed in ethical philosophy, namely, *happiness*, can be justified. Fourth, we shall make a coherent statement of a personal ethical standpoint as a substantive development of the formal notion.

Moral Values

As we enter into moral relationship with others, both our own moral values and theirs are publicly observable. Our notion of moral values excludes any supposed 'private morality' which refers to such things as 'being true to ourselves', or 'making something of ourselves as an obligation to humanity'. Inasmuch as they are *moral* our values are necessarily oriented toward others. Honesty, truth-telling, promise-keeping, impartiality, liberty, all make sense in this way, and make no moral sense with respect to the self alone. In other respects moral values share the characteristics of all our other values. They represent our personal preferences in the same way as in our reading, our choice of sport or of music, and indicate, with some degree of commitment, those things which we stand by and use as standards in the areas of conduct to which they relate. When they relate to morality, they incline us toward considering others' interests in a practical way, and place checks on impulses toward malevolence and malefaction, especially with respect to others' suffering. As our moral preferences our moral values state what *is*, but they are also our judgements of what *ought* to be – for ourselves and for others – in moral conduct. Our moral values then have a normative dimension, but since they are personal, we may find, despite large areas of agreement on values in our own community, that some of our moral values may be in conflict with those of others. Then, as we shall convey in Chapter 5,

our task is to explain and defend them in discussion, and if we find
that others are able to demonstrate moral weaknesses in our values,
to be ready to adjust, to modify, but not necessarily to abandon,
except with good reasons. One moral value espoused by Kant – as we
have seen – which has influenced much of subsequent ethical thought,
is *respect for persons*.

Apart from the personal, committed nature of our moral values as
we hold fast to them as standards of conduct, it is important to note
that they *are* modifiable. Indeed, without an assumption of freedom
and the possibility of changing things as they are, even against the
strong contrary pull of deeply entrenched attitudes and values, there
would be little point in discussing morality except descriptively of the
way things happen to be, and no point in presenting a normative
morality, with reasons why we ought to do this or that.

Moral Principles

We have to recognize first that since the formal notions themselves
relate to certain acts (moral acts, acts of justice or of education), each
may be expressed in the form of a primary or fundamental principle.
Given the formal notions, the primary moral principles are self-
evident, simply translating the former into the style of the latter.
Thus the primary moral principle is that we should live by a practical
consideration of others' interests. The primary principle of justice is
that those with power or influence over others should treat them
fairly as persons. The primary principle of education (like justice,
also an expression of a moral principle) is that whenever possible,
relevant members of society should help others in the developing of
their potentialities, in ways consistent with social values. This principle applies particularly, but not only, to the young.

Various secondary principles are deducible from these. For reasons
already given, the first of the secondary principles is that in our
practical consideration of others' interests we should not neglect our
own interests. The second of the secondary moral principles is that
whenever possible we should avoid, or prevent, the infliction of
suffering on others. In defence of the second of these, we support a
case for a condition of freedom from suffering as one of the interests
all people have (as indeed other sentient creatures also have). It is
part of their well-being which is the central notion of *others' interests*.

We shall now seek further justification for the first of the secondary moral principles referring to our own interests. If we could divest ourselves of all personal values and assume a purely intellectual stance, we would face a practical situation of individuals, each with desires and emotions, each with needs, such as for the development of potentialities, for understanding the self in relation to others and for a measure of confidence in planning the future – all interacting in a social group which reflects both harmony and discord, agreement and conflict. Principles are needed to guide conduct toward conflict reduction or resolution, principles which will help individuals to consider others as well as themselves as they go about their inevitable goal-seeking activities. To consider themselves individually, to be exclusively egoistic, would aggravate conflict. To go about considering others' interests and excluding their own entirely – if this were possible – would mean that every individual in the social group would be without active personal goal-seeking, leaving it to others to attain his ends for him. A would be serving the interests of B and C for instance; B those of A and C, and so forth, extending to as many members as there are in the social unit. In each case individual desires, motives and goals would be assumed or inferred, or would need to be explained to a number of other individuals. What follows from this imagined external stance? It is that we cannot ignore our own interests: we must consider them as we consider others' interests. A practical consideration of others' interests, without neglecting our own, is therefore central in our moral lives if we assume, from our supposedly detached intellectual stance, that morality is a matter of living together in social groups in ways which will be conflict-reducing.

Now let us more realistically consider the persons we are, with both reason and values. If we now open the door between the two, in metaphorical terms, we recognize that we are in general persons of some *sympathy* toward our fellow-men. We exclude psychopaths, those who are pathologically cruel, bestial, totally indifferent to others' interests, as psychologically abnormal, and not merely as uneducated. Undoubtedly these exist, in both war and peace. We shall leave open the question of whether sympathy is part of our natures, innate therefore, as Hume and some other Eighteenth Century moral philosophers believed, or whether it is learned, or whether learning supplements a dispositional tendency toward it. Empirically there may be no categorical answer to this question. We do know, however, that through the experience of living with others in family groups, in schools and in communities, we do *learn* attitudes and values relating to others. There are dispositions which develop, much as reason develops, and often in conjunction with reason. In the same way self-interest develops as part of maturation, for as individuality develops, so do personal desires, motives and goals, and part of our growing into adulthood is the increasing awareness that our interests and others' interests are sometimes in conflict, and that adjustments have therefore to be made. That rational perception is strengthened by sympathy for others as we perceive that they have interests similar to our own, they too are beings who are desiring, feeling, striving, at times deliberating on goal fulfilment, so we have among us a human kinship which is the basis of our sympathy.

We must recognize that a justification in terms of avoiding or reducing social conflict is no more than a pragmatic one. A further justification relates to a value or sentiment of benevolence which we assume to be widely shared among us, a conviction that since others are so much like us in their desires, emotions, motives, goals and so forth, we should regard their interests as in need of satisfaction as much as our own, and therefore to be considered by us along with our own interests. This is a rational and value justification, and a stronger justification than the merely pragmatic. Its weakness is that if a value of benevolence is part of morality then we are again arguing circularly, justifying a primary moral principle by an aspect of morality itself. If we agree that the first of the secondary moral principles simply expresses the way we are, with limitations of reason as well as of values, but with all of us (or nearly all) entertaining some sympathetic attitude toward others, we have an argument from nature which has no moral implications, for we may not reason from the way things are to the way they ought to be. We are not able, then, to claim an absolute justification for this secondary moral principle on grounds of what we find to be the case in experience.

In the last resort we must accept it as a substantive extension of the formal notion of morality, with the second part of the principle (referring to our own interests) a practical proviso to take account of particular circumstances in social relationships when it would not be rational to ignore our own interests. We can never rest entirely satisfied, though, with a private appeal to reason.

We shall now return briefly to the second of the secondary principles referring to suffering. The notion of benevolence often assumes significance in experience as non-malevolence, and benefaction as non-malefaction. A strong element in malevolence and malefaction during childhood and adolescence is cruelty, cruelty to others and to animals. Among normal individuals – excluding again the psychopathic and the psychologically immature – some degree of sympathy is a general human propensity, as is some degree of aversion to suffering. If it is right to consider others' interests, it is wrong to inflict suffering unnecessarily, for that is presupposed by a practical consideration of others' interests. The infliction of suffering unnecessarily is cruel, and cruelty is wrong. (In this we acknowledge that some inducement of suffering is necessary – as in surgery – as a means of eventual alleviation or elimination of pain.) That physical and mental suffering is wrong whenever inflicted unnecessarily on any creatures which are demonstrably sentient and sometimes capable of experiencing mental suffering as well, can be sustained only if we extend the notion of morality to include non-human sentient beings within our environments. We shall develop this point when we consider rights in the next chapter. For the present we are justified in supporting the secondary moral principle that whenever possible we should avoid, or prevent, the infliction of suffering on others.

Moral Values – Objective or Subjective?

We have presented individual moral values as matters of personal preference and commitment, and therefore as subjective as an individual's values in cultural activities, clothes or companionship. The analogies are not close: moral values are usually much more stable, for instance, and our commitment to them is usually more tenacious. In most circumstances we open our values to criticism more readily with respect to clothes and companionship than to moral values, despite a common defensiveness and protectiveness applying to all. More importantly in the present connection, we perceive that our choices in clothes and companionship, according to value criteria pertaining to them, are our *individual* preferences, whereas with moral values this preferential character is often obscured by an objectifying tendency to regard them as common to all, universal obligations relating to rules to which we are all subject, and to which the element of preference is irrelevant. When legislating for ourselves, as Kant insisted, we legislate normatively for all others too. It has been observed by some moral philosophers that the language of morals, with terms such as 'duty' and 'obligation' to which Kant attached special significance, has overtones of authority which we carry with us from childhood. It is part of the child-rearing practices of most cultures to associate moral good and right with rules, authority, obedience, punishment or reward, and indeed, before children develop the capacity to reason there is no alternative to the habituation of rules by some means or other as the beginning of moral education. We trail from childhood a widespread inclination to objectify 'good' and 'right', to recognize them as objective properties and as such external to the mind, things for everyone to seek, to discover, to become committed to, before we can all live morally. The language of the school continues the tenor of moral authority and the strong suggestion of objective moral properties. 'It is wrong to cheat' is not for an individual offender only to have stamped on his memory. It is universalized for the school community, to be remembered always, something that 'everyone knows' (or ought to know); a pupil is stigmatized as somehow imperceptive for failing to recognize its supposed objectivity, as he is similarly stigmatized with respect to telling lies, breaking promises, stealing, and so forth. Even the morality of school tradition, in the Headmaster's injunctions, is there, outside the mind, in the past as in the present, more indestructible than the school building.

Our task is to find whether this common tendency to objectify moral values is capable of justification, or whether it is illusory. If moral values are not objective they are subjective, part of an attitude – value complex if they are held with strong conviction. We shall review the objective – subjective dispute but endeavour to keep it in proportion, since whether we hold one view or the other, the character of moral conduct – its deliberations, judgements, decisions or conclusions, and the moral action that follows from them – seems not to be significantly affected. Values may be equally strong and action-tending whether we regard them as objective or subjective.

An Objective View

In his *Principia Ethica* G. E. Moore argued that *good* is a unique property (and so objective), rather like 'yellow' and equally indefinable. While particular light vibrations which stimulate the normal eye are natural, he explained, the actual yellow that is perceived is *not* natural. In a similar way *good* is perceived differently from the way we perceive objects such as good persons: the first is non-natural, the second natural, and when we confuse the non-natural with the natural, believing falsely that we are perceiving good when in fact we are perceiving a good person, we are committing, he asserted, 'the naturalistic fallacy'.[12] Moore claimed apprehension of knowledge beyond what may be derived from sense experience, referring to a class of objects or properties of objects which do not exist in time and so are not parts of the natural world. *Good* does not exist in time, it has no duration, no beginning or end of an existence; nor does *two*. Yet 'two' *means* something, just as good does. What exist in nature are only good things, or good qualities. While rejecting any supposition of supersensible reality as having a bearing on ethics, he defended the claim that not everything that *is* is locatable in nature (p.110–11, and 113 ff). The strongest criticism of this view of good as a unique property came from those of scientific impulse who objected to claims of indefinability or irrefutability, inasmuch as they tend to obstruct rather than promote enquiry. The case for the objectivity of good, if there is one, is to be made with arguments that are discussable, refutable and non-dogmatic. It has seemed to those of this contrary persuasion that to be generally intelligible, *good* has to be locatable clearly in the stream of experience, perceptible as something in nature, not as a presumed non-natural property. Thus some have argued that *good* might be observable in particular *activities* such as cooperating with others; or in activities expressing love, sympathy, benevolence, courage, truth-seeking, and so forth.[13] Then we may understand it, discuss it, find out how to improve it in experience if we find it inadequate or deficient. Yet it is not at all clear how cooperativeness, for instance, must be regarded as an objective quality to be found in a particular class of activities, rather than an expression of a personal, or subjective, value. That many might value some things similarly is not itself an indication of the objectivity of moral values.

Subjective Viewpoints

Subjective approaches to good have taken two main directions: first, that which claims that ethical terms such as 'good' and 'right' simply express attitudes of approval and disapproval; second, that which holds that ethical statements merely express (and excite) feelings, without cognitive content and without asserting any proposition whatsoever. Supporters of the first approach are sometimes called 'orthodox subjectivists', and those of the second 'new' or 'radical' subjectivists. Between their respective approaches there is a substantial psychological gap, since attitudes have a cognitive basis which emotions do not have. Those in the second group believed that they detected serious weaknesses in orthodox subjectivism, specifically since it led, so they argued, to contradiction. Approval as expressed in favourable attitudes on the one hand, and on the other hand convictions of moral rightness or wrongness, are not identical. There may be approval of capital punishment, of the massacre of prisoners of war or of their exposure to highly dangerous situations, and a simultaneous moral conviction that the approval is not morally right. Without self-contradiction a person could approve of the use of grossly deforming and painful diseases to kill certain animals, it is said, and at the same time admit to the wrongness of such acts. The critics of orthodox subjectivism have themselves missed a fundamental distinction: that between formally approving of, or giving approval to, and having *attitudes* of approval. We are not justified in using 'attitude' in the former sense if we wish to avoid ambiguity. A person with a moral conviction that capital punishment is wrong would not be able to say at the same time, 'I approve of it', unless he were speaking under duress. It is only the person who has not arrived at a moral conviction on the subject, who is vague or apprehensive or confused or prudent or conformist, who is able to say, 'I approve of capital punishment, but I have a feeling that it is wrong just the same.' If some in the community who have genuine moral attitudes and values are able to impress others to the extent of having them assume similar attitudes on moral questions, there can be no guarantee of the authenticity of the attitudes so assumed.

What was radical in the 'new subjectivism' was the belief that the ethical language of good and right, ought and obligation, and so forth, merely expressing or exciting emotion, states no proposition to be examined for truth or falsehood, and the ethical terms have no cognitive import whatsoever. This is an extreme view when related to experience, and savours of presumption and inadequate respect for persons. Those who use no more than emotional expletives to condemn acts of violence and wanton destruction, brutal cruelty or depravity, are not necessarily devoid of ideas on the wrongness of the acts: inarticulateness is not to be mistaken for cognitive emptiness. We shall not devote further time to this view, except to note that much ethical language may be emotional and persuasive while still expressing an individual's moral attitudes and values; and it may be emotional and persuasive without expressing *any* authentic attitudes and values.

Subjectivism refers, in the most defensible sense of the word, to notions of good and right as reflections of personal moral convictions: that is, to genuine moral attitudes and values. In this sense, good and right *do* have cognitive content, but it is not content which is discoverable in the external world. It is a subjective view in the sense that it refers to an individual's personal moral preference and commitment, regardless of how that moral value has been learnt, and regardless of how many might hold similar values. This subjectivism accounts for all moral values and not only for some; it excludes the possibility of some moral values being objective, however many might share particular values.

Doubts on Objectivity of Values: Ethical Relativism

It is the observation of some values being similar among a number of persons, and some classes of activities having similar characteristics, such as cooperative activities, or benevolent activities, or selfish activities, that seem still to give credence to notions of moral values as objective. The error lies in descriptiveness. To observe a similarity among all activities which we describe as cooperate, or as benevolent, is not to detect an objective quality of cooperativeness or of benevolence in each of the activities, but simply to note that our value of cooperativeness, or of benevolence, has application to many separate activities. Multiplication of cases does not give support to the objectivity of moral values. Sociological descriptiveness may be still more misleading: the view that ethical terms refer merely to whatever values members of a culture find generally acceptable. In many separate activities a value of loyalty to fellow workers may be observed, as though individuals were simply playing out the values of their culture. But what any society accepts widely as values among its members is irrelevant to the question of what 'good' and 'right' are in themselves; that is, irrelevant to the question of value objectivity. Ethical relativism – as this viewpoint is called – merely describes the values in a particular social situation, those conveying a distinct measure of uniformity among individual members, and offers no account of the moral character of the values. Whether or not individuals comply generally with social values has nothing to do with the moral justification of the values themselves.

Ethical relativism has relevance in our present discussion chiefly for the doubt it casts on the objectivity of moral values. There is sufficient empirical evidence to show that social mores have some influence on the formation of an individual's moral values: that what we learn as right in the family and the school is *partly* a reflection of social expectations. In the minds of some individuals what is socially approved is what is right, and moral development does not progress beyond what is sometimes called 'socionomous' conduct: that which seeks social approval and shuns social disapproval. To some extent these values differ interculturally, but they are learned and accepted by some individuals as the only standards they have for their individual behaviour. But what is true of some is not necessarily true of others.

The objectivity of moral values is much more difficult to defend than their subjectivity, based on individual attitudes and values. We must acknowledge again that a simple account of our moral values does not itself express an ethical standpoint, referring merely to what happens to be the case and not to what *ought* to be the case. We make our subjective values normative by justifying them for others as well as for ourselves, preferably in reasoned discussion with others. What conforms best with reason will be the highest form of justification we can achieve, but it will not be infallible, and we may need to make adjustments to our personal moral stance in the light of others' criticism of it. On the other hand, without the mutuality of discussion, others may criticise our moral values by the standards of their own, but such external evaluations, without public criticism of the various standards used along the way, can have little value. The subjectivity of values has no ethical justification unless their standards are open to public scrutiny. The ethical oughts proposed for others in our subjective moral values require both to be understood and accepted by them if they are to have effect in practical morality for others, as well as for ourselves. We shall return to the question of the subjectivity of our moral values when we present a personal ethical standpoint.

Purpose of Morality

Moral values, standards, or preferences are themselves indicative of purposes in morality: as values have many possible substantive variations, so too do the purposes which individuals give to morality. In contrast with value-based purposes is a category of social purposes from a sociological perspective which we shall consider first.

Social Purposes of Morality: Conflict Reduction

When we move into the social context and see individuals interacting with others, we observe the tension between altruism and egoism, between considering others' interests and disregarding them. Since there is a *prima facie* opposition between them, we assume that total egoism is immoral (though egoism as a theory of morality has been supported by some from a rational, rather than a value posiition, or from one which combines the two.)

Hume approached the altruism – egoism tension from his impression of man as characterized by selfishness and limited generosity, as we have noted, and of his social condition as characterized by scarcity of resources. Historically there has been much to support Hume's position: the interaction of these two has invariably increased competitiveness and strengthened self-interest, whether in small hunting tribes, in more stable agricultural settlements, or in the immensely more complex industrialized societies that have developed from them. At each stage it would have been in society's interest for every member to be benevolent toward others, distributing food and burdens evenly, and in ideal communal spirit giving according to his ability and receiving only to fulfil his needs. But as Hume observed, the practical difficulty in moral living has been consistently that benevolence has been in short supply, and so have material necessities. The greater the strain on the means of basic subsistence, the heavier the demands have been on benevolence. So in a sense selfishness has been pressed on man by the circumstances of his life, and morality as a system of social rules and regulations has become necessary in the interests of all, just as, in a state of nature, prior to social regulation, the strongest survived over the weakest and made necessary a system of laws. That at least was the view of Hobbes in the Seventeenth Century, in his impression of man as fundamentally selfish, seeking the gratification of his own desires but frequently in situations where many have 'an appetite to the same thing'. Then, as he explained, before the institution of law, the object of appetite or desire was invariably seized by the most powerful.[14] From moral reflections such as these in the Seventeenth and Eighteenth centuries the notion of morality emerged with a clear social purpose – a morality which was tied to the need for regulation in the general interest. Hume's observation of a common human sympathy was an advance on Hobbes' position, for sympathy itself would presumably help to reduce man's single-minded selfishness in Hobbes' understanding of it.

Subsequently, in the last and the present centuries, egoism has been given a different complexion by some, following experiences of social conflict in complex industrialized societies which would not have been considered in the Eighteenth Century. From a socialist perspective, for instance, egoism is an inevitable by-product of fierce capitalist competition for limited resources, and its immoral social influence is to be removed only by an unselfish outlook of collectivism.[15]

For those who hold moral convictions similar to Kant's, the search for a purpose for morality is unnecessary: morality is obedience to moral duty; it is its own end. For those consequentialist in outlook who consider the social effects of morality, its purpose may be seen as reducing conflict among individuals by means of self-imposed checks on desire or self-interest, strengthened by positive concern for the interests of others. It would contradict the very concept of society to claim that in a particular case all its members are egoists who require no interaction with others. Societies are for interacting people, and morality takes its meaning from the kind of interaction that ensues. A morality of total egoism is self-contradictory. But we must repeat that a moral purpose which seeks its main justification in conflict-reduction is pragmatic only, an external justification rather than one relating to the fundamental character of morality in its formal statement and the secondary principles derived from it. It is sociological rather primarily moral.

Value Purposes of Morality: the Instance of Happiness

Moral values derive their quality from their degree of affinity with the formal notion of morality and its primary and secondary principles. We shall examine one value as a general purpose of morality, an end to which individual moral acts and activities should be directed. *Happiness* has been the subject of most discussion in moral philosophy which has looked toward an end for mankind, since Aristotle proposed it in his *Nicomachean Ethics*. There it was seen as a general goal by ordinary people, he observed, as well as by those of 'superior refinement', yet was interpreted differently by them. His own answer on what constituted happiness was then given in terms of 'eudaimonia', referring both to doing well and to the way one conducts oneself. It does not consist in amusement or bodily pleasures, but in the exercise of the highest virtue which is contemplation. It is this which satisfies the two notions of doing well and of conducting oneself well, by taking thought of 'things noble and divine' (Book x, ch.6, 1177^a). Happiness of this kind is beyond animals, beyond slaves too according to Aristotle. At much the same time Epicurus thought of happiness quantitatively as any pleasure, and the Greek word for pleasure – hedone – has given us 'hedonism' to describe his outlook. So to the Greeks happiness did indeed mean different things, but to modern hedonistic philosophers such as Jeremy Bentham it was the *quantity* of total pleasure, not its *quality* which was the significant goal to be pursued. In *An Introduction to the Principles of Morals and Legislation* he explained his view that we are all governed by the two masters of *pain* and *pleasure* and then proposed his principle of *utility* which acknowledged this common human subjection. By utility he meant 'that property in any object, whereby it tends to produce benefit, advantage, good, or happiness, (all this in the present case comes to the same thing) or (what comes again to the same thing) to prevent the happening of mischief, pain, evil, or unhappiness to the party whose interest is considered: if that party be the community in general, then the happiness of the community; if a particular individual, then the happiness of that individual' (ch.1, III, pp.1–2).[16] A thing promotes the interest of an individual, or is *for* his interest, when it adds to the sum total of his pleasure or diminishes the sum total of his pains (ch.1, v, p.2). Bentham even explained how to measure pleasure and pain: simply 'sum up the values of all the *pleasures* on the one side, and those of all the *pains* on the other': if the balance is on the side of pleasure, it expresses 'the *good* tendency of the act'; if on the side of pain, 'the *bad* tendency' (ch.IV, v, p.16). An act is good in so far as it promotes the greatest good of the greatest number, each person counting as one, and good being measured in terms of happiness or pleasure which are synonymous, and significant only in terms of *quantity*: pushpin to Bentham was as good as poetry in this respect. From this notion of utility we have derived the name *utilitarian* to apply to philosophers of a similar persuasion to Bentham's.

As a utilitarian, Mill's task was to defend criticism of the viewpoint and to offer some amendments, such as to acknowledge that pleasure or happiness is not all of a kind. 'It is better to be a human being dissatisfied than a pig satisfied; better to be Socrates dissatisfied than a fool satisfied' (p.284).[17] But Mill's defence was not totally adequate. He pleaded against utilitarianism's critics that the happiness to which it referred, and which it used as a standard of what is right in conduct, is not merely the agent's personal happiness but that of all concerned. The agent is required to be strictly impartial – 'a disinterested and benevolent spectator' (p.291). Mill's ultimate defence lay in human nature: we are so constituted that we do not desire anything 'which is not either a part of happiness or a means to happiness', (p.312) and therefore happiness is the natural end of human action. This was indisputable from his own observations, though he did concede that the matter was one for empirical investigation.

Mill was asking too much of utilitarianism: to be a disinterested and benevolent spectator on the one hand, and on the other hand to be a desiring individual *naturally* seeking his own happiness, but interested also in the consequences of his acts in so far as they contributed to the greatest happiness of the greatest number. The main weaknesses of Act Utilitarianism (referring to the consequences of individual acts for all concerned, in terms of their happiness or unhappiness) are these. First, it is vague: it is not always clear what is to count as happiness. Bentham's lumping together of benefit, advantage, pleasure, good and happiness aggravates the problem. If it is not clear what happiness consists in, it is to that extent not clearly measurable, and certainly individual's experiences of pain and pleasure are not objects to be quantified by any numerical means, or to be put in any balance to be weighed. How are we to determine the comparability of one person's experience of pain or pleasure with another's? Bentham's criteria of intensity, duration and so forth are themselves imprecise: what to one person is intense is not necessarily so to another (*Introduction to the Principles of Morals and Legislation,* ch. IV, ii, and iv, p.16). We have no means of assessing when, from a single act, an individual's happiness begins, and when it ends. It makes a great deal of difference whether we accept happiness in a specifically Aristotelian, *qualitative* sense, or whether we regard it hedonistically and quantitatively. The position is further confused when happiness is used in an undifferentiated way as it was by Bentham, or when it is used, as it has been by some, to convey general social ideals or practical preferences. Under Act Utilitarianism so much is possible.

A second major weakness of Act Utilitarianism is that it is apt to lead to moral contradiction from its claim that our primary obligation is to promote the general welfare, or happiness. An act of murdering a violent husband and father may lead to a great imbalance of happiness over unhappiness. Does that make the act morally right? The moral convictions we hold such as killing is wrong, keeping promises is right, expose our moral values. It is they which play a conspicuous part in our deliberations leading to action. But there are many situations where the consequences of an act in terms of general welfare cannot be easily predicted, and careful deliberation becomes necessary, even calculation. Do Act Utilitarians expect of us that we should suspend our moral convictions, allowing a calculating reason to plan the act which will attain the greatest happiness of the greatest number? In some circumstances such an approach would be Machiavellian: in almost *all* circumstances it would be impracticable, since it would contradict the meaning of moral values and practical morality based on them. The only conceivable situation, indeed, where a calculating reason could so prevail would be that where the agent was not at the same time a *moral* agent; where he had no moral values at all, and no notion of the meaning of morality. In such circumstances, by manipulation or design an act could be planned to bring immense satisfaction to some and untold misery to others. Historically such circumstances prevailed under slavery, serfdom and some forms of colonialism, and it is not difficult to imagine now a calculating individual with power and devoid of moral scruples, making a nice judgement on how far to go with suffering in order to produce a small balance in favour of general happiness (assuming that for some odd reason, such as for giving a plausible explanation of his policies and practices to the people, he gave formal support to Act Utilitarianism). In similar vein some might be tempted to use a utilitarian justification for refusing to pay their debts, urging that their giving the money to those in impoverished circumstances would produce more total happiness. Husbands who became tired of marital obligations to wives and families might calculate that, with their wives working, they might effect much more total happiness by marrying younger women in need of happiness. Cavalier rationalizations such as these may clash with personal moral convictions. The fact is that we do have moral obligations based on our moral values, other than the single utilitarian obligation to promote the happiness of all concerned. Bentham attempted to reply to his critics in a variety of ways such as by elaborating on his initial formulation with 'second

– order' consequences, and showing that the breaking of contractual arrangements would lead to general unhappiness. Moral philosophers continued to find contradictions in utilitarianism. Moore's attack in *Principia Ethica* (ch.III) set out to show some of its inconsistencies and contradictions.

While Mill had strengthened Act Utilitarianism by his acknowledgement of the *quality* of happiness as well as its *quantity*, he left the theory still vague on the question of how quality could be measured against quantity: that was a matter, he said, for those best fitted to make the comparisons (p.286). Bentham believed that general happiness could best be achieved by each individual following *rules*, but the rules were still an individual's own rules, and it was the individual act – in so far as it led to general happiness, which was significant to him. Others changed the focus from single acts to the general application of such acts, asking what would be the effect of Act A on total happiness if it were made *a rule for everyone to follow*. An Act Utilitarian would consider an act of murder justified by its consequences for the general welfare, but in this modified approach the *Rule Utilitarian* would consider an act of murder as falling under a general rule, reflecting on what would be the effect on total happiness if acts of murder were generally committed, or not generally committed. A judge who feels that capital offences are increasing in the community and that he should make an exception of the very next case to come before him with an unduly severe penalty is thinking of the judgement as a separate act and of its consequences for the general welfare. Another judge who follows a rule that all cases of capital offences will be punished by every member of the judiciary with equal severity – allowing for the individual circumstances of each case – is following a principle that the general welfare is best determined not by the happiness potential of single acts, but by the happiness potential of implementing rules governing all relevant acts. In so far as each is a utilitarian in outlook at all, in the first case the judge subscribes to Act Utilitarianism; in the second to Rule Utilitarianism. Vagueness with respect to 'happiness', 'welfare' and similar terms still remains, as well as contradictions in the notion of moral value inhering only in the consequences of acts; so that if marital infidelity could be shown to produce the greatest amount of happiness for the greatest number that would be made a rule for everyone to follow, and the infidelity would not be considered right or wrong in itself. Further, short-term happiness (such as might be developed in some progressive schools) may contrast with long-term benefit or eventual well-being, so that in the formulation of rules sometimes complex qualifications or specifications become necessary. And as long as the general principle of 'the greatest happiness of the greatest number' remains, the problem of the quantification of happiness remains also under Rule Utilitarianism, as does the problem of how to avoid a submergence of *individuals* under totals or balances of happiness.

We have not found utilitarian arguments sufficient to justify the view that the ultimate end of all morality is happiness – our own and that of others affected by our acts, or by general rules of conduct based on them. By concentrating on consequences, either form of utilitarianism is liable to conflict with moral values, especially in situations of oppression: slavery, apartheid, political detention and so forth. We stand by our personal moral convictions of what is right and wrong, and these are generally much more persuasive of what we ought or ought not to do than are any secondary considerations of consequences. Yet utilitarianism has raised a point of central moral concern to us. As soon as we are able to recognize in others something of ourselves, to respect them as persons, we do have sympathy for them, some interest in their desires and goal-seeking, and so the consequences of acts must be weighed in practical morality. The formal notion of morality as a practical consideration of others' interests presupposes a concern for their *well-being*. This too is vague, but it expresses the tenor of our moral outlook. If we are moral at all in our outlook, consistent with this formal notion and the moral principles derived from it, we will not need a philosophy of utilitarianism to guide us toward a concern for others' well-being, since that concern is already built into our notion of morality. To have this concern is at the same time to have a concern for the consequences of our acts, inasmuch as they affect others.

A Coherent Ethical Standpoint

Our last substantive consideration is to present a personal ethical standpoint and to justify it. This will serve to test again the fundamental nature of the formal notion, to review and consolidate some of the substantive emphases already made, and to provide a basic rationale for ethical standpoints taken in subsequent chapters. Our personal standpoint is itself subject to discussion as one of a number of possible moralities, others constructed perhaps with different assumptions, but each of them requiring justification. The important thing for each of us in practical morality is to work out a moral standpoint which we can justify by rational and non-dogmatic means, subjecting it for criticism by others and prepared to amend it as indicated by reason. To this point we have supported the general view of morality as having a social purpose inasmuch as it is concerned with our relations with others in social groups, while retaining the individual character of moral values and their expression in personal moral convictions; we have been left with doubt on the question of objective moral values, giving our subjective views a basis in attitudes and values; we have found a similar difficulty in supporting a goal of happiness as proposed by utilitarians, but acknowledge the morality of considering the well-being of others which is presupposed in the very notion of our having a moral stance.

Our ethical standpoint is based on a rejection of objective values. The moral values which we have are learned personally by us, and we are to some degree committed to them. In the strongest sense they become our moral convictions. But the values we hold do not become *moral* values simply as expressions of our attitudes and values, for then *any* values could be regarded as moral for no other reason than that they are individually held. We have to defend them as morally good, justifying them rationally according to our formal notion of morality and our moral principles, which in our case refer to a practical consideration of others' interests as well as our own, and to the non-infliction of suffering on others whenever avoidable or preventable. Our own subjectivism refers neither to orthodox nor to radical subjectivism, but rather to personal attitudes and values which we justify as morally good first from rational criteria, second from our moral principles which are derived from the formal notion of morality. Our moral judgements, decisions or conclusions thus do more than state what the values are, for this could be done merely autobiographically by stating an attitude to war, or to famine or to family life, for instance. To make a moral judgement from our subjectivist standpoint is to declare that war, for instance, is wrong, and that would imply that we have reasons for the judgement we make, reasons that are open for explanation and discussion. If a person were to say, 'My attitude is that the aggressor should be pushed out by force without any opportunity to negotiate, but I know I'm prejudiced; it's simply the way I feel', he would then be making no more than an autobiographical statement. There would be a recognition, that is, that the statement does *not* express a considered moral judgement, and is not, then, a matter for justification or discussion. With respect to our subjectivism we believe that our minds are never free of value influences: there may be, on a certain issue, attitudes to killing or to war generally; to political parties or dictatorships inducing a situation of war or at least not preventing it; to colonialism; to aggression or to the use of force to oppose it; to sophisticated weaponry; to motherland; to the suffering of wives and families; so that to make and justify a moral judgement is also to take into an explanation something of our own attitudes and values, just as in discussion of the moral judgement the attitudes and values of all other participants enter and are impossible to exclude. To re-iterate, the purpose of discussion is to enable collective reason to reveal any entrenched preconceptions and prejudices and to refine the rational and moral status of the judgement itself. Thus from our subjectivist stance we do not regard the good as something to be discovered in the world outside our minds, but something to be worked out individually by us according to reason, the formal notion of morality, and the moral principles we relate to it.

Our own ethical position relies partly on what we find to be the case in experience, but when we ask, what is the case? we do so not in an expectation of locating or identifying good, but simply to guard against ethical prescriptions which are impossibilities according to empirical evidence. This approach is fraught with difficulties and confusions relating to various philosophical 'isms'. We shall illustrate with naturalism, empiricism and psychologism, and then with rationalism, but beyond this chapter we shall not refer to them again, since it is only specific *individual* points of view which are significantly discussable. 'Isms' form from general agreement with a particular viewpoint, followed by variations and amendments, and eventually to positions that bear only broad resemblances to the original.

Naturalism has taken various forms, such as Rousseau's naive declarations that everything in a state of nature is good and that evil enters the world only from the corrupting influences of human societies. To the progressivist in education freedom is natural to the child, and the imposition of authority unnatural and therefore reprehensible. By some, original sin has been viewed as natural, justifying authority and punishment to exorcise evil in children. Each of these is reducible to the analytic statement that whatever is natural is good (or bad) the predicate of which does not enlarge on what is already conveyed in the subject. Other common expressions of what is natural have been highly selective, such as a natural tendency toward benevolence or sympathy. Hobbes was less speculative in his attributions of good, presenting what he believed has evidence from experience, namely, that man is fundamentally selfish and that nothing is more natural to him than his desires. Therefore, being natural, desires are good, whatever they are. Thus two forms of naturalism emerged: the first is illustrated in Rousseau's viewpoint, that what is in a state of nature, so-called, is therefore good and ought to be followed; the second, as illustrated in Hobbes' viewpoint, that whatever is natural to man in the sense of being common to human nature, such as desire or self-interest, is therefore good. In the first instance there is usually an error of selective convenience, with particular virtues or ideals such as unselfishness found to be in a state of nature, to suit the purposes in mind at the time; in the second, a narrow interpretation of human nature, based on an expression of what appears most dominant in experience. Each of these illustrates a fallacy of reasoning from *is* to *ought*. Counter-examples are too obvious to warrant any elaboration of the fallacy. In our own view we have not sought the nature of our attitudes and values as a direct route to the good, but merely as a means of rejecting certain claims and assumptions about reason as in some kind of superordinate relationship with supposedly more 'natural' things, such as desires, emotions, motives, attitudes and values. From the elevation of reason has come the ethical advocacy to resort to reason and to reason alone in our moral deliberations, conclusions, decisions and judgements, constituting, in the light of empirical evidence, a counsel of impracticability. Our stance may be described in part as empirical, in the sense that we believe we may fall into prescriptive error if we do not take account of knowledge from experience, but *empiricism* has had a variety of meanings, from the view that matters of fact are grounded in sense-experience (as with Locke, Berkeley, Hume and Mill, for instance) to sophisticated contemporary approaches to perception. Another presently misleading label is *psychologism*, a pejorative term in ethics, levelled particularly at theorists who use psychological laws and psychological explanations to justify ethical or other philosophical standpoints. It is thus an instance of the fallacy of sliding from *is* to *ought*.[18] In a wider sense 'psychologism' is used to refer to a supposed confusion of function between the factual descriptiveness of psychology and the reasoning and evaluations of philosophy. The philosophy of mind has clear relationships with some aspects of psychology, and ethics too (though it pursues a different kind of enquiry) must take into account what is relevant to it in the Aristotelian spirit of a regard for 'observed facts'.

Consistent with our opposition to the exaltation of reason both as capable of casting off the imperfections of our 'natural' state and as a higher-order and even ultimate justification for our moral maxims, we have assumed an ethical stance which relates our moral activities to one plane of experience. This enables us to examine our moral beliefs, opinions, judgements and so forth according to reason, but not to appeal to any perfect or pure Reason, and not to justify anything in its name by any transcendental assumptions or procedures. There are not two classes of reason, we believe, but one only, as there are not two levels of experience, but one level only, though there are many different kinds of human experience. The contrasts drawn by Aristotle and Kant between the pure, theoretical or contemplative, on the one hand, and the empirical, imperfect, practical on the other, we believe are untenable if they imply not a difference of function, but different reasons operating. We reject Moore's assumption that good is non-natural, a uniquely objective property, and as such something that defies discussion and the possibility of refutation. From our standpoint that was *his* naturalistic fallacy: the elevation of the good, which we locate in our subjective values as part of our experience in the natural world, to something non-natural; but from *his* standpoint the fallacy was to give a natural status to something non-natural.

Despite our objections to the elevation of reason to a transcendental status, reason remains the corner-stone of our ethical position. It is the common reason which we recognize in our empirical world: the activity of reason, not any higher-order Platonic reality which is beyond the reach of most mortals. It is what is *within* reach of us all which is important to our moral deliberations and conclusions, and to the critical evaluation of others' moral deliberations and conclusions. We have made use of our naive intuitions in our formal notions of justice and morality, especially inasmuch as these have brought to the surface common impressions of childhood, but we do not accept the notion of a moral intuition with supersensible powers, sometimes called *conscience*, which prompts us in our moral actions or pricks us if we err, for that too, like a higher-order Reason, implies (unless we are speaking merely metaphorically, as we often do) something above or beyond the level of reality which we experience ordinarily.

The reason that is the corner-stone of our ethics is imperfect, as are all our natural powers or capacities, including – as the corner-stone of our morality – our capacity for considering others' interests with sympathy. It was the striking contrast presented by the Greeks between what is, and what might be, that gave moral thought its most basic insight: one exposing individual and social imperfection. Our own ethical viewpoint recognizes, beyond Hume's perception of our selfishness and limited generosity, a variety of other limitations which are relevant to a practical morality: the ability to reason, to empathize – at least to the extent of perceiving the shape of others" attitudes and values – and the reflective and introspective power to understand our own, including the extent of our own egoism. Reason itself is not sufficient to control our egoism, and combined with our dispositions, especially attitudes and values, we still have imperfect control over it. The Eighteenth Century philosopher Hartley observed, as we have noted, the tendency 'of self-interest to exercise benevolence, and reciprocally of benevolence to lessen self-interest" (*Observations on Man,* ch.III, Section VI), but how much of the association of happiness with that of others was of a self-referential character, referring to the happiness or welfare of one's own immediate family, was not intimated. It is beyond that circle of dependants, or close relatives and acquaintances, that Hume's 'sentiment of humanity' is put most rigorously to the test. It is a big jump to associate one's own happiness with the happiness of those whom one does not know, with whom one has made no personal contact of any kind. From our own ethical perspective we see altruism and egoism as in continual tension, and reason alone incapable of reducing the tension significantly. Many moral philosophers have agreed with Sigdwick, as we do, that it is equally rational (excluding our attitudes and values entirely) to support egoism as it is to support benevolence[19]: acting for advantage to self is just as *rational* as acting for advantage to others. If egoism is to be constrained it will be constrained by a unitary rational-value effort; that is, by moral attitudes and values working in unison with reason.

The force of the value components in this process may be a matter of the greatest importance to any successful extension of altruism and reduction of egoism. Our own ethical viewpoint returns, in this respect, to Kant and his moral imperatives, for though his appeal to transcendental justifications of reason we find untenable, the *deonto-logical* character of his ethics, with its imperative call to *duty,* is compelling. It is when our personal attitudes and values have themselves the force of moral imperatives in their call to action that they, with reason, are most likely to constrain egoism and increase altruism; that is, when our moral attitudes and values bind us, with the force of law, as reason did presumably to Kant as he expressed his categorical imperatives. His 'law from within' had a much stronger moral demand than one imposed from without, for a law from within was a law to oneself as well as to others, a law which made superfluous any externally imposed law. From an ethical position, this law-like character can conceivably be part of moral convictions which are rooted, not in reason as Kant believed, but in our personally-held moral attitudes and values. But what we lack is the *necessity* which Kant claimed was given to moral law by reason. Ours is a more contingent matter, and apart from that, since we advocate discussion of our moral deliberations and conclusions with others, there is some danger that if *all* our moral attitudes and values had the force of law we should find less readiness to modify them if rational pressures were brought to bear on them by others. The moral judgements we make, regardless of whether we believe ourselves under the influence of reason or values or of both, are intended for others as well as for ourselves: hence the attempt to give them the strongest possible rational character by proposing them for scrutiny by others whenever practicable. Although subjective in our approach to morality, we hold, as Kant did, that in making our moral judgements we legislate for all, not for ourselves alone, and for that reason our judgements are made, not tentatively, but with confidence, unless the demands of a particularly complex problem defy a single rational solution. We need to caution further, with reference to Kant's emphasis on moral *duty*, between a genuine deontological character in our moral convictions and a false deontological ring which is part of the persuasiveness of some moral language of duty or obligation. Some expressions heavy in formal administrative emphasis may be correspondingly light in moral conviction. 'Don't you know you have a duty to respect public property!' may carry little conviction to a vandal being addressed from a magistrate's bench.

While rejecting both Act and Rule Utilitarianism for the reasons we have given, our ethical standpoint is distinctly oriented toward others' well-being. But we are consequentialist in a secondary, rather than a primary sense. Our first thoughts are for the immediate responses to our moral attitudes and values, or the reactions to our moral convictions. We recognize the vagueness of expressions such as 'well-being' and 'human flourishing', but in contrast with their opposites they are sufficiently clear to be action-guiding in a supportive way to our moral attitudes and values. They do not refer, obviously, to acts positively prejudicial to others' well-being, such as destroying their homes or taking away their livelihood, or causing grievous bodily harm, or seriously impairing the prospects of their

dependants. Since well-being is presupposed by the formal notion o
morality, there is no need for us to assume any separate consequen
tialist stance, since as long as our stance continues to be a moral on
we will be concerned partly for the well-being of others in our socia
group. From an Act Utilitarian stance we might face comple
situations involving us in seemingly endless deliberations on th
effects on various persons of possible courses of action open to us
before we reach a conclusion on which of these will yield the greates
happiness of the greatest number. From a Rule Utilitarian positior
the deliberations might be no less protracted. In our own ethica
position our subjective moral values place a demand on action *now*
though not without relevant prior deliberation. Only the mos
introspective of persons, such as Hamlet, stand off and use reason tc
appraise the possible courses of action open to them, then moralize
on the consequences of each according to their particular mora
values. Much more commonly we are carried forward toward actior
by our moral convictions, deliberating at some length only when we
face moral dilemmas or when we need to consider the best *means* tc
the fulfilment of these moral convictions in action. In moral situations
action is usually called for as soon as possible: consideration o
others' interests is practical in purpose. Utilitarian calculations are
likely, in some situations, to be tedious to the point of impracticability.

This account of our own ethical stance, though sketchy and
incomplete, is sufficient to establish a coherence in our moral point of
view and to satisfy the other purposes which we have stated. We shall
have more to say on morality in Chapter 5 when we consider moral
education, and in particular the important question of *autonomy*
which we have deferred because of its supposedly developmental
character.

REVIEW AND CONCLUDING COMMENTS

In the first section of this chapter (p. 34) we have considered the
formal notion of morality and in the second section (p. 45) the
substantive questions, leading to the statement of a personal ethical
standpoint. This ethical position has taken account of the failure to
justify as universal particular purposes for practical morality, such as
the various positions taken in utilitarianism to justify happiness or
satisfaction as an end of morality. All such interpretations are

substantive rather than fundamental. It has taken account also of man's condition from a perspective similar to Hume's, from which there has been deduced a notion of a constant tension in our individual lives between egoism and benevolence, as well as between good intentions and a capacity to act. We are concerned with a morality of good acts and activities, not a morality that ends with good intentions. From the perspective of a subjectivism which gives a central position to moral convictions whose dynamic source is attitudes and values, we are the better able to see some of the relationships between morality, justice and education in our practical lives.

To prevent misunderstanding of the ethical position we have taken there are three emphases to be made: the first refers to moral scepticism, the second to naturalism, the third to ethical relativism. First, it is a fallacy to argue from our subjectivism, which is based on personal moral attitudes and values, that because they differ from person to person there can be none which can be morally relevant to others as well as to ourselves; that morality, in other words, is a matter of an individual having his own values, which are good for him, but meaningless or morally irrelevant if applied to others. Such naive subjectivism is aggravated by doubts on the ability of reason to justify any moral viewpoint, even one for ourselves alone. Our standpoint is that by reasoning we *are* able to reach and justify moral conclusions, that the best judgement we can reach in any given circumstances is an interpretation offered for public criticism by anyone who wishes to evaluate it. That criticism may be helpful in further refinement, but in practical decision-making of any kind we cannot go on indefinitely with prospects of refinement. We must be satisfied with the conclusion we have reached, even if subsequently a better one is worked out, perhaps in the light of other experiences which we hadn't been able to anticipate. Morality attracts to itself a sense of perfection through its affiliation with ideals, but reason, though imperfect, must be relied upon in our moral deliberations. We can reject reason only by reason itself, and that is as contradictory as to reject reason from any other branch of philosophy. As in the practice of the law, when some judgements are reversed on appeal, there is simply no way of reaching rational or moral perfection in our judgements, decisions or conclusions, but that observation is to be kept in proportion by reflecting on the *achievements* of our practical deliberations, and the confidence that is justifiably placed in them.

The second warning is against unwarranted attributions of a naturalistic fallacy, in one of its forms, whenever we argue that personal moral values themselves constitute the good, since this is *not* what we are arguing. Our attitudes and values may be described as 'good' for all sorts of reasons: they are certainly not good because they are part of our natures, or characterize us as individuals. They have to be argued for as good in the best way we can, and then evaluated in discussions with others. Individual reasoning requires an external monitor because of its relationship with personal attitudes and values, and the best monitor we can have is a form of disciplined a-personal discussion which we shall elaborate in Chapter 4.

Third, in the formal notion of education as a developing of potentialities consistent with social values, we are *not* espousing an ethics of relativism which assumes that whatever society approves is good, but rather stressing education as a social process. The prescription of consistency with social values is not in any sense a concession to relativism, and does not conflict with our subjectivism based on personal moral attitudes and values. Education becomes moral for a quite different reason from that proposed by ethical relativists. It is moral because as an on-going activity it involves a practical consideration of others' interests. First, from this formal notion – in so far as we are considering *human* others– we have a moral demand to respect learners as persons, particularly as individuals who are different one from another, with their unique patterns of needs for the developing of potentialities. Second, it is in their interests (especially in the case of children) not to be subjected to educational programmes that will lead to appreciable difficulty and embarrassment in social adjustment. It is in their interests to learn social values which are positive and unambiguous even in a pluralistic society, such as may be the case with respect for parents, respect for property, non-violence, and so forth. To be individually accepted as moral values even these would need to be defended with reasons; with respect to some values in some societies the reasons may not be difficult to find. Other social values may be examined, challenged or rejected, such as a value of white supremacy in a population including blacks. Indeed, rejection of some values, with appropriate reasons, might itself be a moral decision, with a practical consideration of others' interests. Our ethical standpoint goes beyond merely describing social values and declaring the good to be whatever society accepts.

The formal notions of justice, morality and education stand as constant references, and have immediate value in this way in many situations. Brutal flogging of prisoners, extermination of millions of people in gas chambers on racial grounds alone, reprisals against hundreds of innocent people in war by mass executions, these are obvious cases of a failure of justice and morality in their fundamental senses. So too is segregating a group of migrant children in a classroom because they do not understand the language in which others are being taught, on the pretext that the class teacher has no time to help them, or is not equipped for the task. That is just as obviously a case of justice, education and morality all combining in their formal senses to demonstrate a violation of each. There are many such instances in educational practice of relationships between the three, and this is not surprising since justice and education in their formal senses are also moral inasmuch as they involve a practical consideration of others' interests.

There are other situations where substantive notions may be more strongly and more immediately directive of their relevant acts or activities than are the corresponding formal notions. For instance, just as we have personal values which are consistent with the formal notion of justice, so too we have personal substantive values which give content in our interpretations of concepts of *fairness* and of *persons*. The architects and supporters of apartheid deny that their laws and practices are either unjust or immoral, claiming that through them they *are* considering the interests of both white and black people. In the last resort we must accept that there is no *absolute justice* to be discovered by us all which stands above any of our personal values. Certainly the formal notions of justice and of morality establish no absolutes. Ever since the Greeks distinguished between freemen and slaves, various criteria have been used in treating individuals differently rather than alike, and in supposedly undiscriminatory ways. Despite all such substantive variations, the formal notions of justice, morality and education remain unchallenged as fundamental to each of the respective activities. It is the substantive interpretations themselves which need to be defended with reasons, and in this process it is the formal notions which form a necessary and indestructible last line of defence – though procedurally it will normally be a first one.

Such a conclusion is not to be taken as suggesting that our subjective approach to values condones practices which violate our personal moral convictions: on the contrary, we stand by those reasons which to us are the strongest reasons. The onus is on us, should a conflict of moral values occur which at the same time accounts for conflicting attributions of justice, not only to assert our own position with the best reasons we can adduce, but also to point to flaws which we see in opposing points of view. But in this process we must guard against a confusion between logical flaws involving false inferences or internal inconsistencies, and merely substantive disagreements on what constitute justice and morality, as we extend our formal notions of these to include further values. In this, we must remind ourselves, values themselves are not to be upheld as either true or false.

There is much yet to be explained on the relationships between justice, morality and education, especially with reference to individuals as persons. There is much more to be explained also on the complexity of our mental states prior to action, involving more than the values which have so far figured prominently, with their associated attitudes. We shall explain this increasing complexity in Chapter 4. Our broad perspective in this chapter has been to see justice as general and closely related to morality, and law as particular, without a *necessary* connection with morality. When we consider practical matters in Chapter 5 we shall be concerned with questions of legal practice and educational practice and their relationship with morality. Some of our considerations will be connected with a large area of common concern to justice (as well as the law), education and morality – namely, *rights and duties*. It is to these that we now turn.

3 Rights and Duties

RIGHTS

We shall state at once the conditions applying to legitimate moral rights, and then consider certain pseudo-rights from the literature of ethics, law and politics which do not fit these conditions, whatever other moral significance they may have.

Legitimate Moral Rights and their Conditions

We commence with the division of rights into claim-rights and liberties – a distinction derived from law.[1] A claim-right expresses the notion that a right that is claimed by a person calls on others to acknowledge that the person has a right to it, and to allow him to have or to do whatever the right pertains to. Liberties refer mainly to ideals of personal freedom, such as freedom of thought and expression. They express the notion that the person who is under no obligation *not* to do something, such as speak freely, has a liberty to it. A right confers *obligations* on others to respect it, whether it is a claim-right or a liberty right.

At this point we reach a difficulty with the kind of subjective morality espoused in the previous chapter. If morality is not absolute or objective, but a matter of subjective choice or of learning particular attitudes and values expressed as personal moral convictions, how can others be said to have moral obligations? It would be much easier to justify claim-rights if morality *were* objective, for then the standards would be positive for all members of the social group who could understand them. If A violated the moral standards in his relations with B, the community could support B in a claim against A. That is, B could exercise an unequivocal claim-right against A. But if in fact A has one set of subjective moral standards and B another, how could B ever justify a claim-right against A? Two considerations help to rescue this situation from increasing perplexity as we extend this case to all others in the community – each with his own subjective

73

standards. First, we may allow ourselves to be influenced to some extent by Kant, arguing that if we envisage a *rational* community, there will be appreciable agreement (but not complete consensus) among its members on moral standards. That is a beginning, but a complete consensus on moral standards is not necessary. Our subjectivity is based on the *need* to defend our moral standards or moral points of view with other rational persons, especially in disciplined discussion groups. In this way initial disagreement is itself not as important as the capacity to weigh all points of view and to determine which is the better case. Second, we may envisage a community in which, by such rational procedures, a large measure of agreement *is* reached on moral standards, so that there is at least a core of standards which are not variable and uncertain. Then we may justify B's claim-right against A by arguing that each understood the standards and accepted them, and that therefore B had a justifiable case against A (such as for breaking a promise). If a community accepts the fundamental notion of morality as a practical consideration of others' interests, a parent may be said to have a claim-right against a Headmaster or Principal for not being advised that a child is working distinctly below capacity. The Headmaster may be said to have a moral obligation to the parent. Whether we consider a rational community, or a moral community with broad agreement on values and principles, or preferably one that is rational *and* moral – each member having some personal moral values but prepared to defend them in discussion with others – in every case we require moral rights to be set within boundaries of a certain agreement in principle. In the area of moral claim-rights ignorance of the moral standards *is* an excuse, whatever the law may say. A and B must not only be moral agents, but – since we support a subjectivity of values – moral agents who agree on certain moral boundaries. In this, if they are to follow the rules they must know what the rules are. Moral boundaries are not as indeterminate or perplexing as a subjectivism of endless differences in values might suggest. But the boundaries are not fixed or stable, and continued rational discussion on such matters as liberties in individual-state relations is required to give members of the moral community an understanding of what their liberties in fact are. All that we need are rules understood and agreed upon by all parties who are involved in a moral-rational community in which claim-rights and liberties have a legitimate place.

When rights do have this legitimate place in such a community they become some of the interests which individuals of the community have. But not all interests qualify as rights. All persons with wants or desires, motives and goals have *interests* and some of these are related to *needs*, such as for food, or for affection. Clearly not all individual needs can be claimed as rights: because A has a car and B has the confidence and trust of others, there is no obvious justification for C's right to both, even though he may feel he needs what A and B have. From naive egalitarian standpoints, rights claims are sometimes made on an assumption that whatever needs are individually experienced by comparing oneself with others can be justifiably translated to rights. On the other hand if persons of the kind of community we have in mind share a moral value of respect for persons, they will acknowledge the rights of individuals to such respect as they go about their various activities of forming plans and striving to fulfil them, whether in routine daily activities or in deliberations and decisions to change their life directions, for these may bring them into contact, or even conflict, with others.

We shall take a positive view of rights in moral senses, ruling out proxy rights or custodianship rights, although for reasons of protection of certain individuals these are recognized, and need to be recognized, in law. The specific expectations we shall make of moral right-holders are first, that they must understand the right and so be able to assert it or claim it against an appropriate person or persons; second, that they recognize the right as theirs to waive or relinquish if they wish. In some circumstances the second will be seen as an odd condition, but there may be unusual circumstances when a person is prepared to sacrifice some rights, such as a right to be advised of bereavement at home, for the sake of continuing uninterruptedly his humanitarian work abroad.

Pseudo-Rights

Formal

There are some rights which are merely formal, such as those associated with official responsibilities. Thus it is sometimes said that a lecturer has an academic right to prescribe a formal written examination for his students, rather than have them assessed by essays alone, and there is an administrative right – governed by precedent or regulation – to apply sanctions against a student who does not submit an essay within the prescribed time limits, and without adequate explanation. There are rights such as courtesy rights connected with formal responsibilities, such as the rights of a convenor of a committee to be advised if a member is unable to attend; and a Headmaster's right to be advised if a teacher is unable to take his classes.

Legal Rights and Natural Rights

Legal rights have no necessary connection with morality, as we found similarly with legal justice in the previous chapter. Thus a legal right may authorize a white employer in a particular society to pay subsistence level wages to black workers, but not to white workers, but the moral right would be for the black to be treated, on grounds of colour alone, no differently from the white, a question of *prima facie* justice, of fairness in the treatment of persons. That is also sometimes called a 'natural right', or 'natural justice', the basic right of an individual to be regarded as a person, without discrimination. In many cases legal rights are also moral rights (legitimate claim-rights or liberties), providing a sanction to protect an individual's rights from certain forms of interference. Generally a right which a person can claim as having the support of the law is readily recognized by others, and so legal rights and obligations are usually mutually respected. In a formal sense legal rights are the more binding, but for persons with strong moral convictions moral rights are the more compelling, particularly when the two conflict.

The idea of *natural rights* is associated with visions of a *natural* state where individual are free of formal constraints, and as moral agents are able then to make moral judgements concerning relations between or among persons. In this natural state there are supposedly opportunities for what we might call *natural justice*, and entitlements under natural justice are entitlements to a consideration of interests and to respect as persons. From such assumed principles much generality has developed in the formulation of natural, human and fundamental rights. In their defence reference is sometimes made to the increasing complexity of social living with its consequent narrowing of sectional interests, increasing competitiveness among groups to maintain supposed relativities, combined with increasing articulateness in asserting and defending individual and group rights. In such sociological accounts of the state of affairs as it is perceived to be, there is implied a *need* for protection of the natural rights of individuals – their rights under a kind of universal *natural justice*. Our task is not moralistic in the sense of moral advocacy in the interests of common people the world over, but rather one of justifying wide-sweeping claims to natural rights as moral rights at all. When we apply to them the criteria we have set forth for such rights, we find that the mutuality of a moral-rational community of understanding and acceptance of rules is not evident. Instead we have one-sided pronouncements.

Natural rights under natural justice apply to no more than the fundamental notion of justice as fairness in the treatment of persons, often drawing attention to the inadequacy of the law. What the law leaves out in its comprehension of possible wrongs inflicted by some and suffered by others is very considerable indeed, partly through increasing social complexities. One of the distinctions drawn by Aristotle was between natural justice and conventional justice: the first he thought had universal validity, with the same force everywhere, regardless of 'people's thinking this or that'; the second, by contrast, is what is laid down by law. Since the constitutions of different states differ, what becomes conventional justice by human enactment in different societies is not the same. It is only natural justice which is everywhere the best (*Nicomachean Ethics*, 1134^b – 5^a).[2] The universality of natural justice, regardless of personal viewpoints and the values of different societies, would depend on an absolute view of morality, rather than the subjective values on which we have based our moral viewpoint. It is not difficult to show that the constancy which Aristotle believed to characterize natural justice does not hold between and among societies, and differs within the one society over a period of time. But the distinction he made was an important one, for he saw a difference between moral law which he called *natural*, and conventional law which was as changeable as man's legislation; between the natural justice of treating equals equally, let us say, and the conventional justice of declaring by law that a prisoner's ransom shall be a *mina*. The first referred to a universal, in his view, the second to a particular. But what he was referring to was no more than justice in our formal sense.

We shall illustrate this point in other contexts. Returning to our intuitive notions of morality in childhood, we may say that many of the rights claims made nowadays are on the basis of a presumption of equality, and the sense of injustice is apt to be felt when presumed equals are treated differently, leading to allegations of arbitrariness or a denial of natural justice. Such naive or intuitive rights claims are not always groundless, however, so that, as one jurist has explained, in the idea of justice there is first a precept to 'Treat like cases alike'; but second, a varying criterion used in judging whether the cases are alike or different.[3] Yet in natural justice an underlying sense of equality persists, if on no other ground than that of common humanity, demanding an equal respect for persons. There is frequently a tension between this sense of fundamental equality and a suspicion of arbitrariness, and in egalitarian societies a shifting of the criterion for judging supposedly like cases toward a blurring of the differences. It is at that point that acknowledgement of natural justice on relevant grounds tends toward confusion or misapplication of the criterion for treating like cases alike, and the concept of natural rights under natural justice loses much of its practical significance. But the fundamental criterion to be used in such considerations is simply the formal notion of justice as fairness in the treatment of persons.

Natural justice as sensitiveness to arbitrariness or discrimination has had its most blatant expressions historically in autocratic abuse of power, with a high-handed disregard of the law as it is displaced by decrees to suit arbitrary purposes: punishment under laws which are not published or change from day to day, or are made retrospective for convenience; imprisonment without trial, or execution without reasons. This kind of denial of natural justice is also a denial of the idea of law.[4] Thus deficiencies in the law have given rise even to some acceptance in law of the concepts of natural rights and natural justice, but not without opposition or reluctance.[5] The formal notion of justice as fairness in the treatment of persons suggests that two of the rules sometimes attributed to natural justice in law, the right to a hearing, and the judge's freedom from bias, should be observed. Yet in England over the last two decades some jurists have been concerned at the extension in case law of the notion of natural justice, giving an increasing flexibility and uncertainty to its use, so that judicial attitudes tend to be expressed in a reluctance to set rules for others' guidance. The complexities of individual cases before the courts indicate to some that to give substance to the formal notion of justice as fairness in the treatment of persons cannot be as firm an undertaking as the notion suggests. Fairness is not as determinate, in practical situations, as it appears. What seems obvious to laymen, that fairness requires that the accused be given a hearing as a natural right, is not so obvious always to lawyers: in some circumstances it is difficult to grant a hearing as a *natural right*, particularly an oral hearing.[6] If we confine challenges in the name of natural justice to instances of arbitrariness and discrimination, various natural rights that have been claimed in courts exceed the boundaries of natural justice: a right to legal aid, for instance: a right to an appeal from a decision; a right to have reasons given for decisions. The desirability of the last, for instance, is widely recognised, but in some circumst- ances in law it is easier to give a correct decision than to supply adequate reasons, in particular reasons that will avoid serious embarrassment to a party. So the concept of natural rights under natural justice has become embarrassing even within the law itself. The formal notion of justice would in all circumstances have provided a clear and constant reference.

We have considered the law in its attitudes to natural rights and natural justice only to the extent that its interests are *moral* interests – that is, expressing a practical consideration for the interests of others. This moral concern has been shared by some philosophers and jurists. We shall illustrate this briefly to demonstrate again that the central concern is none other than a concern for fundamental justice as fairness in the treatment of persons, and that natural rights are no more than *pseudo-rights*.

From Aristotle's distinction between natural law and conventional law through the centuries to our own time, there have been attempts to find a law which can command universal respect, as Aristotle believed, to set against the variability and particularity in time and place, of positive law. One interpretation of this yearning for a higher law is that it is part of a widespread inclination, which we noted in the previous chapter, to look for objective values to which all law can subscribe, based on a belief which is nevertheless difficult to justify rationally,[7] and which is contrary to our own belief in the subjectivity of values. Natural law, or justice, is reduced to a sociological level by another jurist who offers various suggestions for the nature of man in society. This suggests to him, intuitively as one of his critics observes, that there is a certain minimum content of natural law which takes account of man's condition in these five respects: vulnerability, approximate equality, limited altruism, limited resources, and limited understanding and strength of will. This constitutes, it is claimed, a 'core of good sense' in natural law which is required for a common understanding of law and morality,[8] but it is not obvious in what way positive law would take account of these supposed aspects of man's condition. For our purposes it is sufficient to note that 'natural justice', 'natural law' and 'natural rights' are now used in at least three different ways: first, to refer to justice as fairness in the treatment of persons, which makes it indistinguishable from justice itself in the formal notion which we have taken; second, to refer to a higher law which unites law and morality in a kind of Aristotelian universality, above any particular law; third, in a minimum content sense, to apply to all men alike in their social circumstances. But the last two interpretations share with the first simply a fundamental concern for justice in its formal sense. To add to the confusion in law, substantive interpretations of natural rights under natural justice differ from society to society, and sometimes from judge to judge. In one society a court of appeal may hold a judge in breach of natural justice when accusing a group of witnesses of collective lying, since they have no right of reply; another society may permit such accusations when consistent with the evidence. Similarly, rules of natural justice in law are never absolute, even the rule against judicial bias, for in a strict sense no one is capable of perfect impartiality. Every judge is subject to the influences of his own attitudes and values, as well as to changing social values. Questions may even arise, as one writer has indicated, as to ' which biases society wishes its judges to have'. In matters of controversial legislation the known biases of some judges are matters of concern.[9] But substantive considerations such as these do not alter the point we have been making, that natural rights under natural justice are no more than pseudo-rights, and that the entire discussion of such rights refers simply to justice in its formal sense, without invoking a community of moral-rational persons who understand and accept rules of conduct and therefore might have legitimate claim-rights and liberties within that community.

Human Rights

A similar conclusion is reached in considering those rights that are called Fundamental Rights or Human Rights, or both, but which we shall henceforth designate as Human Rights. They are one-sided statements of moral advocacy out of concern for adequate standards of living and for fair treatment for all peoples of the world. As such they are a significant part of practical morality inasmuch as some of their articles have been translated into statutes which have increased much individual well-being. But to be moral inasmuch as they are directed toward the well-being of others does not justify them as legitimate moral rights, for they do not refer to any mutuality of understanding and acceptance of rules of conduct within a moral-rational community. Therefore neither claim-rights nor liberties may be claimed under them.

First we shall demonstrate this moral orientation, and then show how it leads to generalities which provide no foundation for claim-rights or liberties. If we assume with Eighteenth Century moralists that we all have some degree of benevolence, it is understandable that we should put others into the same human context as ourselves, giving them basic opportunities to make their way in life, to plan their futures and to carry out their plans for what they see to be their well-being. Thus in this minimum universal sense it is easy to deduce a Human Right to education, by which is meant formal professional assistance in developing individual potentialities. From the secondary moral principle referring to the need to avoid or prevent the infliction of suffering on others, we might similarly deduce various Human Rights relating to satisfaction of basic needs for survival and for a minimum at least of life satisfaction beyond mere subsistence. The defence of such rights is usually made on grounds of individual human worth, and then the argument is a peculiarly anthropocentric one. It leads to doubts about the worth of lives such as those responsible for suffering on a national and international scale, and of those irremediably brutish and depraved in the family unit. The notion of equal human worth is indeed almost meaningless. If equal worth for mankind, why not for animals too? Is it sensible to speak of horses as having equal *equine* worth, and dogs equal *canine* worth? The statement that men have equal human worth says no more than that all men are human, and that is a purely analytic statement: having said 'men', human worth follows. The general principle is simply that the worth of everything that is, as a member of a species, inheres in its existence. There is a further difficulty in that if fundamental Human Rights are to be related to an individual's well-being and freedom, they cannot be as fundamental in a universal sense as is usually supposed: criminals and others may be deprived of each to protect the well-being and freedom of many others.

When Human Rights refer to non-discrimination on various grounds such as sex, religion or race their justification is to be sought in the formal notion of *justice*. This becomes apparent when we refer again to the law. It has become difficult enough to accommodate natural justice in the courts, and a strong tendency exists in some countries such as England to avoid its mention by referring instead to other expressions such as 'common fairness', 'fairness of procedure', 'the fundamental principles of a fair trial'. [10] There could be no accommodation within national law of Human Rights which referred simply to the equal worth of all individuals as human beings, except in so far as it refers to respect for persons and the possible intersection of legal justice with morality. In practice the function of lawyers is generally to perceive differences between and among persons, not merely to comprehend uniformities. A perception of common humanity is no more than a raw beginning to practical morality too, for specific moral obligations to others would be pointless if we were obligated equally to all. There seems very little point even in asserting a general human right as a claim against any other person, for all one can assert in a *general* human right, *as such*, is that one's worth as a human being is equal to that of the person against whom one is making the claim. It makes sense only in a situation where one is *not* being respected as a person; that is, in a situation where one individual is treating another unjustly. That again returns us to the formal notion of justice, without any indication that Human Rights belong to a moral-rational community of common understanding and acceptance.

Some specific rights that have been classified under Human Rights for their assumed universality may be capable, nonetheless, of independent justification as moral rights under the rights conditions we have outlined. One is a right to education, another a right to privacy. If formal education contributes to well-being by promoting a developing of an individual's power in continually *improving* directions, and consistent with social values, then assuming no other means to this end are available it is self-evident that everyone should benefit from it. Apart from instrumental benefits, there is satisfaction to be derived from the developing itself, regardless of individual differences in abilities and capacities. At this point the justification is again on grounds of justice, of fairness in the treatment of persons. But if we belong to a moral-rational community in which education is valued for its capacity to contribute to every person's well-being, then a claim-right might be made against persons responsible for providing it should it be in any way deficient.

Privacy may be defended, like education, as a universal need according to the values of a particular community, in so far as it relates to the individual as a unique person, with his own values, goals and plans to achieve those goals. Therefore on grounds of elemental justice – of justice in the formal sense – a person may claim privacy as a legitimate right against another person or persons, egarding himself as distinct from other selves, perhaps distinct from thers' external perceptions of him. But a legitimate claim-right may e made only when there is an accepted rule within a moral-rational ommunity that privacy is to be respected, and the moral grounds of uch agreement may well be that the self-image or the uniqueness of idividuality is to be respected. The right to privacy would then relate o any activities or procedures (such as the use of electronic devices) vhich are seen by the individual himself as threatening, or doing arm to, the integrity of his unique individuality.[11]

When the right to privacy is protected by law and written into onstitutions as it is in China and the U.S.S.R.[12] formal legal anctions may have an unstated moral justification with respect to the iviolability of the person. Even with respect to presumed Human Rights which have a social, political or economic purpose, and an leological basis, such as the right to work, it is difficult to exclude a noral purpose as well. But in this case there is a notable *difference* in he claims that are made: here the stance changes to the stance of the uling party, and statements of the right to work as a basic universal ight reflect a paternalism and a political motive,[13] rather than a noral justification of the right to work based on a practical considera- ion of the interests of others. In these politically-oriented statements f Human Rights there is a one-sidedness which prevents their ranslation to claim-rights within the kind of moral-rational commun- :y we have assumed. With respect to privacy it would be difficult to laim that the people of China, for instance, constitute such a ommunity of mutual acceptance and agreement on moral values as ules for conduct. Unless subscribing to the rights conditions we have ssumed, rights under constitutions are not moral rights in our sense, ut pseudo-rights only.

It is not everything that is demonstrably moral in purpose that may e claimed as a moral right. The proliferation and politicization of luman Rights may proceed from genuine moral impulses in a ractical consideration of others' interests, but it is usually unclear to vhat extent they refer to shared values or rules within an identifiable ommunity, with mutuality obtaining rather than unilateral pro- iouncements. Certainly the history of Human Rights statements hows that people value, or think important, rather different things in lifferent ages, and value them with such personal attachment that hey become to them both 'inalienable' and 'imprescriptible', to use he catch-words that have come to us from the French Revolution. 'hey are 'inalienable' inasmuch as the owner cannot transfer, forfeit

or waive them; and 'imprescriptible' inasmuch as he cannot *lose* them
by prescription, such as by the edict of a despot, or by his own
negligence in failing to assert them. Following oppression under
autocrats or a degrading colonialism, it is understandable that some
socialist states should feel that values of freedom and equality are
widely shared.[14] But what it is precisely that is shared is another
matter: it is likely that neither freedom nor equality could be reduced
to commonly understood and accepted rules. Similarly it is under
standable that following the American and French Revolutions there
has been a preference for liberty, security and property.[15] Yet apart
from the problem of clarity of definition sufficient for practical rules
to be formulated, the difficulty of identifying a moral-rational
community on such a national scale – with many of the population
illiterate or barely literate – precludes any translation of such
declarations into legitimate claim-rights. This situation is compound
ed when international communities are postulated. In these there
appears no prospect of mutuality, no common understanding or
acceptance of rules.[16] Thus the politicization and unilateralness of
Human Rights statements give no indication, though couched in the
form of agreements, on how much agreement there is among the
peoples to whom they refer, and for this reason it is impossible to
accept them generally as legitimate moral rights. Specific Human
Rights such as education and privacy *are* capable of independent
justification in moral-rational communities, to the extent that there is
wide understanding and acceptance of them as contributing to
individual well-being. But such a justification has nothing to do with
their supposedly universal nature as appropriate for all mankind
nothing to do, that is, with the generic class of Human Rights.

Children's Rights

There are two particular applications of rights which compel atten
tion: first Children's Rights; and second, Animal Rights. In this
chapter we shall consider each from a general ethical standpoint, and
shall defer more practical considerations to Chapter 5. The two
aspects of children's rights which call for comment at this stage are
first, the relevance of children's immaturity to their rights; and
second, the tendency – already observed with adults – to use merely a
biological or species criterion in referring to them, rather than a
moral criterion. The two aspects are related. In approaching the

question of children's immaturity we face a problem of definition: what is childhood? what is to count as immaturity? On childhood itself the various perspectives from law, sociology, education and ethics have limited common ground. It is largely a matter of administrative convenience in law to lump together as children all of those within the span of formal schooling, though with the lowering of the voting age in some countries and the extension of schooling to eighteen years of age the threshold of adulthood has been correspondingly lowered. The general implication of associating childhood and immaturity with formal schooling is one of dependency while students are still in the custodial care of parents and teachers. But the vague assumptions of dependency and immaturity ill-fit some individual students, in the senior years of formal schooling at least, and therefore legal and moral perspectives on childhood are in conflict. Noting the conspicuous abilities of some students, their capacity for rational thought, the breadth of their knowledge, observers are justified in comparing them with the inferior qualifications of many adults who are classified legally as mature. The philosopher Mill, in his essay *On Liberty*, failed to face this problem squarely. Echoing the sentiments of the 1791 version of *The Declaration of the Rights of Man* in France, 'Liberty consists in the power of doing anything that does not harm others', Mill asserted that 'the sole end for which mankind are warranted, individually or collectively, in interfering with the liberty of action of any of their number is self-protection', adding that the exercise of power against any member of a civilized community against his will can be justified only 'to prevent harm to others' (p.68).[17] Yet the liberty from interference which this principle entails excluded children on grounds of their immaturity, a situation which he found 'hardly necessary' to explain. In the context of his time, when some children did not attend school at all, and those who did often attended irregularly and ceased schooling after a few years, it was understandable that he should have had young children in mind in his reference to 'those who are still in a state to require being taken care of by others' (p.69). But legal dependence continued after schooling, and the category of children 'and other young people' was much wider than those of school age. Mill's error was to lean too conveniently on whatever the law happened to fix for manhood or womanhood, without a serious attempt to distinguish moral immaturity from legal immaturity, readiness for assuming moral responsibility and self-direction from unreadiness. In this there was then, as there is now, a denial of natural justice, or justice as fairness in the treatment

of persons, to some with intellectual and moral developmen
appropriate to the assumption of independent moral roles in their
relations with others: a denial, that is, of respect for persons, or a
failure to recognize that some who do not qualify legally for
adulthood are *persons* in the sense in which we have used the word
When they are persons they are capable of holding legitimate mora
rights in the sense that they can understand their rights as members o
a moral-rational community, and so can make claims against others in
the same community who equally understand and accept the rules.

It is that consideration which leads to the second general aspect o
children's rights, namely, the tendency to ignore the particular and to
think of children in the general, as a class of the young of the human
species. This is the effect, though not the intention, for instance, in
the United Nations Declaration of The Rights of the Child (1959)
which shares the generality of the Universal Declaration of Human
Rights. The child is to be accorded special protection, with full
opportunity to develop in various ways. He is to have the benefit o
social security. His health and the health of his mother are to be
safeguarded. Those in need of special treatment – the physically
mentally and socially handicapped – are to receive it. Whenever
possible the child is to grow up, under his parents, in an atmosphere
of affection and security, both moral and material. Free and compul
sory education is to be offered to all in elementary stages at least. The
tenor of the Declaration is plainly that of a welfare document for the
child, a prescription of adequate minimum standards for the nations
of the world. But these are nominal rights for all children without any
indication of how, or against whom, the rights can be claimed.

Instead of setting out children's rights and justifying them *as* rights
individually held, thought important, claimable by them, and so
forth, the document is a manual for parents or custodians or
standards of child care, ensuring that they grow up healthy in mind
and body, are not neglected or exploited or cruelly treated, and for
the sake of humanity are not nurtured in an atmosphere of racial
religious or ethnic discrimination or prejudice. These are things that
are good for them all, for the young of the human species as a whole
It is by no means an empty or a futile document, for children have
been, and continue to be, maltreated, and proper standards of
child-nurture are everywhere needed. The misconception is to state
these as children's *rights*, when children – if immature intellectually
and morally – cannot possess them, value them, assert them or claim
them. If parents or custodians claim them as rights, it is then parents

or custodians who experience the valuing, asserting, and so forth, and this experience cannot be transferred to children. To say that parents or custodians value a right to education for their children is to say two things: first that parents value education or think it important; second that they desire it for their children. If they value education as a *right*, it may be a right for themselves to education, and if they value it because it will enhance their children's life prospects, and for no other reason, it is still education that is being valued by them or thought important by them, and claimable by them. It is a confusing and improper use of 'right' and 'right claim' nonetheless, to speak of claiming a right *for* someone else. The person who has the right can make a claim against another person or persons violating the right, a person or persons morally obligated to the holder of the right. The relationship involves both the holding of a right and the duty by some other person or persons to respect the right. Under the conditions we have assumed for the holding of moral rights, it is only *some* children who may be said to have them: those who are intellectually mature enough to become members of a moral-rational community which understands and agrees on certain rules of conduct.

To attribute or impute rights to others, or – to use the language of philosophy and the law – to *ascribe* rights to them, is sometimes to use rights in a pseudo or quasi sense. But it is not always the case that ascribed rights are merely *supposed* rights and not rights in the proper sense, as we shall see, for there are some rights ascribed to children which may be at least partly understood by them, but with respect to which they nevertheless do need assistance from adults in asserting and claiming them. This situation may be approached from the legal perspective offered by a philosopher of law.[18] In this explanation, when we ascribe ownership by using such operative, non-technical expressions as 'This is mine', 'This is yours', we recognize such rights whether they are claimed or not. So used, our ascriptions are said to be related to the facts that support them in much the same way as is a judge's decision. That is, we decide as a judge decides, *on* certain facts before us, that another person has certain rights, and the judgement we make, like a judicial decision, is a blend of fact with rule, regulation or even law. To illustrate from a case of contract, the judge's function is that of deciding, *upon the evidence put before him*, whether there is or is not a valid contract. He does not use any legal touchstone of an ideal interpretation of contract to which a particular case is simply referred. If a party fails to make a successful case, the judge decides entirely on the evidence before him: that is what is expected of him, and he can do no more. So his judgement may be either a right or wrong decision, good or bad, affirmable or reversible, and it may be quashed or discharged. But it cannot be either true or false. In this sense, the legal concept of contract, like other legal concepts, is said to be *defeasible*. The explanation is then made that the description of ownership is defeasible. In making statements such as, 'This is yours', on the evidence before us we make a decision that some person has a right to ownership, but we make it as a judgement which is neither true nor false. In this we are not referring to merely descriptive uses, as when we point to a house and say, 'This is ours', or to 'casual ascriptive' uses, so-called, as when we hand a wallet to a person who, we noticed, had dropped it a pace or two ahead of us, with the words, 'This is yours'. Even in the latter circumstance, though unlikely, the ownership is capable of annulment, or is defeasible, for *prima facie* ownership can be defeated by further evidence. (The wallet may in fact have been stolen from someone else.)

What relevance has this explanation to the ascription of rights to children? Within the broad category of children we need to make a distinction between those with, and those without, sufficient maturity to understand what the rights mean to them, to be able to claim them and to be aware against whom they may be claimed. For those too immature to fulfil these conditions we regard the nominal ascription of rights to be misapplications of the positive concept of rights which we have adopted. But for the others both legal and non-legal rights may be properly ascribed. Legally ascribed rights would include a right to protection from abuse such as parental cruelty, and the ownership of this right by such children could hardly be classified as defeasible, whatever the evidence. But many non-legally ascribed rights, those imputed to children by teachers, parents or community leaders may have a defeasible concept of ownership. Let us imagine the case of children claiming a right to the use of a community library after it has been ascribed to them by a community Library Committee. The Committee had previously canvassed opinions and made the best judgement of which it was capable in the light of the evidence then available. Children of a certain age, it was argued, may be regarded as capable of participating in community activities, and ought therefore to share some of the community's privileges. Subsequently further evidence is adduced: children have been noisy in the library and there have been complaints from adult readers; in addition, some adult books have been damaged and the evidence points to children acting irresponsibly. The Committee reverses its earlier decision, and the children's ownership of this ascribed right is proved defeasible. In this, it is explained, there is a mixture of fact and rule or regulation, as there is in judges' decisions on questions relating to contract. It is important to recognize that the children involved have understood the meaning of the right, the fact that it was claimable against the Community Librarian, but as non-ratepayers themselves and non-citizens, have needed someone to *ascribe* the right to them. The Library Committee had taken it upon itself to ascribe the right to children, announcing it with the words, 'This right is yours'.

The ascription of rights to some children may be therefore a demonstration of the conflict between the law and morality, for some children – by virtue of their intellectual and moral maturity – may be capable of membership of a moral-rational community where moral rules are understood and accepted. If some fail in the trust placed in them and the ascribed right is shown to be defeasible, their moral eligibility for right-holding is not in any way thrown into doubt: moral failure is not confined to children.

Animal Rights

The natural sympathy which Eighteenth Century moral philosophers attributed to all of us was probably not an innate sentiment but rather one that was learned as in various ways our attitudes and values are, but the impression of its naturalness to man as a probable inference from its widespread manifestation in that century would undoubtedly be strengthened in ours, when sensitiveness to cruelty, human and animal suffering, distress or neglect is generally much more wide-spread than it was then (according to social history and the literature of the period). There are now strong demands for *rights* for all those who need society's protection, for infants and children of all ages who have to make their way in a competitive world, for imbeciles and the handicapped of all kinds, and, increasingly, for animals which have suffered in many ways such as by cruelty, neglect, destruction of habitats, indiscriminate slaughter in the name of sport, and animal farming. In other words, individual attitudes and values may be changing social values too, inasmuch as significantly large numbers of individuals in various social groups appear now to share them. In this process individual attitudes and values with respect to animals understandably transfer to the objects themselves, and animal rights we imagine to be held by us as surrogates. From the intensity of our pity or compassion we wish to strengthen their status by attributing rights to them, presumably in the expectation that this will draw public attention to their suffering and lead to legislation in their favour. There is no question that we may speak of *legal* rights of animals, just as we do of the legal rights of infants, children and imbeciles. But on moral rights we have taken a positive approach, insisting that for rights to be held they must be valued by the rights holders themselves, as well as, in normal circumstances, be assertable or claimable by them, within a moral-rational community of mutual understanding and acceptance of certain rules of conduct. There is no point in ascribing moral rights to animals, for they are obviously powerless to claim rights when they are unable to understand what they mean. It is only legal rights that may be ascribed to them, which convey our legal obligations with respect to them. Whether these obligations are *moral* as well we have yet to decide. Rights are affixed to them, but because the two-way relationship of mutual understanding and agreement on rules does not hold in their case, claim-rights and liberties are beyond them.

The idealist philosopher Bradley explained that the having of moral rights implies that the person with the rights sees himself as a *subject*, one who possesses moral rights and is able to claim them; and also as an *object*, an object of others' duty to him (*Ethical Studies*, pp. 207–8).[19] Further, since duty and right are simply different sides of the same thing, to say that we have a duty to act with respect to another's right is to say at the same time that it is *morally* right for us so to act. To have a moral right then is to have the capacity for entering into an active relationship with another person or persons, not merely to be a passive recipient of another's duty. As *subjects* we can assert our claim rights. As objects, we expect others with whom we are in this kind of moral relationship to respect our rights – our right to a free choice of vocation, for instance, or our right to marry if we wish and whom we wish. To qualify as moral rights we thus require an understanding of the relation involved in rights and duties from both sides. Moral rights, we repeat, are held by moral individuals; moral individuals are persons capable of understanding moral relationships between themselves and others. Though individually held, our values are shared by others in the moral community in which we live. Otherwise the moral subject–object relationship of which Bradley spoke would not be practicable. Some conflict we can expect, but the moral system of rights and duties cannot tolerate total conflict, or even a high degree of conflict, in our relations with others. It is clear that animals fall outside such moral relationships. Whenever legislation is introduced in their favour, for reasons of conservation or prevention of cruelty, it is the government, acting for society, which accepts the trust. In these legal rights those accepting the trust are not acting in response to any right claim (which in these cases can't be made). In declaring that animals have rights they are adding nothing in meaning to what is already conveyed by declaring their acceptance of a trust. It is a similar external, one-sided declaration to some non-legal declarations, such as those of the United Nations, but unlike the latter, it is not setting up standards and urging nations to follow them; it is enforceable. This use of legal right is as meaningless, from the point of view of ownership of the right, as a statement made by a mother to her infant in presenting it with a new garment, 'This is *yours!*' The infant does not understand the meaning of the words and the attribution of ownership to it is artificial. The garment is still not owned by the child in any positive sense of ownership; the mother is unable to transfer ownership merely by using a form of words, as though affixing a label of ownership to the garment, for others – but not for the child – to see and understand.

The arguments for animal rights generally founder on loose applications of rights such as this, and such as those used in some legal rights. One is an argument from pity, noting man's presumption, as Montaigne did, or as Bentham did from a utilitarian standpoint: some animals can suffer and therefore we should accord them the rights 'which never could have been withholden from them but by the hand of tyranny' (*The Principles of Morals and Legislation*, ch. XIX, IV, p. 143).[20] We agree on a number of observations of animals which are not relevant to this question: first, that some can experience pain (as well as enjoyment)[21]; second, that according to their nature they are actively striving beings with wants such as those relating to basic survival needs; third, that some are capable of emotions, of affection for young and distress when separated from them. The question for the attribution of rights to animals is not, in Bentham's words, 'Can they suffer?' but rather 'Can they ever understand and claim rights?' All we can do in artificially attributing rights to animals is to do as the mother does in attempting to bestow ownership on an infant who has not the capacity for ownership: that is, affix labels of rights to them.

But if animals are not capable themselves of moral agency, may we regard them one-sidedly as objects of our moral duties or obligations? If we may, then despite their incapacity for right-holding, they may still belong to our moral sphere though themselves unaware of it. This is a question we have deferred from the previous chapter.

We may imagine an artificial separation of our attitudes and values into two categories, one comprising moral values and the other comprising non-moral values. In the first category we put all those attitudes and values which relate us to others according to our moral principles as we have stated them; while in the second category we put all our attitudes and values which either relate us to others in non-moral ways – as when we value things in common, such as particular recreational activities – or relate us to things, animals, the environment, and so forth, all of them of a non-personal kind.

Our attitudes and values in the first category are not necessarily more intense or action-oriented than those in the second. One individual may value diamonds, gold, cars, a bank balance, a large house more strongly than he values any moral relationships, or personal relationships of any kind.

The two categories overlap, and we may represent them by intersecting circles. In the common area of intersection there are locatable such general attitudes and values as concern for others (their well-being, rather than insecurity, anxiety, suffering), applying equally to human beings and to animals. This does not entail *identical* attitudes with respect to both humans and animals, since both cognitive and affective components may vary according to the object. But, given a degree of human variability in this regard, we may be equally concerned and equally compassionate about animals in pain as about humans in pain; we may value their well-being as much as we value human well-being. Further we are apt to use the language of morals to express these values: our revulsion of feeling, for instance, when we see humans inflict suffering unnecessarily on animals, and declare it is not only cruel, but *wrong*, or wrong because it *is* cruel. In this we express a deep-seated conviction, or attitude-value, relating to the wrongness, so-called, of all unnecessary suffering. But it is a value that we may express either in our moral relationships with others, or with respect to animals, or both. Further, there may be a connection between the way we regard animals and the way we regard human beings.[22] It is the area of intersection that is in question, for if we have a conviction that an act is wrong which relates to a human treatment of animals, it is merely definitional to classify it as non-moral on the basis of an earlier determination that morality is restricted to our relations with other human beings, and our relations with animals are therefore non-moral. The fundamental flaw in any argument that morality refers only to inter-human association is that such a distinction is no more than stipulative.

Since our attitudes and values are personal or subjective, if we do in fact express them in the language of morals there is no reason to deny them as part of our moral convictions. Subjective moral values pertaining to animals cannot be explained away by a classification system which arbitrarily excludes them: the task is to change our classification so that it fits the situation, not vice versa, for classifications are made by us for convenience. We shall maintain that we may have moral duties to sentient animals, obligations for their well-being, including particularly a duty not to inflict unnecessary suffering on them, which do not require that there be correlative rights held by the animals: that nothing is gained, and much indeed is lost, if we attribute artificial rights to them, as are attributed to infants and imbeciles also, simply to protect an assumed correlativity between duties and rights. Our reasons for supporting the view that we may have moral convictions expressed as moral duties to animals is that animals, which are sentient beings capable of experiencing pain (we do not include all animal life, some of which is insentient) have interests by virtue of this, and need therefore to be protected against human cruelty and neglect; that they have interests as well peculiar to their species, including enjoyment of their young, and their protection; that it would be contradictory to argue that pain is evil in man but not in animals; and that animals are in any case brought into man's moral sphere whenever the infliction of suffering on them leads to a brutalizing of man's relations with others.

As we have noted, avoidance and prevention of unnecessary suffering is presupposed in our very notion of morality as a practical consideration of others' interests, and does not entail a total acceptance of the utilitarian argument. Whenever we consider others' interests we consider generally their well-being, inasmuch as this is served by the satisfaction of their interests. To enable a person to go about his normal activities in which we recognize his personhood – desiring and planning, making decisions and acting – it is important to him that he be not *hindered* as a person by physical or mental suffering. Similarly to enable sentient animals to live out their lives according to the interests of their species, it is important for each not to be hindered in the satisfaction of its interests by avoidable or preventable physical or mental suffering. A moral stance toward animals is partly dependent on becoming acquainted with their natures without being anthropomorphic in our attitudes toward them, just as to have a moral stance of respect for persons is partly dependent on understanding human nature.

There can be no firm conclusion on whether the allowance of sentient animals into our sphere of morality is merely idiosyncratic unless appropriate empirical studies are undertaken to ascertain the distribution of these attitudes and values throughout society. While an individual who is prepared to justify his moral attitudes and values with reason is free to stand alone, and may influence social values rather than be influenced by them, an ethical position regarding man's relations with sentient animals gathers some confidence when it is indicative of changing social values. Montaigne and Bentham were still prepared to stand alone, and this is the strongest ethical position to take, since moral values are essentially personal, and morality is not merely a description of social values. Our normative conviction is that the interests of sentient animals ought to be considered, and therefore the statement of the formal notion of morality in the previous chapter remains unchanged, as does the statements of the primary and secondary moral principles. 'Others' refers to sentient animals, as it does to human beings.

DUTIES

At several points in this chapter we have indicated that rights have another side to them which we call *duties*, and the implication seems to have been that whenever we have rights we have correlative duties. That is one link between right and duty, and another is in the contemporary emphasis on Fundamental Rights or Human Rights, with its corresponding Fundamental or Human Duties. We shall introduce our discussion of duty by considering briefly each of these, commencing with the latter, using Human Duties as we did in the case of Human Rights to cover what are also regarded as Fundamental Duties. Human Duties, like Human Rights, refer to a moral context in so far as it relates to human beings: an association of individuals in social groups in which there is a practical consideration of others' interests. Apart from being moral duties in this sense, they are also seen as broadly in common to all human beings, obligations which we owe to others simply because they are human. These duties are *ascribed* responsibilities, based on the species assumption that all human life has worth, or is deserving of others' efforts toward maintaining well-being and freedom, without putting obstructions in the way. It is clear that these Human Duties must allow of exceptions, and so have a *prima facie* status as duties, just as Human Rights do. We do not have a Human Duty to promote the well-being and freedom of a psychopathic killer. There is a link too between Human Duties and natural justice in its concern for non-discrimination, returning to the formal notion of justice as fairness in the treatment of persons. As a Human Duty we might speak generally of a duty to treat all citizens alike, regardless of ethnic background or colour of skin. For reasons which we have given in connection with Human Rights, we might refer to a Human Duty to respect others' privacy, or to provide education for all children. Human Duties can be justified as long as they remain moral in character, and are not merely expressions of a species viewpoint which values anything human, simply because it is human.[23] What we have been saying of Human Duties parallels what we said earlier of Human Rights.

Duty is simply part of the two-way relationship in the moral-rational community we have described. But we have already observed that in the case of young children and of animals the relationship cannot be reciprocal.

Correlativity with Rights

We must now look more closely at the relation between the two, in particular the notion that rights and duties are correlatives, the one presupposing the other. Are we able to claim that given a right there is always a corresponding duty? This seems sufficiently clear: if A has a claim-right it is claimable against a person or persons who in turn have an obligation to A. With respect to liberties such as freedom of speech there are others who have obligations to respect those rights to freedom. But if B has a duty or obligation to A, does it follow that there is still a mutuality in the relationship: that is, that A has a right that is claimable against B? We may, as we have seen, speak of a moral duty to protect sentient animals from harm and suffering, but because they do not understand what it is to have a right and are incapable of claiming it, it is not reasonable to argue that they have rights. There is in fact no mutuality in our relationships with them. We are unable to justify the general proposition that a duty of A to an animal (or similarly to an infant or an imbecile) implies that the animal (or infant, or imbecile) has a corresponding right which is claimable against A. But what is the situation within the narrow framework of morality of human association in which A is capable of understanding his rights and of claiming them against B? Is it invariably implied that if B has a duty to A, then A has a right against B? In many situations the mutuality holds: if a doctor has a moral duty to advise relatives that a patient is terminally ill, the relatives may be said to have a right against the doctor to be so advised. In many ways it may be in their interests to know the facts. On the other hand there are notable exceptions which show that the relationship is not an invariable one. According to our moral attitudes and values we may have a duty to be charitable to the poverty-stricken in our community, but this does not confer on the poverty-stricken a corresponding moral right to our charity. Again, we may assert, according to our personal moral values, that we have a duty to be Good Samaritans in helping someone we find in distress, but it is straining our understanding of 'right' to say that the person lying by the roadside has a moral *right* to our help. Similarly, in response to an act of beneficence from A, we say that we have a moral duty to express gratitude to A, but that duty should not involve any correlative right held by A against us. When we have a relationship of trust and affection with close relatives we may be said to have a moral obligation to them to protect ourselves from death or disabling injuries, except in war or other emergencies, but this does not entail a moral right held by our relatives against us. What we perceive as our moral duty has its source in our moral attitudes and values, and the moral convictions that express them. It is contradictory to speak of *ascribing* moral duties: the ascription of duties refers to the assignment of formal or official responsibilities of a non-moral character. To say to a person that it is his duty to be charitable, if charity is not consistent with his attitudes and values, or to ascribe to all human beings a duty to be charitable, knowing that this is inconsistent with some individual attitudes and values, is to demand the impossible (at that particular time). Instances of moral duties which do not imply correlative rights are further support for the view that our duty to consider the interests of sentient animals does not entail rights held by them, and therefore their inability to hold rights is not a disabling condition for bringing them into our moral sphere.

We shall now consider briefly Kant's distinction between 'perfect duty' and 'imperfect duty', and Ross's explanation of *prima facie* duty

Perfect and Imperfect Duties

No philosopher has given duty a more compelling force in practical morality than Kant. We have referred in the previous chapter to the law-like character of Kant's moral imperatives. He distinguished between desire – instinct – inclination – passions, on the one hand; and on the other hand a moral duty which gives any action its moral worth. To have moral worth, an action must be done from duty; and an action done from duty derives its moral worth from the maxim by which it is determined, not from the realization of the object of the action (*Fundamental Principles of the Metaphysic of Morals*, p.16).[24] It is only rational beings who have the capacity to act on duty, and that capacity depends on the relation of rational beings to one another: all are united in a "kingdom of ends", where no one regards another simply as a means to his own ends. Duty is a practical necessity to act on the principle that the will of a rational being must always be regarded as legislative; legislating, that is, universally. Duty has nothing to do with feelings, impulses or inclinations (p.52). Kant illustrates his categorical imperatives in negative terms: breaking promises, telling lies, committing suicide are things which the Rational Will commands us not to do. In this we rely on no external authority whatsoever. As equally rational beings we are each autonomous as moral agents. The categorical imperative is a moral practical law: '*duty* is the action to which a person is bound' (*Introduction to the Metaphysic of Morals*, p.279). The categorical imperative is objectively necessary, since it is necessary *in itself*, commanded by rational law (*Fundamental Principles of the Metaphysic of Morals*, p.31). By contrast with a categorical imperative not to break promises, rational persons could never subscribe to a principle that they should break promises whenever it suited them, for that could never be universalized. If it were, the mutual distrust established would obviously produce an irrational basis for human association (p.40).

Kant distinguished between *perfect duties* and *imperfect duties*: perfect duties, he explained, admit of no exceptions in favour of inclination; imperfect duties are subject to inclination (p.39 n). Perfect duties are made obligatory by the Rational Will – the will resisting inclination or desire. The perfect duty to obey categorical imperatives lies in the obligation to act as if by the will the action were to become a universal law of nature. This suicide cannot be, or breaking promises, or telling lies. The two overriding moral principles in Kant's ethics were first, the general formulation of all categorical imperatives, 'Act only on maxims in adopting which you can at the same time wish that they should become universal laws', and 'So act as to treat humanity, whether in thine own person or in that of any other, in every case as an end withal, never as a means only' (p.47). Together these principles had the effect of taking the attention away from self-interest, and encouraging a more impersonal view of morality, as well as giving to man a dignity in his moral relations with others which was emphasized by the belief that all rational beings could legislate universally in their moral decisions. Together with the English moral philosophers of the Eighteenth Century who developed the theme of benevolence as a natural sentiment, Kant at the same time, through his exaltation of duty as the product of a Rational Will, took ethics a long way from the declaration of Hobbes that man is a creature of self-interest, and as such unable to depart from his fundamental nature. But Kant's defence of his position is not always a strong one: first, he overtaxed the notion of man as a rational being, and justified reason transcendentally – as we have seen – as requiring no critical examination (*Introduction to the Analytic of Pure Practical Reason*, p.102); second, he did not offer adequate explanation of the supposed obligatoriness and unexceptionality of the laws dictated, as categorical imperatives, by the Rational Will, for they can frequently be shown to conflict. Thus conflicts of duty can arise between truth-telling and saving human life, and it is not at all clear that in all conceivable circumstances we should tell the truth, for instance, or keep a promise, or even abstain from killing someone. It is for that reason that Ross preferred to speak of all duties as no more than *prima facie* duties. In many situations it is difficult to give perfect duties an unconditional stamp. While in some uncomplicated situations the duty before us may be clear enough, complexities are sometimes revealed in our deliberations and the call of duty loses its imperative character. Is patriotism an unconditional duty in time of war, regardless of the individual's responsibilities to others?

Kant's distinction between categorical imperatives, on the one hand, as representing an action 'necessary of itself', and self-regarding acts such as *prudence* on the other, is similarly not as clear-cut as he believed. Kant used 'prudence' in two senses: first to apply to the man who is able so to influence others that he can use them for his own purposes; second, in a more private sense, to a man's ability to choose means for fulfilling his purposes 'for his own greatest well-being' (*Fundamental Principles of the Metaphysic of Morals*, p.33 n). The man who could achieve the first but not the second he considered was on the whole imprudent, rather than prudent, and might best be described as clever and cunning. The prudent person had the care and foresight to act in ways that would be self-beneficial. From this notion has developed the concept of prudence as applying, usually more negatively than positively, to the person who is so narrowly self-regarding as to safeguard himself regularly from consequences harmful to himself. That was indeed the antithesis of Kant's perfect duty and its law-like inviolability. Yet duty cannot lead to the total neglect of self-interest, and it is in this respect that the distinction between duty and prudence is frequently blurred. In some circumstances nice judgement is needed before deciding an appropriate moral measure of each. Then it becomes difficult to speak of a perfect duty: we have imperfect obligations both to others, in promoting their well-being; and to ourselves, as prudence, in considering our own well-being as well. By accepting a moral principle of a consideration of others' interests as well as our own, we depart from Kant's notion of perfect duties and categorical imperatives, and adopt a more generally defensible approach where all our duties are imperfect, subject to modification in our deliberations as we face complex moral situations. To tell the truth in a simple situation may appear to be a response to a perfect obligation, and we may appear to be obeying a moral imperative; but the same obligation loses its binding force in other more complex situations where we have to take account of conflicting interests. In practical morality perfect duties may provide a base-line from which to proceed. Their performance is not always true to them, and in some circumstances there is good reason that it should not be. We have linked our moral convictions based on personal attitudes and values with Kant's elevated sense of moral obligatoriness, but only in an ideal and exhortatory sense. In practice we realise that moral duty can occupy no such consistently sublime position of command.

Prima Facie Duties

Are all our duties then, no more than *prima facie* duties? Instead of viewing duties as unconditional, as Kant's perfect duties were, should we not regard them all as *conditional*? Ross uses *prima facie duties* to refer to 'things that tend to be our duty' (*The Right and the Good*, p.18 n).[25] There is a need to examine a situation which presents more than one prima facie duty, he explains, suggesting that perhaps this is always the case, until we are able to decide to the best of our ability though never conclusively, that one of these duties is more incumbent on us to perform than any of the others. Motive is never part of duty. That which is a prima facie duty in a particular situation is never an arbitrary decision. His classification of *prima facie* duties was wide ranging without claiming completeness. (It included duties of fidelity gratitude, justice, beneficence, self-improvement, and non-maleficence.) While there are simple moral situations in which Ross's duties are unambiguously appropriate, practical morality is concerned usually, and more interestingly, with cases of conflicts of duties, and here we may or may not be in a position to refer to a matter of principle. In some circumstances we are left with a deliberation on the possible *consequences* of an individual action, and then, as Toulmin observes, we conclude that we *ought* to perform an action, but not, usually, that we have a moral obligation to perform it, or that it is our *duty* to perform it (*Reason in Ethics*, pp. 147–8).[26] Duty then becomes less and less binding, more and more conditional, as the complexity of situations increases, and we need to determine on balance which action is likely to have the least ill-consequences. In some circumstances an appeal to the primary moral principles which we have formulated may be of very little help in reaching a decision on the best thing to do in the circumstances. Since our deliberations are both rational and dispositional as we have indicated in previous chapters, the best decisions in complex moral situations are often made in formal group discussions, for the reasons given. Ross's suggestion that *prima facie* rightness becomes self-evident, like mathematical axioms (pp. 29–30), is in conflict with this view, and indeed with the view of some contemporary philosophers of mathematics who themselves challenge the concept of self-evidence. We may feel satisfied that we have reached, by careful deliberation, the best solution to a situation of conflicting duties, but there are usually slender grounds for supporting claims to the intuitive self-evidence of a *prima facie* rightness.

Moral and Non-moral Senses

Therefore while Kant gave *duty* a central place in his moral philosophy, and was not alone in the Eighteenth Century in justifying its aw-like character by appeal to Reason,[27] in moral philosophy to-day ts centrality is seldom claimed. Generally there is little support for he exceptionless nature of moral duties as we move from generalities concerning the powers of rational beings and consider rather the complexities of particular moral situations. Then it is that the force of obligatoriness is lost, and because the status of perfect duties, binding on equally rational beings, is now reduced to a *prima facie* one only, with things *tending* to be our duty as Ross put it, it is understandable that the concept of duty should have a decreasing philosophical significance in contemporary moral discourse. In more general discourse it is much more usual to return to one of the earliest uses of duty, to refer to responsibilities associated with particular offices or positions. These entail rules or expectations, so that we refer readily to parents' duties to their children, teachers' duties to children or to the community, a policeman's duty to the public, a doctor's to the sick, and so forth. In these duties there is no *necessary* connection with morality, but in every case contingent moral obligations may arise: protection of the young from moral danger, for instance: selfless service to those in need. The distinction is clear in official responsibilities between experiencing a moral duty, and being *dutiful*. We are dutiful when we have a strong sense of duty with respect to our formal responsibilities in the roles we are given or the official positions we hold, convinced that it is our *duty* to carry out, to the best of our ability, the functions for which we are held responsible. In our roles as car-drivers on public roads we are dutiful, obedient, conscientious in the formal sense when we carry out the instructions we have learned and are consistent rule-followers. When we exceed such rule-bound behaviour in a practical acknowledgement of others' interests on the roads, being patient, avoiding harrassment or obstruction, we have begun to act with a moral awareness, acknowedging others' rights and our corresponding duties to them at least as far as considerateness is concerned. *Conscientiousness,* we observe, may be used in either non-moral or in moral senses. From the conscientiousness of meticulous attention to the functions assigned to us in our respective offices, we use 'conscientious' in a moral sense when we refer to firmness of purpose in refusing to deviate from our moral convictions. In the former usage our acts are considered meritorious, as we shall see in the next chapter. In the latter the question of merit generally does not arise, as it did not arise to Kant with respect to his duties of perfect obligation. For Kant the Rational Will left no alternative to any rational person; in our view firmness of allegiance to moral principles is an expression of the strength of moral attitudes and values, which though not as binding as Kant' moral imperatives, are sufficient to account for the conscientiou moral conduct observed in us by others.

In moral philosophy duty has become circumscribed with qualifica tions. In our view moral duty is not absolute. Our subjective mora values are generally not so rigid as to prevent change, and the same applies to the broad trend of individuals' values which we call socia values. Complex moral problems do not lend themselves to a application to absolute principles or rules, for there are no infallibl touchstones here any more than there are in the justice of comple hearings in the courts. Kant made the Intellect or Reason absolute combined with the Good Will which resisted desire and inclination We have the advantage of empirical knowledge which has develope after his time, and so have some grounds for holding his position t be a dogma derived from an ideal.

REVIEW

We have viewed rights positively as involving a subject holding a righ and another person or persons against whom the right may b claimed, with the former able to understand the nature of the right that is, able to assert or claim it, and even to waive or relinquish it Moral rights are held within a moral-rational community where ther is agreement on certain values.

Natural Rights and Human Rights are both pseudo-rights becaus of their one-sided declarations, and the lack of the mutualit condition for rights to operate. Particular rights classified unde Human Rights by some, such as the rights to education and privacy are defensible as moral rights quite independently of the classifica tion.

Children's rights raise at least two important questions in th philosophy of rights: first, how is 'maturity' to be defined? second, i it proper to speak of rights being held by others in trust for children The first question leads in some cases to a denial of justice whe maturity is judged, not on individual merit, but generally or arbitrari ly on such criteria as age. When children are viewed broadly as th young of the human species, as they appear to be in the Declaratio of the Rights of the Child, wide individual differences among childre in intellectual and moral maturity are overlooked, and there is littl understanding of them as emerging persons. On the second question, according to our view of positive rights those held in trust on behalf of others who cannot hold them themselves are not strictly rights, despite legal recognition of rights of custodianship.

With animals there is similarly a violation of the usual logical relations holding between a holder of a right and a person or persons against whom the rights may be claimed, but this is because we customarily think of rights and duties as establishing a necessary mutuality. Animals do not have rights, according to the positive rights criteria we have adopted. Our concern for animal welfare is not at all impaired by this disqualification. Since we use the language of morals when we refer to animal suffering, often as a spontaneous expression of moral convictions, it is therefore impossible, except by the arbitrariness of stipulative definitions, to exclude sentient animals from our morality. Though they do not have rights and cannot themselves be moral agents, we *do* have moral responsibilities to them because they clearly have interests. For some children both legal and non-legal rights may be properly ascribed, for they do have the capacity to experience and to understand them. Some of these may have a defeasible concept of ownership, and this is of interest to us inasmuch as it draws attention to a proper ascription of rights to children too young for legal rights but still sufficiently mature intellectually and morally to hold rights.

Rights and duties are often correlative, but not invariably so. The demonstration of moral obligations which do not confer rights, even in human associations, helps to justify the idea of having moral obligations to sentient animals, which similarly can claim no right against us. As for the ascription of duties, this is meaningful in defining the responsibilities attached to offices, but it is contradictory to speak of ascribing *moral* duties, for these are necessarily related to our personal attitudes and values.

The exaltation of *duty* in moral philosophy gained its highest expression in Kant, with his concepts of categorical imperatives, the kingdom of ends for all rational persons, and perfect duties. His prescriptions are seldom defended nowadays because of his failure to account for conflict of duties, and the necessity therefore to relax the austere obligatoriness of moral law in particular complex circumstances. Ross's *prima facie* duties are closer to the way contemporary moral philosophers generally perceive duties, but sometimes duty is given little attention by them now that its law-like character is so clearly in question. By a better understanding of the nature of attitudes and values, and through formal discussion, there are possibilities of giving our moral convictions something of the force of Kantian law, or of compelling duty, but only as personal ideals, and only to the extent that they remain open to discussion.

Concepts of 'dutiful' and 'conscientious' have application in Chapter 5 in both moral and non-moral senses, but especially in non-moral ones. Being *morally* conscientious is not especially meritorious, assuming that it is authentic conduct to which we are referring, and not posturing, since moral conscientiousness is simply an expression of our habitual moral attitudes and values and the strength of our commitment to them.

With the theoretical basis of education, justice and morality completed, we shall now turn to considerations of a practical nature which comprise Part II.

Part II
Practical Interlude

4   Practical Deliberations

We have now reached an intermediate stage of our discussion. Instead of proceeding directly from the theoretical basis of Part I to considerations of social justice in Part III, we introduce Part II as a pause between these two for two main reasons. First, practical considerations are themselves illuminating to the principles that have preceded them, helping to translate abstractions to concrete experiences. Second, rather than proceeding simplistically, we need to show how the simple becomes increasingly more complex. We have already referred to attitudes and values, to values as preferences and standards, and to individual reasoning requiring ideally, an external monitor in a kind of formal discussion, especially when value judgements are being made, though obviously such an external monitor is not always available to us. We have taken these matters largely for granted: now we must probe them further and examine some of their practical connections.

The present chapter is practical inasmuch as it aims to increase understanding of our thinking as we reason on what we ought to do; specifically to explore the complexity of reason and its accompanying dispositional tendencies. It becomes then a bridge to the next chapter by linking these insights with practical situations and enlarging their moral implications. These understandings will be carried forward to Part III when other practical perspectives are taken on relationships between justice, morality and education.

Although it is difficult to speak of a science of ethics, or even to envisage one which could tell us, on the basis of adequate evidence and moral principles derived from it, what we *ought* to do in all moral situations, it is nevertheless necessary that we should approach the *ought* in our conduct with a clear understanding of what is practicable and what is not in human behaviour, and even of what is probable, on the basis of experience, and what is improbable. We are not arguing that what is, is therefore what ought to be: that a person who is murderous in intent *ought* to be murderous in intent. What we are arguing is quite different. It is that *unless we take account of* the is, or the probable is as indicated in experience, our ethical oughts may be ill-founded; so ill-founded indeed, as to render them relatively empty and therefore inefficacious in any practical morality. That has been the case with some ideals, an ideal, for instance, of general submergence of self-interest beneath a universally benevolent social interaction, everyone playing his part to the best of his ability for the sake of something higher than himself – a completely harmonious society or a reified moral state.

We begin this chapter too with an intuition that the full story has not been told – if it ever could be told – about the limitations on our reason as we undertake the kind of activity to which Aristotle referred in his explanation of practical wisdom: we have the intuitive feeling, that is, that as we deliberate on what ought to be done, exercising our reason to the best of our ability, there are influences on our choices or decisions which are both wider and more complex in their interrelationships than are customarily conceded. We are not denigrating the place of reason in these deliberations: on the contrary, we give complete support to normative statements which urge that our practical deliberations be rational. But it is not unqualified support for an invariant dominance of reason. We believe that a philosophy of action can be developed which considers not merely desires, emotions, motives and intentions, but also certain relatively stable organizations of psychological complexes which help us to attain a better understanding of the place of reason in practical morality. To understand that place is to make our normative statements more realistic: to argue for what ought to be on the basis of what is believed, on empirical evidence, to be impossible, or highly improbable, would itself be inconsistent with reason. In other words, normative ethics itself benefits from a foundation of empirical knowledge, acknowledging the limitations which this too might have. *Oughts* become stronger, not weaker, by acknowledging any limitations there may be on practicability of achievement. To recognize ideals for what they are does not weaken any directional or motivational force they may have when they enter into our practical deliberations.

We shall commence our enquiry by referring briefly to the views of Aristotle and Kant, in particular, on the place of reason in practical deliberations. These will give an impetus to our consideration of dispositions, and especially of their interaction with reason.

PHILOSOPHERS ON REASON

Aristotle

Those who have attributed to reason an overriding significance in our moral lives, such as Aristotle (with the aid of learned habits of virtue) and Kant (in his assimilation of moral reasoning to the Rational Will) have had recourse to various means to explain the relation between reason and observable phenomena such as psychological states or tendencies. Aristotle was very well aware that reason, combined with the virtues, was powerless to lead all men to practical wisdom, for in some there is *akrasia*, or incontinence.[1] This refers generally to inadequate self-restraint, or self-mastery, and is either acquired through habit, or is innate (*Nicomachean Ethics*, Book VIII, ch. 10, 1152^a). It is a morally debilitating condition which frustrates attempts to attain practical wisdom, or the state which "issues commands" on what ought or ought not to be done (Book VI, ch. 10, 1143^a). Incontinence takes various forms, Aristotle explained. Sometimes it is expressed as passion, which impels the incontinent man to do what he knows is wrong (Book VII, ch. 1, 1145^b). Sometimes it shows itself as self-indulgence, or weakness of will (Book VII, ch. 3, 1146^b); sometimes as impetuosity, as in 'keen and excitable people'. There are some who deliberate well, but give way to emotion and fail to stand by their conclusions on what ought to be done. Others simply fail to deliberate, allowing themselves to be controlled by emotion (Book VII, ch. 7, 1150^b). Incontinence formed by habit is more curable than incontinence which is innate: the condition is similar to that of people 'who get drunk quickly ... on little wine'. So not all people *can* be rational, or in control of reason to enable them to deliberate to a conclusion on what ought to be done, and to stand by that conclusion. What Aristotle is doing in this explanation of *akrasia* is to challenge the view attributed to Socrates in Plato's *Protagoras* that everyone who deliberates on what ought to be done, acts accordingly; that no one, having made a judgement on the matter, turns around and acts contrary to his judgement. It is a reflection of Aristotle's scientific impulse that he recognized that 'this view plainly contradicts the observed facts' (Book VII, ch. 2, 1145^b). His observations of the limitations on reason in practical wisdom might have been wider, but that was a start. Among incontinent people reason is influenced by emotion to such an extent that either the deliberations fail to reach a conclusion, or when they do, the conclusions are set aside. In his thoughts on practical wisdom, Aristotle considered the possibility of reason leading to a conclusion by deliberation and that in turn to action. The contemplative man is engrossed in first principles and cut off from the affairs of men, but the thoughts of the man with 'the reasoned state of capacity to act' are on the future and what is capable of being otherwise. For the practical, deliberative man, desire and reason lead to an end-in-view; there is a desired end, reasoning which calculates what ought to be done, a choice, and action. Good action requires a combination of intellect and character, but *intellect on its own* 'moves nothing'; 'only the intellect which aims at an end and is practical' leads to action (Book VI, ch. 2, 1139^a – 1139^b). The man of practical wisdom deliberates, not about what is invariable, or about things that are simply impossible to achieve, for both of these would be futile, but about things that can be changed for his own good and for the good of men in general. (Book VI, ch. 4, 1140^a – 1140^b) The *oughts* of ethics therefore, by implication, should not violate what is known to be the case or what is, for that would be equally futile. This is crucial to our argument. If something 'plainly contradicts the observed facts', as Aristotle put it, it should not be permitted to mislead our deliberations on what we ought to do.

Kant

By contrast with Aristotle, Kant held fast to moral law which is dictated entirely by reason. In acting on maxims which are moral imperatives not only for himself but also for every other rational being, the moral person is uninfluenced by any considerations of what is, or is not the case, from empirical observation. The objective law of morality is discoverable only *a priori*, by pure reason. Kant acknowledged that man has inclination and sensible impulses. Inclinations combine to produce feelings of *self-regard*, either self-love or selfishness, but in contrast with these inclinations the 'moral feeling' is produced simply by reason (*The Analytic of Pure Practical Reason*, pp. 165–9). Repeatedly Kant distinguished between psychological influences on conduct, which are subjective, and the influence of moral law, which is *a priori*, objective, dictated by reason alone. Put plainly, 'reason determines the will to action' (p. 131). The difficulty Kant faced was to reconcile man as subject to psychological tendencies, or inclinations, and the kind of higher, rational man who is

under the supreme command of moral law. In the last analysis, for
him the dictates of reason in moral law require no justification or
explanation beyond the fact of reason itself. His position on moral
law is more clearly understood in its contrast with practical reason as
it is directed to non-moral, or empirical concerns. *The Analytic of
Empirical Practical Reason* sets out to show that in this *empirical*
practical reason, so-called, we have a lower faculty of desire, which
has first, an idea or image of some object which becomes an
end-in-view; and second, an urge, or conative impulse. Reason
intervenes in the situation to the extent that it provides an incentive
to the will, which itself relates the action – according to a principle
derived from past experience – to the object of the desire. But in this
empirical practical reason there is no suggestion of law. That is the
province of morality: moral law is prescriptive, binding on all rational
beings. At best empirical practical reason is subject only to maxims,
and its will, being non-moral in kind, refers only to self-love or
personal happiness. Appreciation of moral law comes by discovery of
pure reason (Introduction to *The Analytic of Pure Practical Reason*,
p. 102. Empirical practical reason may be expressed in a syllogism
such as this:

My ambition is to win the election
To slander my rival would enable me to succeed
Therefore I shall slander my rival.

The desire is conveyed in the major premiss, which in Kant's terms is
a maxim, or principle, but not a law. The end-in-view, the elective
position, is linked with the desire by means of practical reason, or
will, which relies on empirical knowledge in the minor premiss. The
decision to act is conveyed in the conclusion. To this point Kant was
in agreement with Aristotle in his theory of action: there is desire, an
object of desire or an end-in-view, reasoning which calculates what
ought to be done, and a choice or decision. And just as Aristotle
distinguished practical reason which is not good from that which is
good, or leads to good acts, so Kant, and Kant in particular,
distinguished between practical reason which leads to mere self-
regard or to happiness, and the immediate apprehension by pure
reason, in the Rational Will, of what ought to be done. In the latter
there was no need for the deliberative process in Aristotle's practical
wisdom. The following syllogism would therefore be redundant:

My duty is to relieve human suffering
To send food to those starving in Ethiopia would relieve human
suffering
Therefore I shall send food to those starving in Ethiopia

Here the major premiss conveys a moral law which the Rational Will
apprehends as such, and the rest follows. The deliberation in this
syllogism would be made by someone who had not yet recognized
pure reason in its intuitive apprehension of moral law: the person
who debated whether or not to relieve human suffering in a particular
situation, or who was hesitant in his decision, would not be compelled
by pure reason. Therefore in pure practical reason as distinct from
empirical practical reason, Kant's theory of action is expressible in
the form: apprehension of moral law by pure reason, its immediate
formulation as an imperative ought, followed by necessary action. In
this there is no need for deliberation of any kind, unless deliberation
is necessary in the calculation of the means.

The second syllogism leads to a possible relation, distinct from
either Kant's thought or Aristotle's, between desire, emotion, and
action, and we shall note this in passing since in this chapter we are
concerned with the limitations on reason in our moral deliberations.
Those dedicated to the alleviation of human suffering have a desire or
wish to help others in this respect, as well as pity or compassion for
the sufferers. In these circumstances we may wonder if there is any
universal need for deliberative practical reason on what ought to be
done. We are not proposing a theory of action which asserts that in all
circumstances desire and emotion lead to action, only that they are
capable of leading to action in some circumstances without reason.
But in this instance at least there is an intervening factor which is not
reason, but *moral value*.

In value-free situations there can be little doubt that desire and
emotion can alone lead to action, as in the case of a child desiring an
object which has emotional significance for him, and spontaneously
reaching for it, or jumping for joy when he has obtained it, but this is
a trivial case without moral import. In these considerations of moral
conduct which take account of what we find to be the case in
experience, we shall be departing further and further from Kant,
whose sharp distinction between empirical practical reason and pure
practical reason left him with a justification of reason by reason itself
which has since been the subject of much philosophical scepticism.

That reason is never alone in moral deliberations is a view which from Kant's perspective is itself sceptical, and he criticised Hume for it. In *A Treatise of Human Nature* Hume had argued that 'morals excite passions, and produce or prevent actions', and on that very account cannot be derived from reason. Reason, as the discovery of truth or falsehood, is 'perfectly inert', incapable of producing or preventing action or affection (Book III, pp. 457–8).[2]

As an expression of moral reasoning, the second syllogism calls for additional comment in that it is formally inadequate, unless we read into the major premiss the moral imperative of a Rational Will, asserting that I, and all other rational persons like me, *ought* to alleviate human suffering. The difficulty in its present form is that it appears to be making a factual *is* statement, as does the minor premiss. From two 'is' premisses there can be no moral conclusion: no *ought* follows from an *is*, as Hume observed (Book III, p. 469). This is the situation in the following syllogism, where an attempt is made to draw an 'ought' conclusion from two 'is' premisses:

There is human suffering from hunger in Ethiopia
There is human suffering from hunger in India too
Therefore we ought to help human sufferers in Ethiopia
    and India.

For Kant, the moral law would be invoked by the first premiss alone and the call for action would be commanded by pure reason. But for those who deliberate according to reason, the reason they experience, the conclusion to this syllogism is false. By including one *ought* premiss the formal situation is rectified:

We ought to relieve human suffering
There is suffering from hunger in Ethiopia and India
Therefore we ought to relieve suffering from hunger in Ethiopia
    and India

With the formal position clarified (but incomplete), we shall now return to the general theme of limitations on reason in practical (moral) reason, as distinct from Kant's empirical practical reason. We shall be concerned with possible influences on reason in terms of desires, emotions, motives, intentions, attitudes and values, showing how these may interact in many complex ways in our practical deliberations, sometimes conflicting with reason, sometimes affecting moral decisions and judgements in ways which go beyond Aristotle's notion of *akrasia*, or incontinence (which is something of a disease or disorder, or a long-standing ailment), and which come into headlong confrontation with Kant's notion of the inviolability of the Rational Will. We shall stress throughout the need for moral action as the end to which moral deliberations are directed and which mark their moral fulfilment much more distinctively than the supposed quality of moral ideas, thoughts or impulses, in themselves.

DISPOSITIONS

Desires and Emotions

Our purpose in beginning with desire and emotion is to show how the simple readily becomes complex, and that what becomes complex in a variety of possible interrelationships in our mental states or activities places ever increasing constraints on reason. There are two general observations which may be stated at the outset. The first is that desires, emotions, motives, intentions, attitudes and values, as well as the deliberative reason itself, all have *direction*. The second is that their interrelationships one with another, and with reason, are not necessary or binding. We are concerned rather to show the possibilities and the tendencies in these characterizations and relationships, so that on the basis of our observations our oughts will not be in open defiance of what we find to be the case empirically, particularly with respect to the power of reason in our practical (moral) deliberations. To desire something is to want it, and it is possible to experience desire in itself, without emotion, though more usually once the conative urge develops the two become inseparable, so that wanting something is to want it with emotion, both desire and emotion being directed to the one object. Though we speak of 'emotional persons' as a way of describing persons who readily give way to emotion, no one is emotional over nothing, or simply emotional without emotion having an object. Both desire and emotion may lead to action: a desire for warmth to lighting a fire; joy to an expression in spontaneous action. Emotions themselves can scarcely be held to lead to deliberative judgements, but desires and emotions may, as the desire for a new house, deliberative judgements on available means, and appropriate action. Normally desire is not compelling: we are free to change our desires, such as for a life-style which is impairing our health. It is the compulsive and addictive who have a direct route from desire to action.

Motives

Some particular emotions such as anger, directed toward a person, may lead to action of a spontaneous kind, but with more control often lead to action when the desire-emotion urge becomes united with motive, such as for revenge. At this point, with the introduction of motive, the state of mind prior to action becomes more complex. The motive itself is voluntary: it would be contradictory to say of a person that he was forced to have a motive of ambition which he did not want. Though the motive, as perceived by others, is used to explain the reason for a person's action, it may not be perceived by the person himself, aware only of desire and emotion. If emotion is strong, it is that which may impair self-understanding, so that motive is obscured. The person who deliberates on the best thing to do when offered a much higher salary in a foreign country, may be so elated that his reasoning becomes a rationalization that is not in the best interests of his family or other dependent relatives. From the observer's standpoint, a person's motive is often more clearly understood in its relation to wants, or desire. Whether or not from the influence of crime-concealment and the difficulty of crime detection, it is sometimes erroneously held that motives refer to the unconventional or the unexpected. We do, it is true, ask what a person's motive is, when we are puzzled and do not expect the answer to be according to recognizable habit or conventional behaviour. In those circumstances the very asking of the question implies an element of doubt and an expectation of the unusual. Yet there are many other contexts where we do not ask questions of doubt about motives, but rather make statements or offer explanations which refer to anything but odd or unconventional behaviour. When motives are attributed in literature or in history it is by no means the unexpected which is always discovered. Othello's motive for murdering Desdemona, and Lady Macbeth's 'fell purpose', as she called it, in spurring her husband toward crime were both plainly human. Any detective who asks himself what was the motive for the crime expects neither the usual nor the unusual, and probably finds as many cases of the one as of the other. It is not unusual in everyday discussion of colleagues to remark that a person's motive in striving for a position was 'perfectly normal', 'understandable', or 'human'.

Motives form an elementary complex with desire and emotion. They have a direction which may be derived from the desire and emotion when the motive is not self-perceived, and when it is, from deliberation or suitable means toward goal fulfilment. Thus reason may interplay with motive, and intensity of emotion may overpower reason, or lead to a rationalization. As a component of total personality, temperament may inhibit reason in the interaction of desire, emotion and motive with reason. Rational deliberation demands a degree of self-mastery which some individuals have and some do not. Thus Aristotle's *akrasia* as innate in some, habituated in others, is consistent with our observations. If we introduce the notion of motive, and for the present exclude moral thoughts which we have yet to discuss, something akin to Kant's empirical practical reason is within reach of some: desire and emotion with an end-in-view, a motive with a conative urge to attain the end-in-view, deliberation from experience of ways of achieving it, and a decision leading to action. Deliberation in practical matters demands of reason that it have direction, that it be oriented toward an object. That is why Aristotle remarked that it is only the intellect which aims at an end that leads to action, not intellect itself. In this inertness of the intellect Aristotle's thoughts were on pure reason in contemplation, as Hume's were similarly on theoretical reason – the truth or falsehood of propositions – in his own comments on the inertness of reason in producing an action (*A Treatise of Human Nature*, Book II, Part 3, p. 414). Empirical practical reason suggests the following action schema:

> Desire with emotion – motive and end-in-view – means to attainment learnt from experience (which may involve choice from among various options) with confidence in the efficacy of the means – decision to act.

In this schema it is motive and end-in-view which give the impetus toward action. Desire and emotion each have direction toward an object, but in some instances reason interacts with desires and emotions to indicate that their objects are unattainable, and no motives are formed with respect to them. On the other hand there are equally non-rational desires, such as those emanating from urges for self-enchancement, which do lead to motives and action: to win the approval of friends and acquaintances by an act of community benevolence beyond one's means, for example. Conversely, and an exception to the proposed action schema, motives and larger ends in view may lead to certain desires, as when a motive to attract someone's attention stimulates a desire for particular material possessions. These then become the means to an end-in-view, but means derived from desire rather than by calculation.

Motives, Intentions and Purposes

Since desire is wanting (something) it is a tendency, or inclination, toward an object, often but not necessarily, combined with emotion directed also toward the object. Motive is distinct from these inasmuch as it has a cognitive component (of knowing, understanding, or perceiving), even though some motives may be vague and poorly articulated; and even though a person may not clearly understand the motive he has for action. There is still the motive, as perceived by observers, which is the accepted reason for his action. In general motive does include perception of self in relation to others, as well as relevant ideas or beliefs. The person with a motive for acting in a particular way is a thinking person, at least in a rudimentary sense, though not necessarily a reasoning person. He has engaged his mind in an active relationship with an object in a fashion which does not describe the mental state of a person who has no more than wants and emotion. Even if he misconceives his own motive, influenced strongly perhaps by emotion, his mind is not furnished only with a desire and an image of the object wanted. To take a more positive view, a person may be so clear on his motive for acting that the motive expresses also a purpose, or intention, as it does when we say that 'his motive in buying a large number of shares was to gain control of the company'. Here there may be an underlying motive of achieving power and influence over others, but even if the motive stops at control of the company, motive and intention appear to be inseparable. On empirical investigation of the particular circumstances of the case it might appear that 'motive' is improperly used for 'intention', that in fact there were other intentions in mind as well as buying shares and gaining control of the company, and that the underlying motive was to attain power and influence over others. Yet in some circumstances, as we shall see, motives are intentional.

Intention is a narrower concept than motive. While some motives are equivalent to intentions, there are others which are not intentions, as Anscombe shows (in *Intention*, pp. 18–20).[3] In this class there are first, backward-looking motives such as revenge which are clearly distinguishable from intentions, in that they are not oriented, as intentions are, toward the future; second there are broad 'motives-in-general' which have no connection with intention, evident when acting out of friendship, or out of curiosity, or out of family kinship, or out of fear of the consequences. The backward-looking motives and 'motives-in-general' are not *causes* of actions.

We shall approach the notion of intention in another way by considering *purpose*. 'Purpose' is used in a variety of ways which have no obvious connection with either motive, or intention, such as in expressions of a yearning for fundamental explanation in asking what is the purpose of life, of national catastrophe or personal bereavement, where 'purpose' has the force of 'meaning' or 'ultimate justification'. It is used in ways which relate to motive or intention thus: first, in the sense of motive; second in the sense of intention; third in the sense of the last or end intention (in a series); fourth, for the thing intended, as when we say 'he could not achieve his purpose'. We shall not comment further on the last usage. It is the third which is of most interest to us in that the notion of ultimacy seems to be transferred to it from the notion of purpose as fundamental explanation. One of the common tendencies in ordinary language is to assign *purpose* to the end and *intention* as the means to the end, as we see when we consider a series of intentions. Our task is to find whether 'purpose' is conceptually distinct from 'intention' in these instances.

An athletics coach plans a training exercise:

A. He intends to make his athletes cover 1500 metres in fast time.
B. He intends to have them run hard and to breathe hard.
C. He intends to have them persevere, despite discomfort to legs and lungs.
D. His purpose (intention) is to build up their stamina.

Anscombe's explanation of such a series (her own illustration is given on pp. 41–7 of *Intention*) is that D, the last statement, is an intention *of* the action as described by any one of the three previous statements. A, B, or C; and D would be stated as an intention with the possibility of extending the series to other statements such as E, or F. Each statement of the series is seen as an intention *in* the action described by the previous statement, so that, for instance, the intention in A, making the athletes cover 1500 metres in fast time, is to have them run hard and to breathe hard; the intention in that, (B), is to have them persevere despite discomfort, and in turn the intention in that, (C), is to build up their stamina. It is difficult to distinguish conceptually between 'purpose' and 'intention' here, for 'purpose' clearly has the characteristics of 'intention'. While its *function* in the series is distinct to the extent that it is expressing an end rather than a means to an end, it shares with 'intention' particular characteristics. Intentions refer to conscious thought, and part of this consciousness is an orientation toward action. This distinguishes intentional acts from those which follow spontaneously from mental events such as shock or fear. A person may close a door and window after a loud thunder clap, but if asked why he did so would not reasonably answer, 'Because I intend to keep out the noise', or 'In case it rains', but rather 'It makes me feel safer', and this would not express an intention. Because of the relative inaccessibility of mind and the privacy of thought, an intention is better known to the person experiencing it than to observers, and it is known to the individual without his personal observation. An intentional act is also voluntary, distinct from a wide range of possible involuntary responses or actions. Except in very unusual circumstances a person would not reasonably say, 'I intended to blink when the light flashed in my eyes'. We shall not proceed further with this analysis of characteristics, since it has become sufficiently plain that 'purpose' may be used in the sense of intention, even when it is the last in a series.

There is an important distinction yet to be made. Suppose the series were extended thus:

E.   He intended to train them to peak condition prior to the Olympic Games.

F.   His ultimate intention (purpose) was to win personal and national recognition.

Here the ultimacy of 'purpose' as distinct from 'intention' takes on a possible alternative meaning, for while E is still clearly an intention and a means to F, the last statement does not necessarily involve any intentional act. An alternative possibility is that the last statement expresses, though the language of intention is used, not an intention but a motive, a motive which is directed to this as a final goal, or 'ultimate purpose'. What seems at this stage to be important, then, in a series, is to ask whether the last statement is extendable to yet another statement involving action. If it is, it seems, it may be construed as an intention, for it can still be used as a means to something else. If it is not, it seems, alternative possibilities are first, that the last statement expresses a motive or an end-purpose in the sense of a goal; second, that the person in fact did have a conscious intention to win personal and national recognition. In the latter event, intention and motive would be one. In the first alternative, since the intention is *reported*, we seem to be acknowledging the difficulty of ascertaining what another person's *intention* actually is, as distinct from a *motive* of which he may be only half-aware. This is a common difficulty in all *reporting* of motives, intentions or goals as 'ultimate purposes' or ends, as distinct from personal statements of motives or intentions which may have greater authenticity. Despite this difficulty, we must now ask if there is a valid distinction between acting intentionally, restricting intentions to the sense of means to ends, and acting with an end-purpose or goal in mind. Do intentions apply to the first case, when motives and intentions are one, and not to the second, when we focus on a final goal? Are not end-purposes also intentions, and are not such intentions also motives?

The distinction we have drawn between acting intentionally as a means to an end, and acting from a motive or ultimate purpose, is evident in our attempted interpretation of other minds. Thus of Stone Age people who have left paintings in caves we ask Why? as we do of intentions. The question of why they made elongated forms is different from the question of why they made paintings at all; that is, what their *purpose* was in painting on cave walls. Anthropologists' answer to the second question gives the supposed *motive* of the painters: to inspire confidence in themselves and in others, or to gain magical control over animals that were needed for food and clothing, yet were often large, powerful, fleet-footed and difficult to kill. That was an end-purpose, as distinct from their short-term intention in depicting spears and arrows protruding from animals. Brutus was 'the noblest Roman of them all' in Mark Antony's eulogy. Though his intention was no different from that of the other conspirators, namely, to kill Caesar, his long-term *motive* was not envy but the 'common good'. It was a conscious state of mind, as well as a voluntary one: oriented toward action, and not open to observation. In these respects it was similar to his intention. But his motive was distinct from his intention, it seems, which was a means to the fulfilment of the motive: that, in turn, had the sense of an 'ultimate purpose' or a goal, an end state to be reached. The distinction between, on the one hand, *intention* as short-term, a means to an end; and on the other hand *purpose*, as a long-term, or final goal, is nevertheless not a conceptual distinction, even though it has practical application to a wide variety of situations such as statements of curriculum objectives. The error in any attempt to draw a sharp distinction between *intention* as means and *purpose* as goal, recognizing motive in the latter but not in the former, lies in the shifting nature of motive and the attempt to give it stability. Intention as means expresses *motive*, just as purpose as goal expresses both *intention and motive*. A purpose *is* an intention. That motive can apply to short-term intentions is evident when we consider those formed spontaneously or with little deliberate thought as a new situation suddenly develops. When an employee sees his opportunity and forms an intention to take another position, with a motive of higher salary and status, motives and intention are one, and the postulation of an additional motive, one that is 'fundamental', 'underlying', even open to criticism inasmuch as it conveys a desire for personal recognition, is conceptually unnecessary to explain his behaviour. Whether there is a deep-rooted, fundamental motive related to such things as self-enhancement, security or affection, is a contingent, psychological question, but it does not distinguish 'motive' from 'intention' in universal terms. While Brutus was very clear on *his* motive in the conspiracy, others were much less clear on their motives of envy. Apart from psychological variability in clarity of awareness of motives, there is variability in their degree of complexity: some motives are simple, and others 'mixed': some are short-term as immediate intentions, some long-term as final intentions or purposes. Motives which are intentions, as Anscombe shows, are forward-looking.

When desires and emotions, motives and intentions are in possible interaction in practical deliberations, it becomes evident that reason, which itself must interact with these, may be subject to a variety of complex influences before decisions are reached. Some motives are intentions and others are not. Intentions are usually strong in a cognitive sense: we *mean* what we say and know what we mean when we state our personal intentions. But even without their assistance, desires and emotions, when linked with end-purposes or goals, may have an impact on our deliberations on what we ought to do, for desires directed toward goals may be effectively sustained by emotion. In this we are beginning to see the development of a complex state of mind which may, or may not, be compatible with or supportive of reason in our practical deliberations. This will be more clearly evident when we introduce other components of that state of mind, namely, values and the attitudes that are sometimes associated with them. If desires, emotion and motives (including intentions) might together constitute a force to be reckoned with, especially in relation to end-purpose or goals, this complex is given still greater direction and influence by attitudes and values. Indeed one answer to the question of why we have deliberated in a particular way in a specific situation is that our reason has been unable to assert a mastery over other influences on our thinking. These influences may be in terms of wants or desires, emotions, motives and intentions, and now, added to these, in terms of our attitudes and values. The argument which we are unfolding does not require a total subjugation of reason: it is enough to show that the influences on reason in our practical deliberations are such that reason is not on its own in these activities but relates to other factors in ways that have implications for our ethical *oughts*.

Attitudes and Values

We shall first describe attitudes and values in general terms to give point to the pertinent characteristics which we shall then delineate. The values most relevant to a person's actions and tastes are those which answer questions such as, What do you value highly in life? What do you value highly in the home? What do you value highly outside the home? To the first a person may answer one (or more) of these: peace of mind, a happy marriage, children, financial security, satisfying work, a garden, friendship, and so forth. To the second he may answer one or more of the following: antique furniture, a grand piano, television, a home library, music, a wardrobe of attractive clothes, a quiet study room, home cooking. To the third, he may answer from these: drinking with friends, watching football, going to church, playing cards, eating out, symphony orchestras, sunbaking on a beach, singing in a choir, amateur drama, browsing in a library, pop concerts. Individual answers to the respective questions tell us something of personal *values*: that is, what are the things which different people attach great weight or significance to in their own lives, and are prepared to stand by or defend in their own interests. They are distinct from ideals in that ideals are at best only partially realizable, while values refer to realized or realizable sources of satisfaction. It is not necessary that answers given to each of the three questions be in unitary terms: we normally value more things than one in such lists, but we may value some things more than others, and even one thing *above* all others. The establishment of a clear hierarchy of values is an ideal rather than a fact of general experience. The first observation to be made is that in normal circumstances people *are* able to state things which they positively value, as distinct from other things which they do not. The second is that valuing involves our preferences, and – in a weaker sense – our tastes, the things we like as distinct from those which we don't like. In values as preferences, at least we reflect the ability to sort out the things which we give some positive weight to, from the things to which we give no positive weight at all, that is, which we do *not* value. The third observation of a general kind is that values indicate *standards*. We oppose material values to cultural values, for instance, and reserve the stigma of Philistine for those in the first category: we oppose some music to other music – orchestral to pop, or vice versa – and imply a standard of evaluation by so doing. With respect to values, implied standards are not absolute.

That values and attitudes are capable of close relationship is evident from the things they may share: they may refer to the one object, with each oriented clearly toward it. The things we do not value are the things toward which we have unfavourable, or at best only mildly favourable attitudes. Since to value something is to have a strongly favourable attitude toward it, our values are themselves attitudinal, and form part of an attitude system. Attitudes are wider than values: it is not true to say that all our attitudes are related to things which we value. To keep in mind the attitudinal characteristic of values we shall henceforth refer to *attitudes and values* in combination, thus referring only to the attitudes – the strongly favourable ones – to which values are, by their nature, related. To express a love of opera is to refer to an attitude and value in combination: to assert a dislike of pop music is to express an attitude, but not a value. Usually the stronger the attitude and value the more resistant it is to change; and when it is involved with personal self-esteem it is usually defended with some obstinacy.

We shall now set forth the characteristics of attitudes and values, first with respect to the things they share with desires, motives and intentions; second with respect to those things that mark them off from these. They are like desires, motives and intentions in that they are not directly observable, but need to be inferred. As such they are subject to empirical investigation, including validation. They are like the psychological states already considered also in their orientation toward action, and in their voluntariness. It is contradictory, in normal circumstances, to say that an individual was obliged to adopt certain attitudes and values: that belongs to coercive situations such as those of the brainwashing of prisoners of war. Of attitudes and values it may be said that as they are voluntary, we are also conscious of them, as we are conscious of intentions, but we must not overlook that the attitude and value combination refers to strongly favourable attitudes. (When attitudes are not part of this attitude-value complex, that is, when they are unfavourable or only mildly favourable, they may be closer to certain motives inasmuch as we are not always distinctly aware of them.)

Attitudes and values are different from other psychological states which we have considered in ways which have a direct bearing on our argument. We have stated that motives have a cognitive component not evident in desires, as such. But motives need something in addition to give them greater firmness and consistency in their capacity for influencing action: if they are to have anything of a law-like character in this respect the cognitive elements need to be further developed. Attitudes and values fulfil this function. They are stronger and potentially more influential than motives as such, inasmuch as they have greater cognitive complexity, are relatively stable and durable, and once learned become habitual.

Again we must emphasize that their efficacy in practical deliberations in one of *influence* on reason, but *not* of causality. There is no necessary or logical connection between attitudes and values on the one hand, and decisions to act on the other, and our argument is not dependent on this kind of requirement. The cognitive core of attitudes and values consists of various ideas, beliefs and opinions relating to an object. Emotion gives a cohesiveness to these, and the total mental complex attains a certain stubbornness and resistance to change, most pronounced when attitudes and values are very strong or extreme (or when they are closely connected to self-esteem, as we have noted). Complexity increases as we consider further possible relationships. The strongly favourable attitudes toward things valued extend to unfavourable attitudes to things not valued, as their opposites: a value of peace implies not-hostility; of liberty not-oppression. Much greater complexity is entailed first by relationships between different values (and attitudes), and second by the relationship of attitudes and values to desires and motives. The complex of desire (with emotion) and motive (oriented toward an end-purpose or goal) may become an integral part of a larger complex whose core is attitudes and values, absorbed within the larger complex, but strengthening its total potential for influencing our deliberations. A desire for peace of mind may be translated from the abstract to the concrete in the form of a rural retreat, an intention (as a forward-looking motive) to obtain a suitable country home, all flowing from an attitude-value system where inner contentment, quiet, clean air, a oneness with nature, are valued, as against tension, competition for material gain or power, noise, pollution, crowded streets and buildings, and so forth. In these relationships there is not always, or necessarily, a harmonious or supportive function for the various parts, but when there is, the total impact on our deliberations is to that extent potentially stronger. That there is no simple, direct, or necessary decision or action that flows from the holding of a particular value is evident when we consider the variability of attitudes and values as held by different persons. A value of liberty may be experienced and expressed differently with respect to specific objects. We need to distinguish between *valuing* an object, or giving it worth, and *having values* in an area covering a class of objects such as in recreation, or art, or domestic architecture, or politics. The value we give to a particular object becomes a reflection of our values in the area of the class of things of which the particular object is a member, but the value may vary from person to person, and may even lead to value conflict in community groups. Thus liberty values may have been held equally strongly by persons who valued in quite different ways the 1980 Summer Olympics in Moscow: on that occasion liberty values conflicted with political values and with Olympic or sporting values. To further complicate the situation, certain motives intruded which were in conflict with attitudes and values relating to the Games themselves. Attitudes and values are always personal, and so valuing occurs according to personal standards, rather than external group or social standards. The values with which we are concerned directly in our practical deliberations on what we ought to do are moral values, but there are many others such as aesthetic values or cultural values which may or may not be related to moral values, and many others again which have no obvious connection with moral values at all, such as values (or tastes) in clothes, or furniture, or cars. An individual may value some things which are strongly opposed to social values: dishonesty or theft as something that serves his self-interest, rather than honesty or respect for social values concerning property rights of others. For him dishonesty is a value, and so is unlawful appropriation of another's property. It is logically possible, though in experience much less common, for a society to espouse values of aggression and hostility toward enemies, and for an individual's values to be in conflict with these values. But whatever external values there may be, to say that those individuals who value dishonesty or stealing, when these are in conflict with social values, have no values, or have false values, is to judge their values by standards of other individuals; as it is when a person is similarly accused of having no values for espousing tolerance in a social context of racial bitterness and violent prejudice. Values may be criticised as good or bad, but not, as we have observed in the first chapter, as true or false, and they may be judged good or bad only by values accepted by the person judging: the onus is on him to justify his own standards by rational means.

INTERACTION OF REASON AND DISPOSITIONS

We shall not become involved with psychological questions of *how* attitudes and values are formed, but shall content ourselves with the all-important empirical fact that they are *learned* and are *habitual*. For that reason, as we have seen, they are relatively stable and long-lasting compared with desires and motives, which may themselves be ephemeral; but as we may change our habits, so we may change our attitudes and values. The learning of attitudes and values has important implications for the education of children, particularly before they are able to reason independently, and for as long as they are susceptible to adult influences or ideological pressures imposed by a political party in power. This is a question we shall consider in Chapter 5. We have now reached the focal point of our argument in this chapter. The fact that attitudes and values are *habitual*, together with the equally significant fact that they form a relatively stable, durable and complex state of mind with both cognitive and affective significance, often strengthened by the absorption into the complex of desires, motives (including intentions) and goals, or by some of these, indicates the possibility, in appropriate circumstances, of a dispositional force of appreciable influence in our practical deliberations. Reason is *never* alone in these deliberations: we are simply never *without* our dispositional states during these deliberations. Reason and dispositions interplay in a variety of ways according to contingent circumstances or individual variability: education, professional training in certain vocations, temperament and intelligence, including mastery of emotions and potential for rational control. But that control is never perfect in complex human situations. As we have indicated in connection with justice, impartiality is an ideal, in most conditions improved by legal, administrative, educational or other practical experience in human affairs, but never perfect, never attaining a condition where reason expels dispositions, so that the mind, as in Aristotle's contemplative or pure reason in mathematics, physics or metaphysics, totally excludes the many habitual thoughts, beliefs and ideas, the predilections and the prejudices, the binding emotional support, the pressures and the tendencies this way and that, that characterize dispositions. Reason alone in justice cannot be enough, and it is the same in all our practical deliberations. Principles of consistency and equity do not flow from minds as reasoning machines, but from minds with supportive dispositions, including humane feelings and a core of appropriate attitudes and values. Rationality itself is a *value*. It is not pure reason functioning, but includes ideals of impartiality and objectivity, humility in recognition of human imperfection and of the impracticability of living up to all values completely, a sense of common humanity and a respect for truth. Justice in law, administration and other situations calling for practical deliberations is a blending of reason and dispositions, especially of reason and the complexity of appropriate attitudes and values.

Dispositional Complex

We have used 'disposition' in a special sense which requires clarification. Since in our practical deliberations we are concerned with decisions and actions which flow from them, the dispositions that are of special interest to us are those which *predispose* individuals to the making of action-tending decisions.[4] We shall therefore not be using 'disposition' in the ordinary sense of a natural inclination as when we describe a person's disposition as equable or irascible, but rather in a sense which is a *predispositional complex* of many different cognitive and affective components including motives, with their end-purposes or goals, and *centrally*, attitudes and values. But each of these is a complex, as we have seen, of various thoughts, perceptions and tendencies, which, when they are in harmony – as they usually are when all cognitive components are given the same direction, with motives, attitudes and values all bent toward a single end-purpose or goal – may constitute a potent support for reason, or equally, a potent opposition. When our deliberations are bent toward what we ought to do, as they are in 'practical reason' as it is understood in ethics, the support of reason toward the best moral decisions will come from the strength of moral attitudes and values; conversely the support of reason toward the worst moral decisions will come from the weakness of moral attitudes and values. In this theory of moral decisions and actions stemming from the interplay of reason and dispositions (that is, the predispositional complex) we are opposing all rationalist doctrines that reason alone – pure reason which is its own justification as Kant supposed, indicates to practical wisdom what ought to be done. What we are not claiming is that the influence of the dispositions in this interaction with reason makes the decisions either good or bad. All is imperfect in this interaction, reason included. The outcome, the decision itself, is subject to criticism from as impartial and objective a stance as possible. But once again, it is not pure reason, in this subsequent appraisal, which is able to cast off the dispositions as merely parasitic, and to make a judgement on what ought to be done in the light of reason alone. However ultimate the judges may be, from first courts of appeal to the highest in the land, judgements are made by individuals who are simply incapable of divesting themselves of supposedly 'non-rational' influences, if this is the way they are viewed. Such a view is in fact unwarranted with respect to attitudes and values, for their cognitive core has already involved, in its formation, reason of some kind. Where comparisons are made prior to preferring some things to other things, it is difficult to see that the preferences could ever be totally blind, for that would contradict the notion of comparing and the degree of understanding implied by it. Further, when dispositions include ideals of impartiality and objectivity, as well as integrity, attitudes and values are necessarily supportive of reason, as is indicated in the description of rationality. The importance to our practical (moral) deliberations of dispositions which are sympathetic to reason is evident to philosophers and jurists alike. If justice is fairness in the treatment of persons, implying consistency in the application of rules or standards, and *equity*, neither consistency nor equity can be dispensed with mechanical efficiency. In the contemporary idiom, no computer could be programmed to accommodate them. Aristotle's arithmetical principles for rectificatory justice had extremely limited application, to the simplest of judicial situations, where compensation might be made for what one person had lost and another wrongfully gained, for instance. But beyond that, the application of rules in complex cases calls for judgement as well; and in equity, making up for an absence of law or even correcting law, where the judge acts largely as a free legal agent guided by legal experience, but with opportunities to set precedent rather than to follow it, his own dispositions – especially his personal attitudes and values – give additional direction to his reason. He must act, not only with clear reason in his grasp of the complexity of the issues before him, but also with humanity. His reason and his dispositions function in sympathy. It follows that every person has not the capacity to act judicially in this way: hence the appointment of some as judges, and the non-appointment of others. Selection is therefore crucial to the maintenance of legal traditions, as well as to proper respect for social traditions, and the ability to influence them. In this selection, as in the selection of administrators and others with influence over people, it is proper, by implication, to give considerable weight to persons of clear intellect, but proper also to take into account the kind of person each one is, inasmuch as dispositions may be inferred in experience from acts or performances.

Reason in Relation to Dispositions

In dispositions as we now understand them, which constitute in each of us a complex mental organization predisposing us toward decisions and action, we are concerned with an active orientation toward objects, which may be immediate – to be reached when specific short-term motives (or intentions) are fulfilled, or end-purposes to which long-term motives are ultimately related. It is the potential energy of the complex, its general motivational thrust when all components are united or in sympathetic inter-relationship, which indicates a force which may influence reason or be influenced by it. In the deliberative process reason has the opportunity to eliminate irrational desires and visionary ideals, for practical deliberation is nothing if it is not practical, concerned with what is to be done in terms of clear achievability. To be otherwise would be contradictory. Reason might also select appropriate means toward the efficient attainment of ends. Indeed it is possible to conceive of a means-end continuum, where possible means are sifted by reason in a process of

continuous evaluation, and to envisage a situation of social ends
(rather than personal ends) which, once attained, become the means
to other ends in a process of ever-increasing social efficiency. That
was in fact the ideal of one philosopher, in the first half of this
century.

Since his personal values were expressed in a democratic conception in reaction to the individualism and moral inertia which he
encountered in industrialized communities, it is a reasonable interpretation that his aspirations for a community of intelligent problem-
solving individuals – each improving the quality of experience by a
constant evaluation of means – illustrated the dominance of the idea
over reason.[5] If the interpretation is sound, it must stand as ironic
for all their dedication to reason, even philosophers may be subject to
dispositional influences capable of clouding reason. In practical
deliberations attainability of the means *must* be considered. It is part
of the action-schema proposed that confidence be placed in the
efficacy of the means. We do want to know what ought to be done in
a way which takes account of clear *impracticabilities*.

There are frequent situations when reason and dispositions are in
tension, rather than in harmony, particularly in instances of passion
and prejudice and obvious discriminatory injustices. Entrenched
racial attitudes and values are cases in point. Attempts to modify
attitudes and values by appeal to an individual's reason often fail
because of the nature of these central dispositional components: they
show themselves stable, well-organized, stubborn and inclined toward defensiveness. They may have already been subjected to
reason, many times, in the process of their consolidation. But they
are modifiable, as group techniques in particular have demonstrated.
These are contingent, psychological circumstances which we shall not
pursue further. It is enough to appreciate the empirical facts which
we need as signposts in our practical deliberations, at least inasmuch
as they can warn us on what roads *not* to take.

Relationships between dispositions and reason may be transcribed
into syllogistic form to convey something of the possible conseque-
ences when dispositions are strong enough to distort reason, or when
reason is weak enough to allow this to happen. The first three
syllogisms are of fallacious reasoning which we *assume* to have been
produced by dispositional influences, but in actual experience
whether they *were* so influenced, or whether reasoning was an
expression of factors such as limited intelligence or inadequate
education, could be settled only empirically. The assumptions we

nake are for the purpose of demonstrating possibilities in the
ontinual interplay of reason and dispositions. The Aristotelian form
s sufficient for our purposes, though not characteristic of our general
easoning. In cases of simple inferences the form appears unneces-
arily drawn out in a lock-step, mechanical elaboration. In cases of
omplex reasoning there are usually many more steps than these, and
o reduction to three – with two premises and a conclusion – appears
equally artificial.

Let us first consider a person imbued with Rousseau-like zeal for
children to be free to grow up naturally (that is, in a state of nature)
to the threshold of adolescence. If his values are sufficiently strong he
may allow them to control his reason to the extent of reaching a false
conclusion in this way, even if he is not translating Rousseau's
thought exactly:

Before adolescence children ought to be given freedom to grow
 according to their natures
Schooling places constraints on their freedom
Therefore children ought not to attend school before adolescence.

It does not follow that given the need for children to grow up
according to their natures (that is, *as* children, not forced into adult
moulds) they should not be given this consideration in a school
environment.

Now we shall convey strong racial prejudice, where again the
conclusion does not follow:

We ought to use our limited resources in education where most
 good will result
It's hopeless trying to get much out of black children
Therefore we ought to spend proportionately less of our resources
 in education on black children.

In this syllogism the second premiss is false, on empirical evidence,
and this makes the conclusion false. If empirical evidence were not
available, the conclusion would still not follow from this premiss, for
an assumed or actual difficulty of teaching black children in a
particular situation might have many possible causes, such as children's attitudes with their source in social conditions. This would lead
to a different conclusion. A different conclusion would follow too if

teacher prejudice were a factor, or teacher incompetence, or scholas
tic retardation for a variety of reasons.

In a third syllogism we shall convey the possible influence o
motives on reasoning:

> For the sake of our reputation we ought not to let our research
>   publications lag behind those of comparable institutions
> Our reputation is suffering from scarcity of publications in recen
>   years
> Therefore we ought to increase the volume of our researcl
>   publications as soon as possible.

Here there is an overriding concern for status or scholarly reputatioi
as stated in the first premiss. The second premiss reinforces this witl
concern at the present level of publication. The conclusion does no
follow since it implies that *any* publication will suffice, that scholarly
reputation is related merely to the number of publications achieved

By contrast with these forms of fallacious reasoning which w(
assume to be dominated by dispositions, and which can be shown t(
be false in their conclusions by examining the respective argument:
informally, we shall state another syllogism where the conclusioi
does follow, this time for *formal* reasons.

> All slow learners require individual attention
> Intellectually-limited children are slow learners
> Therefore intellectually-limited children require individual
>   attention.

In this argument the conclusion is true. The term 'slow-learners' link:
the first and second premises, and the two terms of the conclusion –
'intellectually-limited children' and '(persons who) require individua
attention' – are related by the premises to the third term 'slow
learners'.[6] In each of the three preceding syllogisms the conclusion
does not follow from the premisses for purely formal reasons: the
terms of the premisses and the conclusion are not related as they need
to be before true conclusions may be drawn. But their deficiencies are
sufficiently obvious informally as to demonstrate that reason is not
always the master in our practical deliberations on what we ought to
do: that there is another explanation for poor reasoning in these
deliberations than the more convenient explanation of quality of
intellect as a human variable.

We have used expressions which indicate that reason is, or is not, in particular circumstances, the controller of dispositions, or which suggest, alternatively, that the two are in separate camps, sometimes in harmony, sometimes in tension. In such expressions metaphor is misleading. Reason is not an overlord of the mind, ruling over, as his natural' subjects, desires and emotions, motives, attitudes and values. That would be to imply a dualistic system of the kind the Greeks and Kant envisaged, with reason belonging to a different order from the imperfect world of natural impulses or inclinations or lower desires'. Putting aside these metaphysical assumptions, we hold that reason is as much a part of our mental activities as are our dispositions, and as 'natural' inasmuch as they belong to the one natural order. Similarly, and to extend the metaphor, we do not accept any assumptions of parallelism whereby reason pursues one path in these mental activities and dispositions another, with occasional interaction between them when parallelism is temporarily lost and their paths collide. On the contrary, we hold from experience that our reason is never without dispositional tension of some kind. Even when we are reasoning in pure mathematics, we have an attitude to our task and emotion associated with intrinsic motivation. In our practical deliberations our reasoning is never without dispositions (as we use the term) and our dispositions never without reason. Dispositional reasoning describes the situation as we find it in experience. Reason in the abstract is nothing as far as our practical deliberations are concerned, and even as far as Aristotle's notion of contemplation is concerned. It is related to contemplative wisdom and to practical wisdom only in concrete experience, and then it has an inevitable form of dispositional reasoning.

Deliberations, Decisions and Actions

To keep the matter in proportion we must now stress that the dispositional influence is not necessarily a harmful one to the quality of our reasoning, and that it may indeed be supportive; and that the quality of our reasoning in practical deliberations is not given any uniformity or single characteristic stamp by dispositional influences. At its worst it is influenced adversely by prejudice or passion. As some people reason more efficiently than others, so some people's dispositions are more powerful influences on their deliberations than others'. Another qualification is that by determination or conscious effort we are able to modify our attitudes and values in some circumstances and re-direct our decisions and actions. To reach a decision to give up something, and to give it up, constitute such a re-direction, and this again represents a variable in our human capacities: some are much better at it than others. But whatever the decisions and actions, they are part of our practical deliberations which are always dispositional-rational deliberations. The person who decides to give up smoking does so for a reason: he desires better health without a bronchial affliction, let us say, or to be relieved of the anxiety of possible cancer. In his deliberations he has *concern* for himself and for his dependants. Motive or intention, attitudes and values are all involved in his reasoning or reflections. Kant's notion of the Rational Will as giving unmistakable instruction to equally rational beings on what they ought to do was too narrow a conception. In practical deliberations the Rational Will is an unwarranted reduction from a much more complex rational–dispositional will (We are not using 'will' here in a faculty sense, or as any unifying force controlling both reason and disposition, but simply as a capacity for resoluteness). Such a rational–dispositional will allows scope for wide human variability in propensity for action change. The action schema which we now propose from these considerations is this:

> Desire (with emotion) – dispositional reasoning (involving motives, attitudes and values – decision (with confidence in the efficacy of the proposed means) – action.

Before we finally adopt this schema we need to be satisfied that it fulfils all conditions in experience. What could be said to initiate practical deliberations, for instance, on such questions as giving aid to an impoverished Third World Country? Is it necessary that there be initial wants or desires? Might not a person be impelled entirely by a *value* of benevolence, and his practical deliberation directed toward ascertaining the best means of attaining his goal? Then the action schema would take the truncated form: attitude and value – dispositional reasoning – decision–action. But to act out of benevolence is to act from a motive, and this presupposes a wanting of some kind, a desire to translate the feeling to action, to *express* the benevolence not merely to experience the emotion. Motives themselves, it is recalled, are action-oriented. Aristotle gave desire general application when in the *Nicomachean Ethics* he explained that 'the origin of action ... is choice, and that of choice is desire and reasoning with a view to an end', describing choice as 'either desiderative reason or ratiocinative desire' (1139^a–1139^b). His own observations in the city-state may have shown him dissension and even injustice stemming from the conflicting desires of the citizens. So in practical *moral* deliberations it is only a special kind of deliberative desire, namely that guided by morality as well as reason, which in his view produces practical wisdom. Desire alone could clearly lead to immoral motives, and immoral decisions and actions, expressed as anti-social, conflict-producing conduct, and social injustice. But desire which produces choice or decision from within a moral state of mind aims at good action, which is its end. These moral requirements of Aristotle's practical wisdom we can set aside for the time being, because in a formal sense they do not affect a theory of action presupposed by his ethics. For him action originates in a decision, and decision originates in a desire and rational deliberation: something must be desired for action to result, for action is itself the bringing about of an event in the world. When it follows from choice, decision or intention, as it does in our deliberations, the choice, decision or intention requires some prior wanting. Desire is therefore implicit in the deliberations which lead to a decision, as it is implicit in a motive which appears to provide the initial impulse for the deliberations.

In an extended form of the action schema the desire at the beginning of the deliberative process may have a different object from that at the end, for the original wanting may be modified appreciably in the process of deliberating, and a decision to act will be taken after the deliberative process has indicated that which is, at that stage, most desired. This extended form may be set forth thus:

Desire (with emotion) – dispositional reasoning (with motives, attitudes and values) – decision (with desire and confidence in the efficacy of the means) – action.

Yet in most circumstances the separation of desire and decision prior to action is artificial. Wanting something after appropriate deliberation and deciding to act refer generally to one process and not to two. Another consideration is the fluidity of dispositions: in dispositional reasoning involving the motive – attitude – value complex no general sequential order can be laid down. Motive may develop from desire, and will at least imply desire. The interrelationships among motives, attitudes and values in the deliberative process are psychologically contingent and open to considerable variability. Intention has not found a place, it will be observed, in the action schema. This is for two reasons. First, forward-looking motives, as Anscombe calls them, are intentions, whether short-term as means to ends in a series, or long-term as fundamental end-purposes or goals. Second, decisions are intentions. We do not formulate intentions to act consequent upon our decision-making, with two deliberate operations. Decisions and intentions in this phase of our deliberations are one, just as, at the commencement of the deliberations, forward-looking motives and intentions are one. Henceforth we shall keep in mind the fluidity and variability of dispositional relationships as they interact with reason, but shall refer to the action-schema in a simplified form:

Desire – dispositional reasoning – decision – action.

The ethical implications of our combined conceptual and empirical observations will become more evident in the following chapter. That desires, motives (including intentions), attitudes and values have conceptual and empirical bases is evident from our distinctions between and among them, and as well from empirical research. It is not possible to dismiss attitudes and values, for instance, as merely theoretical formulations, although we do speak of attitude theory and value theory. When we ask what is the case in an empirical sense, we find adequate experimental evidence to indicate that mental organizations which we call 'attitudes' and 'values' are measurable, and that they have the characteristics by which we have described them, such as relative stability and durability and resistance to change. A dispositional complex, an action-oriented state of mind conducive to deliberations and directed toward action, does not necessarily war with reason, but invariably produces a tension which is either supportive of reason or otherwise. But this is again to see dispositions and deliberations mistakenly as separate. Our deliberations are best viewed, not as purely rational, but, as we have already described them, as dispositional and rational. The mental occurrence which we have in mind in practical deliberations is *reasoning with dispositional tension* as a single, integrated process. This does not prevent us criticising that process as insufficiently rational, or urging in others, using Aristotle's language and speaking metaphorically, 'a better command of reason'. Similarly this view of practical deliberation is quite compatible with our introspective self-criticism and consequent resolves to be more rational, and – metaphorically again – not to let our passions or prejudices 'get the better of our reason'. We can and do, as others can and do, improve the quality of reasoning by suppressing dispositional pressures which we perceive as unreasonable. This is part of the deliberative process and may lead to a change of desire, decision and eventual action. But before we move from formal to substantive considerations, it is appropriate for us to consider the possibility of using a formal technique for improving the rational quality of our deliberations in those instances where the dispositional pressures are opposed to clear reasoning. This has been anticipated in the two preceding chapters.

Formal Discussion

We shall begin with the empirical fact of the entrenched character of our attitudes and values, and the possibility in experience of their attracting to a dispositional state motives and desires as well, so that altogether there may be an influence of considerable strength inclining deliberations away from what is the best thing to do on rational grounds. While we are using a rational criterion in so speaking, we are not departing from our assumption and belief that our practical deliberations can ever be entirely disposition-free. What we propose to consider now is a formal technique for reducing the impact of dispositions which are likely to seriously impair the rational quality of our deliberations, particularly when these dispositions have attained an habitual quality and so have become part of our character – more clearly perceived by others than by ourselves. Deliberations lead to decisions, which are judgements on what is the best thing to do in the circumstances, and so it is the quality of our practical judgements which is of greater concern to us, and the further problem of how to improve their quality as well as the quality of the preceding deliberations. This is a matter which because of the very nature of our dispositions we may not be able to achieve independently of others' help and may best achieve with their cooperation. By repeated experiences of deliberating together rather than individually, arriving at what may be better judgements than any individual judgements, we may arrive at a self-understanding, with respect to both dispositions and reason, which may improve our capacity for reaching decisions or judgements of a more distinctively rational character. The observation that many minds are better than any one mind in practical deliberations is as old as democracies. Aristotle noted in his *Politics* that when 'assemblies meet, sit in judgement, deliberate and decide', any single member is seen to be 'inferior to the wise man'.

But the state is made up of many individuals, and 'a multitude is a better judge of many things than any individual' (Book III, ch. 15, 1286ᵃ). Every individual left to himself, he observed when referring to the mass of freemen and citizens who are not rich and have no particular merit, forms an imperfect judgement (Book III, ch. 10, 1281ᵇ).[7] It would be misleading to assert that invariably the best way to arrive at the *truth* is by the engagement of collective minds rather than individually, arguing that it is only in this way that, with our individual imperfections, we are likely to glimpse the reality of the true or correct decision. Though it is tempting to some to speak in this Platonic fashion from a common assumption that reality is something to be discovered in the objective world, we claim for collective deliberations no more than a likelihood of reaching more rational decisions, especially in complex problems, than by individual deliberation. Collective deliberations, viewpoints, decisions or judgements refer to the cooperative efforts of individuals in their respective contributions, *not* to a realization of a 'collective mind', as it is sometimes described, in which individuals do not think as individuals but rather think uniformly according to a common creed or ideology. To improve the *rational* quality of practical deliberations and judgements by collective procedures is partly to achieve a higher level of impartiality and objectivity than is likely to be achieved individually, given individual dispositions and rational imperfections. Although we do not usually perceive in full the dispositional influences in our own deliberations, we do generally perceive them more readily and more completely in others. Even when we are forewarned with an elementary understanding of the nature of desires, motives, attitudes and values, we are often unaware of the extent to which these dispositional tendencies penetrate our own practical judgements. It is well known that group discussion techniques require sympathy among members and good will, including a tolerance of individual imperfections and even temperamental idiosyncrasies, as well as a common goal. That goal is in general terms the best judgement concerning a situation, issue or problem which it can arrive at, but its goal is not *truth* in any objective or ultimate sense; it is *improvement* of the deliberation and of the eventual judgement, not the illusion of finality or perfection. In the expression of his own opinion, each individual stands alone. Evidence of the collapse of individuality is to be found particularly in politicized groups, where conformity to sub-group pressures, external lobbying, conformity under threat reflect a collapse also of group integrity. By contrast, as Mill observed in his time, the person whose judgement attracts confidence is the one who keeps his mind open to criticism, listening attentively to everything said against his opinion, Indeed, receptiveness to a wide range of opinions and willingness to learn from others are means of substantially increasing one's own knowledge (*On Liberty*, p. 80)[8].

With these general considerations in mind, we shall now state the main principles of a formal discussion technique, setting aside contingencies of human imperfections. There are four features to be noted. First, discussion is an expression of more than thought: it is thought and feeling, a statement of individual ideas, opinions, impressions, beliefs, judgements or interpretations, inseparable from the dispositional complex of individual mind, with its motives, attitudes and values. We are generally unaware of illusions or distortion in these expressions, or we would not utter them: mostly we are as unaware of them as we are of illusions in ideological beliefs, which may form part of them.[9] Our expressions therefore are not merely of our thoughts, but of our thoughts caught up with elements of our dispositions, and influenced as well by reason. They are personal, but not private. We present them to the world in good faith as *our* views, as a part of ourselves of which we are not ashamed, but we are not fully aware of how much of *ourselves* we communicate – ourselves as thinkers. As we listen to others' criticisms of our thoughts we recognize that our thoughts are perhaps in need of modification: in various ways they can be trimmed, and we can express them more clearly, accurately and impartially. Imperfection is shared, and for rectification of our viewpoints we depend on others, as they depend on us. Imperfection is the great leveller.

Second, discussion calls for an aesthetic stance by the participants, a deliberate effort to cast off prejudices and irrelevancies of all kinds. With single-mindedness we offer contributions of our own, consider criticisms openly, listen to others' contributions, criticising them sympathetically with the same impersonal concentration on the intellectual objective. We listen, evaluate, speak, listen to others' evaluations, without deviating from the common goal. We assist, along with others, in the formulation of the finally accepted statement of our combined interpretation. If we cannot agree with it, we do not acquiesce, but declare our position as in need of further thought, by us and perhaps by others too. We recognize that majorities are not always right: their interpretations are not necessarily the best. An agreement to disagree is not necessarily uncooperative, mulish or obtuse. If we are unnecessarily obstinate, that may be a dispositional tendency to be exposed by others and accepted by us for appropriate self-adjustment. Whatever our conclusion, it is most likely to be fair-minded if we can shut off all consciousness of self – our own selves and others' selves as well. We are not to be distracted by any consideration of personality, or even of group counselling in the sense of trying to stimulate less able or less communicative group members, whatever might be done by group leaders in counselling *privately* in order to avoid paternalism in humiliating public gestures of encouragement.

Third, in discussion we learn from others. All individual experience is unique in its total personal apprehension. Some experiences we share, but there is usually something we can learn from others even when group members are diverse in ability, age or educational background. In this we need to retain the self-discipline of the aesthetic approach: it is irrelevant who gives us something to add to our knowledge of the world, as it is irrelevant who learns from us. We give and receive, and the benefits are mutual. Mill considered it not 'in the nature of the human intellect to become wise in any other manner' (*On Liberty*, p. 80).

Fourth, conflict of opinion or viewpoint is often more clariying in discussion than agreement. In many circumstances we understand our own viewpoint more clearly if we have had the opportunity to consider a contrary viewpoint, and to work out a personal refutation of it if we are convinced that our viewpoint is the stronger in reason. Some advocates in law have followed Cicero's practice of studying his adversary's case as closely as, if not more closely than, his own, the better to understand his own position. But to study an opposite viewpoint to one's own with the express purpose of overthrowing it, as in debating, may lead to sophistry, the deliberate misrepresentation of the others' view, selecting facts or arguments to suit one's own case and suppressing those which do not support it. Intentional mispresentations are foreign to the spirit of discussion.

CONCLUDING COMMENTS

We have now prepared the way for practical considerations in the next chapter, and before we do that we shall briefly review the approach we have taken, which is closer to Aristotle's than to Kant's. Aristotle did not want to contradict the observed facts, as he said, in his analysis of practical wisdom. While observing the disability of *akrasia*, or incontinence, he still believed that reason gives commands to those not in that way afflicted. We have to acknowledge that there are many more 'observed facts' available to us now than there were available to Aristotle, but it is his *approach* that is significant to us: in his comments on practical wisdom he had to ask first what is the case in the observable world. Some of his observations appear odd in this area as they do in the area of science, but he had at least one eye on things as they are in common perception, concerned lest his recommendations should contradict them. Kant similarly used the language of command, giving reason much more imperative force. In his view psychological considerations belong entirely to the *subjective* world. (Our account of the dispositional complex would have been included). Outside and above that world is the objective world of the *a priori*, the world of pure reason. Psychological states or events belong to 'empirical practical reason', but it is only *pure practical reason* which issues unmistakable moral imperatives.

Such views of reason taking command in our practical deliberations are in opposition to our own. We ask what is the case empirically, and find evidence to justify the claim that in our deliberations reason is always influenced to some extent, for good or ill, by dispositions. These are our desires, motives, attitudes and values, often forming a cohesive complex in which all of these are united; but it is motives, attitudes and values which constitute the strongest potential influence. There are many instances of rational deliberations which do not refer to what we ought to do in moral senses: in 'productive wisdom', the design and construction of a house, for instance; in 'contemplative wisdom' reasoning in geometry toward the solution of a problem; and we deliberate in a wide diversity of everyday activities as we prepare schedules, organize time-tables, plan a holiday, get ready for retirement. We are not interested especially in either productive or contemplative wisdom or the host of deliberations which fit neither, even though we acknowledge relatively minor dispositional influences in all, but rather with 'practical reason' or 'practical deliberation', so-called, concerned with what we ought to do in moral senses, and in which we acknowledge the possibility of relatively major dispositional influences on reason.

It should be observed that in the action-schema we have proposed, we have *assumed* that deliberation is taking place: the schema refers specifically to our practical deliberations in *moral* situations. In non-moral situations, as we have seen, desire and emotion alone may lead to spontaneous action. There may be *apparently* spontaneous action from values too. It is true that a Good Samaritan seems to act spontaneously from his values, his values having an implied motive of benevolence. In the contemporary scene it is the person who stops and helps the injured on the roadside while others go on their way, all acting according to their respective values, no one pausing to deliberate on what he ought to do. Even in such instances from everyday experience it is difficult to claim that reason is entirely absent, or that there is no stage when reason and value do not quickly come together prior to action. We shall extend the notion of 'deliberation' to include these cases, and shall take as standard for moral situations the action schema we have proposed.

The ideal of intellect or reason as espoused by the Greeks and by Kant is not an appropriate guide to a practical morality, and dispositional states are not to be relegated to a status unworthy of humanity or of any section of it. It is characteristic of our practical deliberations that reason and dispositions are united in the one thought process. Normatively we may strive to control those dispositions which function contrary to reason – to continue the misleading dualistic metaphor – but we can never cast them off and deliberate according to pure reason, even by a long process of disciplined training such as Plato envisaged for his rulers. Similarly we must reject any metaphysical assumptions of powers of intuiting first principles in our *formal* notions of education, justice and morality. Our considered judgements on these formal notions are simply judgements, reached in similar fashion to the decisions, conclusions or judgements of practical (moral) reasoning: that is, by engaging our minds already equipped with ideas or impressions from experience, as well as attitudes and values and a variable capacity for reasoning. Such judgements are ordinary human experiences, as are the practical deliberations which we have included in the proposed action-schema, not the preserve of an intellectual elite with highly developed intellects or rarefied perspicacity. Without being intellectually elitist as the Greeks were and as some modern philosophers such as Mill were also, we do not accept completely Descartes' belief that we differ in our opinions (and judgements) not because some are more rational than others, but simply 'because we direct our thoughts along different ways, and do not consider the same things.'.[10] There is some truth in that statement, but there is also, we believe, some truth that our capacity to form judgements by practical reasoning is variable, that we are not uniformly imperfect in this respect but differ one from another as we differ in our dispositions.

5 Practical Applications

In this chapter we shall focus on principles from the foregoing chapters which relate to certain practical aspects of justice, morality and education, selecting for consideration these four topics:

1. Rights and Duties in Education
2. Justice, Morality and Punishment
3. Justice, Morality and Moral Education
4. Justice and Morality in Educational Administration

We may observe initially some of the common ground in practical activities of justice, morality and education. Practical education clearly aims at improvement, and it would not be education otherwise. Practical morality faces a continual tension between benevolence and egoism, so to live morally ourselves, or to assist others to live morally, is to have in mind a moral improvement, an attempt to do better than we have been doing. Practical moral justice is no less an activity of improvement on an original position, not only in simple instances where it intersects with legal justice, such as in commutative or corrective justice in Aristotle's classification, but as well in more complex cases of establishing fairness in the treatment of persons. Similarly, some educational activities – notably the activity of teaching – have common ground with some of the activities of legal justice which we considered in the first chapter: some at least of these activities have a moral basis in a practical consideration of others' interests. Each is influenced by social values, with the capacity for influencing social values – the teacher who undogmatically defends before the community the teaching of evolution *as a theory* no less than the judge who declares unionists avaricious in claiming payment for unworked overtime. At its best each has opportunities for creativity in constructive understanding and judgement as attempts are made to be fair in the treatment of persons.

RIGHTS AND DUTIES IN EDUCATION

Children's Rights to Education

We shall begin with children's rights, and specifically with their right to education as an *ascribed* right. This will establish a link with the notion of ascribing rights as discussed in Chapter 3, as well as with the fundamental question of children's immaturity and whether any rights can in fact be held by them. When we are assured that some children are mature enough to understand what it is to have a right to education, let us imagine that we explain that education is a process of developing their latent powers – intellectually, physically and morally – and then say to them, 'This right is *yours*', or 'This is a right you have'. Part of their understanding is that some of their potential development is contingent on the provision of proper facilities: a gymnasium and an area for games; a music room and a stage for drama; a variety of small discussion rooms where moral problems are discussed under suitable leadership, and so forth. We shall not dwell on the defeasibility of this right, except to note that it is logically possible to defeat the ownership of even this right to the development of potentialities of various kinds: society's values may change, for instance, on the school as an appropriate place for moral education; or a long-term empirical study might produce substantial evidence to indicate that children generally are not improved physically or morally by having these provisions in the school – are no better off than are a control group which has had no physical and moral education at a school. We might then agree that the right to physical and moral education *in the school* is defeasible in the light of changing social values or reliable evidence. Ascription of a right to make their own decisions on a range of matters, such as accompanying partners home after a school dance, may have implications for personal development which can be defended as a practical consideration of others' interests. Indeed to increase their responsibility for their own well-being by according them greater trust while undergoing formal schooling may justify the ascription of a number of rights not at present granted. In these circumstances arbitrary annulment of rights is likely to be as damaging as their ascription without proper regard for a capacity to hold the rights. That indeed is the crucial question for children's rights at school: whether they can understand what it *is* to have rights, or to have particular rights, within a moral-rational community. The answer is an empirical one, and for some who are still children in a legal sense the answer is sometimes not in doubt. Yet the answer is more difficult to give than it appears at first: for while in some instances children may understand what it is to have a right to express any grievances they may have to the principal, and to be given a fair hearing, they may still not understand what it is to have a right to *education*. On aspects of physical development they may be clear enough, as they compare themselves visually with their elders, but their ability to understand what intellectual and moral development denote before they have experienced them will limit their capacity to understand what it is to have a right to *education* in the formal sense. We have considered education as a right in the positive sense of being able to understand what it is to have it, or to own it, and this is a pre-condition for being able to assert it and to claim it against some person or persons. Since this entails an ability to understand the *object* of the right, it is clear that children who have sufficient intellectual maturity to understand some objects of rights may not have sufficient intellectual maturity to understand others – a condition which applies to adults as well, for the kind of maturity we are speaking of is not a function of years or of legal status. One of the practical difficulties in discussion of children's maturity, and of capacity to hold rights, is not merely the variability in rate of maturation among different individuals – some maturing more slowly in all respects than others, some more slowly in some respects only – but particularly the fact of uneven individual development: some children may be advanced for their years physically and even intellectually, but remain morally immature, and this is observable in legal adulthood as well. Since we are concerned primarily with those we classify as children, in the legal sense, the question we should be asking is not whether they are generally mature enough to understand what it is to have a right, but whether they are mature enough to understand what it is to have a right to a *particular object*. The area of education which presents the greatest difficulty is not the physical or the intellectual, but the moral. But moral education is a gradual process which begins before children are able to understand what it is about, so that unless we limit this activity to moral *instruction*, we face a contradiction with the *understanding* condition which we have proposed for the having of rights. If by a right to *moral education* we imply at least some capacity to act as a moral agent, we must then include the capacity for independent reasoning and for control of passion, as well as a commitment to personal moral values, an understanding of moral values held broadly in common in society, a recognition of others' rights, and a capacity to consider others' interests generally, with a respect for persons. All of these may be in a developing stage, with much room for improvement, but the total demands are such that this particular right, the right to moral education, if it implies an understanding of what it is, is one that we should have most hesitation about before agreeing that children have it as a right which they can sensibly assert and claim. With respect to intellectual education, many who are children in the legal sense understand what it is to improve in reasoning and in other cognitive functions, without an understanding of what it is to have a 'liberal' mind, tolerant and open, and as free as possible of error and illusion; but it would obviously be asking too much to insist that a person has no right to intellectual education until he can comprehend what he has never experienced. All we can reasonably expect is that a right to education, before it can be said to be assertable and claimable by the holder, requires *sufficient* understanding to make the assertion or the claim a sensible one; that suggests that we should specify the kind of education that we are referring to – intellectual, moral or physical, or two or more of them, so that in fact we are not referring to the abstraction 'education', but to specific educational activities. Unquestionably some legal children do have sufficient understanding of these to be in a position to claim a right to them, with the underlying notion of a developing of potentialities, or a *becoming*, in particular directions.

These considerations emphasize that when we weigh the rights of children there is no justification for denying them moral rights which they have the capacity to have, simply because they are children by legal classification. That is to treat some legal children unfairly, as we have seen, to deny them natural justice; or simply, for this amounts to the same thing, to be unjust to them. Between moral rights and legal rights there are important differences. Legal rights are entitlements to certain things which have the backing of the law, requiring others to recognize the entitlements by refraining from action which is prejudicial to them. But to assimilate moral rights to legal rights, to endow moral rights with the character of an entitlement, so that we can say that young children have a *right* to our protection, or to certain welfare provisions, is again to fall into the *error of ascription*, which is to ascribe rights to beings incapable of holding them except as bearers of affixations. We have seen that to some children moral rights may be sensibly ascribed, because though legally children, intellectually they have sufficient understanding to know what it is to have the rights, to assert and to claim them against others in the moral-rational community. Mere *recipients* of ascribed rights who have not this understanding do not have moral rights, or rights of any kind, except by a misleading, metaphorical ascription in the case of so-called legal rights, held in trust for them by their custodians. It is not enough to argue that a being qualifies for a right through being able to receive and enjoy it. Even if society confers it as a 'right' so-called, in the sense that it is not seen as charity or favour, some beings receiving it, such as infants and other very young children, and seniles, may be no more than passive recipients. While it is proper that parents and other citizens should claim education for the children of the community, it is improper to claim it as the *right* of all children. It is contradictory to speak of rights opening up opportunities for their possessors, if to possess a right is merely to have attached to one an ascribed entitlement, for opportunities can be realized only when the eyes are open. It is contradictory to speak of infants or other young children as possessors of rights, simply because they have the supposed *potential* for understanding and claiming rights, which will be realized when they are sufficiently mature. To *have* a right is to have it *now*, not at some time in the future when the capacity to have it may be expected to develop. It is contradictory also to assert that a right is a claim upon someone, or upon individuals comprising a state, for things which certain beings *ought* to have. An *ought* statement does not create a moral right: a convicted killer does not have a moral right to freedom because a statement is made that he ought to be free.

Rights of Parents

We shall return to children's rights which may be sensibly ascribed to them, but since we have been referring to education as a provision, normally by the state, we shall consider at this point an alternative view of a right to education, namely, that it is not the children's own right to education which can be claimed, but the right of parents *for* them. We have been insisting that a right be assessable and claimable by the owner of the right, who understands its significance, including the person or persons against whom it may be claimed. From empirical evidence it is clear that some parents cannot satisfy these conditions with respect to education, through insufficient understanding of its implications. For instance, those who view it in consequetial terms only, as a means to employment and attractive remuneration, do not understand education sufficiently to claim a right *to* it. But for those parents who do fulfil this condition, they are strictly able to claim the right for themselves, not for others, as we have argued in Chapter 3. Some have sought to overcome this difficulty by referring to parents' rights not *to* education, but *in* education, for their children. Then what is being asserted is that parents, who in most circumstances have custody of their children and are responsible for their upbringing, have legitimate expectations of society. They themselves have certain legal and social obligations to discharge with respect to their children, including a responsibility to send them to school, though not a responsibility to educate them. But part of their expectations is that the state, or independent institutions within the state, will undertake that function satisfactorily for them, so both as guardians of children, and as taxpayers or as fee-payers, these legitimate social expectations are translated into rights *in* education for their children. If this distinction between a right-to and a right-in is sustained, we have still to determine what the parent has the right *to*. Various ancillary rights in the field of education have been proposed, and each is capable of adequate defence within particular social contexts: a right to choice of school, a right to choice of a type of education, a right to freedom of conscience, so-called, referring to personal beliefs in a preferred type of education for children. A right to type of school is sometimes argued against the state as the education provider, on the grounds that some schools are of distinctly poorer quality than others, in terms of teachers, material resources and facilities. The second and third rights are sometimes argued against the state as provider, by those who hold particular beliefs which are not adequately catered for in the state or government schools. These are matters which touch on the liberty of the parent, and in some countries have legal or quasi-legal sanctions to support them. At this point we must note an important distinction in the use of 'duty'. The duty to educate children refers to a recognised *function* of government, along with other duties of this functional kind such as the provision of health services and social welfare. Individuals in government do not ordinarily initiate such functions on taking office, out of consideration for the well-being of children and others, but assume duties already there, attached to their offices. They are not *moral* duties, though they may have moral implications. They do not, as moral duties *usually* do, have correlative rights. From the duty of members of a democratic government to provide for the education of the state's children, there is no right conferred on parents against the government, except those of a legal kind. But parents do have corresponding legal duties as the guardians of children, namely, to ensure satisfactory attendance. The assimilation of duties of governments as welfare providers to moral duties with correlative rights is therefore improper. Articulation of legitimate expectations of governments does not itself warrant the use of rights language, and when 'duty' is so used it should be used unambiguously to refer to the formal functions of government; without, that is, a confusing metaphorical association with moral duty.

Liberties of Children

The attempt to transfer rights from children to their parents or to other guardians on grounds of children's immaturity raises problems of justification with respect to both parents and children. But now we must ask if there are rights which we may properly ascribe to those children who have sufficient maturity to fulfil the rights conditions which we have proposed. In this regard the area of most interest is that of liberty rights, and with respect to these it will be sufficient for our purposes to refer to Mill's threefold division: first 'liberty of thought and feeling, absolute freedom of opinion and sentiment on all subjects'; second, 'liberty of tastes and pursuits, of framing the plan of our life to suit our own character', while avoiding harm to others; third, with the same condition, 'freedom to unite for any purpose' (*On Liberty*, p.71).[1] As already noted in the previous chapter, Mill was summary in his disqualification of children from rights on grounds of a supposed immaturity: this he had imperfectly analysed, especially with respect to its relevance to particular rights and to particular children. On the first of his liberty rights he had some doubts, since liberty of 'expressing and publishing' concerns other people, he acknowledged; yet ironically after his time, the right to freedom of thought and expression has in fact been claimed and successfully exercised by students of some schools. Both the problem and the achievement have been to reconcile immaturity of judgement with educational opportunities perceived by educators, and unobtrusive guidance with an avoidance of paternalism and the use of children merely as means to educators' ends. Morally the educators' task has been to see them as emerging persons, deserving of respect in their own right. Educational opportunities have again been seized by educators with respect to liberty of assembly and association, and similar remarks apply. This is associated with political liberty: the right of students to form their own councils, to participate in decisions which affect them on the management of the school, and to appeal against one-sided decisions which affect their own welfare as students. Part of the justification for this right is that children do have interests, some of which need to be understood from *their* (different) standpoint. Another is that as developing persons they are as sensitive as adults to slights, to deprivations and discriminations, which are recognized and articulated as unfairness or injustice. It has often been an educator's presumption, as it was Mill's by implication, since he excluded them from liberty rights, that because of immaturity and insufficient understanding children require decisions to be made for them. Some educators are capable of turning children's participation in decision-making to their own educational purposes, in the interests of children's development, perceiving in mutually trusting relations the foundation for increasing self-mastery and responsibility toward others.[2] In this they are also creating a basis for moral education and for the development of individuality. It is to the latter which we now turn, suggested by Mill's second liberty.

If education is a developing of individual potentialities, consistent with social values, a developing which is without any finite end, at least we place a *value* on the developing, the gradual increase of the individual's abilities and capacities, since the developing is at the same time the observable shaping of unique individuality. That too is without any finite end, changing over time in adulthood, yet sufficiently stable and consistent in its various expressions to give each a recognizable identity. Mill's second liberty was prompted in part by a concern that any general state education 'is a mere contrivance for moulding people to be exactly like one another (*On Liberty*, p.177). If that were to be permitted to happen it would be in opposition to natural tendencies of growth. Mill had been impressed, as we have seen in the first chapter, by Humboldt's views on the importance of human development 'in its richest diversity' which required both 'freedom, and variety of situations'[3] (p.57 and 121). That was the keynote of Mill's second liberty: not likenesses but differences, not uniformity but the immense range of variations of which human individuality is capable when it is permitted the liberty to develop without unnecessary interference. But individuality is not a matter of externals, of school uniforms or hair-styles: some children's rights claims have been trivialized by such digressions. It is easy to defend such claims with questionable arguments that to interfere in these matters of externals is to interfere with children's self-regarding inclinations to present themselves to the world as they please, according to their developing self-images. It is not that externals of dress and hair-style are necessarily matters for uniformity, but rather that they are relatively unimportant to individuality, which will develop rather from freedom of mind. What is of far greater significance is the mutuality of trust, responsibility and respect for persons which some educators have shown to be achievable, with a gradual relaxation of control but always, in the background, the ready availability of experienced guidance. Then it is, given optimum conditions of professional skills, that the liberty of interference with developing individualities which Mill foresaw can be practised successfully even during formal schooling.

Legal Aspects

From the standpoint of justice and morality we shall now consider the law as it pertains to both parents and children in areas of education, offering an opportunity to compare legal justice and moral justice. In this we shall be selective, referring first to statute law[4] on the transition from childhood to adulthood; second to the general welfare status of children; third to cases on miscellaneous matters affecting parents and their children; fourth, to the law as it affects teachers. We shall defer the question of corporal and other punishment to the following section.

Children's Immaturity

Mill's error in categorical assertions of children's immaturity is not uncommon, and tends to be aggravated by legislation. Children do not undergo definite states of metamorphoses, emerging like insects from their pupal prisons to the full realisation of the imago. Unlike insects, their precise transformation from childhood to adulthood is not perceptible, either physically or mentally. There is simply no point in the individual's stream of experience which we can seize on and say, *there* is the definitive emergence of the adult state. When given responsibilities such as caring for siblings, or when sent out of the home to work and to earn their own living, some children behave as adults, as historical circumstances have shown. In fact protection of children from exploitation and early work experience has in some respects frustrated and inhibited individual development. Some who are legally adults, especially without responsibilities and work experience, behave as children. Variability in human development, intellectually and morally in particular, poses a problem for the law, since in some respects, such as voting eligibility and criminal responsibility, a line needs to be drawn for purely practical, administrative purposes. To contemplate the task of testing every individual for sufficient intellectual and moral maturity in order to qualify him for electoral responsibility, or to disqualify him from criminal responsibility, is enough to indicate that neither is the sort of area where it is practicable to give either a certificate of competence or a certificate of exemption. Therefore in setting legal limits to adulthood a degree of arbitrariness is unavoidable. But the extent and implications of the arbitrariness are another matter, and raise questions of moral justice. There is arbitrariness in reducing the legal age of adulthood to eighteen years, with the powers it may confer such as those of making a will, of voting, of owning and disposing of property, of entering into contracts, or of acting as plaintiff or defendant in civil cases, such as those of tort.[5] Here the arbitrariness lies in not treating equals with equal consideration according to relevant criteria. For if adulthood is to confer certain legal entitlements, with assumed powers of exercising the rights implied by them, what is relevant above all is whether the recipients – in this case eighteen-year-olds – have the capacity to match the entitlements, and whether others such as sixteen-year-olds have not the same capacity. Why should eighteen-year-olds be allowed to sue in court, while fifteen, sixteen and seventeen-year-olds are required to be represented by an adult? Would not an educational qualification be less arbitrary than an age qualification for adulthood, at least to admit some to adult status before they reach the legal age by which all may be admitted? Arbitrariness which discriminates against some unfairly is seen as a denial of the fundamental or formal notion of justice: it is degrading of some as persons as they compare themselves with others, and as they are perceived by others. At present legal age qualifications for adulthood tend to treat unequals equally. Those who are unjustly treated are legal children who are capable of assuming the legal responsibilities of adults by virtue of suffficient intellectual maturity. The conflict is not only between the law on the one hand, and justice and morality on the other; it is also a conflict between law, morality and education. In those cases where teachers and headmasters or principals establish trust relations with students, and increase the responsibility given to students in decision-making, there is a positive preparation for the roles of adulthood. For such students to be told that they are still juveniles and therefore not ready for the assumption of the roles of adulthood, to infer from this that their educational preparation does not really prepare them sufficiently for adulthood but is some kind of curriculum exercise with the status of a game activity, is in conflict with the educational objective and with what the students know of themselves. It is in ironic contrast too with what they perceive of some eighteen-year-olds who have been early school leavers, perhaps with inferior ability or capacity to fulfil adulthood roles: indeed, in some cases, it may contrast with what students perceive in their own parents. Ill-founded discrimination is unfairness; unfairness in the treatment of persons is injustice.

There is a conspicuous arbitrariness also with respect to criminal responsibility. There is a presumption that below a certain age, whose variability among and even within countries is a sufficient indication of arbitrariness, a child is not criminally responsible: does not know, that is, that what he has done, or has omitted to do, is wrong. Usually evidence is admitted above this minimum age of exclusion of responsibility, but until the juvenile has advanced into adolescence and reached another variable limit, he is not held to be *fully* responsible for criminal acts. Again, to treat equals equally in relevant respects, and unequals unequally, would be to apply criteria with a factual rather than a presumptive basis, in so far as this is practicable: to consider the kind of moral education the juvenile has had, the influence of home, school and environment, and empirical evidence to indicate wide variability in relevant respects of moral attitudes and values and degree of self-mastery.[6]

Welfare Status of Children

Indeed in some countries these are some of the issues that are being increasingly recognized by the law, so that arbitrariness is tempered by an emphasis on the juvenile's *welfare*. In this an *educational* perspective is sometimes taken – a view of the juvenile as a *developing* individual, and therefore one who needs sympathy and practical guidance[7], based partly on a study of his home and social circumstances. In this context the child is perceived as an individual with his own life prospects, an individuality yet to be developed; and welfare is not merely reform, but primarily the setting of a course that will give him the best opportunities to build on his abilities and capacities, consistent with social values. To that extent the perspectives of law, education and social welfare merge. A much more difficult problem in law is in giving practical support to the notion of some welfare rights, such as the right to education. Some jurists hold that the enactment of rights to such welfare provisions as education faces insuperable difficulties in their enforceability, since the courts would find it impracticable to decide whether or not a child had received what was his supposed entitlement.[8] It is for this reason that statute law on educational provisions is usually restricted to what *is* clearly enforceable, notably attendance at school. Though regularity of instruction is readily determinable, efficiency of instruction is not, at least by the courts.

Children and Parents

It is within the competence of the courts to decide some matters which are referable to particular enactments outlining educational provisions, such as the parents' right to an education of their choice, their right to object to certain activities in the curriculum, and to withdraw their children from those activities. In matters such as these there is a growing awareness in law of the developing nature of the child as a person, and an increasing reluctance in some countries to recognize the right of the parent over the child. In this there are also fundamental moral implications of a practical consideration of children's interests by avoiding the possibility that the parent is using the child to his own ends.

The rights of the child tend to be supported also in matters of school uniforms and homework,[9] but in these respects the moral connections are not obvious. When we reject the notion of vicarious right-holding and focus instead on rights which children themselves have the capacity to understand, assert and claim, we move closer to the formal notions of justice, morality and education. Then we may realise that we have given too much weight, in our social attitudes and values, to parents' entitlements in law, and correspondingly too little weight to children's moral rights and to the conditions of morality which require those with sufficient maturity to be respected as persons, and all others as emerging persons. Our special concern from perspectives of justice, morality and education is with the rights of children who *do* have the capacity to hold them. Should a parent claim the right to withdraw his child from a curriculum activity which opposes his personal beliefs, and his child is sufficiently mature to have made up his own mind and disagrees with the parent, any legal or quasi-legal entitlement which the parent may have is not consistent with justice, morality and education. For it is the child's powers that are being developed by education, under professional guidance, and when he has attained sufficient intellectual maturity to be able to make choices of his own which affect his developing individuality it is contrary to both justice and morality to deny him liberty from interference. Similarly it is conceivable that some legal juveniles, such as those beyond junior adolescence, have formed personal beliefs which conflict with those of one parent or of both, and, assuming the same sufficient intellectual maturity, have a moral right to have their views respected, and not to be directed to a school of their parents' choice purely on grounds of personal belief.[10] Parental entitlements have been disproportionately strong compared with children's liberty rights. We still carry with us some of the traditional social attitudes and values of our not very distant past, when children were the property of parents. That supposed property right, from the perspective of the juvenile of sufficient maturity, is virtually an enslavement of a human life, in conflict with justice, morality and education when it is used to hamper the continuing development of his potentialities and individuality, or turned toward parental ends rather than his own.

Teachers and the Law

We shall now consider the law as it pertains to *teachers* in their relations with children and parents, confining ourselves first to teachers' professional liberty; second to the law governing negligence; and third to the question of criminal proceedings for assault of children, which will lead into the next section on Justice, Morality and Punishment. On the first question teachers' professional liberty has been challenged in cases where the community has sought to intervene in the teaching of content which has threatened fundamentalist or other beliefs. In some instances the courts have reversed earlier decisions. Justice as fairness in the treatment of persons suggests that the onus of justification for any restriction of a teacher's liberty as a qualified practitioner is with the objectors. The Federal Courts of the United States have upheld teachers' liberty of thought and expression, acting on 'due process'.[11] Challenges by individual parents which have the purpose of constraining the teacher are often misconceived in their understanding of curriculum – its nature and its objectives. The development of intellectual aspects of individuality requires the teacher to encourage critical thinking; that in turn, calls for a free exchange of opinions and viewpoints on social and other matters between teacher and children. Odd cases of teacher indiscretion are not relevant to this formal situation. Both children and teacher require freedom to think and to express their thoughts. The teacher who aims to develop critical thinking cannot do so if he is to set an example of reticence on controversial matters; cannot himself be a critical thinker if he is to develop a habit of closing his mind to some subjects, and cannot contribute to children's awareness of changing social attitudes and values if areas of change are, by reactionary community sentiment, walled off as dangerous to immature minds.

Teachers or their employing authorities have been sued by parents for negligence in two different ways: first for alleged educational negligence, or for failing to promote the child's development in specific directions; second for alleged carelessness in supervision of children, where serious physical injury has ensued. If either could be substantiated it would at once confront the fundamental or formal notions of morality, justice and education. In the first sense of negligence, the basis of charges laid has been generally that elementary skills, such as reading, have not been developed, and the child has suffered serious impairment of his life prospects. Where negligence is claimed over a period of years, in fairness to teachers many other factors need to be weighed as possible contributions to failure, factors in the child's own attitudes, and in the home environment particularly.[12] 'Due process' would therefore find some difficulty in establishing teacher responsibility. That is a practical matter, but the fact that in some instances there can be years of apparent neglect when children's special learning disabilities have not been properly diagnosed, draws attention to an important social problem with moral, judicial and educational implications. Every teacher charged with the task of setting a young life on an optimum course for the fulfilment of its potentialities, as far as practicable, assumes as high a moral responsibility as society can entrust to any of its members. Though compensation may be claimed in courts for educational negligence, the damage that is done may be irreparable: compensation cannot properly be measured in monetary terms when an individual's life fulfilment is involved. Justice as fairness in the treatment of persons also requires that schools be provided with adequate teaching resources and adequate facilities for the diagnosis and proper education of those with learning difficulties, as well as with a sufficient number of teachers so that class sizes are at a suitable level for individual attention. Teachers may be sometimes held responsible for such administrative situations which prevent or inhibit their effective teaching of every individual child, so that the attribution of educational negligence to them may be unwarranted.

The more usual case of negligence faced by teachers or administrators is that where parents sue for compensation under the Law of Tort, alleging that a wrong has been done through failure to observe proper care in the supervision of a child. The ease with which accidents occur, the difficulty of achieving complete vigilance in the playground, on the sporting field, on excursions, even in the classroom, are all complicating circumstances which it is the duty of the courts to acknowledge. The teacher's duty is to exercise care, but the duty of care is not merely a duty of vigilance but one of prevention as well, so that an alleged negligence may relate to inadequate administrative arrangements.[13] Aristotle's notion of corrective justice, as distinct from distributive justice, sought to apply a mathematical formula, as we have seen in the first chapter, to ensure objectivity in rectifying an imbalance brought about by an act of wrong-doing. The Law of Tort is an instance of such corrective justice, and in contemporary societies there is generally as much concern as Aristotle had that the courts restore the balance between right and wrong with as much objectivity as possible: that is, to ensure that the person wronged is compensated to the full amount of the loss. With respect to injuries incurred at school, or elsewhere under the supervision of teachers, there are two complex and difficult problems in attempting to meet the requirements of justice and morality: first, in attributing culpability; second in making compensation. An injury leading to permanent disability or incapacity such as blindness, from educational negligence, is not something which can be compensated in monetary terms, and lesser disabilities can be severely inhibiting in the fulfilment of individual potentialities. In the Law of Tort some wrong-doing is assumed to have occurred before action is taken with respect to the loss incurred by it. From the standpoint of a teacher on supervisory duty at the time of an injury to a child, the charge of liability would be unjust if he had committed no wrong; that is, a wrong of negligence in failing to prevent the injury. From the standpoint of the parent, the child who suffered the injury may have done nothing himself to bring it about, and on that account may be seen to deserve some compensation, yet that consideration is irrelevant to the central issue of whether a wrong had been committed, as is the question of whether either teacher or child was insured against loss or injury. The wrong-doing assumed in the Law of Tort may include an *omission* to act, even – as we have noted – *before* the injury occurred.[14] As with educational negligence, there are no scales by which to weigh corrective justice in cases of injury to a child. The teacher's duty is clearly a moral duty, not merely one of carrying out official duties as formally prescribed responsibilities. The other side of the problem is the responsibility of the courts to ensure that justice is done to teachers by ensuring that liability is related to an *established* wrong of negligence. For the teacher to be used merely as a means and not an end, a means of achieving compensation for the parents of an injured child regardless of actual liability, would be contrary to both justice and morality in their irreducible formal senses.

We shall now consider the third aspect of the law referring to teachers in their relations with parents and children, namely, that which is concerned with criminal proceedings against teachers for assault. We shall here simply record the facts as an introduction to the next section of this chapter, on the justice and morality of punishment. Since the principle of *in loco parentis* has been found an unsuitable guide to the courts, the courts themselves in some countries have been obliged to determine whether corporal punishment administered to a child is beyond what is 'reasonable'. If it is deemed 'unreasonable' the teacher or principal involved may be liable either under the Law of Tort, or under criminal law. Excessive corporal punishment may cause physical injury, but its effects on the attitudes and values of the child may be such as to seriously impair both his intellectual and moral development. In that sense it may be considered contrary to both justice and morality in its failure to consider the long-term and fundamental interests of the child.[15] Perhaps at least as significant for its effects on other children in his charge, is the damage which brutal and excessive punishment causes to the teacher's self-respect, and to the respect of other children for him, so that the curiosity and will to learn may both suffer irreparably. We shall consider moral and educational aspects of punishment, and of corporal punishment in particular, in the next section.

JUSTICE, MORALITY AND PUNISHMENT

The philosophy of punishment has been concerned almost exclusively with the punishment of adults, but we shall ask whether it has application also to children, especially those at school. Our first task is to enquire into the meaning of punishment; our second to ask what are its purpose and justification according to various philosophical standpoints; the third to ask what is the purpose of punishing children at school, and whether that punishment can be justified. In the last question we shall be concerned with corporal punishment in particular.

Nature of Punishment

In offering his definition of punishment, Hobbes took a legal standpoint. It is 'an Evill inflicted by publique Authority, on him that hath done, or omitted that which is Judged by the same Authority to be a Transgression of the Law'. Its purpose is to make the will of men 'better disposed to obedience'.[16] Hobbes has asserted that punishment is experienced as something unpleasant, suffered by an offender against a public authority, who is responsible for upholding a system of rules recognized as law within a society. He specifically excludes those 'evils' which are experienced privately between men and which do not come within the ambit of public authority. For the same reason he excludes those which are natural consequences of wrongdoing as when a man is hurt when assaulting another. Punishment may be the unpleasantness of physical pain, as in corporal punishment, or of mental pain, such as the anguish of ignominy or exile. Again from the standpoint of the law, Hobbes insists that punishment requires a public hearing: otherwise the infliction of the unpleasantness is no more than an act of hostility. If we may set aside such peculiarly legal perspectives, Hobbes' analysis of punishment has wide application, even to the school. Punishment is an unpleasant experience inflicted by an authority on someone who offends against a system of rules publicly promulgated within a society, including the society of a school. If a system of rules is not known by a person suffering an inflicted unpleasantness, then the sufferer has not offended: that is, he is not an offender within the meaning of the rules. The infliction of the unpleasantness in such circumstances is not strictly punishment, but in Hobbes' language, an act of 'hostility'. Its arbitrariness stems from the fact that the sufferer could in no way be held responsible for what he had done. If punishment depends on rules, and a knowledge of the rules, ignorance of the rules is a legitimate reason for claiming that the act in question does not constitute an offence.

Purpose and Justification of Punishment

In proceeding now to the second question, concerning the purpose and justification of punishment from various philosophical positions, we shall keep in mind Hobbes' legal perspective on the disposing of offenders to obedience, but substitute for it a moral perspective. Punishment to instil obedience to rules, or to the law, is not necessarily a moral justification for punishment, for rules or law may be immoral. There are two general problems of punishment which we shall mention before turning to particular philosophies on the subject. The first is a procedural difficulty, the second a difficulty of restricting the punishment to the offender. The procedural difficulty refers to desert. Justice is never far from the concept of equality, of treating equals equally in relevant respects. But before we are able to give equal punishment for equal offences, we have to be able to measure how much each offender *deserves*. Justice suggests that we should not punish *excessively*; that is, that the punishment should fit the offence. Over-punishment as a warning to others may have salutary social consequences, but most would see it as unjust to the offender, who should receive in punishment no more than he deserves. The metaphorical scales of justice have presented many problems – problems much greater than the scales which Portia demanded for the literal weighing of a pound of flesh. The determination of punishment would be greatly facilitated if it were possible to *quantify* desert and proceed according to Aristotle's corrective or commutative justice. But the mind is relatively inaccessible, accessible to others only inferentially, and the detection of the *mens rea* and the assessment of desert are sometimes perplexing, as reversals of legal judgements indicate. Further, assuming that punishment is justified, and that in general circumstances offenders deserve differential punishments according to their various offences, desert is not always evident from the offence itself, but may be contingent on various personal circumstances as well. The student who steals a book from a library as an act of petulance and contempt of borrowing procedures, and who already has a well-stocked home library, may be considered by some to deserve greater punishment than another who steals a book compulsively and aggressively from a sense of deprivation and injustice, coming from a home without reading material of any kind. We might feel on safer ground in justifying differential punishment for similar offences if we had an accurate mirror of the offender's dispositions at the time of the offence, his wants or desires, motive – including intention, his attitudes and values, and reliable techniques for measuring awareness of guilt. Once we accept the principle of excusing conditions a new set of imponderables emerges: how much weight is to be given to these in the assessment of desert? The second general moral problem of justice and desert is that in punishing offenders it is very often impossible to exclude unpleasantness in innocent parties. The suffering spills over to others, so that the act of punishment breaks its own rules. The anguish of mothers and wives may be much greater than that of prisoners. In the case of a child disturbed by punishment at school the emotional involvement of parents frequently exceeds his own suffering.

Retributivism

Those philosophers who link punishment with desert are generally known as *retributivists*. To them the *purpose* of punishment is repayment by the offender for an offence against society. In this approach they do not seek revenge for a wrong committed: on the contrary their stress is on human dignity, and not on human debasement. Kant rejected all consequentialist views of punishment, such as punishing for the good of society, or for the good of the offender himself. He was concerned particularly with punishment in law, and the penal code under which the criminal must be punished without exception, 'for no other reason than because he has acted criminally'. A guilty person must receive 'the due of his deeds'. The sequence of law – breach of law – punishment is inexorable. The dignity inherent in such Hebraic sternness is that punishment annuls the crime. It is a matter of keeping faith with a moral order, of giving out what is deserved. 'We pay the penalty', explained Bradley a century later, 'because we owe it, and for no other reason' (*Ethical Studies*, p.26).[17] Ross rejected the argument that not to punish an offender is to break faith with him, to fail to trust him with the respect due to him as a moral agent, but instead insisted that the state has a right to punish the guilty, and that this right is supported by the general feeling in the community that promises should, in a *prima facie* sense, be kept. The two considerations together account for the moral satisfaction in the community when the guilty are punished, and the indignation felt when they are not punished, or when the innocent are.[18] Those who do support the view that punishment keeps faith with an offender refer at times to autobiographical reflections of criminals on the honour, dignity and equality with others which they experience when they are punished for breaking the rules. But selected cases establish nothing at all of a generalizable nature: there might well be at least an equal number of criminals who have rejoiced when they have escaped capture and punishment. It would be contradictory for criminals to seek to evade detection and punishment if punishment were to guarantee honour, dignity and respect in their treatment as equals with others. The central weakness of the retributivists, however, is in their emphasis on the very aspects which defy accurate assessment – responsibility and desert. It is as though they hold an offender's guilt, responsibility and desert to be self-evident. But even in criminal cases, from which retributivists draw much of their argument, the law is generally much more doubtful about the self-evidence of the *mens rea*, considering as defences or exceptions such things as mistake of fact, accident, coercion, duress and provocation. One or more of these may be sufficient in some cases to exclude liability, in other cases to reduce it. These are some of the complexities Dostoyevsky introduces in his *Crime and Punishment*: desert is established only in a *prima facie*, legal sense; for a sensitive person punishment appears to be needed to give peace to a mind tortured by guilt. But the implications of guilt and responsibility go far beyond a simple retributivist interpretation. If on the surface severe punishment is the only means of expiation, below the surface, Dostoyevsky shows, there are many troubling questions of desert that remain unresolved.

Consequentialism: Individual and Social Benefit

It is partly for the very reason that it is often difficult and sometimes impossible to be clear on an offender's guilt, his responsibility and his desert, that some philosophers have agreed that the focus on punishment should shift from the retributive to the reformist. The latter is a consequentialist view, with the stress now on punishment that is likely to *benefit* the offender. In some retributivist views there

re consequential applications, it is true, in that the consequences of
punishment for human dignity and self-respect are taken into
account, but in these the primary purpose of punishment is to annul a
wrong, whereas reformists suggest that punishment should not be
given as a matter of moral necessity, but when, and only when, it is
likely to *benefit* the offender. The measure of success is in the
consequences, but it is frequently assumed that short-term benefits
amount to fundamental changes in moral outlook. Punishment as
deterrence is another consequentialist standpoint: here the consequences are considered, not for the reform of an individual, but for the
good of the social group to which he belongs, or for the good of the
wider society. Punishment is again instrumental. But to treat others
merely as means and not as ends is contrary to the spirit of Kantian
moral philosophy. Hegel was one who objected to this instrumental
approach to punishment, regarding the offender as 'a harmful animal
who has to be made harmless, or with a view to deterring and
reforming him', rather than holding him a rational being who
understands his offence and the measure of punishment which is his
due (*The Philosophy of Right*, pp. 70–1).[19]

   The conflict between retributivism and consequentialism in punishment is brought to a head in the utilitarian approach. As consequentialists, utilitarians attempt to justify acts as good in so far as they
contribute to total happiness or satisfaction, but all punishment is in
itself evil by definition, since the concept of punishment includes the
notion of a reduction of happiness or satisfaction in the offender.
Therefore punishment is to be justified only if it can be shown to have
good consequences. Evil though it is in itself, if it prevents something
happening which would result in still *greater* loss of satisfaction or
happiness, on balance it is useful: it is the lesser of two evils. It is easy
to distort the views of utilitarians on punishment by arguing that if
punishment is justified only by valuable consequences, then even the
innocent might in some circumstances be justifiably punished, but the
inference is fallacious since the concept of punishment requires an
offender. In other ways utilitarians pose serious moral threats in their
views on punishment. The first is that, given the offender, his
punishment might not be kept as commensurate as possible with his
offence, for in some circumstances greater total happiness might
ensue if it exceeds his desert. In criminal cases judgements that are
made unduly severe to protect society from crises of violence are such
instances. The second moral threat is from a Rule Utilitarian
perspective. If society were to develop a widespread *practice* of

punishing as a means to supposedly valuable consequences, there is the likelihood of a correspondingly widespread reduction in a practical consideration of the interests of others, with an associated loss of respect for persons. A more general objection to the utilitarian approach to punishment is that it suffers from presumptions about the predictability of the consequences of acts. In fact, predictions that punishment will lead to an excess of good over evil cannot afford to be wrong, because punishment itself is accepted as an evil by utilitarians. Punishment serves the argument of utilitarians most effectively when it leads to an acknowledgement by the offender's society of the wrongness of the offence. The widest deterrence to wrong-doing may come from the social disapproval of peers. Indeed one philosopher has suggested that the most appropriate punishment is social disapproval, and that it is this which should fit the crime.[20]

The social consequences of punishment are of obvious interest to the law, but they are of interest also to recent philosophers such as John Rawls whose general views we shall consider in more detail in the next chapter. Rawls believes, from a social contract and not a utilitarian standpoint, that penal sanctions should be seen ideally as a stabilizing device in society, and that responsibility is best understood in the context of a system of public rules for rational persons 'to regulate their cooperation' (*A Theory of Justice*, p.241).[21] This he believes is similar to the perspective in criminal law, that punishment is to give protection, order and social stability, not, retributively, to right a wrong, to give an offender what he deserves. Hegel had seen the *offender* as a rational being, able to understand the justice of punishment according to desert. Rawls shifts the perspective to that of cooperating members of a society, for whom it is rational to observe public rules, and when they are *not* observed, punishment is needed to restore stability.

Punishment of Children at School: Pre-Rational and Rational Distinction

We now move to the third question in this section, namely, what is the purpose of punishing children at school, and whether that purpose can be justified. In the centuries of punishment that has been a feature of schooling from Greek and Roman times it is probable that the reasons individual teachers have had for punishing pupils have been varied and often confused, with strands of retribution and

ven the exorcising of original sin, as well as of consequentialism in
eform and deterrence. If any had, as a reason, the utilitarian notion
f punishment leading to a happier or more satisfying *school* society
hey would have been dull indeed. Schoolboys of Sixteenth Century
England had good reason to creep like snails 'unwillingly to school',
n Jaques' description; and by all accounts those in France fared no
etter with 'the outcries of boys under execution, and the thundering
f pedagogues, drunk with fury (Montaigne, *Essays*, p.70). A century
r so later Aubrey gave his ideas on education, referring to the
tyrannical beating and dispiriting of children from which many
ender and ingenious do never recover'.[22] What is of particular
nterest is not so much the brutality and apparent incessancy of the
unishment as that its *value* was questioned by those who wrote
bout it. For its harmful consequences Montaigne urged the removal
f the violence. Brinsley was satisfied that 'cruell and continuall
eating and dulling' takes from the mind 'all the helpes which reason
ffers' (*The Grammar Schoole*, ch. XXVI, p.277).

Aubrey noted that tyrannical beating of children broke their spirits
nd left them 'confounded with fear'. By the Nineteenth Century
dministrators had begun to make a stand against such punishment,
hough it persisted, with cane, stick, ferule or ruler, strap or taw, or
irch rod.[23] The challenge to corporal punishment was on consequen-
alist grounds: effects on the child's nature and on his attitude to
chool and capacity to learn. For retributivists there was little to be
aid: if a wrong had been committed it had to be punished. Yet from
ach standpoint there was room for compassion. Montaigne and
ubrey were certainly sensitive to the well-being of children. It is
ley who raised the question of whether, on moral grounds, punish-
ent of children can be justified. We shall pursue the question from a
oral standpoint, considering children's interests, including their
apacity for suffering. We hold the retributivist view simplistic that a
rong committed means a right to be rectified by punishment, as well
s the retributivist justification that punishment annuls a wrong,
ipes the slate clean, gives the offender a fresh start and leaves him
ith the dignity of a rational being, rather than, say, the indignity of
abmission to paternalistic reform.

Yet children may need to be considered in a different light. If they
re not *capable* of a mature rationality, including a capacity for
asoning and for self-mastery, if they do not *understand* the rules of
ooperation required in society, if the consequences of corporal
unishment are not beneficial to individuals, why do we submit them

to it? Clearly we need both argument and evidence, and the first step must be to recall that children are *not* all of a kind, all immature intellectually and morally as well as physically, but that some of them are in fact capable of distinguishing between right and wrong according to their individual values just as adults are, and are as intellectually mature as they, given the degree of intellectual variability that obtains among adults. We may therefore divide all legally acknowledged children into two groups, each with considerable variability within it: first, a group of those intellectually and morally immature; second, a group of those intellectually and morally mature, where maturity refers to a sufficient development to regard them as rational and responsible beings, comparable in these respects to legal adults in a broad and general sense which allows for individual variability.

Justification of School Punishment

Pre-Rational Children

Since punishment is by definition an infliction of unpleasantness, what justification can there be for punishing children in the first group? There is a *prima facie* contradiction in punishing someone for an act or omission for which he cannot be held responsible. Even if we have doubts about his *total* responsibility, we should ordinarily hesitate to punish, if only because there is no way of removing the doubts: no way of confidently measuring the degree of responsibility. But children are in the first group for the very reason of their incapacity for total responsibility for their acts, both in terms of reasoning ability and in terms of self-control. We can therefore dismiss the notion of punishment for purposes of *reform*, for this implies a lapse from a rational state which in fact has never existed. Following the law with respect to the criminal responsibility of children, we have no alternative, if we are to take a retributive standpoint, to accepting the immaturity of children in this group as an excusing condition. But if we are to take a consequentialist standpoint, which is also moral *and* educational, we shall consider as central to any justification of their punishment their own well-being, regarding them as individuals who are in need of our guidance as they develop intellectually and morally. Here the fundamental notions of justice, morality and education are united in one perspective. I would be just to punish only if punishment were needed, in individual instances, to remove mental impediments to progressive development, and with very young children that is sometimes the case. In this regard the principle of *in loco parentis* has some application. As we shall see in the next section on moral education, before children can reason there is a period in which they are instructed in social and moral habits, a phase which some prefer to speak of as 'training' to distinguish it from educational development with understanding. Before there is self-control there is need for external control, and in some individual instances a demonstration of the superior strength of the teacher. Where, as a last resort, physical means are needed, only the most sensitive perception of the likely consequences for the individual and the rest of the group can give it adequate justification.

Transitional and Rational Children

The most serious issues in justice, morality and education are raised in connection with the second group – those who have advanced sufficiently to have some reasoning capacity, as well as to have personal moral attitudes and values which are generally consistent with, rather than generally in conflict with, the values of others to whom they relate in their social group, so that some moral communication is possible. A particular complication occurs with those in a transitional stage, for there is no sharp break between immaturity and this specified degree of maturity. Intellectual and moral development are not always strictly in sympathy: when some adolescents can reason effectively, there may be a moral lag, a period when clear moral attitudes and values have not been formed. Then, for purposes of the following argument on punishment, such transitional children will be considered closer to the first group than to the second, not yet ready to make moral judgements, and therefore not to be held morally responsible for their acts. We must admit that by virtue of their reasoning capacity and their degree of self-control, it is within their capacity to observe and understand what *others* regard as right and wrong, and therefore to avoid punishment if they wish. Indeed to invite punishment would be contrary to the rationality we acknowledge in them. Yet to punish because such transitional children violate what others regard as wrong, without perceiving the wrongness of the acts themselves, must be regarded as unjust and immoral, using them merely as means to the teacher's ends, such as ends of

deterrence. Educationally this punishment runs the danger of thwart-
ing moral development by reinforcing what is no more than socially-
approved behaviour. Are we to assume, from what has been said,
that those who fall squarely in the second group, as being rational,
and to have formed clear moral attitudes and values, are therefore
totally responsible for their moral acts?

We shall not enlarge on the traditional philosophical debate
between liberty and necessity, between free will and determinism,
between those who hold that, in a broad sense, man is free to choose
his acts and therefore responsible for what he does, and those who
hold that man is not free, that freedom is an illusion, that man's acts
are caused by influences bearing upon him. Both Hume and Mill
were advocates of *necessity*.[24] Under criticism Mill was obliged to
acknowledge that 'necessity' is not as binding as it sometimes
appears. We do in fact have the power to resist particular motives we
may have, he confessed, and are not obliged to obey them as though
we were under a magical spell. To William James this was being
evasive (*Essays on Faith and Morals*, p.149)[25]; but Mill felt bound to
reject any determinism dependent on compulsion and irresistibility.
To borrow Hume's terms neither 'liberty of spontaneity' (or freedom
from constraint) nor 'liberty of indifference' (or the power to do
otherwise) is incompatible with some versions of determinism,[26]
and in fact the supposed opposition between determinists and
libertarians – so-called – usually melts away on close investigation.
Thus libertarians acknowledge the forces of habit which influence
many of our acts, limiting their recognition of acting freely in a moral
sense to the instances where they have good reason to recall a
successful opposition to desire or inclination. Certainly the fact of our
dependence upon tradition, convention, and habit for many of our
acts, is not relevant to the *capacity* for freedom which adults and
sufficiently mature children have. Similarly that capacity is not
disproved by any empirical evidence of *antecedents* for our wants or
desires, motives (including intentions), attitudes and values. We shall
assume that children in the second group *do* have the capacity for
acting freely in their moral conduct, and that deterministic arguments
do not provide grounds for absolving them from moral responsibility
for those acts. But the question of *how much* punishment is deserved
for wrong-doing, if punishment is to be given, is a very different
question, for them as for adults. Desert is not easily measurable, as
we have noted: some believe its measurement is beyond the powers
of any man on earth.[27]

Therefore retributive grounds for punishment of these particular children are not strong. Moral responsibility and desert are related to influences in the home, peer group influences, temperament, state of health, fatigue, provocation by teachers and many other variables, so that their assessment is an individual matter, usually beyond the capacity of teachers to fathom, especially within the time constraints placed on them. It is no argument in support of corporal punishment to use the viewpoints of some senior students, that it is swift, clean, fair, restoring the balance while treating offenders with respect and dignity, instead of demeaning them with paternalistic counselling. Those opinions, as we have noted, are selective and non-generalizable. Further, subjective feelings are unacceptable as justificatory in themselves: what an individual feels about a particular practice cannot be regarded as a rational justification for it, and this is the case however many subjective feelings are canvassed. On the other hand, if corporal punishment is used for deterrent purposes it is unjust and immoral, since it is making an example of individuals, again using them merely as means and not as ends. If another consequentialist view is taken, that corporal punishment is justified by its beneficial consequences for offenders as well as for the social group to which they belong, these two must be clearly separated. The only possible justification is in respect to the beneficial consequences for offenders. But how can this be? Intellectually and morally, corporal punishment will not benefit the offender, for it will not give an understanding of right and wrong which children of the same group already have. Physical benefit is out of the question: the only possibility is harm. In a pragmatic sense corporal punishment may have a temporarily beneficial effect on particular senior students, those who prefer corporal punishment as an act of speedy moral rectification, but it can hardly be said to be educative except in the unlikely event of its inducing greater self-control. Otherwise corporal punishment inflicted on children in this group can only be educationally damaging: first, as Brinsley observed nearly four centuries ago, it may affect attitudes and values in education, developing unfavourable attitudes to teachers, schools, particular aspects of the curriculum or learning generally. It may damage class or school ethos if practised extensively, and beyond that may have an effect on aggression in society. It may be self-corrupting to teachers administering it, impairing their self-respect and their moral capacity for considering others' interests. From a utilitarian standpoint it is morally dangerous, opening the possibility of punishing excessively for the sake of a supposed total amount of satisfaction in the school society, as well as the possibility that the supposedly valuable consequences will attain a higher importance in the minds of teachers than the interests of the individual offenders. Such utility-oriented attitudes to punishment are objectionable fundamentally for a viola-tion of the formal notion of morality with respect to others' interests, and also because they suffer from presumptions about the predicta-bility of consequences. Those who *threaten* corporal punishment aggravate the hazards of predicting consequences by inducing fear or apprehension, and constant repetition of threats may have the effect on some children of stifling moral development. If wrong-doing is associated with anxiety and punishment there is the danger that some children will become morally stagnant as rule-followers, unconcerned about developing their own views on what ought to be done in particular situations, or about their freedom as independent moral agents. Mill held that punishment can be justified if it first, benefits the offender; and second, protects others in the offender's society.[28] This utilitarian viewpoint founders primarily on the imponderability of the consequences.

For the second group of children who are sufficiently mature to be considered rational and to have personal moral attitudes and values, we can find no justification for punishment in terms of their individual well-being. Any beneficial consequences are probably short-lived, pragmatic and circumstantial, to give temporary relief to tensions in the classroom for instance. Justice and morality are both in question when we consider some other forms of punishment, such as deten-tion. When a number of offenders are confined collectively regardless of the nature of the offence, and supervised by rostered teachers at the end of the normal school day, the practice savours invariably of arbitrariness and retribution: offences are different, teachers' de-mands and standards are different, and there is an obvious breach of fundamental justice as fairness in the treatment of persons. Sentences may be handed down summarily without concern for the offender's motive, degree of provocation, involvement of others in the offence, and so forth. In such cases the teacher's motive is usually deterrence, and in this situation we again note a failure to respect offenders as persons, for those in the second group are both rational and sensitive to slights and unjustified discriminations. For those in the first group, as emerging persons, an awareness of unfairness in comparisons with others is evident long before rationality develops. In all cases, justice demands that where the reason for the penalty is not clear, the student has a right to request an explanation. If this is denied, or if to preserve the respect of peers he does not request it when he knows he has been unjustly accused and penalized, his detention has the moral status of a curbing of personal liberty without justification, and in some interpretations the legal status of false imprisonment. Cases before the courts of improper punishment have been concerned generally with corporal punishment, but in some countries legal action may be taken with respect to other school penalties as well.[29]

Conclusion on School Punishment

We may sum up our views on justice, morality and punishment by applying the fundamental moral criterion of a practical consideration of others' interests, considering children's interests primarily, and not those of the teacher as punisher. If corporal punishment proceeds from retributive impulses, from primitive motives to repay offenders, it is demeaning to teacher and children alike. If it is based on a philosophy of retribution which holds that wrongful acts need to be rectified by punishment according to desert, that it is somehow dignified to treat rational beings in this way, it seems to be misguided in both belief and practice, since desert is difficult to estimate in the best of circumstances and often impossible, and there is no evidence to establish that punishment is rational – the expectation of all rational offenders and non-offenders alike. If it is based on conse-quentialist views, it runs into the difficulty of establishing that any consequences are beneficial to *individual* offenders, and the further difficulty of establishing that its consequences on the school society are beneficial. All consequentialist theories which distract attention from the interests of the child as a *developing* individual, and make him merely a means to some other end, are contrary to the fundamental notions of morality, justice and education. The only corporal punishment that can be justified is that used by the teacher of children who are still pre-rational in their development, the teacher acting *in loco parentis* when all other control procedures fail. Then it may be fairly claimed as action in the child's best interests, assuming moderation in its administration. In all other circumstances it is at best a stop-gap, a pragmatic relief measure; but since aggression generates further aggression it is self-defeating, without long-term benefits of any kind to the offender or to his peers. Children who are rational are not totally so in their daily conduct any more than adults are. All are under dispositional influences, as we have noted in the previous chapter. All are influenced by, and sometimes provoked by, teachers and parents, as well as by the attitudes and values of their peers. School counselling is paternalistically hollow to sensitive victims of deep-seated social ills: corporal punishment may merely exacerbate injustices whose roots lie outside the school. In those situations teachers too are victims of circumstances beyond their control, and to that extent outside their responsibility. As for other forms of punishment, the penalty of detention in out of class hours is open to abuse in the secondary school especially, with teachers' motives often mixed, in part retributive and in part consequentialist. As such, detention is subject to the general criticism of all retributive and consequentialist punishment, in its worst forms arbitrary to suit administrative convenience.

In general terms, teachers' prescriptions of penalties are contrary to our assumptions on morality when they are not intended for children's well-being, but for their own; and when they lead to unnecessary suffering, including the mental suffering that may extend to parents as well. The onus is always on punishers to justify the *necessity* for punishment, on criteria of elemental justice, morality and education. Punishment of any kind which is perceived by children as unjust is a poor basis for moral education, the subject of the following section.

JUSTICE, MORALITY AND MORAL EDUCATION

We have already noted certain connections between justice, morality and moral education, in particular the danger of inhibiting moral development by using procedures designed to instil, or with the effect of instilling, unquestioning obedience to law or to school rules. We shall keep in mind the major emphases of Chapter 2 as we proceed, since notions of moral education are necessarily dependent upon notions of what constitutes morality. In this section we shall be concerned first, with the importance of attitudes and values in moral education; second, with the possibilities of autonomy; third, with principles of a methodological approach; fourth, with questions of content.

We shall begin with several preliminary observations. First, in a practical activity such as moral education we cannot afford to ignore the empirical question of what is the case, for to ignore it may mean to substitute ideals for a factual foundation – as we have found also in practical morality. So although we may not leap from what is to what ought to be, the *ought* must at least take account of the *is*. Second, lest again we be transported unrealistically by ideals, though recognizing their motivating value, we need to be sensitive in moral education as in our personal practical morality, to general human limitations. It is better to perceive imperfection than to set children on a course of impossibilities which will impair their faith in the integrity of the objectives. It is proper therefore for children to acquire a balanced realisation that man is limited in all his morally relevant powers and propensities: limited in generosity and in altruistic impulses, leading to the regular tension between benevolence and egoism; in the ability to reason; in the ability to control impulse or inclination which is contrary to moral attitudes and values; in his perception of others' dispositions and in empathic insight generally; in self-understanding; in his comprehension of relevant facts significant to a particular moral situation. From this it follows that practical morality requires an *effort*, and moral education needs to take cognizance of this simple fact. Third, from what has been said of morality and what we shall say of moral education in this section, successful guidance in moral development is dependent in a very large measure on the moral quality of both parents and teachers. Either they become mutually supportive, or – if one is conspicuously inferior to the other – there is conflict, loss of faith, the one vitiating the contribution of the other. Teachers who posture, who are *not* expressing authentic moral attitudes and values, readily become transparent to children. The high qualifications needed by moral educators are as much qualifications in personal moral standards as in knowledge – knowledge of our psychological and social condition, of child development, and so forth. In addition each requires a degree of rationality that can be an example to others, an ability to reason openly and dispassionately, and to control emotion; personal qualities of sensitiveness and discretion; a skill in unobtrusive guidance of others, and an unaffected zeal in helping them to see and to feel according to *their* values, as long as their judgements are subjected to critical evaluation by others. Yet in all of this there is no more than a counsel of perfection unless *all* teachers are mutually supportive. Conflict or indifference can quickly shatter the ethos which moral education in the school demands.

Attitudes and Values

We shall now proceed with the four themes we have set for this section, beginning with the importance of attitudes and values to moral education. Since to morally educate is not merely to provide relevant knowledge but in particular to develop a capacity for moral *conduct*, we must re-state our simplified action schema: Desire – dispositional reasoning (including motives, with intentions, and attitudes and values) – decision – action. Our present task is to draw attention to the central significance of attitudes and values in this schema, and specifically of *moral* attitudes and values to *moral* action. It is a common ethical observation that good intentions (motives) are not enough: that there is often a gap between intentions and action. What is needed is a catalyst: and in fact there are *two*, or at least two components of the one: *reason* and our *attitudes and values*. It is the latter which in many circumstances constitute the most potent dispositional force prior to action. United with reason in rational-dispositional deliberation, they lead to decisions, and to action; but between decision, or judgement, and action, there is no faculty of will to provide the impulse for action. The catalyst is reason and dispositions: sometimes reason interacting primarily with motive, at other times with attitudes and values, but the action schema indicates the general situation of the place of attitudes and values in predisposing the individual, in his deliberations and decisions, toward characteristic action. It is reason which sometimes moderates the tendency of the attitude and value; at other times the reverse influence is evident. Returning to the explanation in the previous chapter we now re-emphasize our reasons for using attitudes and values in combination rather than separately. Valuing an object implies having a strongly *favourable* attitude toward it. We do not value things toward which we have unfavourable attitudes: that is, unfavourable attitudes do not express values. But *favourable* attitudes toward an object may be relatively weak or relatively strong, and it is only the relatively strong ones which identify with values as they relate to the same object. We use *attitudes and values* in combination to remind us that values are attitudinal inasmuch as they are combined with strongly favourable attitudes to their objects, and to have an *attitude* extends the sense of valuing to the notion of a cognitive and affective core, with a set of ideas, beliefs or opinions which have relative stability and durability, and a stubbornness, defensiveness and resistance to change (especially when self-esteem is involved).

Our attitudes and values occupy a central position in the action schema proposed since, although they are like our desires, motives (including intentions) in being oriented toward action, they have greater cognitive complexity than motives, and unlike desires and motives which are often more ephemeral, they are *habitual*, the most deep-seated of our dispositions. Attitudes and values are learned in various ways. As distinct from our desires and motives which may be relatively blind or irrational – especially our 'backward-looking' motives such as revenge – our attitudes and values, expressing our preferences and attitudes toward them, cannot be blind or irrational, though some of the reasons we have for our preferences may not be strong.

We shall discuss shortly the importance of habit in moral development when we discuss in particular the beginnings of moral education in early childhood, and shall now recall the views of Aristotle on habit to which we referred in the first chapter. Not only did he record his belief that moral virtue comes about by habit, but also his conviction that if moral habits are to endure it is best that they be formed as early as possible and that they be of the right kind, for habits may be good or bad. 'It makes no small difference, then, whether we form habits of one kind or of another from our very youth; it makes a very great difference, or *all* the difference' (*Nicomachean Ethics*, Book II, ch. 1, 1103^b).[30] We shall use this as a link with the second theme in this section on moral education, confining ourselves to three questions arising from empirical studies: first, the continuing significance of habit in moral development; second, the limitations of theories of moral development; third, the concept of moral autonomy. Moral education is not a process of reason taking over from habit; it never does completely. At a pre-rational phase moral education is *all* habit formation, for by definition it cannot be otherwise. Even then the *how* may be of lasting significance to moral development, for in the very early years of childhood, if habit is formed totally without affection, there is some evidence to suggest that the consequences may be irreparable in emotional instability. We shall not dwell on the incidence of such abnormal psychological states, or on habit formation in normal circumstances of child rearing, but rather on the two-sided effects of habituation, both in the pre-rational and rational phases of intellectual development. While it is natural for children to have 'anger and wishing and desire', Aristotle thought, for these are implanted in them from birth (*Politics*, Book VII, ch. 15, 1334^b)[31], reason and understanding develop as they become older. That is obvious enough. But as he noted in the *Nicomachean Ethics* (Book X, ch. 9, 1179^b) the ground has to be prepared for them to be influenced by reason. If it is not, they may continue to live as passion directs them, not listening to argument, not amenable to our influences on them designed to change their ways. What is needed is a kind of habituation which will still leave the mind open, receptive – when the time has come to understand reasons – to dissuasion from immoral activities. The kinds of habits that are formed in children are, then, of the first importance. Even at the pre-rational level, Aristotle believed, to love what is noble and to hate what is base can be instilled, so that a kind of moral character is developed which is 'already with a kinship to virtue'. For 'character' we shall substitute 'dispositions', in particular moral *attitudes*, for these may be formed by habituation before the child is able to reason, and so before he is able to make independent preferences of moral *values*. Particularly at the pre-rational phase, Aristotle's observations are pertinent to the relationship between teachers and young children, affection and trust facilitating the habituation of moral attitudes to such things as cruelty, truth-telling or helping others.

The other side of moral habituation is perverse, for a trusting relationship between educator and children can be used to the educator's own purposes, and not necessarily in children's interests. This is the side which we call *indoctrination*, a word derived from the Latin *doctrina* which had no original sense of abusing the opportunities educators had, before children could understand what was happening to them, but referred to no more than to *teaching*. Simply to implant a set of ideas, beliefs or opinions by habituation, persuasion or coercion, without engaging the critical minds of the learners, at once raises questions of the educator's own motives, including his intentions and long-term purposes, as well as of his personal attitudes and values. The core of indoctrination in the pejorative sense, as it is now used, is thus dispositional. As Aristotle was suggesting, the habituation may be no more than a preparation for moral education *with understanding*, but the situation is entirely different if the motive, or intention, of the educator is not to leave children's minds open for the reception of moral ideas *with reasons* (when they are old enough to consider them), but rather to fill them with one particular set of ideas which excludes all others, closing the mind to other possibilities, using threat or fear, perhaps, or affection and an unquestioning trust relationship, to suggest that practical morality is an area of our lives, unlike intellectual activities, which is not one for individuals to reason about, but is rather one for obedience, trust in

lders, unquestioning acceptance. The indoctrinator is not an educa-
or, inasmuch as he is not promoting a developing of the individual
norally and intellectually. The indoctrinator is dispositionally, in his
personal attitudes and values, an immoral person, though he may
believe his purposes are moral. He is fundamentally immoral in-
smuch as he is not considering the educational interests of children,
but his own interests; and apart from violating our primary moral
principle he violates as well the moral value derived from it, of
respect for persons, which has application to the rational phase of
children's development. In his own attitudes and values he is not a
person of integrity, though he often believes otherwise; he is
primarily a manipulator, one who is prepared to regard children,
even when they are old enough to reason, merely as *means* and not as
ends. The indoctrinator violates justice at the same time, for to strive
deliberately to close the minds of rational persons, and to use various
reinforcing psychological procedures as techniques to that end, is to
take advantage of his superordinate position, and is obviously not
being fair in the treatment of those who require the liberty to think
and feel and strive and plan, as persons, in their own way. Since
children do in fact learn many things which teachers want them to
learn, the test of indoctrination lies partly in the truth status of the
beliefs that are being imparted, and partly in the motives, including
intentions, of the instructor. The teacher is an indoctrinator if he
teaches Darwinian evolution, not as a theory with relevant supporting evidence, but as final and indisputable knowledge. If he teaches
as knowledge something which is not only believed, but is also true
according to the present state of knowledge, at least, with adequate
evidence to support it, then he is not indoctrinating. On the other
hand if he teaches as indisputable knowledge what is no more than
belief, and makes no attempt to distinguish between knowing and
believing, he is imparting dogma no less than is the indoctrinator of
Darwinian evolution, and is, in this instance too, indoctrinating. He
is indoctrinatory in motive, or intention, whenever he strives to
implant particular beliefs, his own beliefs, in children who are too
young to appraise them critically, deliberately taking advantage of
their immature plasticity.

Autonomy

In discussions of autonomy the terms most commonly in use are
heteronomy and *autonomy*, the first referring to law or morality

imposed by others, and the second to law or morality deriving from the self.[32] The most influential empirical researchers in moral education have focussed on concepts of autonomy. Piaget's research led him to believe that autonomy comes from mutual respect in peer relationships. By contrast with heteronomy, whose source is constraint, 'autonomous rationality' has its source in *reciprocity* (*The Moral Judgement of the Child*, pp.395–6).[33] Kohlberg claimed to find a hierarchical order of child development, requiring an invariant one-way progression, although not all were expected to develop fully, especially in the last two stages. It is logically impossible, he believed, for anyone to reach a higher stage before a lower one. The final stage represents the individual's development toward *autonomy*: it is the culmination of every preceding stage, each one of which is a higher cognitive organization than the one preceding it.[34] Now he has worked out a personal code of ethics, his own set of values, and follows it without concern for others' judgements of it. He is his own moral master and answerable only to himself.

By commencing with certain assumptions and preconceptions, both Piaget and Kohlberg have misconceived the nature of moral development as centrally rational, rather than as rational *and* dispositional. In Kohlberg's view moral apprenticeship culminates when the individual forms the ability to think abstractly and to make generalizations, so it is fundamentally *intellectual* development which he has in mind. It is this which gives the individual the power to stand alone in working out his personal ethic. But there is no point in having a person *intellectually* equipped to stand alone if by that time he has to cast around for moral values: otherwise, proud of his newly-won independence of authority and convention, the autonomous individual might prefer a highly competitive egoism to any form of cooperation or consideration of others' interests. Kohlberg therefore includes, at the sixth stage, a value of respect for the individual, and it is this which supposedly gives to the morally educated the entitlement to rational *moral* autonomy.

But what is this 'autonomy' of which the empirical researchers speak? It is often assumed that reason is the guide to morality, that the man who is a law unto himself, disregarding others' interests, for instance, has simply lost rational self-mastery, and when he returns to reason he will return also to the moral way. As we have seen, that assumption leans heavily on a Kantian transcendental justification. Kant held as his fundamental principle of morality that we achieve an autonomy by which the will to action is determined by reason alone.

The Analytic of Pure Practical Reason, p.131). Sufficient has been said in Chapter 2 to refute any claim to a necessary connection between morality and rationality: rationality and an all-out egoism are not incompatible.

Similarly we may wonder whether the conjunction of 'moral' and 'autonomy' is a necessary one. Can we live morally without being autonomous, or be autonomous without being moral? Kant's use of autonomy had regard for the Greek derivative *autonomia*, a self-governing community, one whose law (nomos) was literally self-imposed. To him the person of good will was governed morally by pure reason as a kind of executive power. But in the literalizing of the metaphor of self-government serious difficulties arise, especially when the government is in the hands of a unitary force such as Reason: there are common deterministic arguments, for instance, of being unaware of the many possible influences on our behaviour, with the implication that reason is only one of them; there is the impracticability of having everyone in a society autonomous, if by that is conveyed the notion of everyone making his own laws to suit himself, for then the bases of both society and morality would be destroyed; there is the added impossibility of ever knowing that either we or others are autonomous, of being able to validate claims to autonomy, for which subjective or autobiographical statements would give no firm support; and there is the psychological considera-tion that a life of continual self-legislation, even if it were confined to moral matters alone, would be in practice intolerable, if not simply inconceivable.

If we shed from autonomy any implication of an inner power which enables self-legislation, we may still ask simply, and without metaphorical confusion, in what ways an autonomous, or indepen-dent, individual may be said to be independent in his moral decisions or judgements. It is only in a limited sense, and certainly not completely, that a person may be independent of others in his community; or independent of the law, or of external authority; or independent of the rules of social institutions or of social mores generally. He can never be independent of his central attitudes and values, his desires, motives, or intentions, independent of habit, or independent of his reason: all of these will play a part in his moral decisions or judgements. It would be contradictory to refer to a capacity to be independent of these components of his own self, for that would be to take away much of his individuality; so that it is only of certain external constraints or influences that we may speak sensibly of limited independence. Yet if a person may be said to be autonomous, or independent, in his practical morality (to the extent that he is true to his dispositional structure of ideas and ideals, beliefs and standards constituting his moral attitudes and values), and may be said to reason with a high degree of independence of external influences, any logical nexus between morality and autonomy still eludes us. It is clear that morality does not *make* a person autonomous, or independent, and autonomy or independence does not *make* a person moral. A person of clear moral values – oriented toward considering others' interests – may still be a slave to habit and tradition; another with a high degree of independence of external influences may have attitudes and values that are either immoral or a-moral, and these may exert a dominant influence in his rational-dispositional deliberations.

We conclude that morality and autonomy, or independence, draw close together only under conditions which permit relevant personality attributes, such as self-assurance and self-mastery, to combine harmoniously with moral dispositions and reason. While moral autonomy in a perfect sense is unattainable, we may recognize something of the limits of attainability if we interpret autonomy in the ordinary sense of relative independence of external influences, and practical morality as the interplay of reason with a dispositional structure of moral attitudes and values, which includes principles and rules in its cognitive core, beliefs, ideas and standards, all with affective support. Autonomy in the metaphorical sense of an inner government is misleading, since it implies that we have within us a hidden power which makes us do what we do, think what we think, decide what we decide, whether the inner force be pure reason, in Kant's sense, or inclination, or a composite of dispositions including our central attitudes and values. None of these govern us to the extent of *making* us moral, either in thought or deed. Morality is the outcome of reason interacting with our moral dispositions, especially our attitudes and values. Limited moral autonomy is achieved when we have sufficient self-understanding and determination to act independently, in appropriate moral situations, in accordance with our moral convictions, whose source is our moral attitudes and values. Moral autonomy has most application to the state of *authenticity*, where the individual is consistently true to his own moral attitudes and values, with sufficient courage, determination, self-mastery, imagination and moral enthusiasm to live up to them. As for the empirical research of Piaget and Kohlberg we find it misleading particularly for its assumption that moral education is in close relationship with the progressive development of reason, with rational autonomy as the culmination of a moral maturity, without acknowledging the dual significance, with reason, of the development of moral attitudes and values. With respect to reason, it is significant that some who link it with the autonomy metaphor of self-government acknowledge that reason is not alone, that there must be something for reason to relate to, something which we have referred to as attitudes and values with their associated cognitive components of ideas, beliefs, principles, rules and so forth, and that without this content the entire notion of autonomy as self-government would collapse.[35]

Methodology

At an appropriate phase in the development of children's rational powers, we believe that formal group discussion with peers is a necessary but not a sufficient method for optimum moral education during school years. We believe that without it, normally, children who are mature enough to reason will not develop their moral potentialities in adolescence, although some will compensate in other ways on leaving school. It is probable that only in very exceptional circumstances of suitable critical discussion occurring in the home will this not be the case. What is of the greatest importance is the probability that some, on leaving school, will never develop morally *without* such a programme, for reasons that lie both in the home and community environment, including the environment of the work place.

In the previous chapter we have given formal group discussion a rectifying function, helping participants to understand themselves better as inveterate intellectual habits are exposed sympathetically by others. In this respect all are equal and the aid is mutual. That perception helps to encourage contributions in the exchange of moral viewpoints, which are not secret or private but for public scrutiny, so that the illusions or distortions which are common to all of us may be gradually, though perhaps never completely, removed. Ideally the formal group discussion is an activity of self-discipline by all participants. Its purpose is moral also in its emphasis on integrity, on the exclusion of irrelevances, and – in a moral context – in the single-minded pursuit of the best moral solution to a problem or situation.

Respect for other persons extends to a willingness to learn from
others, a ready perception of merit in others' viewpoints once
cooperation replaces the common competitiveness of the classroom
It leads ideally also to an appreciation that a contrary viewpoint to
ours often helps us to see our own more clearly, and that many
individual and different viewpoints are often more useful to the
collective effort than similar viewpoints. The ideal situation in
discussion can be *approached* but not fully attained because of
contingent circumstances: some members may remain inhibited
others may be exhibitionist or disruptive, but attitudes of peers may
have a corrective influence. It is this peer influence which (given
sensitive discussion leadership) may be most beneficial in the learning
of moral attitudes and values, or in the modification of those which
have been subjected to adverse influences in unfortunate home and
neighbourhood environments.

We have described group discussions as formal, not to characterize
their leader-participant relations, but rather to distinguish them by
the formal qualities as we have presented them from other discus
sions in groups which are not characterized by integrity of purpose
group cohesiveness, and a moral basis of respect for persons. There
are, as we have noted, other means of eliciting the facts of a situation
or problem such as in debating the issues, in the adversary system of
the law – with counsel for the plaintiff and counsel for the defence –
and in conferences the presentation of a paper followed by its
defence. At their *worst*, each of these takes on the form of conten
tion; at their best competition remains and the underlying moral
structure of mutuality and respect is often wanting. For children in
particular, whose personalities are generally immature, there are
seeds of moral values in cooperative truth-seeking which one-sided
competitive procedures lack. In its ideal form the discussion proce
dure provides for moral education of both *reason* and of *attitudes and*
values in a practical engagement of the two, avoiding direct moral
instruction of any kind.

Content

Guiding Principles

Our main concern is still with children able to reason and to articulate
independent viewpoints. With this in mind we summarize the follow

ing principles governing content. First, in the education of teachers elementary courses in moral philosophy, sociology, and both individual and social psychology are needed, to be adapted by them – as discussion leaders – to the needs of the discussion situation. Second, selection of content areas must take account both of children's capacities and of relevance to their experiences. Third, in so far as moral education is aimed at improvement in an understanding of ourselves and of others, it needs to have proper regard for dispositional reasoning, or to reasoning influenced by desires, motives (with intentions), and attitudes and values; not merely to a supposed unitary force of reason. Fourth, children are to be guided towards values of rationality, referring especially to fact-finding, impartiality, respect for truth, and tolerance. Fifth, understanding is to be developed of individual liberties with the moral implications of their responsible exercise. Sixth, children are to be led to appreciate first, that some moral situations are of such a complex nature as to defy simple or summary solutions, demanding that they sit down like a jury, and in number of about original jury strength, and work things out together as equals; second, that the verdict or solution is likely to be better than the original opinion of any single member. Seventh, the distinction is to be clarified between moral values and situations and non-moral ones, thereby contributing to an understanding of morality. Eighth, as far as possible material for discussion is to be drawn from contemporary social issues or shared experiences, with a reconsideration of some of these in ever-widening complexity as maturity advances and experience widens.

Content Areas

The following content areas suggest themselves at once, though moral educators in touch with children's interests and experiences are to be free to select their own content in so far as it is devoid of indoctrinatory intention: rights and duties; the underprivileged; discrimination; moral obligations to sentient animals.

Under rights and duties liberty rights are of immediate relevance to senior adolescents in particular, as are questions of privacy and civil rights. The conflict between legal maturity on the one hand, and intellectual and moral maturity on the other, raises many questions of justice as fairness in the treatment of persons. Questions of distributive justice will be the main focus in the area of the underprivileged, with justice, morality and education in their formal senses providing fundamental criteria in discussions. Situations of discrimination also provide opportunities for fact-finding and for emotional control in discussion of such topics as employment prospects, housing, recreational and educational opportunities, and – as Mill noted in *The Subjection of Women*,[36] sex discrimination. In all these areas morality is to be learned as practical and actively self-involving, not an imposed code to be externally applied. In the fourth area – moral obligations to sentient animals – again there are opportunities for research and rational reflection on ascertained facts: on the nervous systems of higher and lower animals, for instance; on man's infliction of suffering on animals by exploitative farming,[37] including high-risk farming in areas prone to drought or flooding; and on the destruction of natural habitats. From reflection conflicts of interest become obvious, as well as the anthropocentricity of some of our attitudes and values relating to sentient animals. Moral sensitivity is sharpened as posturing and rationalizations are exposed.

At this point we must recognize procedural impracticalities in many schools which lack facilities for small-group discussions. This is both an administrative and a moral responsibility with relevance to the following section.

JUSTICE AND MORALITY IN EDUCATIONAL ADMINISTRATION

We shall consider aspects of justice and morality in this section in five topic areas: first, decision-making; second, leadership and communication; third, administrative presumption and the challenge to person; fourth, moral responsibilities of administrators, as in curriculum provisions; fifth, moral duty and prudence.

Decision-Making

As a basis for discussion of decision-making we shall set out three different action-schemas where the moral status differs one from the other, extending each for comparative purposes. The first is identical with the action schema already proposed, in which the dispositional and rational orientation toward action is entirely *moral* throughout

This must be regarded within administrative contexts as very exceptional, but still logically possible.

(i) Moral schema (a practical consideration of others' interests):
Desire – moral motive (or intention) with goal – moral attitudes and values – rational–dispositional deliberation – moral decision to act – action.

(ii) Administrative schema (considering institutional interests or goals):
Desire – non-moral motive (or intention) with goal – non-moral attitudes and values – rational–dispositional deliberation – decision to act – action.
(In this the goal is impersonal, such as a production target, or business efficiency, or optimum use of resources including human resources. The rational–dispositional deliberation is without the influence of moral attitudes and values.)

(iii) Administrative – moral schema (considering both individual and institutional interests or goals):
Desire – mixed motives (including intentions) with goals – mixed attitudes and values – rational–dispositional deliberations – decision – action.
(Here there is the possibility of conflict between different motives and between different goals. Tension can be expected between the moral and the non-moral in motives, attitudes and values.)

Depending upon the relative forces of the moral and the non-moral, in motives as well as in attitudes and values, various kinds of decision outcomes are possible. In (i), conflict would be avoided because the administration would be insisting that moral ends be pursued at any cost to institutional ends. Non-moral ends are suppressed. In (ii), conflict would be avoided because the administrator would be insisting on non-moral impersonal ends at any cost to moral ends. Moral ends are suppressed. But in (iii), conflict is unavoidable in most circumstances: the exceptions are first, the fortuitous situation of all personal and moral ends being fulfilled at no expense to administrative ends, such as efficiency; second, the situation of administrative ends being fulfilled *by means of* the fulfilment of personal ends. That is, by concentrating entirely on personal ends of individual satisfaction, the administrative ends take care of themselves: optimum effort and efficiency are achieved almost as by-products of personal fulfilment. In large organizations in particular this kind of union is very much an ideal, and still contingent in small organizations on personal compatibilities. The much more general situation is of personal rivalry and conflicting interpersonal motives and goals, and of individuals striving egoistically without more than token concern for others' welfare. Then decision-making and leadership merge, and the quality of leadership is related to the moral quality of the decisions that are taken by the leader as mediator or moderator, and when the occasion arises, as the supporter of some over others for advancement in the organization. In that situation, where there is more than one contender for a position and selection is necessary, the administrator cannot use entirely moral criteria in his deliberations. If he is to use a criterion of concern for others' interests, he is placed at once in the contradictory situation, in deciding on the most suitable candidate, of serving the interests of one and necessarily *not* serving the interests of some others. But at the same time he is a moral agent to some extent, despite the non-moral motives, attitudes and values which influence him toward a strong concern for institutional ends, and he is an agent of *justice* too. For in assuming the responsibility of choosing the most suitable person for a position, among a number where discrimination among them is difficult, he must be fair in his treatment of persons, consistent in his application of criteria, and with regard for equity in maintaining what he perceives as a proper balance or proportion among members of the organization. If, on the other hand, he allows himself to be influenced by nepotism, or yields to threats or irrelevant pressure, he is an agent neither of morality nor of justice, and will be so perceived by most subordinates. In terms of institutional efficiency his action then becomes self-defeating. Morale has often a moral core, and is usually most lasting when it has; but morale and morality in some circumstances are not directly related, as in factitious work-value claims which temporarily increase worker morale with prospects of excessive wage increases.

The administrator who is guided predominantly by *moral* attitudes and values in his decision-making is frequently in a state of conflict. Out of respect for persons, seeing others as individually striving toward personal goals, planning their lives as he has planned his, his deliberations incline him toward satisfying *their* goal-seeking as much as possible, inasmuch as it is not oriented toward harming others. He would have no great difficulty in meeting a situation when an individual had distinctly immoral motives, or intentions, such as in spreading false rumours to discredit other contenders for a promotion position. But in other cases the goals may be morally genuine yet unrealistic, and to promote them would have an irreparable impact on the morale and efficiency of the institution. In academic institutions there are possible economic considerations which are compelling, and running counter to moral considerations. In times of scarce resources financial constraints may pose administrative dilemmas: morality and justice may both be strained in decisions affecting the interests of staff members, and though of strong moral convictions the administrator may have no alternative to acting pragmatically and prudentially, with his own decisions morally irksome to him. Whenever institutional ends and moral ends are in conflict, a priority given to the first requires to be justified.

The administrator cannot escape decision-making. If he is so overwrought by conflict between moral and non-moral motives or intentions and values that he is rendered vacillating and indecisive, his inadequacy is apparent. He is morally inadequate too if in his dispositions he is predominantly self-regarding, fundamentally concerned with his own reputation rather than with decisions likely to satisfy personal staff ends or institutional ends. In a third sense he is morally inadequate as a decision-maker if staff members become merely means to impersonal ends of organizational efficiency. And in a fourth sense he is morally inadequate when rational-dispositional deliberations are allowed to be swayed by threatening but fundamentally irrational forces from within the institution. Some student activism in the last two decades has reflected a lack of moral education of the kind suggested in the preceding section, confronting ideals of scholarship and patient research with direct action of violence and intimidation.

The observation that egoism is just as rational as altruism or benevolence may be applied to the administrator as egoist, one who is neither a moral person nor a just one. A Nietzschean *will to power* is rational when viewed externally as a principle of life,[38] a determination to achieve total self-interest by crushing opposition by the swiftest and surest means available, including deception and intrigue; to be even cunningly creative in such devices, stamping on existing moral values, seizing power and influence by out-manoeuvering, out-witting every opposition. Nietzsche's *superman* proceeds from desire and motive to action, without rational-moral deliberations. In contrast, the Kantian unity of rationality and morality, with an acknowledgement of the capacity of rational persons of good will to exercise tolerance, compassion and imaginative insight, provides a moral basis of individual participation in committee deliberations, with mutual respect and rejection of individualistic dominance. But the authentic morality of administrators is put to the practical test in the nature and extent of their actual cooperative decision-making: the morality of some may prove to be a superficial facade to disguise self-regarding control of authority and responsibility. In large bureaucratic departments or offices of education a common observation is that delegation of decision-making may be no more than paternalistic inducements to subordinates, with those in the highest hierarchical positions reserving for themselves the right to make far-reaching policy decisions, those in the middle of the hierarchical structure entrusted with procedural decisions; and those lowest in the order left to make decisions which are routine and can in no way affect the direction of the organization as a whole. Status and quality of ideas in decision-making may correlate very poorly.

Leadership and Communication

The administrator is often best judged as a moral leader by his style of communicating with other members of his organization. If he is predominantly self-regarding, jealous of his authority and protective of his status, he may withhold information to impress others, or to make them feel inferior. If he creates an atmosphere of fear or anxiety, rather than of mutual respect and understanding, he may achieve the kind of response to his communications that he seeks, inasmuch as it is conducive to a distancing of himself from others; but in other respects the communication may be self-inhibiting inasmuch as its reception is half-hearted and its retention by others short-lived. Formal communication downward to subordinates is demeaning to individuals as persons, tending to reinforce authority structures. Where relations between leaders and subordinates are distant, without mutual trust, the flow of communication is not free; from subordinates it is forced, undertaken only as a last resort. A free flow of communication between superordinates and subordinates is an indication of a mutuality of respect. While we have focussed on the moral motives, and the moral attitudes and values of *leaders*, those of subordinates must be expected to share some of their imperfections. When communication is horizontal and informal, based on an assumption of equality, in a *prima facie* sense there are optimum conditions for personal satisfaction, unity and cohesiveness; but immoral motives, immoral attitudes and values, self-regarding among subordinates no less than among leaders, may produce a deliberately false communication to serve individual or sectional ends. The assumption that immorality is confined to leaders is a false one. Moral responsibility is as reciprocal as the free flow of communication.

In order to share decision-making as widely as possible, the leader again acts as a moral agent when he organizes committees, trusting members to handle a problem delegated to them, not attempting to override or influence their judgements, and certainly not intruding into their deliberations with an authoritative judgement of his own. Part of the leader's communication in such situations is to define the problem clearly and to remove possible ambiguities, to provide access to all relevant information, some of which he may have accumulated and jealously classified as confidential. Nothing can serve the leader better than authentic respect for persons; nothing worse than paternalism and posturing.

Administrative Presumptions and the Challenge to Person

To Montaigne, presumption 'is our natural and original disease'[39], and it is not too much to say that its manifestations in administrative situations are very extensive. The literal accomplishment of empathy can be no more than approximate, but there are no instruments by which to measure its proximity to another's *actual* state of mind. What is more evident to observers, at times, is how far some are from understanding others, some who presume to know them, to be in a position to penetrate and to evaluate them, to compare them with others who have been similarly understood with assurance and (groundless) indubitability. The presumption is to be found in those in either subordinate or superordinate positions, though there is some evidence to suggest that the affliction is apt to increase in the latter as they achieve goals of higher status and influence over others. From a perspective of moral sensitivity, presumption in evaluating others is in every instance a challenge to personhood. We shall consider its incidence first, in the evaluation of teachers; second in judgements made on persons within some universities, such as in selection and promotion procedures. In those countries where school inspectors or supervisors report on teachers' efficiency or suitability for promotion, keeping dossiers that can be used for or against teachers, personal perceptions weigh heavily, with their biases, preconceptions and subjective impressions. Some regard it as presumptuous for anyone to undertake the task, especially in making judgements over a short period of time, and in abnormal rather than regular situations when the visiting observer threatens through a known capacity to influence teachers' careers by his determinations. Staff cohesiveness tends to be disrupted by the element of chance in success, the gains occasionally made by opportunists who are dutiful in observing expectations; and conversely the occasional failures by others who refuse to be theatrical, or with moral revulsion do not perform at their best. Frank professional exchanges are difficult in such circumstances: communication is often inauthentic, tense and distanced. If there is presumption among some inspectors and supervisors that they have unique powers of perception, the capacity to see things which ordinary teachers are not able to see, it is ironically discredited from the perspective of teachers in daily contact with colleagues over a much longer period. It is the presumptuous ones whose attitudes and values are in question, and whose capacity for empathy is especially limited. But again, morality and justice, in their opposites, are two facets of the one situation. What is unjust is the fundamental failure of fairness in the treatment of persons, making evaluations of other human beings which by their nature cannot be made with sufficient validity and reliability. The criteria of teacher effectiveness are still unclear, except in superficial respects. The impact which a teacher of moral quality may make on the moral attitudes and values of children and adolescents, by his own personal example, his fairness, interest, willingness to help others, his sensitivity and understanding of others, is progressive, and there are no techniques available to inspectors and supervisors by which to measure it. Although there may be agreed assessment criteria, these are formal in character, and are given substance in a variety of ways. The personalities of teachers, though these may be excluded from agreed evaluative criteria, do influence evaluators, and again influence them in different ways.

Lack of respect for teachers as persons is evident also in accountability procedures.[40] These are demeaning of teachers inasmuch as they attribute responsibility to teachers for children's achievements which are properly a shared responsibility, among teachers, parents and children themselves. But their most significant moral and educational defect is that they are based on a fundamental misunderstanding of education, which is a developing of various powers or potentialities, consistent with social values. Accountability tests miss the important yet tangible achievements in moral attitudes and values. They tend to reduce the teacher and the child to technological instruments, the teacher inserting into a child – as into a machine – testable pieces of information or simple measurable skills, while overlooking other teacher accomplishments flowing from moral and intellectual relationships between teacher and child, and which are continuous processes, never reducible to mechanical teaching and testing of specifics.

In some universities the presumption of members of academic committees, at their worst, formed to select new staff members or to select those suitable for promotion, is apt to violate the high ideals of the liberal mind which Newman and others have attributed to a university training, especially in objectivity, impartiality and clear-thinking – ironically exhibiting summary and superficial judgements without supporting reasons, sometimes swayed by subjective impressions of personalities, disregarding important evidence, and with a democratic mix of laymen and academics giving some weight to uninformed opinion, against a background of inadequate representation of persons informed in the candidate's own field. Promotions Committees at their worst may function with similar presumption, composed of academics standing high in the hierarchical order of the institution, apt to have a misplaced assurance of judgement born of status and influence, again ironically disregarding principles of objectivity which they espouse in their respective disciplines and in research, as they rely on summary impressions formed during short interviews, together with relevant but sometimes biased documentation. Contempt for person, rather than respect, is evident also when administrators misconstrue personality differences among committee members, confusing reticence with obtuseness and volubility with perspicacity; in presuming to know more of others' specialized fields than they know themselves, merely by virtue of administrative control over them; in academic dispute yielding to prudential institutional protection, even when a dispute has to be settled in ways contrary to reason, evidence and morality; in denigrating another's discipline and presuming to make informed judgements on it; in the allocation of resources, presuming to judge some faculties, schools or departments as more important than others; at all times, in pursuing personal aggrandizement before attending to the interests of others.

Other Moral Responsibilities of Administrators

Our concerns have been primarily with the moral failure of some with administrative functions in education to respect the persons of others whom they presume to have the capacity to judge. Apart from the failure to perceive others as persons, with desires, motives, goals, attitudes and values of their own, and to insist on justice as well as morality by fair and equitable administrative procedures rather than summary ones (which may be neither valid nor reliable), there are other moral failures in educational administration to which we shall briefly refer. We must be clear at the outset that moral perfection is unattainable, that between moral ideals and administrative practicalities there will always be tension to some degree, just as in practical morality in our individual lives we require consistent effort to reduce the balance of egoism over benevolence which is characteristic of most moral conduct. It is an ideal for instance that effective leadership unites the need-satisfactions of individuals with institutional goals. In practice there are many tensions, and many conflicts. Openness in communication, with an accord of mutuality and trust between leader and subordinates, is an ideal: in practice, and for a variety of reasons, confidentiality is unavoidable. Rationality is itself an ideal: administrative practice necessarily falls short of it. We can nonetheless observe moral failures in administrative responsibility which are difficult to justify simply on grounds of human imperfection. Serious misfits may occur in staff recruitment even for senior positions, because an academic administrator in another institution is prepared to put his own motives before integrity in forwarding a false testimonial. It is because selection committees are unable to ascertain enough about the dispositions of candidates, as well as their academic qualities, that a relationship of trust among universities is needed, but sometimes broken. Administrative motives and goals are similarly in conflict with morality when non-moral goals assert themselves, a goal of high First Year enrolments for instance, to sustain a suitable staffing level, regardless of the quality of all entrants and the consequences for those who eventually fail in their courses. In such ways students become merely means to administrative ends.

It is in the area of curriculum provisions that the educational administrator responsible for the provision of formal schooling has the heaviest moral and educational responsibility. Since the curriculum provided in the schools is the framework for the fulfilment of educational purposes, it is in contempt of the morality of considering children's interests to fail to make adequate provision for their continuing development. It is similarly immoral to regard them merely as means to other ends such as national ends, in insisting for instance that all secondary students – regardless of ability – undertake a rigorous course in mathematics and science, or in technology, to satisfy the needs of the nation in the future. If he is a moral agent, there is only one course open to the educational administrator concerned with schooling, including the administrator as policy-maker, and that is simply to provide all the facilities and resources required for developing the potentialities of all the children, reducing, as far as possible, *inequalities of educational opportunity* which may be socially-based, providing for the underprivileged as well as for the privileged, the handicapped as well as the normal. Justice demands fair treatment for all and neglect of none. The primary educational ends are not national ends but individual ends, the developing of unique sets of potentialities. Even the provision of small discussion or seminar rooms which we believe to be necessary for moral education in the school, especially in adolescence, is a moral responsibility of administrators, as is the recruitment and preparation of suitable teachers for the purpose.

Moral Duty and Prudence

We shall end this section on Justice and Morality in Educational Administration by referring to questions of duty and prudence. Between these two, as we have observed in Chapter 2, there is not always a clear-cut distinction, but in some administrative situations there is, and where moral duty may demand moral action, it is prudence that reflects a moral failure, and a failure to act. The Vice-Chancellor, Headmaster or Principal who yields to self-regarding impulses in protecting his own personal reputation and that of the institution with which he identifies, rather than responding to a moral duty with respect to serious staff misconduct, for instance, demonstrates to others his lapse from morality and from justice, and every such failure has its impact on the moral ethos of the institution. In other cases situational complications may warrant the administrator regarding moral duties as *prima facie* duties only, in Ross's sense, with the impossibility of ascertaining fully all the relevant facts, which – if they were ascertainable – would lead to perfect duty. The onus is on the administrator to remove suspicions of acting prudently by justifying to all concerned his view of the *prima facie* nature of moral duty as it pertains to a particular situation.

Moral duty is often a matter for careful deliberation. To pursue duty for duty's sake is usually a matter of an administrator resorting to rule-following according to an official prescription of his duties. To give absolute obedience, as a duty, to another, is to surrender liberty of thought and expression. To consider moral duty as a matter of fulfilling various commitments according to institutional or external expectations is not to assume the role of an independent moral agent. The *right* course of conduct has usually to be worked out in the light of accepted moral principles and a patient investigation of facts relevant to the case. Educational administrators are generally not chosen specifically for moral attitudes and values, for any indications of moral motives, for moral understanding or sensitivity: if they have these characteristics they are usually revealed after selection, and in these respects selection is fortuitous. For their moral background they may be ill-equipped to make moral decisions: intellectual suitability alone can lead to the princely drive for power and status that Machiavelli described,[41] or a posturing approachability whose purpose is manipulation, or a regard for others' interests that is not genuine but turned reflexively to self-regard. It is easy to pick up the forms and outward signs of moral conduct, leaving the administrator's moral attitudes and values threadbare: his acts of convenience and expediency condemn themselves when there are moral issues at stake. By contrast, the administrator of an institution who has voluntarily assumed a moral relationship with all staff members on taking office, finds unambiguous moral duty *obligatory*. Prudence is not involved in every instance of an administrator considering his own interests; in some circumstances practical morality requires that we do not neglect our own intersts. Prudence is expressed when he disregards obvious and uncomplicated moral imperatives, such as to tell the truth in favour of imperfect duties of mere inclination, in the Kantian sense, in the protection of personal reputation.

SUMMARY

We shall not review in detail the four separate areas in this chapter in which we have considered justice, morality and education in practical perspectives, but shall draw together some of the major emphases only. Though there are connections between and among the topic reas, such as in our dispositional reasoning, some of the content is isparate and relevant to the respective sections.

On *Rights and Duties in Education* a necessary distinction is drawn etween young children at a pre-reasoning state who are unable to nderstand the meaning of education as a developing of potentialities nd therefore unable to assert or claim a right to education, and older hildren still at school, especially senior adolescents, who *can*; though ifficulties remain with respect to moral development which does not lways keep pace with intellectual development. Some senior adolescents, at least, are acknowledged as having undoubted capacity to xercise legal rights, and the arbitrary age threshold for legal dulthood is in tension with fundamental notions of justice and iorality for failing to give them the respect they deserve as persons. eachers' negligence in the proper care of children at school falls nder both legal justice and moral justice. Just as teachers have a ioral duty to children, parents and to the community in this regard, o the courts have a duty to ensure that teachers are justly treated in he proper establishment of negligence. Parents cannot deputize for hildren in claiming a right to education on their behalf: rights are to e claimable and assertable by their owners within a moral-rational ommunity of two-way relationships. But parents are generally onceded to have liberty rights with respect to their children: the arents' own right to send their children to a particular school on rounds of 'conscience' or personal belief. This right becomes uestionable as soon as children are sufficiently mature intellectually nd morally to develop their own personal beliefs.

In *Justice, Morality and Punishment* the general purpose and ustification of punishment is considered, especially from retributivist nd consequentialist perspectives. The retributivist viewpoint that ociety should insist on offenders being punished to repay a debt with lignity, and punished according to desert, raises the practical difficul-y of fair assessments in each case. Consequentialists are divided ccording to whether the impulse for punishment comes from notives of reform, of deterrence, or from utilitarian considerations. Reformists face the difficulty of justifying the consequences as eflecting lasting change in moral outlook, for the consequences bserved are usually those occurring very soon after the punishment. Deterrent consequentialists incur the moral fault of regarding offen-lers as merely means to others' ends, while utilitarians raise ques-ions of disregarding the interests of offenders as long as total atisfaction of a group is increased by the punishment; each of these violates the fundamental, formal notion of morality. The purpose and justification of punishing children at school is subject to similar criticisms, exceptions being made in the case of very young children unable to understand the *reasons* for rules of behaviour. Punishment of children, especially adolescents, who *are* able to reason, i generally pragmatic. It is difficult to justify any consequentialist view of punishment, since consequences, except occasionally with very young children, and then as a last resort, are generally not beneficial. The onus must be on punishers to justify punishment as *necessary*, in the child's best interests.

Justice, Morality and Moral Education draws attention to the importance of attitudes and values in moral education, to the centrality of attitudes and values in our dispositions, for their cognitive complexity, habitual character and relative stability and durability. The importance of habit has been emphasized at the pre-rational level, but under-valued – with respect to our moral attitudes and values – subsequently. The perverse side of habituation is indoctrination, with children used merely as means to an indoctrinator's ends, so that not only is the truth status of beliefs morally questionable in acts of indoctrination, but so also are the motives of intentions of the indoctrinator. Moral attitudes and values appear to have been under-valued as well in the assumptions underlying the research of Piaget and Kohlberg, both of whom had rational ends for moral education. Autonomy appears to be best justified when it applies to individual *authenticity* rather than to a presumed independence of influences, whether external or from within: authenticity in the sense of being true to moral attitudes and values, with sufficient courage and determinatioin to act on them after appropriate deliberation. For most children able to rēason, especially in adolescence the formal discussion technique is believed to be a necessary but not a sufficient means to moral development during school years. In content, again for senior school students, prominent social issues with clear moral relevance are proposed, providing opportunities to develop moral attitudes and values with an informed cognitive core as well as confidence in standing alone as moral agents.

In *Justice and Morality in Educational Administration* consideration is given to decision-making, leadership and communication administrative presumption and the challenge to person, and the moral responsibilities of administrators, with respect to curriculum provisions especially. An administrative–moral schema with mixed moral and non-moral motives, attitudes and values, shows the

ossibility that the administrator as leader will be in a state of
requent conflict. The presumption of administrators in evaluating
thers, often on insufficient evidence, sometimes exhibits both a lack
f perspicacity and of self-criticism, and a moral insensitivity. Admi-
istrators are morally ill-equipped for their task when they act on
rudence and fail to perceive the obligatoriness of moral duty in clear
nd unambiguous circumstances.

Our study of administrators and their responsibilities in education
s incomplete. We have in fact stopped short of the heaviest moral
esponsibilities of all by concerning ourselves with institutions and
he government bureaucracies which control some of their functions.
Beyond these there are the policy-makers and the ultimate distribu-
ors of resources: members of government constituting the *state*.
Distributive injustices cannot be levelled at bureaucratic officials who
ave inadequate resources to distribute. Inequality of educational
pportunity is beyond the power of teachers, headmasters or princip-
ls, and departmental officials themselves to rectify. From the
ractical applications of justice, morality and education in this
hapter, when we have already considered some questions of social
ustice in family and school contexts, we enter the wider field of social
ustice in Part III when we consider relations between the individual
nd the state. We carry forward a confidence that the formal notions
vith which we began have served us well as responsive touchstones:
he practical applications we have selected have demonstrated their
undamental relevance. They may also have served to increase our
noral sensitivity in questions of justice and education as a prepara-
on for the increasingly more complex questions now to be faced
vhen we consider the individual in relation to the state.

PART III
Social Justice:
State–Individual Relations

6 Philosophical Perspectives

The purpose of this chapter is to develop a resource of ideas on social justice from traditional and contemporary thought to serve as clear but *substantive* references in Chapters 7 and 8 in much the same way as the fundamental ideas of justice, morality and education have functioned as *formal* references after their initial formulation. The latter have given continuity; the former will provide contrast.

In the previous chapter we considered education as a provision by the state, and the expectation of parents that the state provide, and provide adequately, for their children. We have noted a liberty right claimed by parents against the state, to send their children to schools of their choice on grounds of personal belief. We have noted too that the state has sometimes attempted to hold teachers accountable for efficiency of children's basic learning, measured by results. That suggests that the state has power over the individual, as the earlier instance suggests that it is rather the servant of the people, amenable to their expectations, or to social values. These are some of the relations between state and individuals already foreshadowed. Further, in Chapter 3 we considered the right to education, and the obligations of governments to provide at least an elementary education for all children. We have noted these as moral recommendations, standards for all civilized peoples. Since morality has its basis in a practical consideration of others' interests, there are far-reaching moral obligations on those in government to consider the interests of individuals which, through education, may make or mar their futures. A polar opposition in social philosophy is between those on the one hand who are gravely apprehensive of conceding to the state a power over the individual and his *liberties*, advocating a strict curtailment of state authority; and those on the other hand who are prepared to put their trust in the state as a universal provider, with unlimited powers over the individual, supposedly in the interests of all.

This is too sweeping a view however, to characterize specific philosophical perspectives on social justice, such as in viewpoints on state–individual relations. We shall therefore turn to a comparative method which highlights, by contrast, what appear to be antithetical

standpoints. This approach involves a degree of simplification of
individual thinkers without distorting either their major emphases or
the general plan for the chapter, inasmuch as it leads to further
considerations of social justice in the succeeding chapters. In our
simplified approach we present three groups of philosophical viewpoints on social justice: first, those of Hobbes, Locke and Nozick;
second, those of Plato, Rousseau, Kant and Rawls; third, those of
Humboldt and Mill. The dominant emphasis of the first group is the
preservation of self-interest; of the second, a consideration of the
interests of all social members; while the third group represents a
mid-position where both self-interest and the interests of others are
considered, but where again there is deep concern for the power of
the state in overriding individual liberties.

Social and political ideas are as inert as Hume's notion of reason in
practical deliberations if they are conceived merely in the abstract.
By relating ideas to the concreteness of time and circumstance we aim
further to put to rest the persistent dogma that certain social and
political values or preferences are either true or false. In the process
there may develop a more tolerant understanding of the nature of
judgements on social justice.

PHILOSOPHERS WITH A DOMINANT SELF-INTEREST

Hobbes: *Leviathan*

Hobbes was not concerned with fundamental morality as a practical
consideration of others' interests, or with education as a developing
of individual potentialities consistent with social values. His fundamental concern was for his own interests. Social justice was to him
a matter of the state having only so much power and influence over
the individual as was needed to guarantee individual security. It was
self-interest that counted above all else.

Hobbes admitted that his major work *Leviathan* was 'occasioned
by the disorders of the present time' (p.728).[1] It was these that gave
him an excessive concern for personal life and limb which precluded a
wider focus on human societies in general. His views on justice and
morality were expressions of his conviction that all men pursue
self-interest. Consideration of others' interests was to him not a
significant issue in practical living, or fairness in the treatment of
persons. The fundamental task in managing one's own affairs, or in

managing the affairs of the nation, was to understand human nature and its preoccupation with self-interest.

Human Nature, Power and Sovereignty

Hobbes' argument from human nature led him from desire, to power, to conflict, to the need to transfer individual power to a sovereign power for the common good. Desires and their opposites, aversions, cover a range of inclinations – pleasures of sense, pleasures of the mind, and passions included. When a person refers to something as *good*, he means no more than that it is the object of his appetite or desire (p.120). Benevolence is recorded merely as one of the many simple passions which some may experience (p.123). When we deliberate, we are moved by appetites or desires, and by aversions, to consider the consequences of actions (p.129). We all have a compelling urge to satisfy our appetites or desires. The next step in his argument is that it is characteristic of each of us to strive toward some degree of *power*, which is our means 'to obtain some future apparent Good' – for ourselves individually (ch. X, Part I, p.150). The value of every man is no more than his *price*: he is worth whatever 'would be given for the use of his Power' (p.151). Men differ in their natural endowments, as well as in riches, reputation and friends, and it is these, or the balance of these over what others possess, which accounts for the power of any individual. But since all men are alike inasmuch as they seek power, conflict among them is inevitable, and the situation is aggravated by the fact that some desires are almost unlimited. The 'perpetuall and restlesse desire of Power', ceasing only in death (ch. 11, p.161), with its constant competitive struggle among men, is a danger to every individual in society, and there is therefore a need to obey a *common* power. Those who desire leisure to pursue knowledge and the 'arts of peace' certainly seek protection from the power of other individuals (p.162). Those who fear oppression, or injury or death, seek similar protection.

The argument for transferring power to a common power, for the sake of individual peace of mind and bodily protection, gives way then to an argument, leading to a similar conclusion, from a state of nature. He begins (ch. XIII) by asserting that men are by nature equal, qualifying himself with the observation that differences among men in body and mind are not appreciable. All have prudence, for instance, and all learn it equally from experience, given equal time (p.183). Each man too has a *Right to Nature*, a liberty to use his own power 'for the preservation of his own Nature' (ch. XIV, p.189). Hobbes then introduces two 'fundamental laws of nature', as he calls them. The first is 'to seek Peace, and follow it', and 'by all means we can, to defend our selves'. The second is to lay down the right to all things which a man would have if still uncivilized, in a state of nature, and to 'be contented with so much liberty against other men, as he would allow other men against himself' (p.190). The transferring of a right is a *contract*. The third law of nature he calls *justice*, which refers to the faithful keeping of covenants made (ch. XV, pp.201–2).

Hobbes refers to the Aristotelian concepts of justice, in the commutative and the distributive, in the context of his earlier assertion that 'the Value or Worth of a man, is as of all other things, his Price' (ch. 10, p.151). Commutative justice he acknowledges as the equality of value of the things contracted for; distributive justice as the distribution of equal benefit to those of equal merit (ch.15, p.208). But when he reflects on man as a market commodity, with his own price, he considers that his value, like the value of other commodities, depends on what contractors are contented to give, influenced by their appetite or desire, so commutative justice is the justice of the contractor. Distributive justice is more properly equity, giving every man his due, and this is another law of nature, that whoever judges between man and man 'deale Equally between them' (ch.15, p.212).

Hobbes speaks of the right to perform any act as an *authority*. No man is obliged to adhere to a covenant unless he freely enters into it himself. It is reasonable that men should voluntarily give up their individual 'rights of nature', or their liberty, to exercise their own power, and in the common good yield it to a sovereign power (ch.18, p.238). The liberty of the individual lies in being able to do, without hindrance from anyone, what he has the will, desire or inclination to do (ch.21, p.262). But as the subject of a sovereign power he is obliged to obey as long as, and only as long as, he is given protection (p.272). Self-interest predominates in all relations among men. The sovereign power may be one man, as in a monarchy; or an assembly of men, as in a democracy, or aristocracy. Laws of nature consist in equity, justice, gratitude and other moral virtues which themselves dispose men to peace and obedience, but they are not enough in themselves. Civil laws as the ordinances of a sovereign power are needed, as well as punishments for disobedience to the laws: indeed the purpose of making laws is to impose a restraint on individuals, without which peace is impossible (ch.26, p.315). All unwritten laws are regarded as laws of nature. Hobbes now extends his notion of justice: it is more than what he said it is earlier, the keeping of covenants. In legal justice he sees the possibility of fairness and equity inasmuch as he acknowledges that judges may err in their decisions and therefore are not obliged to be consistent subsequently in a similar case: 'no man's error becomes his own law'; and 'no Injustice can be a pattern of Judgement to succeeding Judges' (pp.323, 324). While *right* is *liberty*, civil law is an *obligation* (p.334). In these respects he is registering his acquaintance with the law of his time.

Contemporary Relevance and Limitations

What is the contemporary relevance of Hobbes to questions of social justice? From our perspective he may appear narrow in his perception of individual relations in society, but he can never be accused of dishonesty or inconsistency. He interpreted exactly what he saw in the selfish middle-class society that had emerged in England, with its evident materialist interests, and its increasing influence against the privilege of the aristocracy. Hobbes was frank, forthright, impartial and discerning. His interpretation stems from his perception of the centrality of *self-interest* in the society he knew. In the much more complex industrialized societies of to-day, many of his observations are pertinent. The society he depicted, fundamentally selfish in outlook, given to individualistic desires and goal-seeking, obeying laws, keeping contracts, accepting formal duties and obligations, had limited scope for social cohesion except in times of national danger, and that, some believe, is not markedly different from our contemporary situation. But this is to justify the *is*, not the *ought*. Hobbes' account of individuals impelled by appetite or desire was basically an account of an a-moral society, where people unashamedly had obligations to civil laws and duties of justice in keeping covenants, but were neither moral nor just in outlook according to our understanding of these notions. They subscribed not to morality, but to *prudence*. Though Hobbes acknowledged equity in the tradition of the law, *justice* was not an integral part of the society he described. Though he recognized in 'natural law' certain moral virtues, they were perceived as useful for their consequences in disposing men to peace and obedience, and *morality* was not an integral part of the society he described. What kind of respect for persons was invoked in his notion of the equality of men, each free to set his own price for giving up some of his power in return for the protection and security he craved! Yet Hobbes was going much further than our advocacy, in Chapter 2, that we need to *take account*, in our moral prescriptions, of whatever we find to be the case. His purpose was scientific throughout, not normative: to explain and justify a system of government tied firmly to the realities he knew; to depend on the workable, always in the interests of prudence. His philosophical weakness was in failing to apply his own distinction between philosophy and prudence: in confining himself too much to his own experience, and the tensions and fears of his own times, rather than reaching out to comprehend all societies, to move closer to the 'general, eternal, and immutable Truth' of universal generalizations (ch. XLVI, p.682). While he was a close observer of the social scene of his time, his was a one-dimensional view, lacking a perspective of social justice based on morality.

Locke: *Second Treatise of Government*

Locke was influenced by Hobbes' notion of the need for people to come together, in a state of nature, for their personal security and the protection of their property. This was the basis of his contract theory of government: an agreement between the people and the rulers – the former giving up some of their power *as individuals* to a ruler or sovereign power, who would in turn guarantee them what they wanted most of all – personal security and protection of property. Fundamentally Locke's primary concern was as much *self-interest* as was Hobbes'. Like Hobbes he was familiar with the law of his time, and so gave formal recognition to the need for equity and non-discrimination.

Human Nature and Natural Rights

On human nature Locke was as unromantic as Hobbes: as is evident in a state of nature, men are competitive, warring, untrustworthy, driven by fundamental self-interest to achieve their desires by violence if necessary; for though there is reason in the state of nature, here is no common judge with authority to settle disputes, 'no appeal on earth to right them'. The need for 'quitting the state of nature' is therefore obvious (*Second Treatise of Government*, ch. III, 19–21, pp.348–50).[2] Hobbes' notion of man's natural right to self-preservation was conveyed by Locke as a natural right 'to preserve his property, that is, his life, liberty and estate, against the injuries and attempts of other men' (ch. VII, 87, p.387). He had devoted a previous chapter to the theme of *property*, and the need to protect it: and, he asserted, was a gift to the industrious and the rational (ch. V, 34, p.357); a man's labour, what he does with land, puts a value on it (40, p.361). Indeed, in a state of nature it is labour which gives a right of property (45, p.364). Freedom is a natural right, and the notion of equality has application only to this equal right to natural freedom, for in fact there are substantial differences among individuals, and some are superior to others by nature (ch. VI, 54, pp.368–9). So the protection of life, liberty and estate (or possessions) concerns everyone. He agreed with Hobbes that prior to a social contract this protection cannot be assured, though Hobbes had not, as Locke had, argued for a natural claim to property, a claim that could be made in a state of nature.

The Social Contract

The notion of a social contract was introduced from the realisation that life, liberty and estate – all comprising man's 'property' – could not be adequately preserved in a state of nature, which then had to give way to civil society. In this transition the characteristic feature was that the individual gave up the power he had by nature to protect that property, resigning it to the community or the political society. Then everyone was united under 'a common established law and judicature to appeal to' (ch. VII, 87, p. 388). A community is formed, he explains, by the will and determination of the majority; everyone who so unites in a community gives up all the power the majority need to carry out their functions of civil government (ch. VIII, 96, 99, pp.395–6). Nothing can make a man a member of the independent community which he calls the 'common-wealth', though referring to no specific form of government (ch. X, 133, p.416), but an act of consent, a *social contract*, an 'express promise and compact' (ch. VIII, 122, p.411). He re-iterates that 'the great and chief end' in the formation of such common-wealths by social contract is the preserva-

tion of property (ch. IX, 124, p.412). The powers he gives up (again
echoing Hobbes) are first, the power needed for self-preservation,
which in the common-wealth is safeguarded by laws; second, the
power of punishing by using his 'natural force' (ch. IX, 129, p.413).
Political power is also given up: by the social contract this power the
individual has in a state of nature is handed over to the governors of
the society, those with executive power, with a tacit trust that it will
be used entirely for the common good (ch. XV, 171, p.441). When
despotic power is exercised there is a clear forfeiture of the individual's power 'to lords for their own benefit' (ch. XV, 173, pp.442–
3).

Nature and Purpose of Government

On the nature and purpose of government the main lines are already
drawn in so far as they relate to the social contract. Thus as Hobbes
had also explained, laws are necessary to protect men's liberty, to
give them freedom from others' violence, and freedom in the
enjoyment of their own property rather than subjection to another's
arbitrary will (ch. VI, 57, p.370). It is his concern for property which
in large measure turns Locke away from the option of absolute
monarchy and toward a form of constitutional government: absolute
monarchy is 'inconsistent with civil society' (ch. VII, 90, p.390). In a
common-wealth no one in power has a right to deprive a man of any
part of his property without his consent, but this is an ever present
danger when power is vested in one man, as in absolute monarchies,
for then the arbitrary seizure of a citizen's property for personal
advantage is always possible (ch. XI, 138, p.421). Certain conditions
apply regardless of the *form* of government, and flow partly from the
social contract: people are to be governed by 'promulgated established laws', with consistency in application, applying to all alike
without discrimination; the purpose of government is entirely the
good of the people; taxes are not to be raised on property without the
people's consent; the legislative body is not to transfer its proper
functions of making laws to anybody else or to any place other than
that recognized by the people (ch. XII, 142, pp.423–4). When the
social contract is broken by the legislative body, inasmuch as it
assumes arbitrary powers over the lives of the people and so breaks
its trust with them, the people have the right to choose a new
government for their own safety and security (ch. XIX, 222, pp.

69–71). Small mistakes can be tolerated, but not a succession of abuses: it is these that justify revolution (ch. XIX, 225, p.472). Locke concludes his *Second Treatise of Government* with a veiled reminder of the dangers of absolute monarchy: the power to change governments when necessary must be retained by the people (ch. XIX, 243, p.485).

Justice and Morality

Locke's preference for constitutional government was distinct from Hobbes' preference for monarchy, yet it is doubtful if considerations of justice directed this preference. Locke emerges strongly as a man of prudence, as Hobbes was. The self-interest each saw in others was dominant in himself: in Locke's case it was an ever-present concern for his 'estate' in particular, as well as for life and liberty. Yet justice as fairness in the treatment of persons was at least a formal acknowledgement, for the conditions he imposed on the legislative power of every common-wealth was that it should make one rule for rich and poor alike, court favourites and farm labourers (ch. XII, 142, pp.423–4). Again, it may have been acquaintance with the legal concept of equity which prompted a formal acknowledgement that laws are sometimes imperfect, that they cannot be expected to cover all possible contingencies, and that power should be given to rulers to mitigate the severity of the law in particular circumstances: 'therefore there is a latitude left to the executive power, to do many things of choice which the laws do not prescribe' (ch. XIV, 160, p.435). Hobbes had made a similar point in *Leviathan* (Part II, ch.26, p.323). As for morality, though Locke speaks formally of the common good, it is very doubtful if he was any more impelled by considerations of benevolence than was Hobbes, and the views of each on moral standards are again similar. In *An Essay Concerning Human Understanding* Locke explains that 'things are good or evil only in reference to pleasure and pain' (Book II, ch. XX, 2, p.231).[3] That which we call 'good' is apt to cause or increase pleasure, or diminish pain; what we call evil is apt to produce or increase pain, or diminish pleasure. Pleasure and pain, and the good and evil that cause them, are 'the hinges on which our passions turn', which he then proceeds to define separately. Hobbes had given a similar account of the relationship between desire and good (*Leviathan*, Part 1, Ch. 6).

As a man of prudence, like Hobbes, rather than of moral princi
ples, Locke thought it was not the function of society to distribute
resources equitably but rather to protect what everyone had gained
for himself, chiefly by his own efforts. Rich and poor might be bound
by the same law, but it was not a *moral* law which sought to ease the
burdens of the poor or the disadvantaged, or in any way to express
benevolence in practical terms of distributive justice. Politically, life
was still uncertain: the Glorious Revolution had just occurred
vindicating some of Locke's views on government, but the final
outcome was still unclear. For both Hobbes and Locke the observa
tion of man's preoccupation with self-interest was also a personal
value. Locke's advocacy of morality in *Some Thoughts Concerning
Education*[4] contrasted with his general lack of moral concern in hi
ideas of government. In this essay he was partly prescriptive, cautious
still not to exceed what was practicable. Virtue has its foundation, he
asserted here, in a man's ability 'to *deny himself* his own Desires
cross his own Inclinations and purely follow what Reason directs as
best, tho' the Appetite lean the other Way' (p.21). This is something
which can be improved by custom, or habit. Such a moral advocacy
was in conflict with the social and political values he expressed
elsewhere, suggestive of a gesture to the influential moralists of his
time rather than conversion to an authentic moral standpoint.

Nozick: *Anarchy, State, and Utopia*

The Hobbes–Locke tradition of fundamental *self-interest*, with scant
regard for any social justice which involves sacrifices by some for the
sake of others' welfare, has been kept alive in our own time by
Nozick. While he has little concern for a practical consideration of
others' interests, or for a developing of individual potentialities
consistent with social values, he professes a very strong concern for
justice – as he sees it – in the treatment of persons. His own
substantive interpretation of justice is based on the supposed fairness
of the state in not interfering with an individual's *entitlements*. These
are things he has acquired by legitimate means and so has a moral
title to. Any recognition of others' interests is formal only. There is a
return to the notion of the minimal state with powers and influence
over the individual no greater than are needed for personal security
and protection of property.

The Minimal State

The minimal state allows individual freedom to flourish in its own way. This night-watchman state is the one favoured in classical liberal theory, its function limited to protection of individuals against violence, theft and fraud, and other basic functions such as enforcement of contracts. Inasmuch as it obliges some people to pay for the protection of others it appears to be redistributive (that is, serving to re-distribute social goods more evenly among citizens), but this redistributive function is taken no further (ch. 3, pp.26–7).[5] The basis for the minimal state is Locke's social contract theory, whereby the individual recognizes the inconveniences of the state of nature and elects with others to enter a civil society for protection of rights (ch.2). Those rights are inviolable, as is the integrity of the individual (ch.4, p.57). This principle of the integrity of the individual is central to Nozick's view of morality. Rights of individuals are circumscribed with moral boundaries which neither the state nor other individuals may cross. There are rights related to the individual's life and physical safety, his freedom from coercion or imprisonment, his possessions or his 'holdings', as Nozick calls them. It is the last of these which, with something of Locke's zeal, he is particularly concerned to protect from the encroachments of state power. In the name of distributive justice an individual's property, such as his accumulated savings, may be (wrongfully) appropriated by the state for redistribution among those with less property. The right any government has to coerce the people, or to impose moral prohibitions, must be a right already possessed by the people. Any coercive powers the state might have, in other words, are given legitimacy by people's individual rights and duties (ch.1, p.6).

Moral Boundaries and Justice

The moral boundaries which in particular should not be transgressed, according to Nozick, are those relating to freedom from coercion, and to property entitlements. Justice in holdings refers first to their original acquisition, second to their transfer from one person to another, third to rectification of injustices with respect to them (Part II, ch.7, pp.150–3). In an ideal form, a distribution is just when all citizens are entitled to their respective holdings under the distribution. The third raises problems he cannot answer, problems with implications, for instance, to historically displaced persons such as North American Indians and Australian aborigines, with the question of how far back one should go to wipe the historical slate clean of injustices. His main focus in distributive justice is an entitlement, and his entitlement theory of distributive justice is *historical* inasmuch as an entitlement's justice depends upon how it came about. He rejects both the *end-state* and the *patterned* principles of justice: justice in the former depends upon the *structure* of the distribution, such as the extent of equality in it; in the latter upon some kind of pattern, such as having holdings proportional to moral worth, or need, or intelligence, or in patterned combinations of various natural dimensions such as these. An entitlement includes what an individual may choose to do, to make, what others choose to do for him, and choose to give him (p.160). Equality of material condition can only be achieved by re-structuring social institutions in ways that violate individuals' rights to holdings. There is no provision for equality in the entitlement conception of justice. In questioning one view that the only proper criterion for distribution of social goods such as medical care is medical *need*, Nozick replies that the perspective should be changed from a single concern for allocation, to a concern for where the things or activities to be allocated and distributed have to come from (pp.234–5). Rights are indeed inviolable. Holdings may not be seized, even to provide equality of opportunity for others, on the condition that their acquisition is legitimately based. The overriding of people's entitlements – even to improve opportunities for some in society – cannot be justified. When people have rights and entitlements to certain things and activities, no one else has a right to them. That is the major objection for Nozick to equality of opportunity, for any right to equality of opportunity invokes a substructure of things, materials and actions which *other* people may have rights and entitlements over (p.238).

Limitations of Theory

Because of the tension with human nature, we have insisted that practical morality frequently requires some effort, some clear sacrifice of inclination. Nozick's central assumption is the inviolability of the individual, what he is entitled to and his freedom from coercion. To him what the state can properly do is *not* to ease the burden of the economically and socially disadvantaged, but to protect all indi-

iduals from such things as killing or physical harm, destruction or
eizure of property, or deprivation of personal liberty. Inequalities
which happen among individuals as they acquire holdings, without
nfringing the rights of others, are just, not unjust. Therefore our
ssumptions on justice, founded on the formal notion of justice as
airness in the treatment of persons, are not shared by Nozick. To
im inequalities as imbalances in the distribution of social goods are
ot inequities but, if holdings are properly acquired, merely legiti-
nate inequalities. From our standpoint, but not his, he is making a
alse assumption (one that can be shown from empirical research to
e false) that all have a fair and equal opportunity in the competition
or resources, or holdings. From his standpoint, ideals of Human
Rights, which aim at an improvement of the lot of the underpri-
ileged, at a degree of equality which guarantees a minimum
tandard of well-being for all, regardless of particular social condi-
ions or the 'natural lottery', cannot be implemented without trans-
ressing moral rights, or crossing, as he says, moral boundaries. The
tate's provision of education, health care, housing assistance
chemes, and a guarantee of a minimum standard of living, can mean
nly interference with some individuals' rights. To use a distinction
ometimes made in contemporary *political philosophy*, Nozick is not
beral, but *libertarian*, inasmuch as he puts individual freedom of
ction above the power of the state, individual rights to hold what
ney have above the claims of the state with welfare ideals to
edistribute in the interests of the disadvantaged or underprivileged.
he liberties of the individual which Mill outlined in his essay *On
iberty* are liberal ideals, and these Nozick accepts in general. It is
when the state wishes to translate ideals to achievable objectives that
Nozick sees danger, for to give to some is inevitably to take
omething away from others to which they have a proper entitlement.
o him the question of whether they can *spare* what is given up is not
elevant to the overriding question of their *rights*. It is his theoretical
ustification of individualism that is novel, not the expression of
ndividualism itself.[6]

The implications of Nozick's standpoint for education are obvious
particularly for equality of educational opportunity. Those who are
orn fortunate shall remain so, protected by the inviolability of their
ights and entitlements; those born unfortunate shall remain unfor-
unate, and shall have a good chance of passing on their ill-fortune to
neir children. The best educational facilities shall be open to those
who can pay for them, denied to those who can not. It is fair,

presumably, in Nozick's view, that children should suffer for the sin
of their fathers when fathers have been improvident, and should
suffer in any case for the condition of parents who have not inherite
property, even when there has been no improvidence. The very poin
of education as a developing of individual potentialities, and th
irrelevance to this of questions of parental holdings, seem to b
nonchalantly ignored.

In Nozick's propositions there *is* a consideration of others' interest
but the others are a selective group, those with entitlements. To clair
that in a formal sense all have entitlements of one kind or anothe
would be to divert attention from extremes of social disadvantage
Nozick is not concerned for the underprivileged. He forces into hi
scheme a superficial view of Kantian respect for others, a respec
which is based on never seeing others merely as means, and hi
conviction is that those with holdings are used as means to other
ends in any redistributive schemes. He is not concerned with respec
for persons in the sense of trying to see them and their striving
toward goals, their motives, plans, or needs, from their individua
standpoints. The one standpoint he assumes is that of the person wit
entitlements. That some in a society may suffer mentally an
physically from social conditions which do not allow them even basi
material provisions is ignored. Yet Nozick's perspective is direct an
unambiguous, like Hobbes'. A similar perspective had been taken fo
two centuries at least, from Hobbes and Locke to Herbert Spencer
His assumptions are the fundamental assumptions of individualism
His morality is based on a specific notion of *freedom* for th
individual, freedom to acquire, to hold, to transfer; and a staunc
opposition to state coercive authority. What is fundamentally immor
al to him is the act of taking from anyone something to which he i
entitled. There is implicit in this much of the outlook of Herber
Spencer, that work makes character, that individual effort is re
quired, that a man is entitled to keep what he can get by legitimat
means, that state welfare provisions are likely to be self-defeating
and that a state which takes from a man what he has earned by hi
own efforts is merely introducing a form of slavery.[7]

Hobbes, Locke and Nozick are representative of many thinkers o
social justice in state–individual relations whose concern is fun
damentally self-interest, even when they profess a general interest i
individual liberties. We shall now contrast with these another grou
of thinkers whose main orientation is toward a practical consideratio
of *others'* interests, and who therefore appear to be assuming a mor

strictly moral stance as they reflect on social justice. Now the outlook is from the self to all others in society. When justice as fairness in the treatment of persons is thus extended to become *social* justice, it refers literally to everyone – not merely to a select group with personal acquisitions to protect. Social justice applies no less to those *without* 'estates' or possessions than to their more fortunate fellows. It is something to be *distributed* throughout society, without fear or favour. The primary impulse for its advocacy in social philosophy is a moral one – a motivation which gives direction to a practical consideration of others' interests, including their well-being or general welfare.

PHILOSOPHERS WITH A DOMINANT CONCERN FOR OTHERS' INTERESTS

Plato: *The Republic*

Plato's ideal society was one where stability was produced by recognizing that individuals are *different*, and where social justice is achieved when each is doing what he is best fitted by nature to do. All will be given opportunities to demonstrate their capacities by an appropriate education, but only the most highly gifted intellectually will qualify as philosopher-rulers of the state. Others will recognize their superior gifts and respect them. Thus social justice for all depends – in Plato's view – on the prior organization of a just society.

Three Classes of Citizens

Citizens of the *Republic* were divided according to natural endowment. It may be true that Plato was strongly influenced by an ideal of social stability and harmony, in contrast with the dissension that occurred within and among Greek states in his time, but to view *The Republic* as primarily a lesson for his own society, and not a serious attempt to explain a viewpoint on social justice, would require much further evidence than we have; and such a view tends to be discredited by the fact that his last work, *The Laws*, shows considerable amendment to the standpoint taken in *The Republic* (produced in his middle period). We may think of *The Republic* as ideal theory, not in the sense that Plato is here espousing merely a personal ideal of social harmony, but in the different sense that he is presenting a universal theory of social justice which is not confined to Greek city-states but has application to states everywhere, based on constants in human nature. What he is proposing is that if people will be what they are by nature, instead of striving to be otherwise, to be better than they *can* be, and confine their activities in the state to what they *can* do instead of having ambitions toward other activities which are beyond their capabilities, they will be just in their acceptance of themselves for what they are, and in their recognition of others for what *they* are. But social justice somehow comes first: the just society is established by just rulers who are educated for their roles, and it is these who see that others fit into theirs strictly according to natural endowments. Members of the first two classes, the artisans and labourers, who satisfy society's material needs, and the soldiers who defend society, do not merely assume hereditary functions, for they may have qualities different from their parents'. Thus those in the first are like iron and copper, those in the second, like silver, and members of the elite, the philosopher-rulers, are like gold: it is the responsibility of the last 'to guard and watch zealously over the offspring, seeing which of those metals is mixed in their souls' (Book III, 415).[8] Then each will be given 'the honour proper to its nature' in being placed, after an appropriate education which will be a means of identifying or confirming their true nature, in the relevant social and occupational class (Book IV, 434). Similarly with respect to the tripartite division of the soul which accounts for this threefold classification of abilities, the just man is true to himself, recognizing what is dominant in him, controlling his own soul with a self-mastery that suppresses any inclination to exercise *courage* as an auxiliary, or soldier, if what is dominant in his soul is desire or appetite; or *reason* if what is dominant in his soul is the courage of the soldier (Book IV, 443–444). That those of the lowest class in particular, dominated by desire or appetite, are able to achieve this degree of self-discipline, is rather contradictory. Plato's conviction is that we can all live with satisfaction, with internal government of the parts of the soul, by accepting ourselves as we are, and the roles in society for which we are best fitted. Social justice is then sustained, under the watchful eye of the rulers who alone have the capacity for ultimate pleasure in 'the vision of being' (Book IX, 582). That final leap gives reverence to their rightful authority, but other classes would respect them for their knowledge, reason and goodness.

Assumptions and Inadequacies

In this ideal theory, based on the notion of every citizen playing his part according to his nature (though with proper control of his own soul which could be as internally warring as the external political state), justice, morality and education were functional aspects of a single harmony. Social justice of this kind was not a description of any known social order. Given human imperfection it could not be regarded as an account of what was completely attainable, but it was a model of social justice, a model for social and moral improvement. Later in *The Laws*, Plato changed the emphasis from an education of the rulers (which took up much of *The Republic*) to an education of others in virtue, for it seems to have become evident to him in the intervening years that their conduct required moral training: their control by the wisdom of philosopher-rulers, and by their own self-government, could not be taken for granted. Their understanding was still so limited though, that such a moral preparation was to be fundamentally one of habituation. It was their moral dispositions which counted: they might be expected to act from virtuous motives, or intentions, or other learned dispositional states, all as the product of moral habits. Their action schema might include desire (controlled by moral habit), moral motives or intentions (habituated), moral attitudes and values (also habituated), and action. This would show them devoid of rational-dispositional deliberation: close, indeed, to automatons.

The Republic has been condemned as a pattern for totalitarianism. To some in our times it is seen as both presumptuous and paternalistic, but Plato's concern was stability, as he reasoned toward a better society than any the warring Greeks had practised. His main weakness was to ignore the facts: with a distinctly stronger scientific inclination, his pupil Aristotle took much more account of the way things were to *observation*. Certainly there are large and significant differences among individuals; certainly too the matching of vocations to abilities and aptitudes is desirable, and vocational misfits are without doubt a source of social disruption. But Plato's solutions to the problems of the individual in his relations with authority appear to us fanciful, and almost innocently simplistic. As for the morality of his system of social justice it was a one-sided benevolence with benefaction, handed down by those in the highest places of authority, but contradictorily leaving no room for the personal liberty of ordinary people – the farmers and craftsmen, and the soldiers. The ordering of the good society gave the opportunity for contributory involvement of these: the social structure remained settled as long as there was the obedience of ordinary people, an acquiescence in leaving things to those who knew better, and could be implicitly trusted as members of a superior class who would guard the common interest. Plato's scheme was class-based: there was simply needed, to demonstrate this in his time, an articulate artisan or an articulate soldier to present a scheme of social justice from his own equally biased standpoint. It is not that the intellect can be set aside in practical affairs of government, but that it is much more broadly shared among citizens than Plato assumed it to be, and can scarcely be held to be correlative with occupations. When later in *The Laws* he spoke of a suitable education for those outside the elite class of rulers, his presumptions remained: the less gifted could be made good by habit, but not by understanding. So although Plato considered social justice with both moral and educational connections, there were fundamental flaws in his argument. First, he provided no substantial reasons for an occupational immobilization, or for the mutual exclusiveness of abilities and aptitudes. (Why should not a farmer become a soldier, a soldier a ruler, except on the false dogma of definitive class abilities?) Second, his notion of education as finite, to satisfy clear parameters of potentialities which found their outlets in particular classes of occupations, showed little understanding of human capacity for continuous development. Third, his dogma of whole classes of people as dominated by desire or appetite, with no chance of developing their rational powers, in morality creatures of habit but never of understanding, would probably have earned opprobrium in his own time had literacy been more widespread, and inequality of educational opportunity been substantially reduced. (How distant he seemed himself from the market-place, prescribed experience nonetheless for his philosopher-rulers!) Fourth, the relationship of paternalism between rulers and ordinary citizens was poorly based in human understanding, and it is a little surprising that Plato should have proposed it in apparent defiance of the experience of Athenian democracy. Little wonder that his rulers had to be elevated almost to divine status, with supra-rational powers of pricking through the crust of earthly imperfections to a higher realm. But with all his deficiencies, Plato set the stage in western thought for curiosity in the problems of the *just society*, including the liberties of citizens and the limits of authority. He had not quite moved to a contract theory of government, but in the relationships between rulers and ordinary people there was nonetheless an implicit agreement in the form of a common understanding of each other's firm and unequivocal place in society. This understanding made senseless any challenge to the authority of rulers, or to the rightful social functions of anyone once he had been reliably classified by the rulers. It is one of the many ironies in Plato that questions common in political theory today such as those of authority, liberty, obedience, power, were all effectively turned to non-questions by giving to the various classes a self-perception and perception of others in the social organization, with no ordinary degree of tolerance and understanding, while holding reason dominant only in the rulers, and leaving artisans and labourers under the influence merely of desire or appetite. His answer to the problem of morality and justice in human relations was to create a just society. Then fairness in the treatment of persons, and a practical consideration of others' interests would both follow. It was the means, not the end, that proved insubstantial.

Plato's false assumptions do not detract from the sincerity of his moral convictions as he sought a just society. Social justice ensued from a consideration of others' interests, not from a single-minded pursuit of self-interest. The contrast with Hobbes is striking. Plato was visionary and far from practicalities. Hobbes was preoccupied with self-interest in the society he knew, and this prevented a wider focus on human societies as a basis for generalizations on social justice. He was not interested in education, as Plato was, as a developing of potentialities and a means of improving social relations, especially morally, for Hobbes took people as they are (so he believed) and the moral situation as it is. At least he attempted what Plato did not: he did take careful account of what he found to be the case in his own experience. He had no reason to argue from what *is* to what *ought* to be, and was limited inasmuch as he relied on his own observations and his own impressions of human nature; for scientific in impulse as he was, he saw no need to compare those observations with others'. Yet he was much closer to the market place of daily human intercourse and material interests than was Plato, who assumed something of an Olympian detachment as he contemplated the structure of a just society that would form the basis of social justice for all individuals.

Rousseau: *The Social Contract*

In contract theory Rousseau's main departure from Hobbes and Locke was to realise that the agreement between the people and their ruler or sovereign power gave them the opportunity to establish voluntary moral relations with others. They would thus not merely be *using* the agreement for their own security and for the protection of their property, but would find themselves in a civil society where genuine moral demands would be placed on individuals in the fundamental sense of morality as a practical consideration of others' interests. Thus they would develop as moral beings in a moral community. Compared with their former state – the state of nature – where individuals lived by the rule of force, now they would be in a position to live by agreement on moral principles and rules.

The Moral Interest

Rousseau was still prepared to say, in much the same vein as had Locke, that the object of any political association 'is the protection and the prosperity of its members' (*The Social Contract*, ch.9, p.130)[9], yet transcending that commonplace observation, Rousseau saw the civil society as an opportunity for man to develop as a free moral agent, in the familiar paradox that constraint under a moral law gives freedom. He established a moral connection between law and freedom: both justice and morality move closer to the formal notions we have given them, and are no longer tied to self-interest and prudence as they were in Hobbes and Locke, with their concern for peace and strong government for the protection of the individual's interests. He was not concerned with problems of distributive justice, as we shall see, but for reasons quite different from Locke's (as a man of property himself).

Justice and Morality

Rousseau's views on justice and morality are related to his distinctive notion of the social contract and the moral transformation which he saw ensuing from it; and to his notion of the general will and the connection between law, morality and freedom. The 'social pact', as he sometimes called it, becomes necessary when men can no longer preserve themselves in a state of nature, which, if persisted in, would lead to their self-destruction. As he states the problem he begins clearly under the influence of Hobbes and Locke, but then changes direction toward personal freedom. The problem is to reach a form of association which on the one hand defends the person and the material property of each member, but on the other hand leaves the individual as free as he was originally, obeying no one but himself. In words which have become adapted to some contemporary social theory, since everyone gives himself and his rights to the community, 'the conditions are the same for all, and precisely because they are the same for all, it is in no man's interest to make the conditions onerous to others' (*The Social Contract*, Book I, ch.6, p.60). In the social pact everyone gives his person and his powers to the *general will*, but the pact is different from the social contract as seen by Hobbes and Locke in that there is no transference of power from the individual to a sovereign power: sovereignty belongs, as always, to the people (pp.60–1). The moral change in man from the state of nature to the civil society is profound: indeed, it is his very membership of a civil society that transforms him from a creature of physical impulse, desire and self-interest, to a moral being. We may overlook Rousseau's enthusiasm for the ennobling of sentiments and the enlargement of mind; it is clear that he wants to say something afresh about the social contract, something which Hobbes and Locke had missed, that man in a state of nature is a relatively 'narrow, stupid animal', and assumes a new condition of moral freedom, dignity and intelligence as he submits himself voluntarily, and again paradoxically, to the freedom of a law which he prescribes for himself. That is *moral* freedom, which his membership of a civil society gives him. His *civil* liberty is limited by the general will (Book I, ch.8, pp.64–5. The general will is normative inasmuch as it is inclined toward the public good, but while it is 'rightful' in this sense, and does not intentionally corrupt the people, it is prone to human error (Book 11, ch.3, p.72). Therefore the lawgiver is necessary, a man of superior intelligence, but as legislator he must not have executive power (Book 11, ch.7, p.85). At all times, he repeats, sovereignty is with the people. Rousseau shifts easily from one perspective and one emphasis to another. He can quickly put aside the great moral advantages of the social contract, as the individual moves to a civil society, and return almost to the traditional and much more limited perspective of Hobbes and Locke. The social contract, he sums up, leaves the individual much better off than he was in the state of nature: he has given up an uncertain and precarious life for a more secure one; given up natural independence for freedom, physical strength for protection by society. It is only his reference to freedom that here distinguishes him from his two predecessors (Book 11, ch.4, p.77).

Difficulties and Disillusion

At other points Rousseau's moral perspective is clear, especially in reference to the general will, equality of rights, and the law. The social pact establishes equality among all in civil society: all are bound by the same conditions, and all enjoy the same rights (ibid., p.76). Laws are acts of the general will and so by definition cannot be unjust: it would be contradictory for the people, the proper authors of laws, to be unjust to themselves. Not even princes are above the law. But since the general will is not always enlightened, specialist 'lawyers' become necessary (Book 11, ch.6, pp.82–3). So central is morality to the law that it may be appropriately called 'its immovable keystone'. Though in civil society the law has high moral status, there are problems facing the individual as a *free moral agent*. Rousseau sees no answer to the difficulties he has reached: in a nominal and theoretical sense the members of civil society have sovereignty under the general will; they are authors of their own laws. In practice they have to delegate law-making to those with appropriate talents, and to be free moral agents they require the opportunity to make moral judgements even with respect to government and legislation. Corruption of legislators who make laws in their own interests is even more serious than abuse of the law by governments, or those with executive power. He believes 'there has never been a true democracy, and there never will be' (Book 111, ch.4, p.112). Representative government leaves the individual in a morally passive state instead of the morally active one which he should assume for his own moral development. The 'voice of duty' should be given opportunity for individual expression, but in representative government, as in England, people are free to elect members to government and are then 'enslaved' (Book 111, ch.15, p.141). He concludes that unless the republic is very small, as in the case of Greek states where the people assembled in the market-place made their own decisions, there seems no way for individuals in a civil society to exercise their rights and maintain sovereignty in their own hands. That leads to further pessimism on the civil society being able to maintain its moral cohesion. It spells also the limits to Rousseau's notion of social justice. For any government, paternalistic or authentically benevolent, to regard itself as an agent of *distributive justice*, allotting benefits according to resources, in education or elsewhere, is to restrict the people's individual opportunities for *active moral involvement*. And it is in the benefits to the individual, in terms of freedom and moral development, that Rousseau's contribution to the social contract theory lies. We shall ask shortly whether Rawls' theory of social justice is able to bridge the gap which Rousseau left, changing the emphasis from individual moral well-being to the moral well-being of society as a whole. In the end Rousseau saw the possibility of the general will being silenced, the social bond broken, selfish interest flaunted in the name of the public good (Book IV, ch.1, p.150). The social pact had not lived up to its early promise. Rousseau had nonetheless made a significant contribution to social contract theory. Despite his misgivings about human nature and a form of government that would allow man to go from a state of nature to a state that paradoxically was *more* natural to him inasmuch as it provided an opportunity for his free moral development, Rousseau added a moral perception that was largely lacking previously, and at least the first tentative suggestion that a contract might be the means to a more moral society, and thus to *social justice*.

Kant: *Fundamental Principles of the Metaphysic of Morals*

Although sometimes classified as a contract theorist, Kant cannot be brought into such a category with Hobbes, Locke and Rousseau without straining the sense of 'contract' and ignoring fundamental differences in viewpoint with theirs. While they had the idea of a civil society in which members would see it as in their interests, or to their advantage, to unite with a certain agreement on the kind of society they wished to live under, any union for personal advantage was foreign to Kant's morality. The ideal union he had in mind was the outcome of rational persons legislating morally for themselves and for all others. By implication, social injustice could simply not occur as long as rational persons followed moral laws directed especially to considering others as ends, never merely as means. In his ideal there is a union of rational persons, each autonomous (or independent), legislating morally for himself and for others, following the imperatives of *duty* as each responds to the direction of a Good Will. Rousseau had seen the possibilities of men associating for mutual benefit while motivated by a moral sense. Kant gave this strength by arguing that the Rational Will left no alternative to each person acting morally in relations with others, regarding every other as an end in himself. This union which demanded moral relations was hardly a contract. It was a state of common rational and moral inevitability once the Rational Will was developed. In contrast with Rousseau's notion of a morally oriented civil society, Kant's philosophy led inwardly to an intensely personal morality. The consequences for an ideal society are too obvious to elaborate.

The Moral Law and Autonomy

Rousseau's enthusiasm for the paradox of freedom on the one hand, and on the other hand a moral law imposed by the individual upon himself as he moved out of the original state of nature into the free submission to constraints of the civil society, was in broad respects similar to Kant's notion of autonomy; but Kant developed this basic notion into an ethical theory, modifying as well Rousseau's idea of the sanctity of the general will, itself with the force of law and of a moral imperative. Kant begins the *Fundamental Principles of the Metaphysic of Morals* with the assertion that nothing in the world can be called good without qualification except a Good Will (p.9).[10]

In the Second Section he explores what he calls the transition from popular moral philosophy to the metaphysic of morals, explaining that everything in nature works by laws, and that it is only rational beings who can act according to laws, or principles; that is, who may be said to have a *will*. To act from principles requires the functioning of reason, and so the will may be said to be practical reason (p.29). An imperative is a command of reason, referring to an objective principle which is obligatory for a will. The imperative may be either hypothetical or categorical. If an action is good, not in itself but only as a means to something else, the imperative is hypothetical. If the action is good in itself, perceived as such by the rational will, then the imperative is categorical. Thus the categorical imperative declares an action to be objectively necessary, without reference to any purpose (pp.30–2). *Prudence* (in Kant's sense) is an example of a hypothetical imperative, for the action is commanded as a means to another *purpose*: that of influencing others to use them for one's own purposes, for temporary or lasting benefit (p.33). *Duty* has moral significance only in the context of *categorical* imperatives, for these alone have legislative authority for our actions (p.42). With respect to categorical imperatives, the idea of willing that a subjective principle of action, or maxim, should become a universal law is to convey the self-discipline of excluding all personal interests, all external purposes, and of assuming a morally aesthetic stance.

Person and the Legislative Will

Kant sees all rational beings as persons: by their very nature they are ends in themselves, not merely means to be used arbitrarily by another. To this he adds the idea that the will of every rational being is a universally legislative will (p.49), thus freeing the will from any suspicion of self-interest. If the will of a rational being were not regarded as legislative, it would not be conceived, Kant thought, as an end in itself (p.52). The union of all rational beings by common objective laws, under the principle that each must treat himself and all others never merely as means, but at the same time as ends in themselves, constitutes what Kant calls a kingdom of ends. *Autonomy* of the will is opposed to heteronomy, which is acting on the false assumption that the moral life consists in aiming at some end (such as happiness). It is autonomy that confers human dignity (p.54), with the rational being an end in himself. Autonomy of the will is thus the supreme principle of morality (p.59).

Problems of Justification

In the Third Section, Kant explains another transition: from the metaphysic of morals to the critique of pure practical reason. Here he claims that it is the concept of freedom that explains the autonomy of the will: freedom must be presupposed in the will of all rational beings (pp.66–7). But for a variety of reasons his arguments in this section are difficult to justify. When faced with a circular argument he attempts to establish the existence of freedom by means of the distinction between the world of things in themselves, or *noumena*, and the world of appearances, or *phenomena*. It is this very distinction, as a means of justifying the freedom of acts described as noumenal, which has been widely challenged by Kant's critics,[11] and which is at the same time inconsistent with his views on freedom in the *Critique of Practical Reason*. Kant begins by drawing attention to impressions of things that come to us voluntarily through the senses, but which do not give us an understanding of what they are in themselves: all we can attain by such impressions is a knowledge of *appearances*. Thus between the world of sense and the world of understanding there is a distinction which is given significance by reason, showing how far the world of mere sensibility is transcended by the world of the intellect. Inasmuch as a rational being belongs to the world of sense he is subject to the laws of nature, or to heteronomy; but inasmuch as he belongs to the world of the intellect he is subject to laws which are independent of nature, with their foundation in reason, making possible an autonomy of the will. It is the idea of freedom which enables him at the same time to conceive of the idea of autonomy. This argument removes, Kant believes, the circular reasoning from freedom to autonomy, and from that to the moral law (pp.70–2). He then asks, how is a categorical imperative possible? The problem he sees is this: he must show that the contradiction between man's freedom of will, and a determinism which makes him subject to the laws of nature, is apparent only. These are simply two different ways of looking at man's condition, and it must be shown that they are not incompatible (p.76). But the speculative philosophy of reason cannot explain freedom, any more than it can explain how pure reason can be practical. Explanation requires laws of nature to which things can be referred, but freedom is an abstraction, an 'ideal conception' (p.79). A categorical imperative is seen as possible only by giving to it the idea of freedom, but human reason cannot itself go further than asserting the validity of the imperative and of the moral law. On the hypothesis that the will of a rational being is free, its autonomy necessarily follows (p.81). But in the last resort Kant claims that any failure to establish the absolute necessity of a categorical imperative must be due to the nature of human reason in general. His deduction of autonomy as the supreme principle of morality remains unquestioned. At least, by taking his argument as far as he can, 'up to the very limit of human reason', he is able to comprehend the incomprehensibility of the categorical imperative (p.84). On the power of reason to determine the will to action he had no doubt: without that he could not defend autonomy. This it can do independently of anything empirical (*The Analytic of Pure Practical Reason*, p.131).

From time to time Kant is faced with a similar problem of justification, though sometimes with more confidence in reason than appears in this conclusion to the *Fundamental Principles of the Metaphysic of Morals*. His transcendental justifications have been noted earlier: left with nothing by which to justify reason itself, it has to be elevated to a status which requires no justification. His attempt to justify noumenal man as rational, free, autonomous, belonging to world of the intellect, in contrast to phenomenal man as subject to causal laws of nature, and so determined, leans heavily on intuitive convictions of freedom. But Kant is satisfied that the noumena-phenomena distinction has enabled him to establish freedom independently, as he had sought to do.

Kant could leave social justice, or justice for all individuals in society, simply to follow from man's rational nature, as it was to be expressed in the noumenal self. By contrast Plato believed that social justice would eventuate from the establishment of a justly organized social system. We shall now turn to a contemporary philosopher, John Rawls, as one of the foremost exponents of social justice in our time, and one with supposedly close connections with Kant's moral theory.

Rawls: *A Theory of Justice*

In his own explanation, Rawls' *A Theory of Justice* belongs to a contract tradition with its definitive antecedents in Locke's *Second Treatise of Government*, Rousseau's *The Social Contract*, and Kant's ethical works beginning with *The Foundations of the Metaphysics of Morals*.[12] Rawls claims that his notion of justice as fairness is similar to Kant's notion of autonomy, his original position being seen as a procedural interpretation of Kant's autonomy and the categorical imperative; that his own procedure whereby parties arrive at their choices together as free and rational persons is a means of avoiding heteronomy (as distinct from autonomy) and of preserving the means–end distinction which Kant had made: that his principles of justice are categorical imperatives in Kant's sense (pp.251–3). He refers specifically to certain aspects of Kant's theory in addition to autonomy and categorical imperatives, such as legislation for a kingdom of ends, noumena as distinct from phenomena, the connection between freedom and moral law. We shall now turn to Rawls'

theory, but shall note at the outset that Kant, like Rousseau, offer
no guidance with respect to distributive justice: each is concerne
with individual man's determination to live freely under a sel
imposed moral law. Rawls has made significant departures from
Kant's theory: in particular he has something to say on distributiv
justice, and equality of educational opportunity.

Rawls builds his ideal social theory on a perception of inequities i
the actual social order, especially in good or bad fortune both in one'
natural endowments and in the social conditions into which one
born. So he begins to construct an ideal social system which make
equity out of inequity. In this he has none of Plato's fanciful flights o
of his visionary generalities. It is the society he knows – the society c
these inherited inequities – that he takes as his starting point, so it is
matter of rubbing out and writing in amendments until he finishes u
with what he considers an ideal balance. Plato's approach was mor
radical – a different society created from very broad impressions c
the one he knew. While Rawls' fundamental concern is for notions c
morality as a practical consideration of others' interests, and fo
justice as fairness in the treatment of persons, with respect t
education he fails to perceive it as a developing of *individuc
potentialities, consistent with social values. In his claims to be clos
to Kant in other respects – in Kant's notions of autonomy, categoric
imperatives, and noumenal and phenomenal selves – vague corre
pondences conceal substantial differences between them.

Like Kant, Rawls constructs an *ideal* theory of moral relationship
He borrows from Kant the notion of persons coming together unde
reason and a good will. He borrows too from Kant the notion c
moral principles having universal appeal to all rational persons c
good will, and in this sense becoming universally binding. But whe
Rawls refers to the original position of rational and imparti
deliberation, he leaves an uneasiness about a supposed uniforr
direction of rationality, and we are left with an impression that hi
comparison of persons in the original position with Kant's noumen
selves is strained inasmuch as there are clearly various intellectu
positions to be taken in it and Rawls' contention for one ration
position only is implausible.

Main Features of Theory

Rawls asks us to imagine what it would be like if 'free and ration
persons concerned to further their interests' were to work out th

rms of their association, in a kind of hypothetical contract, thereby
tablishing principles of justice which would serve as a basic structure
r regulating all future agreements, specifying the kinds of social
operation that are acceptable as well as acceptable forms of
vernment (p.11). Putting ourselves in this position, we would
gether work out what is just in the sense of being fair for all, but we
ould be operating, in the original position, from what he calls 'a veil
ignorance', for none of us would know our place in society, or our
atus, or how we would fare subsequently in the distribution of
ods within society. We would not know our relative intellectual
ilities, our respective conceptions of the good, or anything of our
ecial psychological tendencies such as liability to optimism or
essimism. But the veil is not such as to produce total blindness, for
this situation it is assumed that we do have general knowledge
out human society such as the basis of social organization, and we
have a general knowledge of psychology. Indeed there are no
strictions on general knowledge which has a bearing on the choice of
inciples of justice (pp.137–8). We are rational, equal and mutually
sinterested – equal inasmuch as we have the same restrictions
aced on us all, with the same access to relevant general knowledge,
ne of us interested in others' interests, all of us rational egoists. But
e force of the *rational*, we learn subsequently, is that it has a strong
antian connection with the moral, so that selfishness in the original
sition is out of the question. We are asked to imagine this
pothetical situation so that we can compare a rational formulation
fairness for all with what our actual moral convictions happen to be
such fairness, or social justice. Even our moral dispositions, our
titudes and values in particular which our moral convictions reflect,
n then be adjusted. We can draw together the rational model and
e actual, making adjustments to each until we arrive at a comprom-
acceptable to us. Thus by 'working from both ends', as Rawls
ys, and 'going back and forth', we eventually reach a stage where
feel that no further adjustments are needed: we have reached a
age of 'reflective equilibrium' (pp.19–20). In the process we may
ve found it necessary to modify not only our *prima facie* moral
dgements or convictions, but also some of the *prima facie* principles
fairness reached from behind the impartial (but rational) veil of
norance. The status of the compromise reached is that of a
bjective moral judgement, based on whatever modification we
ve made to our personal moral attitudes and values. All we can
hieve, in Rawls' words, is to 'strike a balance by intuition' (p.34).

The imaginative exercise of assuming the original position to wor
out our terms of association, and then comparing these terms wit
our conception of justice according to our *actual* moral conviction:
enables us to achieve a measure of our own egoism and of our limite
benevolence. As soon as we return ourselves to the actual world, an
our actual selves in it, our dispositions come into full play, and ou
deliberations are, as they normally are, rational *and* dispositiona
Benevolence probably shrinks to some extent: we may no longe
want to perceive others as equals. If we accept the assumptions of th
original position and the procedure of working towards a reflectiv
equilibrium, we may expect that reason alone will expose gro:
egoism at least. Although Rawls acknowledges that we are mor:
persons in the initial situation – rational, with our own ends an
capable of a sense of justice (p.12) – he assumes that a rational an
moral perspective continues as we deliberate or reflect toward a
equilibrium between the original position and our considered convi
tions of justice. In arriving at our notion of justice, nonetheless, it
not *necessary* that we should simulate the reflections of persons in th
original position; that is said to be useful in attempting to account fo
our moral judgements and helping to explain our sense of justice, bu
it is an entirely hypothetical situation (pp.120–1). If we do in practic
simulate such reflections, we exercise something of a discipline
imagination. No more difficult, it would appear, would be a direc
widely-informed approach to social justice, assuming an equall
impartial judicial role, in so far as impartiality is within our power
as we consider all the relevant facts of the situation: not only facts o
social organization and of psychology, but the multiplicity of interes
and motives, ideals, attitudes and values, abilities and aptitudes, an
so forth – without, that is, the veil of ignorance of an origin:
position. On the other hand, if we were to assume an original positio
whereby we met with others to work out our terms of association, bu
with our eyes open so that we could take into account all the facts w
could ascertain about others, as well as about ourselves, Rawls woul
have some grounds for believing that this procedure would be le
likely to be fair to others, and so less likely to reach a ration
position which could be used as a basis for further considerations o
social justice. For Rawls seems to be tacitly acknowledging the forc
of our dispositions (in *our* sense of the word, as referring especially 1
motives, attitudes and values) in our deliberations. If we try to leav
them out, in the imaginary original position, and then return to th
actual situation where our deliberations are rational *and* dispositio

al, we are likely to be fairer in our conception of justice through coming to realise the strength and influence of our personal dispositions, and of our personal interests as well. His imaginary original position opposes the perhaps unconscious tendency in all of us to rationalize in such reflections *in our favour*. If we can assume a veil of ignorance in our reflections on principles of justice, then move to a position of equilibrium as he has described, the suggestion is that our conclusions, though subjective as always since they are inevitably related to personal dispositions – however strong the rational contribution – will not favour our own respective conditions: we shall be justified in regarding the principles of justice which we formulate as fair for all persons in society. That is a big claim, to which we shall return. First, we shall consider Rawls' own principles, arrived at presumably in this way.

Inequalities and Distributive Justice

At the outset we are asked to accept his social perspective on justice: he is not approaching justice from the standpoint of individual morality, on the assumption that if individuals in society can be somehow educated morally, or habituated with understanding to relate morally to others in a practical consideration of others' interests, a just society would follow: individuals would see to it, that is, that society is so organized that moral relations would obtain among them as persons. Rawls' assumption, like Plato's, is that we must concentrate first on the basic structure of society: only if the structure is just, will individuals have an opportunity to live morally. His reason is that even from birth, individuals are affected inasmuch as they begin with different life prospects. We should therefore attempt to formulate principles which will reduce these inequalities (p.96). From a contract point of view, the purpose is to assume a perspective on justice as fairness, working from an original position of equality toward principles which will enable subsequent specification of forms of social cooperation and forms of government (p.11). Stated very generally, we may say that injustice refers to those inequalities which are not to everyone's benefit. All social goods, everything we value in society – liberty, life prospects of various kinds, education including cultural interests, opportunities for leisure or recreation, and so forth – ought to be distributed equally, unless it can be established that an unequal distribution with respect to one or

more of these is to everyone's advantage (p.62). This general
statement, and the initial statement of his two principles of justice
(p.60) are made more restrictive by the supposition that the rational
person in the original position would consider the situation of the
person *least advantaged* in society: it is he who becomes the
base-line for Rawls' formulations. The two principles of justice for
institutions which he believes are dictated by reason from the original
position are now given. (Rawls explains an institution as a public
system of rules, and this is the basic structure of society, p.55.) The
first principle is that the most extensive system of equal basic liberties
is an equal right for every person, in so far as each system of liberties
is compatible with those of others; the second is that the arrangement
of social and economic inequalities must confer the greatest benefit
on the least advantaged, and must be attached to offices and positions
which are 'open to all under conditions of fair equality of opportunity'. The first principle is ranked higher than the second. If any liberty
is restricted it must strengthen the total system of liberty in the
institution; less than equal liberty must be acceptable to those with
the lesser liberty. The second principle ranks higher than a principle
of efficiency. Another condition is that an inequality of opportunity
must enhance the opportunity of those with the lesser opportunity.
The general idea is that the distribution of all social primary goods
(including education) must be equal, unless an unequal distribution is
to the advantage of the least favoured (pp. 302–3). Future generations are also considered. In the original position those making the
agreement assess what is a fair contribution to make to following
generations, while at the same time acknowledging what they have
received fairly from their predecessors, but this 'just savings principle', which becomes a qualification to the second principle of justice,
provides for a fair rate of saving according to the existing condition of
the particular society: where saving is difficult, as in Third World
countries, a lower rate of saving is to be expected.

Equality of Opportunity

We shall now consider what provision is made by the theory for
equality of opportunity, and particularly for equality of educational
opportunity. What makes Rawls emphatic on the need to begin with
the basic structure of society, to make it *just* at the outset, is the
perception of inequality in present societies, where many individuals

from birth have had reduced life prospects that our societies have tolerated. Social inequalities that are not deserved are those that stem from social conditions, as well as those related to the 'natural lottery' of individual endowments. So much is obvious, as are certain substantive considerations, such as that social conditions should not inhibit the chances of those with equal talents and equal motivation, and that class barriers should not inhibit anyone's chances to acquire cultural knowledge and skills. More contentiously, and optimistically in some societies, comes the suggestion that the school system, whether public or private, should be designed to even out class barriers (p.73). We shall confine ourselves in this chapter to the formal theory or ideal conception, as Rawls calls it, of social justice for institutions, with their public rules, rights and duties and so forth, and consider whether it is adequate to provide a framework for substantive considerations concerning equality of opportunity. In this connection our main focus will be on the *difference principle*, and the rational and moral aspects he gives to the theory as a whole.

Evaluation

Rawls' difference principle refers to institutions offering equal basic liberties and fair equality of opportunity. In these some members are more fortunate than others in social background and in natural endowments. It would be just, according to the difference principle, to support the expectations of those better situated only if they improve the expectations of those less well situated (p.75). Since the influence of social conditions is so pervasive, affecting the fundamental motivation of children's learning, there is need for this principle, Rawls argues, to mitigate the arbitrary effects of the natural lottery in its various aspects. Certainly, as he has recognized, those with similar abilities and talents should have similar life chances, the same prospects of success if they are prepared to use their abilities and talents, regardless of the social class into which they are born. But the difference principle attempts to cope with two separate problems: that of social disadvantage, and that of less fortunate abilities and talents. Rawls believes that from the original position of rational disinterestedness, parties to the contract would arrive at the difference principle. This is doubtful. It is not at all clear that everyone, in such a situation, would agree that fair equality of opportunity would be reached by ensuring that social schemes do not adversely affect the opportunities of the socially disadvantaged. Would it not be rational in the original position to consider the interests, based on *needs*, of everyone in society, without any suggestion of positive discrimination? It is in a consideration of distributive justice applied to education that the difference principle is seen as most inadequate, and even irrelevant to the problem of equality of opportunity. Rawls illustrates how the difference principle would allocate resources in education, to improve the long-term expectations of those less well-endowed. His difference principle regards the distribution of natural talents as a common asset. The benefits of the distribution are to be shared. It is agreed that education is to be considered not merely in terms of economic efficiency and social welfare, but also, and at least as importantly, in its cultural aspects, and its preparation for participation in society's affairs (p.101). The significant consequence of the allocation of resources on education is that the better endowed should gain from their good fortune *only* if the situation of those less well endowed is improved. The weakness of this consequentialist perspective is that it does not satisfy the principle of education as an improving of *individuals*, for on this principle the development of the potentialities of the more able is an end in itself, as the individuals themselves are ends on the Kantian principle which Rawls subsequently accepts, and not to be regarded merely as means to others' ends. To tie the fortunes of the able to those of the less able is not only discriminatory and therefore unjust, but in the last resort it is also impracticable. Those better endowed will generally gain from their good fortune in many ways which do not affect the situation of those less well-endowed: in curiosity and intellectual satisfaction, for instance.

We may assume that resources in education, in terms of teachers and materials, are always restricted: when they are so, it is arguable that each should have an equal proportional benefit from whatever resources are available. It is true that in this, the better endowed may become relatively better off in that they can help themselves, rely more on their own resources, but nothing can prevent this happening except by measures of denying them fair opportunity for their individual development. With a background of knowledge about what education is and what it entails (and Rawls has admitted that *any* relevant knowledge may be used), persons in the original position, as rational egoists and from a position of mutual disinterest, might take the view that all individuals should have resources provided for them for the progressive development of their potentialities, *according to their various needs*, and that where total resources are insufficient to meet all needs, the resultant disabilities should be distributed as evenly as possible among all those being educated. If the difference principle were adopted in a situation of extremely limited resources, attempts to improve the education of the less well-endowed might prevent attention to the needs of the better-endowed. From the standpoint of the formal notion of education as a developing of *individual* potentialities consistent with social values, combined with the formal notion of morality as a practical consideration of others' interests, no conditions (such as those imposed by the difference principle) can be allowed which might inhibit the developing of potentialities of the better-endowed.

Projection from Rawls to Amended Principles of Social Justice

The projection from Rawls' theory to amended principles of social justice is partly a continuing evaluation of Rawls' position, and partly the construction of a foundation for a further consideration of social justice in the succeeding chapters.

Rawls' first principle refers to an individual's equal right to the most extensive total system of equal basic liberties, subject to the compatibility condition stated earlier. This principle we must accept as fundamental, as also its priority over the second principle, which in its now reduced form refers to the accessibility of offices and positions to all under conditions of fair equality of opportunity. Rawls has outlined the basic liberties as political liberty, referring to voting rights and eligibility for public office; freedom of speech and assembly; liberty of conscience and freedom of thought; freedom of the person along with the right to hold personal property; and freedom from arbitrary arrest and seizure (p.61). Not only is it clear that these basic rights should be held by all citizens in a just society, but it is also clear, and unnecessary to elaborate, that the justice of accessibility to all citizens of public offices and positions cannot be secured unless basic liberty rights are first guaranteed. It is sufficient to note the many instances in some societies where discrimination in the filling of public offices, in education and elsewhere, has been achieved from positions of the political and religious values of those in power. The basic liberties are safeguards against arbitrary government which might fill public offices and positions by favour or prejudice. They are a basis for a fair distribution of resources, including educational resources, according to community values, for if these are ignored by representative governments, or biased to favour sectional interests, citizens have an opportunity to exercise political liberty to restore a proper balance. In other words basic liberties support the formal notion of justice which we have expressed as fairness in the treatment of persons. Distributive justice in the allocation of educational resources implies a fair balance or proportion among recipients, so that not only the talented and the socially advantaged but also the slow-learners, the handicapped and the socially underprivileged receive proper attention, quite regardless of their benefits to society in economic or cultural terms. Because of the wide variety of educational provisions required for these various situations, the only criterion that will satisfy our principles of justice is that of *need*. Any consequentialist considerations are purely secondary. So too is the just savings principle. We do not set out as educators to deliberately develop the cultural heritage, to add something to it to pass on to the next generation, so that we in our generation will have played our part in the historical tradition. Whether it *improves* is irrelevant to the matter of change: that will be a value judgement made by the next generation according to its particular standards.

We are now in a position to amend Rawls' second principle of justice for institutions. While retaining his reference to the openness to all of public offices and positions, we shall replace his reference to the difference principle with the following:

> Each person is to have an equal right to basic social goods according to need.

Thus in the allocation of resources, again assuming that in every society these are limited, education – as one of the social goods to be distributed – will serve the needs of individuals as developing persons, and whenever resources are insufficient to satisfy their needs completely, no one group of learners – talented, disadvantaged or handicapped, those of average ability or otherwise – will receive a lower proportion of need satisfaction (in resource terms) than others. Every general principle of justice must have sufficient flexibility to accommodate exceptions which can be justified on grounds of a consideration of others' interests, and fairness in the treatment of persons. The 'equal right' principle does not assume that all individuals will receive equal benefits in terms of basic social goods, or things *valued* as a whole by society, for apart from the need criterion there are other determinants of what is actually received by individuals, including motivation and effort. What is implied is rather an adequate minimum for the fulfilment of individual needs, and some of the social goods are so articulated that the attainment of one is dependent upon the prior attainment of another. Thus with respect to education basic social goods must include an appropriate minimum level of material welfare in such things as housing and food, and a certain level of satisfaction with an individual's social condition relative to that of others. Motivation and effort required for learning are seriously eroded by poverty and social dissatisfaction. Education can only work effectively in developing individual potentialities from a base of sympathetic dispositions – favourable motives, attitudes and values.

Vocational preparation presents a special difficulty. It *is* in the interests of individuals in society to have persons trained for their vocations as tradesmen, technicians, or professional workers of all kinds. The needs that are satisfied in such education are both individual and social (with the social given a special ideological accent under socialist governments). In free enterprise societies there is a point beyond which the individual benefits more than individuals of society, regarded collectively, from an education *above* the basic provisions required to satisfy his strictly *educational* needs (in terms of his developing potentialities). Those who have a need for tertiary education to further develop their intellectual potentialities are considered to have a right to it; but the argument is apt to be strained with respect to those tertiary students who are pursuing specialized vocational studies from which they will be the major beneficiaries, and which exceed their educational needs according to our formal notion of education. Here judgements of distributive justice are required to be made by administrators of scarce public resources: with respect to some it may be argued that they fall into the exception category, on the assumption that expenditure on their tertiary education has a high probability of benefiting individuals in a society as a whole. This argument may be applied, for instance, to the professional preparation of teachers at all levels, and of members of some other professions whose earnings are not regarded as excessive by community standards. But with respect to some others, public funding of tertiary courses is of dubious justification according to the modified principle now proposed, with the need criterion apt to be used factitiously in sectional interests.

We recall that part of Rawls' second principle of justice refers to the justification of social and economic inequalities when attached to offices and positions which have been open to all under conditions of fair equality of opportunity. Each person is to have a right, that is, to stand for offices and positions on a basis of fair equality of opportunity. Since this is already embodied in the first principle, as part of political liberty which he acknowledges (p.61), there is no need for it to be re-stated. We shall therefore simplify Rawls' statement but no longer proceed with amendments to his formulations. The two principles of social justice which we propose are these:

First principle: Each person has an equal right to basic liberties provided that he does not infringe the liberties of others.
Second principle: Each person has an equal right to basic social goods according to need.

With respect to basic social goods we take a relative view of need, since it is influenced in part by social conditions, and society's capacity to provide.

Criticisms of the arguments Rawls uses do not necessarily invalidate principles of social justice which are similar to his.[13] We shall summarize briefly some of the areas of our disagreement with his position, specifically those relating to rationality and morality and a tendency to appeal to authority in Kant, while disregarding the more trivial criticisms that have been sometimes made, such as the artificiality of the original position with its veil of ignorance, which seem rather to depend upon a misunderstanding of Rawls' intentions. First, on the relationship between rationality and morality Rawls leans heavily on Kant as he wishes to demonstrate in his Kantian interpretation of justice as fairness (pp.251–7). He claims that his theory is based on Kant's notion of autonomy which supposedly refers to a person acting on principles chosen by him as a free and equal rational being, the veil of ignorance in the original position making it impossible for heteronomous choices to be made: that is, from considerations such as social position or particular wants. He claims further that principles of justice are categorical imperatives in Kant's sense, claiming that what Kant understands by a categorical imperative is a principle of conduct derived from a person's nature as a free and equal rational being. He notes certain correspondences between his views and those of Kant, such as the assumption of mutual disinterest according with Kant's notion of autonomy. He refers to the original position as the point of view from which noumenal selves see the world, noumenal selves having complete freedom to choose whatever principles they wish. He believes he is following in the tradition of Kant whose aim he asserts as deepening and justifying Rousseau's idea that liberty is acting according to law, a moral law, which we give ourselves. In all, he sees the original position as a procedural interpretation of Kant's conception of autonomy and the categorical imperative. The correspondences Rawls claims are not close when we put his theory against Kant's notion of the Good Will. What is missing most in Rawls' theory is the sense of moral obligatoriness which Kant's notions of autonomy and the categorical imperative dictate. The link made with Kant in aspects such as noumenal selves is tenuous and unsupportive of Rawls' position, inasmuch as these have proved vulnerable to criticism in Kant himself.

Second, Rawls' claim that rationality has the capacity for moral directiveness needs to be examined. There is an assumption that the rationality of the original position continues to exert a controlling influence in the deliberations toward the reflective equilibrium, and in this, as elsewhere, the place of dispositions is ignored. It is possible that in some circumstances these might contribute strongly to an equilibrium that is not a moral one. The mediating influence of dispositions opposes the free and rational stance of the *noumenal self*, which may be no more than an expression of a rational ideal. The original position is itself something of a rational game, although – as we have seen – it has a clear purpose; part of this game is the exercise of benevolence, Rawls claims, since the combination of conditions governing it forces each person to take the good of others into account (p.148). But beyond this artificial assumption of the original position, the link between rationality and morality in repeated references to the original position tends to leave a misleading impression that to be rational is to be moral. 'A good person', he says, 'has the features of moral character that it is rational for members of a well-ordered society to want in their associates' (p.437). Rawls' defence of a nexus between reason and morality rests on intuition.

Third, Rawls' social and political values and assumptions are sometimes hidden, but they do have an important effect on his general arguments.[14] Indeed his original position accepts uncritically the situation of inequalities. His reasoning is an attempt to make the best of what some consider to be a bad situation. Why would not rational persons in the original position consider the possibility of an initial situation *without* serious inequalities and inequities?

We shall carry forward to succeeding chapters the principles of social justice reached to this point. Despite the various criticisms of Rawls' theory of social justice, he stands with Plato, Rousseau and Kant as one with a genuine concern for others' interests, seeking from a moral stance a society where every individual is treated fairly as a person. His self-classification with Locke, Rousseau and Kant in a tradition of contract theory is not as important to an understanding of social justice as his alignment with Plato, Rousseau and Kant in a group which saw in common the immovable moral base of a just society. But in both Kant and Rawls the confidence that reason (and good will) will show the way unmistakably to morality is founded on a rational ideal. If we are to keep ideal theory in mind for what it is, and if we are to be guided in part by asking what is the case in experience, we shall have continuing doubts in this area.

COMPROMISE IN HUMBOLDT AND MILL

From first, philosophers of self-interest, to second, those of more positive moral concern, we now consider something of the tension between egoism and benevolence which characterizes much of the practical morality of everyday relations with others. Humboldt and Mill combine the self-protectiveness of the first group with something of the moral concern of the second. We glimpse the conflict between the two impulses as a powerful individualism asserts itself. Then it is that social justice becomes submerged beneath a defensive and self-interested elitism and paternalism, especially in Mill. The concept of fairness in the treatment of every person in the social group, based on a consideration of others' interests, becomes more and more blurred. The situation of underprivilege and inequality is seldom seen as a threat to social justice.

For a philosopher such as Mill, the Nineteenth Century concern for the individual and his *liberty* was understandable. Humboldt provided him with a supporting argument for liberty in his views on the development of unique individualities. Neither Humboldt nor Mill departed far from pragmatic and practical considerations, each expressing something of the political anxieties of the time. Together they establish a bridge to the next chapter which considers social justice from practical perspectives. There was something savouring of political lobbying and rationalization rather than rigorous analysis in the case for individualism as Humboldt and Mill expressed it. But from the ingenuous egoism of Hobbes, Locke and Nozick, to the forthright individualism of Humboldt and Mill, there is the perennial theme of state power as a threat to the individual. In none of these is there a fundamental relating of ideas to the formal notions of justice, morality and education.

Humboldt: *the Limits of State Action*

For moral support Nozick leaned heavily on Locke, instead of filling in the moral background to his theory which he saw as a yawning gap (p.9). By contrast Humboldt wrote from the centre of society as he observed it, anticipating much of Nineteenth Century liberalism,[15] and giving reasons for his moral and social judgements with confidence (as might perhaps be expected of the designer of the Prussian education system and the founder of the University of Berlin). His argument begins with the assertion that individuality is the true end of man, and that it can be cultivated in its highest form as the individual interacts with others in social groups (ch.11, pp.16–19). That was not an original observation, and what followed was more significant as an expression of his central thought: restricted only by the limits of his powers and his rights, the individual was to develop himself by his own freedom and energy, emphatically without external agencies of any kind (pp.20–1). The bane of all such honest endeavours is the solicitude of the state for its citizens' welfare (ch. 111, p.32). The best political condition for man is to live in a community with great diversity of individualities and the most extensive freedom, each establishing 'profound associations'. On national education he had grave doubts. His theme was the fundamental importance of human development 'in its richest diversity' (ch. V, p.57), a theme which Mill took up, as we have noted, impressed by Humboldt's account of this as 'the grand, leading principle' of his work. He marshalled his arguments against the solicitude of the state for the welfare of the nation. First, such government produces national uniformity, restricts the free play of individual energies and inhibits the vigorous character that comes from a clash of individualities. Second, such positive political institutions tend to weaken the vitality of the nation; the moral character deteriorates as the individual submits to coercion; mutual assistance wanes as it is recognized as a matter for the state to take care of; self-reliance at the heart of individuality is weakened. Third, every individual should strive for the development of his 'inner life', the cultivation of the soul as unified and harmonious. Fourth, government measures are designed for the mass of the people, and may not meet the needs of individuals. Fifth, it hinders the development of individuality in its uniqueness. Sixth, administration becomes self-generating, growing more complex and expensive to the people. Seventh, men are not respected as persons: they are neglected merely as things, their creativity ignored for general results. Collectively they become 'living but lifeless instruments of action and enjoyment' instead of 'active and enjoying energies' (ch.111, pp.23–35). He too is left with the minimal state. His conclusion is that restriction on freedom should be only what is necessary for mutual security and protection against foreign enemies. In these views Humboldt's morality of individualism opposes the paternalism of the state: to him it is a presumption that state measures for whole masses of people can do more for individuals than they can do for themselves by their independent energies and free interaction with other *different* individuals, in a variety of diverse situations. But this is a morality that is compatible with benevolence: indeed, mutual assistance, the spirit of individuals helping others from positions of first-hand acquaintance, is acknowledged, while the false benevolence of paternalistic governments, from positions remote from such knowledge of individual circumstances, is denounced not only as ineffectual, but also as a threat to authentic moral relations.

Despite the occasional romantic flourish on such things as individual energies and the harmony of the soul, Humboldt's liberalism has departed from the concern for property protection found in Locke (and later in Nozick), and to that extent too his liberalism is compatible with our formal notion of morality. As for distributive justice, this is to him no more a practical question than it is to Nozick, though for a different reason: not over-riding self-interest, but a genuine concern for the development of individuality, free from the influence of governments toward uniformity. In this moral advance, on our assumptions, there is also a moral gap, for any assumption that mutual assistance will provide adequately for equality of opportunity, or at least for a radical reduction of inequalities of opportunity, is contrary to empirical evidence on contemporary social situations. There is the further difficulty that the kind of state Humboldt envisaged was neither characteristic of his times nor of ours. It is becoming increasingly more difficult to imagine what such a state would be like, but in addition, increasingly more difficult to believe at equality of opportunity, if left to individual resources in the minimal state, would be greater than is achieved in contemporary societies. Even if societies could be envisaged as minimal in terms of state powers, they have now attained a size and complexity which Humboldt could not have foreseen.

Mill: *On Liberty,* and *Representative Government*

We shall turn finally to Mill's views on the individual and the state as they are conveyed in *On Liberty* and *Representative Government*, taking into account his philosophical background as he conveyed in his essay 'Utilitarianism'. We shall note first, the extent to which he was influenced by, and shared, Humboldt's views, and then the aspects in which Mill was characteristically himself, particularly in his strong intellectual bias which included his views on education in relation to government. Humboldt's work was published in England only a few years before Mill wrote *On Liberty*. In this he paid tribute to Humboldt's emphasis on the need for freedom for the development of individuality (p.121),[16] an emphasis which was repeated throughout Humboldt's work, motivated in part by his fear that national education might be introduced. Mill shared these views, claiming that a general state education was 'a mere contrivance for moulding people' to uniformity. Like Humboldt he ignored the practical implications of *not* having a state education, in particular the implications for equality of educational opportunity. He made no specific mention of this view in *Representative Government*, but in a later work on *Auguste Comte and Positivism* he showed that his view was unchanged.[17] The stamp of uniformity which he feared in state education was an aspect of the general 'despotism of custom' as he called it in *On Liberty* (p.136), which is invariably opposed to the spirit of liberty. In the name of improvement an unwilling people may be subjected to changes which conflict with their individualities, and since the natural tendency of representative government is toward collective mediocrity' (*Representative Government*, p.265), the danger is compounded. It was in the latter emphasis, apart from his utilitarian views, that Mill departed significantly from Humboldt. Mill asserted a strongly intellectual and elitist bias, favouring representative government in principle, but distrusting the masses through an understandable concern for their level of education in his time. He therefore urged that the influence of the best intellects be exerted in

government as a means of offsetting the tyranny of custom (p.195
The superior intellects must be heard, even though they are outnun
bered (p.266); the tyranny of the majority is to be feared. Mill coul
see the need for an informed electorate, through developing powe
of independent, critical thought, but the social situation he faced w;
one where such intellectual powers were not widely distributed. H
insisted that the state should not direct education, even though
should insist that all be educated, leaving it to voluntary organiz;
tions to conduct an education that would preserve and develo
diversity in individuals (*On Liberty*, pp.176–7). The two principles
the need for an informed and thinking electorate and a voluntai
system of education – were not brought together by Mill. One resu
was that he left the question of equality of opportunity unanswere(
even aggravated, it would seem, by the very lack of state contr(
which he deplored. So in *Representative Government* he preferred t
take account of the actual situation rather than recommend any pla
for improving the quality of the electorate by education: he suggeste
that those with educational qualifications should have a plural vot(
giving to graduates of universities and certain other sufficient'
well-educated persons, 'the degree of superior influence' due to the)
(p.287). Later, in *Auguste Comte and Positivism* he commented c
Comte's proposal that all persons, rich and poor alike, girls as well ;
boys, should receive an education of a specialized kind between th
ages of fourteen and twenty-one years, noting that Comte w;
satisfied to produce passive, receptive minds rather than to develc
critical intellects (pp.412–13). Yet Mill saw no need to apply ar
modified scheme of education to English conditions, still unde
valuing ordinary people sufficiently to see the necessity for the be
minds to exert their influence and to be heard by the people. Mill
liberalism was constrained by this intellectual bias. The developmei
of distinctive individualities, free from state control, would t
safeguarded by the wisdom of the few: but in this Platonic thougl
one of the most conspicuous oversights was the limited opportuniti(
which it implied for the many. Equality of educational opportunit
was not a principle which Mill saw any need to espouse. His la
thoughts to be published, except his Autobiography, were containe
in the *Inaugural Address* (delivered as rector of the University of S
Andrews). In this he stressed the need for developing habits of logic
thought in a general university education, and the various subjec
that would contribute to this end. Professional men – lawyer
physicians, engineers – were to be made (as we have noted in Chapt(

) only *after* their intellectual education was complete: professional
r vocational education was not proper for universities[18] (p.5). Mill
ad no suggestions for lifting the educational standards of ordinary
eople by training them to reason clearly, either to prepare them as
iformed and critical electors, or to contribute to the utilitarian end
f the greatest happiness of the greatest number. Two of his major
iewpoints were never completely reconciled: first, a need for the
iost extensive liberties for all, with the proviso that prevention of
arm to others is the only justification for the exercise of power over
iy member of a civilized community against his will (*On Liberty*,
.68); second, a presumption that a select intellectual minority will
est serve the interests of the people in representative government.
etween the two was a principle of equality of opportunity: extensive
berty given with one hand, and taken away paternalistically with the
ther.

EVIEW

n perceptions of social justice the sharpest contrasts are between a
oup of philosophers dominated by self-interest and another with a
rimary moral orientation toward a practical consideration of others'
iterests, and fairness in the treatment of every person in society. A
ore of egocentrism appears to underlie conspicuous preferences for
ie minimal state and resistance to state welfare by redistributive
easures. Humboldt and Mill stand as instances of morality in
:tion, given particular historical, social and political circumstances.
s with Seventeenth Century Hobbes we see them as close to
ractical affairs, unable to cast off overriding personal protectiveness
id fundamental self-interest. Yet each had perceptions of liberal
leals supposedly in the interests of all citizens, as well as a genuine
oral concern for others.

Comparisons between individuals and between groups help to
iarpen distinctive ideas of social justice, leading as well to four
eneral observations: first, on the contrast between a public and
onventional morality, and one that is private and authentic; second,
i wide substantive variations from the formal notions of justice and
f morality; third, on a widespread and almost uniform concern at the
ower of the state over the individual; fourth, on varying assumptions
i equality and equity. We shall reflect on each of these in turn.

First, Hobbes and Locke each knew something of equity in Englis
law in their times, and of the background of inadequacies in Englis
common law which gave rise to it. In each therefore there was
formal acknowledgement of justice as fairness in the treatment c
persons, in the sense of equity and opposition to arbitrary discrimina
tion. This might be considered a conventional morality in the light c
their powerful self-interests. When this is extended to Nozick'
anxiety at the state taking from some and giving to others and s
destroying the principle of inviolable entitlements, there are ground
for reflections on all personal moralities and on the depth and exten
of their authenticity. Who does not experience a moral tension whe
the state demands some of what has been legitimately earned? Th
distinction commonly made between a public and a private moralit
has some relevance in every age: the morality we espouse, such as
morality of considering others' interests, may be different from th
private and more authentic morality which we live by. The wide
spread resistance to payment of taxes, even in the knowledge tha
they will be used substantially for welfare distribution, may reflect
conflict between an individual public moral face and an authenti
private morality that is predominantly self-regarding.

Second, substantive personal moralities vary widely from th
formal notion of morality, as well as of justice, influenced invariabl
by social circumstances. Plato's ideas on individual differences ha
nothing of our present knowledge from the social sciences. Therefor
justice as fairness in the treatment of persons was not destroyed as
formal notion according to the standards he knew. His occupationa
stratification *was* a conception of *fairness*, based on his belief in th
tripartite division of the soul. It conformed to the formal notion c
morality as a practical consideration of others' interests inasmuch a
it considered the interests of all according to what were to hir
indestructible laws of nature. Rawls and Nozick would each claim
morality based on our formal notion, but substantively they varie
between concern for a fair distribution of resources and a considera
tion of the interests of others as holders of entitlements.

Third, on the power of the state as a threat to the individual all
with the exception of Kant – explicitly agree. (Kant was preoccupie
with the state of man, not with the social state.) The stronges
concern was felt by Hobbes, Locke and Nozick, but Rawls too – fo
all his compassion and interest in a fair distribution of society'
resources – argued for a limited state, with extensive liberties fo
citizens. Nozick has written in recent times of increasing welfar

provisions in many societies, with redistributive schemes offensive to some of the more fortunate. Hobbes was concerned for personal security as he observed the growing power of the Commons and the threat of conflict. Locke could never be sure, when he wrote, of the stability or permanence of the English Revolution. Viewpoints on state-individual relations have thus been influenced invariably by particular social circumstances. It is significant that regardless of such differing circumstances, the concern is widespread among social philosophers for a protection of individuals' liberties against the state. Yet if social justice is to be organized in such a way as to ensure that every individual is treated fairly as a person, with those of his interests specially considered which have a positive bearing on his life prospects, the tension between state intervention and preservation of individual liberties becomes obvious.

Fourth, there are various assumptions made on equality and equity which have relevance to social justice. The rough kind of justice foreshadowed by Hobbes and Locke in the social contract was fair in its consistency, but unfair from the standpoint of equity. For what one had one held, and the assumption was made that property distribution was just. That implied a particular way of looking at property. The question of acquisition was covered as far as it need be, by law. But the underlying assumption on property was that there was, or had been historically, an equality of opportunity in acquiring it, and in the class-structured society of England, taking into account the social situation of agricultural workers as opposed to land-holders, that assumption could not be sustained. A morality whose formal basis is a practical consideration of others' interests was largely wanting in each, except for the superficial respect of the contract taking into account mutual protective interests. In this outlook there was no thought of easing the burden of the underprivileged and no thought of uniting morality and education by universal education for the developing of *individual* potentialities.

In the case of Rawls, his ideal theory begins with the premiss that inequalities are part of the social order; it is his own class-structured society that he has in mind throughout. While acknowledging that educational resources are to be used not merely for economic return, but also to provide access to cultural enjoyment, education receives brief mention only in this theory, and there is no suggestion that distribution of educational resources on an equitable basis, and in the sense of a developing of each individual's potentialities, might become a means of reducing social inequalities generally, in accordance with individual need. Nozick too focusses on the social situation as he knows it, assuming as just the distribution of resources as they are found to be in so far as they are moral entitlements. What is unequal in property and life prospects must be defended as just if it is so based. Justice is not a matter of redistributing to improve the condition of the least advantaged in society. Injustice is not a question of poverty co-existing with wealth beyond individual needs. Inequality of educational opportunity is defensible as the outcome of legitimate social processes.

In the individualism of Humboldt and Mill there were also assumptions on equality and equity, especially in the liberal notion that each man should make his own way, earn by his own effort what he gets, and that charity would weaken the morality of the nation through destroying the will to work. Everyone has equality of opportunity in making his way: none deserve more help than others. Mill overlaid these views with a characteristic intellectualism, which impelled him to support university education to develop an elite of individuals able to reason clearly, and knowledgeable as well, not unlike Plato's preparation of rulers. But a combination of distrust of the people, apprehension about the effects of the state's encroachments on basic liberties, and his own intellectual values, all contributed to give his liberalism its characteristic stamp.

It is the last of these four considerations – the assumptions made on equality and equity – that link this chapter directly with the next two, where we shall explore the problem of equality of educational opportunity in relation to our formal notions of justice, morality and education. Ideas which we shall carry forward in our further reflections refer to individual liberty and the extent of state power and authority compatible with it; individual talents and individual needs; good fortune and bad fortune in the start to life; inequalities inherent in social conditions, including inequality of educational opportunity; and through all of these, in their various expressions in historical and social context, a need for tolerance from an appreciation of our common imperfections, even in reason itself. We shall expect a continuing tension between benevolence and egoism, and between privilege and fairness in the treatment of all persons. In social justice we shall be increasingly concerned with *equity*, both as fairness and as a proper proportion holding between and among persons. Our discussion of philosophers' views on social justice has indicated the extent of the tension between dispositions (as we have used the word) and reason, for what is considered just is now seen to be a complex judgement made not with the detachment of pure speculative reason, but rather with a variety of influences on reason including personal values and their associated attitudes, as well as the influences on them of social and political conditions. Relativist views on social justice are nonetheless rejected, for the same reason as were relativist views on moral values. What constitutes social justice in any particular judgement is to be argued for with the best reasons that can be adduced. The exposure of value and social influences may contribute to an evaluation of a judgement on social justice, but there is no objective social justice to be discovered by paring away such influences as these. Hobbes, Locke, Nozick, Rousseau, Rawls, Humboldt and Mill were each subject to dispositional influences. The same may be said of Plato, though with less certainty because of the dearth of biographical evidence; and of Kant – despite his similar dedication to a life of reason. If social justice is not objectively discoverable, in the viewpoints of the various philosophers there are ideas on it which have universal relevance to human societies, as well as relevance to our subsequent discussion. For while dispositions and social conditions are variables, there are still certain constants in human nature.

7 Practical Perspectives

Philosophical perspectives in the preceding chapter have provided ideas for reflection on social justice: we have intimated that justice in a social context is none other than justice as fairness in the treatment of every person in a social group, and that the state cannot evade a moral responsibility for its adminstration. In these respects there must be a practical consideration of others' interests – in particular of the well-being of all others without discrimination – however broad the approach, of necessity, to take account of administrative exigencies and practicalities, for obviously no state instrumentality could afford the time to consider all the interests of every individual. We have glimpsed something of the liberal individualism of Humboldt and Mill, but have not yet developed the inadequacies of this position as social justice. We have referred to the subjectivity of judgements on social justice. This is consistent with our general ethical standpoint, and it is this that links directly with the substance of the present chapter. If subjective, and influenced by dispositional factors in values and their associated attitudes in particular, our judgements on social justice may not always be as strongly rational as we suppose them to be. Further, the object of our judgements may be misperceived for a variety of reasons which we shall now consider as we move from philosophical to practical perspectives. Among these misperceptions none may be more conspicuously in conflict with social justice than *equality of opportunity*, and its vital connection with education.

The plan of this chapter is first, to consider concepts of equality and equality of opportunity, leading to the statement of a principle of equality of educational opportunity; second, to consider the possible sources of illusion in our perception of the social situation. To be clear on concepts helps us to understand the nature of the problem before us, but such an understanding is no more than a start, and may be nullified subsequently by illusory perceptions. The two classes of illusion to be considered are those stemming first from ideologies; second from political deception. The 'practical perspectives' of the chapter title refer to the way social relations are perceived in practice.

250

This approach contrasts with the abstraction of ideal theory as in Rawls and Nozick, and with Plato's vision of an ideal society. It goes further than the realism of Hobbes and Locke as they summed up the political situation of their time, and further than the confident judgements of Humboldt and Mill on the encroachments of state power. This chapter will serve a similar cautionary function to that of Chapter 4 which introduced Practical Applications with an exploration of the interaction of dispositions and reason. That interaction is relevant to the present chapter also, but now we increase complexity by exploring possibilities of the social situation *not* being as we and others perceive it.

INTRODUCTION

Equality

Like Human Rights and Natural Justice, the language of *equality* is often characterized by generalities. What would it be like, for instance, to be *equal* to others under a social contract? Once the terms of association were worked out and the rules made public, justice as fairness would require the recognition of the right for all to equal and undiscriminatory treatment under the rules, for the 'free and equal' principle implies that every individual is to be respected as a person, and assigned equal (the same) fundamental rights. What is implied here is the need Aristotle observed for equality of consideration, and, in addition, an obligation on those who have power or influence over others to apply rules with consistency and impartiality. It is generally not practicable, except for small social units under optimum conditions of compatibility or homogeneity such as those possible for selective discussion groups, for terms of association to be agreed upon as a basis for cooperation that is to be fair for all individuals. We shall set aside particular theoretical frameworks such as the social contract and utilitarianism, though we shall recognize the difficulty of claiming an entirely theory-free stance ourselves since we have already conveyed a set of assumptions, especially in our occasional substantive extensions of the formal notions of morality, justice and education. When we perceive some individuals as having been treated differently from others those differences of treatment are justified, we claim, by impartial considerations, again on an assumption of equal respect for persons. This kind of procedural equality of consideration leaves unanswered certain substantive questions such as what equality is, or what it is to be impartial, or indeed, what justice as fairness in the treatment of persons is. Different administrators, with power or influence over others, each believing that he is acting with equality of consideration, may proceed to judge equality among persons in different ways through lack of common substantive criteria. Rational men and women differ in their capacity to reason, as we have emphasized from time to time, as well as in their dispositions, so that with equally good intentions they can scarcely be equal as moral agents, at least on any assumption of a capacity to deliver identically sound judgements on others. But 'equal' is not to be construed as 'identical'. To speak of all persons as having 'equal intrinsic value' is not to attribute to each an identical potential for moral behaviour, for it says nothing of relevant differences of abilities and capacities, knowledge, understanding of others, values, tastes and ideals. Those who are able to attract equal respect as persons, then, simply by virtue of their being persons and no more, may differ substantively as moral agents, and their moral desert in particular situations – in so far as it can be evaluated by others also morally limited – is related to the differences, the *relevant* differences, between and among them. Generalities about equality, and about treating equals equally, and unequals unequally, tend therefore to beg the question. To ask in what respects persons are equal soon leads to the more pertinent question, In what relevant respects are they *different*? If the treatment of others is different on the grounds that there are differences among them relevant to the moral situation, those grounds must be explained: the onus of justification is on the person alleging the differences. Similarly, impartiality demands that *irrelevant* differences be ignored. Discriminatory practices are morally objectionable generally because they contain elements clearly irrelevant to the situation: when black children are not given the same quality or extent of schooling as white children, for instance.

Equality of Education Opportunity

The notion of equality of educational opportunity invokes the question of what the opportunity is *for*. Those who see the notion in the context of social justice generally have more in mind than the formal notion of education as an improving of individuals, for beyond that there is an end of *individual* well-being (as distinct from a collective or cumulative utilitarian end).

Educational opportunity refers to two distinct ways in which 'education' is used which may be described as the intrinsic and the extrinsic, or instrumental. The first is the formal notion of education as a developing of individual potentialities, consistent with social values; individual well-being is an integral part of this process, with growing satisfaction as potentialities are progressively developed. The second refers to an opportunity for something much larger than the first – including it, but seeing it as a means to wider life prospects in general. This instrumental perspective is assumed by parents and students concerned for vocational opportunities, but as well by theorists of various kinds who are interested in distributive justice, for social goods to be distributed include education itself in the formal sense, but also a range of goods that flow from it according to particular social values – goods such as material possessions, and in a class-conscious society, social advantage. When we move from the intrinsic perspective to a perspective of justice and morality, we find that we can no longer sustain a categorical rejection of the instrumental approach to educational opportunity. For while on the one hand we may deplore society's materialist values, with many seeing education as no more than a means to an end of lucrative employment when intellectual and moral education may often end, on the other hand we find we must take account of empirical evidence in our reasoning, specifically on what is the case as it is ascertained to be by competent research;[1] and this compels us toward a vital connection between the two senses of educational opportunity. That connection is brought forcibly to our notice in considering the fundamental situation of the underprivileged, or those highly disadvantaged socially: their condition is apt to be one of reproduction from one generation to the next, and in this their attitudes and values relating to education's instrumental value in improving their condition, combined with a sense of social injustice as they compare themselves with others, have an inevitable impact on motivation to learn. It is these in particular who are often caught in a web of distributive *injustice*: their housing, their work prospects, their struggle to survive materially, and their consequent dispositions, may leave them with little chance of extricating themselves from the social condition which limits their opportunities to develop their potentialities, and which in turn tends to leave them where they were at the beginning, in a chronic state of social depression. In that situation any attempt at distributive justice is rendered ineffectual.

For education to have a suitable base from which to generate improvement there must be a social condition that offers hope for the future. When that condition prevails, the individual has an opportunity to improve his condition still further by means of education. In this we have little reason to deplore extrinsic motivation in education – the individual viewing education instrumentally, for in many instances motives are mixed, and there is no incompatibility between a student working industriously with an end-in-view of a particular secure vocation, and simultaneously developing his potentialities. From perspectives of justice and morality, a just society would not be satisfied with the distribution of education as a social good in the instrumental sense *alone*, for that would be to foster a non-moral society, or one of low moral standards, in which a consideration of the interests of others would be submerged beneath a dominant and general self-interest, and notions of individual well-being would be controlled by materialist impulses and life-orientations. Yet a just society must have some concern for the distribution of basic elementary and secondary education to develop potentialities sufficiently so that they might lead to more equitable life prospects for all. And it must have some concern for the distribution of social goods on which educational goods partly depend: adequate material conditions of life and a fair comparability with others to remove debilitating emotional effects of envy and a corroding sense of injustice. In some circumstances the instrumental advantages of education may not be set in motion at all because of frustrating dispositional influences of attitudes and values which may be reflected in morbid or angry expressions of hopelessness.

The problem of equality of educational opportunity requires justice, morality and education to be seen together. From our considerations to this point, we may assert that the primary principle of equality of educational opportunity is this: that *each person has an equal right to education according to need, regardless of whether he is fortunate or unfortunate in natural endowments or in the social conditions of his upbringing.* As a formal principle this covers all cases, including that of the individual who cannot, by his own exertions alone, rise above impoverished social circumstances even with the schooling provided compulsorily by the state. Substantively, the state has an obligation to make the principle relevant and workable by social reform and redistributive measures wherever necessary, so that the principle both is, and is seen to be, more than a liberal gesture. No one must be prevented simply by the circumstances of his social condition from undergoing an education according to needs. The formal principle does not imply that equality of educational opportunity will achieve *actual* equality on any specific dimension, such as knowledge or other educational attainments, or respect for the social order, or material benefits when education is viewed instrumentally. This kind of equality expresses the assumptions of naive egalitarians that all persons can be *made* equal by a variety of means such as the levelling of scholastic attainments by suitable compensatory programmes. The facts of individual differences in abilities, capacities, and dispositions prevent such an outcome. Equal opportunity to develop potentialities by means of education can be no more than a *prima facie* principle. There are many contingent factors in individual circumstances, quite apart from ability – factors such as the physical and mental health of the family, the student's own health, personal tragedy and so forth – which may affect an individual's opportunities, factors over which he has no more control than he has over his natural endowments. *Actual* or literal equality of opportunity, in, or by means of, education, is an ideal toward which social reformers may be inclined, but its complete, ultimate or perfect attainment is beyond realization.

IDEOLOGICAL ILLUSIONS:

CONTRASTING POLITICAL IDEOLOGIES

One of the problems is that perceptions of equality of opportunity may not be what they seem, even in the formulation of our ideals. The way we see the social situation depends partly upon the ideas, beliefs and preconceptions already individually held, usually included in the dispositional tendencies of our motives, attitudes and values. In some cases it may be true that we see what we want to see, or what it is in our interests to see. Therefore when we see equality, others may see inequality, and this is significant for society when we consider the perceptions of those in government, for they may view equality of opportunity in ways which serve the interests of their own social class, and not the interests of all individuals in their society. Such are the views of some who interpret social perspectives in terms of ideologies. It is these views which we shall now consider, linking them with the conclusion reached in the last chapter suggesting the uniqueness of an individual's subjective views of society as illustrated in the case of Hobbes and Locke, Rousseau, Humboldt and Mill, Rawls and Nozick. In their views of the overriding importance of individual liberties and the corresponding limitation of state powers over the individual, all conveyed to some extent elements of a classical liberal ideology, with its emphasis on material success by personal effort. This was given bolder lines, and a more personal emphasis, by Locke and Nozick in particular, with their direct concern that a minimal state should protect the personal 'estate' or 'holdings'. Underlying this major strand of classical liberalism (another is support for representative government, which had attracted Mill, for instance) is the assumption, already noted, that there is approximate equality of opportunity among individuals, and if educational opportunity is a factor in achieving other opportunities, such as for material success, it is either assumed or disregarded. More often than not, such assumptions may be undeclared, or suppressed: adherents of this viewpoint may try hard not to think of such things, or may in fact be unconscious of them. In these considerations we are foreshadowing various viewpoints on ideologies. Thus the previous chapter, with its views of philosophers on state–individual relations, and the extent to which these views are influenced by social and political circumstances, will complement this, for each approach draws attention to the difficulty of grasping exactly what the problem is, and of deciding whose perception of social justice is to be supported. We may expect to find confirmation of two matters already discussed: first, the influence of dispositions on reasoning as explained in Chapter 4; second, the status of political and social values as similar to moral values, inasmuch as they are not to be evaluated for truth or falsehood, but rather for having relatively strong or relatively weak arguments in their support.

Characteristics of Ideologies

On what constitutes an ideology there is, as we shall see, considerable divergence of opinion. In a most general and formal sense we may say that an ideology is a belief system, a way of seeing the world. It is thus a conception of the world, but not a theory, if by theory we denote a structure of ideas which attempts to explain the world as it is. While some ideologies convey a political and a social aspiration, and are ameliorative in intention, others are directed at maintaining the status quo, but in each case there is a normative basis. As we would not analyse the attitudes and values of others as true or false, so we would not attempt to evaluate an ideology as true or false, except with respect to particular beliefs which it might include. Indeed ideologies may be said to form part, but not a *necessary* part, of the dispositional complex which we have described in Chapter 4. Belonging to attitude and value systems, that sub-part which is ideological shares their general characteristics: we form an emotional attachment to a cluster of ideas, beliefs and values which make us committed to it not merely in a cognitive sense, but also in an action-oriented sense. The ideology is attitudinal, leading its adherents to respond characteristically to objects relevant to it. These responses may be rationalizations, rather than entirely rational; adherents may become so involved in the ideological commitment that they may, without any sense of presumption or arrogance, believe their action responses to be irreproachable. Thus ideologies may in some measure *mask* perceptions. While various theorists may attain a mutual tolerance and respect as each attempts to explain the world without dogma, and rather, as in science, pursue a common search for empirical knowledge, adherents of various ideologies are not so disposed. Mutual tolerance and respect are not characteristic of ideological believers, but dogma is, and this is characteristic of the *kind* of thinking that is pursued, with the in-built stubbornness and defensiveness of attitude and value systems generally, and their resistance to different ideas which threaten change. This is not to say that ideologies are formed without rational grounds: the reasons given for them may be examined, and some found to be stronger and more supportable than others, with or without a total acceptance of the belief system. Some of the grounds also raise questions of justice and morality, and of education as well, particularly with respect to equality of opportunity. Some of the grounds too may be based in conditions of an historical period, as we noted in some of the social and political theories of the last chapter. As such, ideologies while attempting to universalize social relations for all time, may – through their resistance to change – fail to observe the need to adjust to very different social circumstances in an ever-changing world. Yet over a sufficient period ideologies may change, and their differences from one century to the next, in particular from the last century to the present, are perceptible in some thinkers, even though the basic structure of original formulations are rigidly maintained by some others. There is nothing more binding among some adherents than a sense of social injustice; among others than a threat to their material possessions.

Thus motives, as part of the dispositional complex, are also relevant to ideologies.

Marx and Engels : Founders of Marxist Ideology

We shall now consider the two dominant political ideologies in contemporary societies – the marxist and the liberal – for their bearing on equality of opportunity generally and educational opportunity in particular. We shall not dwell on the early uses of 'ideology', such as those by de Tracy (who first used the word at the end of the Eighteenth Century), or by Napoleon,[2] but it is necessary to present the views of Karl Marx in some detail to give them coherence and relevance to our enquiry. 'Ideology' was opprobrious to Marx, especially in his early writing, where it referred to *false consciousness*, a state of deception in which workers were persuaded to believe what was not in their interests but in the interests of the ruling bourgeoisie.[3] In ideology men and their relations, he held, are an inversion of reality, appearing upside down. Marx used 'ideology' in a different sense when, in *Capital*, he referred to social consciousness as determined by different modes of production, but in this, and in other later works as well, continued to use it occasionally in a derogative sense. In *The German Ideology*[4] Marx and Engels explained how false consciousness is generated by those in power. Those who rule think, have consciousness, and so rule also as thinkers or producers of ideas for a whole historical epoch. Where there is no single ruling class, and various classes such as royalty, aristocracy and bourgeoisie are contending for domination, the doctrine that becomes dominant is one of separation of powers, because that doctrine is in the interests of the various contending parties. When the aristocracy happens to be in power, the dominant ideas are those such as honour and loyalty, because such ideas are clearly in their interests. When the bourgeoisie is in power, concepts such as freedom and equality are dominant, and the ruling class *imagines* that these are properly in everyone's consciousness. What happens in such processes is that the ruling class presents its interests to others as the common interests of all members of society: it imbues in all a *false consciousness*. The characteristic process of a ruling class presenting ruling ideas to all others ends abruptly with a change of social organization; when, that is, society is no longer structured according to the rule of a class. Later in the same work Marx and

ngels attack consciousness of equality as a natural feeling common
all, based upon a feeling of 'natural human affinity and unity.' It is
gain false consciousness: social inequalities of every age have existed
nder such a banner, even feudalism and slavery. It appears natural
r the same reason as Marx had noted earlier: it is a ruling idea, an
istorical product, in the interests of the ruling class.

For those who believe that contemporary capitalist societies
vhich we shall call 'liberal democracies' in ideological contexts) are
lled by particular classes, either the working class, let us say, or –
ore probably – the relatively affluent upper and middle classes
lepending on electoral fortunes), the explanation of Marx and
ngels has implications for equality, and equality of opportunity,
earer to some in the latter case than the former, for then the notion
f false consciousness is more evident to them. In this explanation it
ould be in the interests of socially advantaged classes in power to
ropagate, and to *imagine* as real, the notion that all members of
ciety are free and equal, that all do in fact have equality of
ducational opportunity. If children of workers then, do not advance
s high on the occupational ladder as children of the classes in power,
is not through any lack of opportunity: it is a question rather of
ffort, for all have opportunities for equal education through school-
g provided by the state. All have an opportunity to proceed to
rtiary education, to advance out of their social condition, even to
e more lucrative occupations. We shall return to this point of view
ter: enough has been suggested already to indicate that if such a
onsciousness of freedom and equality exists it is a false conscious-
ess, particularly with respect to extremes of social disadvantage
hich tend to be reproductive. If a working class happened to be in
ower, according to this explanation, it might espouse ruling-class
leas of *inequality* and *inequities* in educational opportunity which
ould be in its interests, and if we imagine such a class in power over
sufficient period, enforcing redistributive measures to destroy
xisting social advantages, and an over-compensation so that working
lasses have better opportunities for education through special
llowances of various kinds – including living away from home
llowances, let us say, and provision of residential colleges with
utors to improve the study facilities for their children – again we
ave the possibility of a false consciousness arising historically,
magined as real and accepted by all, including the formerly socially
dvantaged classes whose children would now have unequal opportu-
ities for education. Such a theoretical possibility would be very

unlikely to eventuate over a generation or two, but Marx and Engels
have in mind ruling classes and ruling ideas over an 'historical epoch'.
Apart from this, the general level of education in society, and its
articulateness on social issues, would reduce the probability of such
an occurrence; though in some societies social awarenesses of
inequalities and their acceptance have not been incompatible. To
Marx and Engels this situation would have been totally unreal:
historically the working class never had been a ruling class. It is
sufficient to note the general point made by Marx and Engels that
social awareness which is conditioned by a ruling class is false
consciousness; and ideas of equality of educational opportunity may
amount to false consciousness. One of the dangers in such a situation,
from the marxist perspective, is that over a long period some
members of society become habituated to such false notions of
freedom and equality of opportunity, so that the ruling class and all
others *imagine* them as true. This becomes part of their lived
ideology, whereby they perceive social situations not as they are, but
as illusions.

So to Marx and Engels ideology refers to an individual's consciousness of society with its class distinctions and distortions of reality
which it is in the interests of the ruling class to instil and to
perpetuate: in time all classes become lulled to a passive acceptance
of ruling ideas which form part of that consciousness. That uncritical
acceptance is supported, thought Marx and Engels, by historical
processes of alienation, with man alienated from his fellows, from the
product of his labour, and from nature. A glimpse of a marxist
economic viewpoint adds a further dimension to this ideology. In *The
German Ideology* the two explained that the historical development
of a system of division of labour has alienated man from his work: it
has appeared as an alien force which he does not understand; he loses
sight of the purpose of production, for it is taken out of his hands.
With the broadening of his activity and that of his fellow workers, all
become more and more enslaved under a power which is alien to
them: it is none other than the world market. Then class warfare
begins; the bourgeoisie develops only gradually, then becomes
fragmented according to the division of labour, but eventually
absorbs all propertied classes. Individuals form separate classes and
at once become involved in inter-class struggles. Thus man is
alienated from his fellows by the division of labour, and personal
relations become transformed to material powers. The fact that
individuals feel freer than before under the dominance of the

ourgeoisie is an indication of the power of ideology as a distorting ocial consciousness: they are in fact less free, but are governed in ways of which they are not aware, by material forces.[5] Freedom and quality in this social consciousness would lead to the blurring of ifferences in educational opportunity, to an acceptance, that is, of iequalities, imagining them in lived ideologies as *equalities*. And om the viewpoint of the bourgeoisie, the ruling class in the evelopment of capitalist production, Marx saw the readiness with vhich some might keep the working class uneducated, committed to n ideology which saw the huge economic machine supported by a oarse division of those who would work with their heads and those ho would work with their hands. From such an ideological stance quality of educational opportunity cannot be for all members of ociety, since the opportunity is given to one class only.[6] And from iis ideological perspective too, the possibilities of illusions fostered y the ruling class widen to include economic considerations: the conomic benefits of including within the belief system the notion iat capitalist production requires a body of workers who are repared to work for minimum wages to keep the production iachine going. The capitalist himself, making profits by buying ommodities as cheaply as possible and selling over their value, ould never succeed in turning his money into capital if he paid ages according to the value of labour. One of the falsehoods then in ie ideology of capitalism, according to Marx, is the belief in the low alue of manual workers,[7] and this is a belief which they themselves ome to share, so that as inferiors they do not themselves expect to be ell-educated, or to share equally in any other social goods.

Critics of Marx seldom disagree that in our consciousness of social elations there may be a degree of illusion. What is often in ontention is Marx's claim that while all social perceptions are false in) far as they are conditioned, this principle does not apply, or pplies with less force, to his own social perceptions. In *The German leology* Marx and Engels stressed that consciousness is a social roduct. It is 'life that determines consciousness'; that is, conscious-ess is conditioned by the material activity of men in the mode of roduction of their material life. History develops as men re-create ieir own lives in this materialist context, and establish materialist onnections with other men, determined by their needs and their iodes of production.[8] It is Marx's view of social consciousness that as attracted non-marxists, rather than his view of historical develop-ent, which is often disputed. Thus Karl Mannheim in *Ideology and*

Utopia acknowledges on the one hand that interests of those in powe
may foster illusions and that Marx has thrown some light on th
historical situation of *Nineteenth Century liberalism*; but on the oth
hand argues that marxism carried forward to a different time ar
place, on the assumption that it offers a *universal* interpretation (
historical development, is untenable, for in this it fails to take accou
of distinctive features within societies that help to explain the
various situations. Further, that human thought occurs within
particular social context does not establish that it is necessari
conditioned by forces in that context, or that its social context
necessarily a source of error and illusion. Is Marx's view of ideolog
therefore too rigid, too much determined by *particular* conditions
have universal relevance? Is it not within our power to dispel illusio
by habits of critical thought? Is there not interaction between or
dispositions and our reason, as we proposed in Chapter 4? Narrow
ness of particular points of view, rooted in preconceptions ar
prejudices, for instance, are not necessarily shared by all, ar
although critical discussion with others may not be value-fre
individual dispositional tendencies in conflict with rational evalu
tions have a chance of being exposed as others view them externall
Critical discussion may also expose the binding quality of language
used by those who follow the *form* of ideologies such as the marxis
worshipping some of the idols which Francis Bacon saw as imped
ments to understanding and science.[9] Marx himself could not claim,
he were to be consistent, immunity from illusion. In rejectir
marxism's universal relevance, Mannheim argued that it is ideologi
al in the illusory sense for failing to take account of what is new in
social situation.[10]

Contemporary Marxists

Since the views of Marx and Engels related specifically to Nineteen
Century societies, we shall select from contemporary marxists on
only to convey both similarity and difference in his views with their
as well as relevance to the problem of equality of education
opportunity. The views of Louis Althusser are similar to Marx's c
equality, inasmuch as Marx's main concern was for inequaliti
masquerading ideologically as equalities: it was in the interests of th
bourgeoisie to propagate the myth of freedom and equality for

citizens, and to live an ideology that imagined a situation of equality of opportunity for all. In *For Marx* Althusser describes an ideology as a system of representations made up of images, myths, ideas or concepts (p.231),[11] but unlike Marx, holds that an ideology, far from being some kind of aberration, is essential to the life of every society: even a communist society could not be without it, for corresponding to the social organization of production, it requires an ideological structure. (p.232) Ideology he says, has very little relationship with *consciousness*; indeed, it is 'profoundly unconscious'. As a structuralist, Althusser believes that ideologies are structures of images, and occasionally concepts, which are impressed on the minds of most men (p.233). An ideology is a lived relation between men and their world. This presupposes, he says, two distinct relations: first the real, second the imaginary (or lived). Rather than describing a reality, the ideology, as an imaginary relation, may express a hope or nostalgia, or a will such as a reformist or conformist will (p.234). While the sense of illusion which Marx gave to ideology is taken over, in most cases, by Althusser, the derogatory notion of false consciousness is lost. In place of that is the positive notion of ideology's indispensability in the structure of society: in a classless society it provides the means for men living their social relations in a way that is to everyone's advantage, in contrast with the situation in a class-structured society, where ideology is a means for men living their relations with particular social and economic conditions to the advantage of the ruling class. Since that is much as Marx saw the situation, Althusser's individual interpretation of ideologies has not substantially changed his view on equality and equality of opportunity. By implication an ideology in a class society would be a system of representations expressing an unconscious imaginary relation between men and their world, and one which conveys a myth of equality since that is what serves the interests of the ruling class.

Althusser has more to say about formal education and its implications for equality of educational opportunity than had Marx or Engels. These judgements are of interest first, for their connection with marxist ideology of the previous century; second, for the speculative quality of the judgements themselves, especially in so far as they convey an opinion on social justice.

Althusser sees societies as complex structures in which ideologies interact with other structures such as the economic, the political and the cultural. Apart from its obvious political and legal institutions the state has also an *ideological apparatus* which includes culture and

education. Since the development of industrialized societies, education, he says, has taken over as the dominant ideological apparatus.
In order to exist every formation must, as Marx explained in *Capital*,
reproduce the means of production.[12] It is the *schools*, Althusser
believes, more than any other influence in society, which have
operated to instil those values which will ensure the continued
hegemony of the bourgeoisie as the ruling class, and the corresponding subservience of the workers. The State Apparatus includes the
Government, the Administration, the Army, the Police, the Courts,
the Prisons: in outlining these Althusser wishes to draw attention to
the repressive function of the state. For the state represents state
power, and has no other meaning (*Lenin and Philosophy and Other
Essays*, p.140). Ideological State Apparatuses are presented to us as
distinct institutions: the religious, the educational, the family, the
legal, the political, the trade union, the communications, the cultural.
The State Apparatuses function predominantly by repression, the
Ideological State Apparatuses predominantly by ideology, though
secondarily by repression (p.145). No class can hold state power
without controlling the Ideological State Apparatuses (pp.146–7). It
is the ideology of the ruling class which provides the necessary
equilibrium for reproduction of the means of production, both
between and among Ideological State Apparatuses, and between
these and the repressive State Apparatus (p.150). Like all ideological
state apparatuses, that of education contributes to this reproduction
of the relations of production, which in capitalist societies are
relations of exploitation (p.154). The ruling ideology interpenetrates
the curricula of the schools from the infant school onward, and when
adolescents are eventually turned out of schools they are already
prepared for particular occupational levels, some prepared as workers, some as technicians, some as intellectuals – to be semi-employed
or to serve as agents of exploitation or repression, or as professional
ideologists (p.155). At that point, Althusser claims, school leavers
will have acquired even some of the forms of behaviour appropriate
to their social roles and occupations (pp.132–3).

It is clear that Althusser's consumer idea of education is at odds
with the formal notion of education as a developing of potentialities
consistent with social values, and that he is not referring to education
in the formal sense at all. For if education in the formal sense goes
on, potentialities may be developed which are beneficial not only
intrinsically, but also instrumentally as they fit the student for
occupations suited to his developing potentialities. Althusser's

claimed socio-political role of the schools with a supposedly stratified vocational outcome may appear extravagantly speculative to some with first-hand experience of particular administrative systems in education, as well as to some who have undertaken historical studies of the development of educational systems in some particular countries. Althusser's claims are at odds too with some empirical research on school leavers, in which a close correspondence between social background and vocations is confirmed only with respect to extremes of social disadvantage. Much easier to establish is an ideological influence on the curriculum, if not always with an alleged persistent infusion of political and social direction. Other marxist criticisms of education in capitalist societies have assumed a similar venturesome speculativeness to his. Thus criticism of education as an Ideological State Apparatus has been made by other contemporary marxists with reference to the differentiation of curricula for girls and boys, or for achievers and non-achievers, or for those who are in a position to proceed to tertiary studies and those who are not. It is related by some to different schools such as independent schools for the privileged, with State Aid to give them additional strength, under-supported state schools for children of the workers, non-selective schools for those who are expected not to continue their formal education beyond the statutory minimum leaving age, selective schools for those destined for university studies. It is levelled by some as well at general indoctrination which serves the interests of the political party in power. Almost any form of educational differentiation in class-structured societies with alleged injustices to some, has been the object of criticism at some time as reflecting ideological influence, a differentiation which is supposedly in the interests not of learners, but of a ruling class. If that criticism can be justified, and equality of opportunity is an ideological mask to conceal the purposes behind a stratified work force to fit into a class-structured society, it is a serious challenge from all three perspectives of justice, morality and education. Yet until it is subjected to comprehensive empirical investigation, the criticism must be held to be largely intuitive. The highly important principle is raised nonetheless that what appears on the surface of an educational system may be different from what is happening beneath it; that equality of opportunity which is taken for granted may be imaginary, and not real, and that its reproduction may be associated with the reproduction of social classes. That situation may exist whether or not the explanation for it is sound.

Liberal Ideology

There can be little doubt that relations between the state and individuals have been influenced by certain basic principles of liberalism, and that equality of opportunity has been part of the liberal idea. To show that this idea is not a static one we shall refer broadly to historical trends in the United States, linking the assertion of rights in its Declaration of Independence, especially to life, liberty and the pursuit of happiness, to John Locke's *Second Treatise of Government*, with its reference to life, liberty and estate. Whereas the original United States Constitution did not declare the equality of all men, some of the separate State constitutions did, but the formal statement and the liberal ideology that developed were contradictory, for equality applied only to some. Those who were seen as equal, in this early United States society, did not include all human beings, certainly not indigenous Indians, or negro slaves in the South, and probably not any workers who depended on public charity or could not make their way by their own efforts. The liberal image was of a society free and full of opportunity to any person with courage, initiative and capacity for hard work. Successful men were achievers by their own efforts, and fully entitled to their material acquisitions, as Locke's viewpoint had already conveyed.

While something of this liberal image of equal opportunity for material success has persisted, the narrow individualism that emerged with rapid industrialisation, especially in this century, led to a liberal image of a different kind, an image of freely participating and adaptable individuals, all on equal terms, where competitiveness was countered with cooperation, and individualism with an ideal of community. The liberal image of freedom, equality and opportunity was amended to include the notion of equality of opportunity by means of equal educational provisions for all.[13] For a time the liberal ideology was centred on the concept of equality of *economic* opportunity, but as soon as Dewey and others saw the possibilities of schools as instruments of social reform, their combined influence infused into the liberal ideology something more than equality of opportunity, namely, equality of *educational* opportunity. The policy-makers and supporters of the liberal ideology showed little understanding of Dewey's strictly *educational* insight into the development of individualities, not unlike Humboldt's in Prussia a century earlier. The ideological stress remained on educational opportunity in the sense of a free and open *access* to education, which, it was implied, was the gateway to equal economic opportunity. The liberal notion of social freedom, social equality and social justice was reinforced with the ideal of a nation made strong by talent that would be drawn from any source, poor or rich, black or white alike, without discrimination. Between the liberal images and the empirical social situation (open, that is, to empirical measurement) the gap has continued to be wide.

Empirical evidence for ideological influence is commonly adduced to support the existence of a *liberal* ideology. While a value-free stance is not practicable, and it is beyond our powers to rid our minds of our dispositions prior to deliberations leading to conclusions, or interpretations of research evidence, the credibility of some researchers is impaired by immoderate or simplistic interpretations to suit their preconceptions.[14] Some of the most pertinent evidence in the United States points to reproduction of inequality in educational opportunity as an outcome of the reproduction of social disadvantage. (Until recently there was an historical disparity between educational provisions for black and immigrant children and those for children from favourable social environments.[15]) The explanation that equality of educational opportunity is now offered to all through equal educational *availability*, is claimed by some as a specifically *liberal* illusion, as they point to contrary evidence from research. To challenge the liberal image of the meritocratic society, with everyone rising by merit alone in free competition with others, research indicates that first, some children are seriously handicapped at the start of the competition; second, that compensatory programmes to remedy the situation have not altered the fundamental social condition of the impoverished; third, that generally family background, including social class, continues to be conspicuously restrictive to the educational opportunities of some, and enhancing to the educational opportunities of others; fourth, and more specifically, inequalities in educational opportunity have their immediate source in marked disparities, from family to family, in linguistic stimulation, as well as in supportiveness of parents, study facilities and so forth; fifth, that regarding *schools* as disadvantaged and in need of supplementary resources, rather than individual *children*, is to miss the point of educational opportunity in both intrinsic and instrumental senses. These failures to provide individual equality of educational opportunity have all been attributed by some researchers to the liberal ideology espoused by the state. But such researchers have made no attempt, out of consistency, to validate their claims with research into the attitudes and values of those constituting the ruling power of the state at the time. With the same stubbornness of preconceptions, there is generally no attempt to find alternative explanations to the ideological for the degree of inequality of educational opportunity established: for instance, in a simple lack of understanding, among those in power, of learning disabilities and the significance of linguistic stimulation in early years of childhood. The complexity of the problem is also not fully acknowledged, such as in applications outside acute social disadvantage.[16] On the other hand, once the research evidence has been established that inequality of opportunity, including educational opportunity, may be directly linked with social conditions, the failure of any government to act on it is more than a failure of educational understanding: it is a failure also to act according to principles of justice and morality. Their rational–dispositional deliberations must, like ours in our normative thinking, take account of the situation as it is found to be, before they reach decisions on the practical moral demands of social justice.

Ideology of Contemporary Marxist States

It is possible that illusions in contemporary marxist states[17] are on the same major dimensions as those of liberal ideologies, relating especially to freedom and equality. Thus, as indicated in their respective constitutions, each socialist country propagates the belief that its citizens are free and equal, with the same fundamental rights, including the right to educational provisions. What may be illusory in this is whether this access to formal education at all levels, subject to sufficient ability, leads to *actual* equality of educational opportunity for all young people throughout the country. In the USSR it is claimed that 'all have equal opportunities to get an education',[18] and this depends largely on the proposition that all types of education are free. Acquiring an education on equal terms with others by going into schools at various levels, is precisely what led to the 'liberal illusion' as it has been designated by some, that universal *availability* of schooling is tantamount to equality of educational opportunity. In socialist countries too there may be relative disadvantages at the starting-point of formal education, and a profession of accessibility may conceal inequalities for various reasons: some may be favoured over others for competitive positions in particular educational institutions.[19] In developing socialist countries such as China, the fact that ideological challenges are sometimes met with compulsory re-education programmes suggests that it is in the interests of the ruling communist party that an ideology of freedom and equality should be lived by the people as an imaginary belief system. The situation is similar to that of liberal ideologies, in so far as such beliefs may be indoctrinated in schools of capitalist societies to the advantage of those in power. In each case, if the marxist interpretation of ideology is correct, the ruling party itself may begin to live the ideology of illusion after a lapse of time: the original deceptions in the indoctrination of the young may be lost by the rulers too as they live the deceptions that are now turned into ideological illusions, such as those of equality of opportunity for all, or basic human liberties held by all such as freedom of speech and freedom of thought, freedoms that are built into communist-socialist constitutions.[20]

Conclusion on Contrasting Political Ideologies

There are differences of opinion as to whether ideologies constitute illusory belief systems which are necessary to all social living – in the form of structures of images and ideas, for instance, as Althusser believes – or whether they are illusory belief systems which begin – as Marx and Engels held – with the domination of ruling classes and then grow on social members until they are accepted by all, or almost all, of them. Most agree that political ideologies begin and end in the interests of the ruling class, and that adherents become unaware of the difference between the *imaginary* social conditions under which they live, and the *actual* social conditions (which may, for example, be conditions of exploitation). There is disagreement on whether political ideologies are susceptible to exposure by critical thinking, or whether they have an opiate effect on the intellect as over a sufficient period whole populations fall gradually under their influence. There is disagreement too on the universal applicability of some ideologies to all societies – such as all class-structured societies – regardless of historical period and of variability in social conditions among different societies.

Substantial difficulties are faced by anyone claiming an objective social reality which can be individually apprehended, something which, if our ideological belief systems could be set aside, would allow us to see things supposedly *as they are*, distortion-free. That has been a perennial human dream: it was Plato's dream of a world of perfection beyond the everyday world of imperfection, with a higher reality glimpsed only by the specially gifted and specially educated few. Individuals make their own value judgements on political systems, sometimes – but perhaps infrequently – deliberating rationally on comparative merits: weighing, for instance, the relative justice of distributive wealth in socialist countries, against the relative morality of personal freedoms in capitalist societies; or from educational perspectives, reasoning under which system there is the greater equality of educational opportunity for all. The compelling force of ideologies is evident among those whose minds are closed to alternative or opposing convictions. It is then that the subjectivity of judgements of *social justice* becomes most evident, determined in part by ideological influence.

IDEOLOGIES OF RIGHTS AND JUSTICE

Introduction

We shall now extend the notion of ideologies as illusory belief systems with widespread social acceptance, and the notion of political ideologies as functioning in the interests of members of a ruling party, by asking whether we may properly speak of an ideology of *rights*. If we show that we may, and rights include such things as rights to education and rights to equality of opportunity in and through education, the possibility is apparent that over a sufficient period people may believe that they have these rights when in fact they do not, or that the rights may apply to some and not to others, or may apply to some *more* than to others. Further, if these espoused and propagated rights have a political purpose they may serve the interests of a ruling party as political ideologies generally do. We would then justify an ideology of rights as one species of political ideology. If they do not serve a particular purpose they may still be ideological, influencing societies into believing that they have rights when in fact they do not, living an ideology of rights as imaginary, and distinct from the actual state of affairs.

Similarly there are possibilities to be examined of an ideology of justice, by which people imagine as real a situation in which moral justice and legal justice are one; or – if separate – where legal justice is inviolable, requiring implicit obedience, or where the judiciary is elevated to a status of near infallibility, giving to legal decisions an unquestioning validity; or where law-makers in their statutes safeguard the interests of all such as by creating equality of opportunity through provisions for free and compulsory schooling; or where legal philosophy fosters the view that the law commands and merits respectful acceptance. Such an ideology – if it exists – may or may not serve the interests of the ruling party, but more pertinently, may be shown not to serve the interests of all individuals in society, or to promote social justice. Since many of these matters are complex, we can do no more than speculate on possibilities from relevant literature and from experience.

Is There an Ideology of Rights?

In considering whether we may properly speak of an ideology of rights we note initially the shift of emphasis in our times from political rights – as Hobbes, Locke and others conceived them in the notion of the minimal state – to rights that are personal and even sometimes private, as conveyed in Human Rights declarations, national constitutions and international covenants and conventions.

National constitutions are generally expressions of aspirations or ideals, without any indication of how they might be realised or any guarantee that they *will* be realised. They have become prominent in newer socialist countries such as China and Cuba for purposes of political education and reform. (Consider, for instance, Article 8 of the 1975 Cuban constitution, guaranteeing 'the full dignity of man' and 'the integral development of his personality'.) They are not quite so conspicuous in some of the older liberal democracies such as Britain, whose constitution is embodied in various acts of parliament and other documents but not in a single comprehensive statement;[21] and in USA, where despite a number of amendments, the constitution would require a more regular re-drafting to keep pace with changing social attitudes and values. In all countries ideological possibilities in constitutions become most apparent from the way the constitutions happen to be *used* by those in power, including those with influence over children. Thus in China the effect of including Article 35 of the 1982 constitution (which proclaims that all citizens enjoy freedom of speech, and of the press, of assembly, of association, of procession and of demonstration') in a programme of political and moral education may be to distort perceptions of the actual situation, encouraging both children and adults to live an ideology of political freedom. Similarly in some schools of liberal democracies (still using the expression in an ideological context reference may be made in social studies to a national constitution which guarantees to all equality of opportunity as though the constitution described the actual state of affairs. Thus the possibility is evident that when turned to indoctrinatory purposes, constitutions may mask social injustices by inducing imaginary perceptions of social conditions and relations which conflict with the actual. Their rights to such things as equality of educational opportunity may become ideological both in intent and in assimilation.

International covenants and conventions may have a similar function. They may be used politically by those in power to mask an internal suppression of rights, for by widely publicizing them at home the intended impression on the people may be that the wide-ranging rights as described are in fact enjoyed, and that a need for remediation refers only to the less fortunate countries such as those with racial discrimination.[22] Part of the deception may be that international covenants and conventions are ensuring that rights apply to all people, regardless of country.[23] In some instances the statement of rights is misconceived, adding further to the possibilities of ideological illusion. Thus in the American Declaration of the Rights and Duties of Man[24] specific mention was made of a right to equality of educational opportunity. Intending to improve the life opportunities of poorer people, the agreement concealed the full dimensions of the social condition of the poor with rudimentary solutions such as proposing elementary schooling for all, without attention to the underlying circularity of inhibiting attitudes and values likely to return the child, in extreme cases, to the social conditions into which he was born. The International Covenant on Economic, Social and Cultural Rights (1966) made a similar gesture, with education to be directed to the 'full development of the human personality'.

The case for an ideology of rights is least speculative when rights embodied in constitutions, covenants and conventions become part of an indoctrinatory programme, particularly in the schools and in adult reformatories. It may well serve the interests of those in power to strengthen individuals' approval of their social situation with illusory beliefs that freedoms stated as rights, including the right to equality of educational opportunity, are in fact enjoyed by them.

s There an Ideology of Justice?

One of the possibilities of an ideology of justice lies in the propagated belief that the state and the law are one, originating in either political or legal philosophy. The view that what the state decrees in its laws is morally just may become a widespread popular illusion, serving the interests of both law-makers and their administrators of justice.

Marx saw the law as an ideological weapon of the bourgeois state, upholding false relationships of workers to bourgeois property owners who exploit them to create surplus value, so that property rights are sanctified in the interests of one class only. In *The German Ideology* Marx and Engels saw civil law developing as private property develops.[25] The *Manifesto of the Communist Party* declared that by revolution all are made equal, the proletariat first overthrowing the bourgeoisie but then sweeping away all class distinctions.[26] Finally, as Marx stated in the *Critique of the Gotha Programme*, when labour is seen as 'life's prime want', society in this higher phase of communism is able to subscribe to the principle: 'from each according to his ability, to each according to his needs' (pp.23, 30,31). It is at that stage, explained Engels in *Anti-Dühring*, that the state dies out, or withers away.[27] And at that stage law withers away too, for despite some extremes of conduct by individuals, as Lenin conceded, these will be controlled by the people themselves.[28] The theme of normative regulation without law has been continued by recent jurists in the USSR.[29] Pending the arrival of the higher phase of communism, in the present socialist phase the state and the law are one, with the law as it is imposed purporting to be just. It is when it is used as a means of educating citizens that its inviolability is staunchly upheld, and the possibility of creating an illusion of justice among large sections of the population becomes most evident.[30] Then although individuals appear to be used as means to political ends, substantive interpretations of ends differ with political perspective.[31]

It is legal philosophy – notably a philosophy of positivism – which in liberal democracies has given much the same emphasis that the state and the law are one, though its influence is much less direct and more speculative than in the case of marxist ideology. The significant difference in the two approaches is that in positivism the law and morality are separated. It is the law that is coercive, the command of a sovereign, with the people obedient subjects; but the question of morality is considered irrelevant to that situation. In his *View of a*

Complete Code of Laws[32] Bentham explained that good or bad, the law had to be upheld. Once reformed, completed and codified, it would not require change in a hundred years; only its language would become obsolete (ch.XXXIV, p.210). In the rigid requirement of obedience to law-makers there was already precedence in Hobbes and David Hartley.[33] Bentham wrote of the law as a command (*Pannomial Fragments*, pp.217,219). He rejected natural rights, declaring that the only rights are legal rights (p.221). One of his disciples, John Austin, re-iterated that the subject-matter of jurisprudence is positive laws 'without regard to their goodness or badness'.[34] Critics of this positivist position in law have pointed to the gap between theory and practice, for judges are not always bound by the rule of law, and this detracts from the view that the only propositions of law which can be held to be true are those based on the content of laws as they happen to be.[35] It also detracts from any ideological influence which the philosophy of legal positivism might have. Of stronger ideological potential may be the central positivist contention that the law is law, with no necessary connection with morality.[36] This vein is continued by a more recent positivist Hans Kelsen, who in *The Pure Theory of Law*[37] also urges that the state and the law be seen as one (p.318). The purpose of the law as a coercive order is to produce forms of behaviour considered desirable by the social order.[38] These would be developed in a science of law which would discover social norms by rational means.[39]

That seemed a clear departure from ideological tendencies, except that if successfully implemented it might increase public confidence in the law to a degree that could not be substantiated as long as the law and morality were still viewed as distinct. But the notion that the law might be a means to social regulation appealed also to some critics of positivism.[40] Roscoe Pound claimed to discern a trend among jurists which began to focus on the harmonizing of the satisfaction of various wants or desires.[41] He gave to law a role in social or distributive justice, adjusting individuals' wants and claims so that social goods are efficiently and fairly distributed without friction.[42] This would develop a respect for law based on sociological evidence, and for this very reason could scarcely become ground for ideological illusion. Philosophy of law moved in this sense from the potentially illusory to the real.

It is primarily the exalted public image of the inviolability and sanctification of the law, as well as opportunities for turning it to indoctrinatory purposes, which in both marxist states and liberal democracies appears to contain seeds of ideological illusion. This situation may be aggravated by wide publicity given to court decisions – a common practice in marxist states – and by a high public image enjoyed by the judiciary, with in some countries illusions of near infallibility.

Speculation on an ideology of justice is not strengthened by widespread civil disobedience, for that is an indication of the law's vulnerability, and an unwillingness of its subjects to accept coercion. Civil disobedience requires action, something more than opposition in principle to the law, and it refers normally to action of a non-violent, demonstrative kind. With the law perceived as distinct from morality, it is believed to be moral to disobey an immoral law. In Rawls' conception of a just society there is a shared understanding of fundamental principles. Whenever a violation of these principles occurs in the law, it is incumbent on responsible citizens to disobey it. Civil disobedience is limited by him to a political act that is public, non-violent and conscientious, performed usually to bring about a change in the law or policies of the government.[43] It is by such a rational control of civil disobedience that inadequacies in the law are brought most effectively to wide public attention, and correspondingly the probability of an ideology of justice (or of the law) diminishes. Indeed it diminishes further when jurists interested in reform of the law themselves point to its deficiencies, some acknowledging legal systems as 'full of uncertainties as to what is their correct interpretation in a great many situations'.[44] Legal reform movements add to respect for the law without encouraging either false images or beliefs on the one hand, or on the other hand a radical contempt for the law such as was not uncommon in Montaigne's time.[45]

It is only an *unwarranted* respect for the law which has danger ideologically, inasmuch as it fails to serve the interests of the people but persuades them otherwise. Some jurists have drawn attention to the force of tradition in common law, especially a tradition in law of learning and rationality. Common law tradition has been seen by some in solid contrast with certain contemporary experiments in dispensing quick justice in new types of court without an historical perspective on the past and the present, looking for quick solutions under the influence of pressure groups, insufficiently informed to be aware of the immense complexity of human affairs generally, superficial in their knowledge of the culture, untrained in reasoning, disrespectful of tradition and learning through limited capacity to appreciate their value. It is difficult to dispute the value of case-law

built up from the judgements of men and women whose wide
experience has given them a first-hand acquaintance with situation
of social conflict, and whose depth of legal knowledge and sense o
responsibility to others have given them, in many instances, a cautior
and degree of impartiality which it would be foolish to exchange fo
more glittering alternatives. One of the strongest supporters o
common law tradition has been Karl Llewellyn,[46] but his suppor
tends to be impaired by speculation, giving to judges a commor
capacity for controlled reason which leads supposedly to simila
decisions in similar situations. Any consistent dedication to the
precedents of case law, or to common law tradition, may itself be ir
disregard of the unique demands of a particular case, as well a
strengthening an impression among the people of the law's inviolabil
ity and of its moral justice. As always it is uncritical acceptance of the
law which leaves it open to ideological purposes of law-makers. Bu
speculation on the force of common law tradition in this regard ha
little foundation in some countries, where in one observation, 'the
higher the court the narrower the range of binding precedents'.[4]
Social and moral values do influence the judges in the interpretatior
of statutes, and in liberal democracies there is generally a regard fo
the individual rather than for the collective or organic state. Ir
general the evidence for ideological influence in common law tradi
tion is not persuasive.

NON-IDEOLOGICAL ILLUSIONS: POLITICAL DECEPTION

One of the reasons we have for regarding ideological explanations a
sometimes highly speculative is that they overlook other possible
accounts of our illusions or misperceptions of the social situatior
about us. Simple prejudices against people of other races or religions
like the passions of war that lead to distorted perceptions of enemies
are obvious sources of illusion. Many of our patterns of illusions forn
without any obvious ideological base. Some may develop even amon;
members of an academic community, or among race-goers or yachts
men, or among members of bureaucracies such as state department
of education. But it would be straining the use of 'ideology' to give i
an extended reference to include all patterns of illusory beliefs hele
by particular sections of the community, without their roots in
broad social acceptance.

Not only do ideological explanations tend to be over-used, with attributions of 'in the interests of the ruling class' made supposedly to expose a wide range of illusory beliefs in class-structured societies, but they also mask a more obvious source of illusion in *political deception*. Assuming in liberal democracies a two-party system of government, and assuming that in this there may be planning, policy-making and decision-making which occur either without an ideological commitment, or at least independently of it if there is one, we may observe many illusions of social relations and situations which have their source in the simple struggle for power and in inter-party rivalry. When the National Assembly of France made its *Declaration of the Rights of Man and of Citizens* (1798) its first three articles comprehended in general terms – as Thomas Paine wrote of it soon afterwards – the whole of the Declaration, and was a basis of liberty for individuals and for nations alike.[48] Apart from declaring that 'men are born free, and always continue, free, and equal in respect of their rights'; and that 'the end of all political associations, is, the preservation of the natural and imprescriptible rights of man' (which were stated as liberty, property, security, and resistance to oppression), the Declaration asserted, in its third article, that 'the nation is the source of all sovereignty; nor can any INDIVIDUAL, or ANY BODY OF MEN, be entitled to any authority which is not expressly derived from it'. In confirming these principles, Paine asked, 'What is government more than the management of the affairs of a nation?' (p.145) and referring specifically to these three articles observed that in them there is no inducement to personal ambition. All that are needed are wisdom and ability to be exercised for the public good, not for any 'emolument or aggrandizement of particular descriptions of men or their families' (p.146). We may note that in one of his early writings, Marx observed that 'the right of man to freedom ceases to be a right as soon as it enters into conflict with political life', referring to contradictions between principles and practice during the French Revolution, such as in the loss of freedom of the press; for then the principle that the function of government is to guarantee the rights of man is set aside for political expediency.[49] If the end of a liberal education is 'a sense of the value of things other than domination',[50] as Russell argued, the solution in liberal democracies may be an educational one for rulers and subjects alike, especially in fundamental morality.

One of the major tasks of those entrusted to manage the affairs of the nation is to distribute social goods, such as education, equitably according to need. To speak of education as one of society's goods is not to take a consumer view of education. What are distributed ultimately are *opportunities* – not merely material goods such as books, buildings and equipment. It is opportunity that helps the becoming that is education – opportunity to promote the developing of potentialities on an individual basis, not collectively on false assumptions of common needs. The state's responsibility is to distribute the means to equal educational opportunities for all. Yet political practice conflicts in obvious ways with an ideal of moral government and social justice. In the struggle for power politicians' personal motives become dominant. We shall illustrate how an explanation of inequalities in educational opportunity which refers to political motives requires no dependence upon ideological explanation. First, we shall refer to the dispositions of politicians. What children's interests are in education is clear enough, and from our consideration of equality of educational opportunity we shall keep in mind that government provision of schooling with all the basic facilities which this implies is not enough to cope with the problem at the extremes of social disadvantage. We shall reflect on the situation of members of governments, ministers of education especially and their senior civil service advisers, as individuals, each deliberating rationally and dispositionally prior to reaching decisions on educational policies affecting planning and opportunities in education. We shall recall the relevant practical action schema:

Desire, motive and goal – attitudes and values – rational–dispositional deliberation – conclusion or decision – action.

In this all the dispositional elements are vital, for when motives and goals are self-regarding and not given moral direction by considering others' interests, reason may be used to devise the best means to achieve ends which ignore individual rights and needs: then belief in the efficacy of the decision may have a cynical connotation. Some decisions in education may have such far-reaching consequences as directing where children will go for their schooling and the type of school they will attend, how long they will undertake formal schooling, opportunities for tertiary education, opportunities for children from severely disadvantaged families to fulfil their intellectual, moral and physical potentialities at school, and so forth. When in office ministerial notions of reputation, advancement within the party by demonstrating a capacity for taking hard or unpopular decisions (even against the advice of the permanent head of the relevant civil service department) may weigh heavily. And though civil service heads of departments of education may in some circumstances be trusted to make decisions for ministers, they too are individuals, with their own desires, motives, attitudes and values, and their deliberations may be influenced similarly by self-regarding interests. The eagerness to be involved in important matters of policy-making may not arise from a concern for educational needs so much as from a concern for public acclaim, or a demonstration of power or dominance. Yet whenever ministers or senior assistants make decisions on policies which they present as being in the best interests of children, or in the national interest, they are making value-judgements, and the quality of those judgements is related to the quality of their own values, as well as to their understanding of education. In other words their moral dispositions are highly important to the welfare of children and others involved in the educational process. By contrast with partisan or arbitrary decisions – with their possible source in self-regarding motives and confused moral attitudes and values – there may be a ministerial resolve 'to fight for the resources necessary to make a reality of more equal educational opportunity', or to 'get away from the situation in which boys and girls are allowed to write themselves off below their true potential of ability': each with a recognizable moral intention, assuming its authenticity, even if the first may seem to miss the point of equality of opportunity with respect to the extremes of social disadvantage.[51]

It has to be recognized that conflict between moral and educational principles on the one hand, and political principles on the other, may be unavoidable: economic constraints may prevent the acceptance of an educational plan, or party priorities may be re-directed in the light of unforeseen social and economic circumstances such as world-wide economic recessions. But the darker picture is to have promises instead of plans, a situation of concealment rather than openness, the standard context for which is inter-party rivalry. Then the overriding concern is to win power and to hold it, and party policy may be as much directed *against* an opposition party as it is *toward* the interests of the people. Once in office economic constraints normally operate; therefore priorities may have to be re-determined. In that situation even the minister of high moral principles may be forced to compromise. But again on the darker side, criteria for Cabinet priorities may be influenced by extraneous considerations of electoral appeal. Internal conflict of values is apt to be short-lived since that leads to

much greater conflict: little persuasion is needed to convince party
rebels of the threat to their retention of office and power. In striking
contrast with this situation of subterfuge and concealment, openness
of policy-making and planning which is not hedged in by constant
pressures from a party opposition, itself manoeuvring to achieve
power, is able to justify its inability to meet all educational expectations by laying out, as impartially as possible, the wide variety of
social needs competing with education for limited available resources.

To achieve power and to hold it under the two-party system of
liberal democracies obviously requires electoral support, and that in
turn calls for promises to an increasingly articulate electorate with
many competing sectional demands, not all of which can be met from
limited total resources. That situation is an invitation to political
deception. Of all the unfulfilled responsibilities of political leaders in
liberal democracies, one of the most conspicuous is to provide
equality of educational opportunity for all: to come to grips with
serious social disadvantage rather than perpetuating the deception
that equal basic educational provisions in classrooms and teachers
means equality of educational opportunity. It is only on the perceived
basis of social justice for all that attitudes and values can be formed in
all children which give to each the motivation to develop his
individual potentialities and to take advantage of common educational provisions. In liberal democracies the problem of social reform to
provide equality of educational opportunity has often proved too
complex and potentially disruptive for politicians to handle with
resolution. Linked with serious social disadvantage is the problem of
discrimination, so that in some countries blackness, ethnic background and female sex may be handicaps in achieving equality of
opportunity. This is nowhere more evident than in the failure of
politicians in liberal democracies to cope entirely adequately with the
problem of equality of vocational opportunity, even for those with
equal educational attainments. To illustrate the significance of this we
shall extend our concept of social justice to include *equality of
vocational opportunity*, which is itself dependent upon a prior
solution of the problem of equality of educational opportunity. This
principle implies that *each person has an equal right to a vocation of
his choice, with selection on relevant grounds*. Relevant grounds may
be educational qualifications, experience, intellectual ability, capacity for hard physical work, adaptability, and so forth: but *not* sex,
ethnic background, colour, religion, school attended – whether

government or independent. This is simply an application of the fairness in treatment of persons principle, or the fundamental principle of justice. If governments meet their responsibilities with respect to equality of educational opportunity – providing secondary and tertiary education for all whose potentialities can be further realised by them, removing serious social disadvantages and so forth – they might then achieve a situation where, from particular socio-economic or ethnic backgrounds, the numbers of individuals in all levels and types of education are not markedly out of proportion to their numbers in the total population to which they belong.[52]

With frequent changes of government and constant manoeuvring for power, politicians find little difficulty in *avoiding* problems whose solution lies in substantial reform, particularly when they can show themselves to be preoccupied with attempts to satisfy more visible but minor problems which consume their available resources. Roots of deception and distrust lie embedded in our use of 'politics' as they did with the Elizabethans' uses of its cognate forms.

The extravagant extensions of ideological explanations that are made at times from particular ideological perspectives such as the marxist do not invalidate all ideological explanations. Our particular concern in the next chapter is again with equality of educational opportunity, and we have shown that this may be misperceived either ideologically, by non-ideological illusions to which we are subjected by politicians or others, or by both. It is because social problems which are also moral problems may sometimes persist as long as legal justice and moral justice are seen as having no necessary connection, and as long as illusions blur our perceptions of social relations, that we return in the final chapter to the notion of social or distributive justice.

REVIEW AND CONCLUSION

We have regarded ideology as an habitual way of looking on the world but one which habituates illusions, so that we may live them, as marxist theorists explain, as imaginary relations distinct from the actual. If we can never know what the *actual* is in a completely objective sense, at least we can recognize distortions in others' ideologies. As with our prejudices which may be better understood by others, and exposed by them to our advantage in formal discussions, *in this interpretation* we may be blind to the distortions of our own ideologies but capable of penetrating, in some cases, those of others' ideologies. The universality of ideological illusion remains, nonetheless, in doubt. We have noted the marxist notion of false consciousness in the ideology of capitalism, distortions of social realities in the conditions of workers *vis-à-vis* their capitalist employers, which serve the interests of the ruling class. It is a fundamental criticism that the interests of the ruling class are always served by them, though not necessarily exclusively. As for the liberal ideology of the capitalist state, Marx's criticism has been to some extent vindicated by research, though some of the interpretations are conspicuously speculative. In particular in some capitalist states there is confirmed a reproduction of inequality of educational opportunity indicated by a reproduction of serious social disadvantage among underprivileged families. Even if this situation refers to a small minority of the population, it violates our principle of equality of educational opportunity: the quantification of the problem in terms of the proportion of the population affected and the cost to the state in remedying it, is not relevant to the *principle*, but rather to practical politics and administration.

On the assumptions that first, the basic idea of morality is a practical consideration of others' interests; and that second, education is one of the individual's interests for both intrinsic and extrinsic reasons (the one concerned with personal satisfaction from the most fundamental or formal notion of education as a developing of potentialities, the other concerned with life prospects to which education leads), the conclusion is self-evident that every individual has an equal right to education. Further, in a class-structured society in particular, where the start to life is influenced by home circumstances, the environment and the school as well as by natural endowment, we have inferred that every individual has an equal right to educational opportunity. It follows that those in government have a moral obligation to every individual to see that the equal right principle is fulfilled as far as practicable, since it would be contrary to morality to serve the interests of some in this respect and not to serve the interests of others. Since education and the opening of educational opportunities for all are practical activities, we need to take account of all the matters included in this chapter: the possibility that in our practical judgements on what we ought to do we may ourselves be subject to ideological illusions of some kind – in particular that we are either accepting, or living unconsciously under, an ideology of rights, believing that equal educational opportunities are there when they are not; and similarly that we are either accepting or living unconsciously under an ideology of justice, believing that statutes making provision for education in the state are in fact opening up equal educational opportunities for all when they are not – that what state laws provide amount to moral justice and deserve both respect and acceptance as in the common interest, not in the interest of those in power.

In legal positivism the emphasis on sovereign authority, on law as command and as coercive, with subjects obliged to obey, and the corresponding stress on *positive* law all have ingredients of respect for the social order, and come surprisingly close to the positive law of the communist-socialist state in this broad approach. The possibility of an ideology of justice being promoted in part by a particular philosophy of law depends largely on how *public* that philosophy has become – clearly more so generally in socialist states than in liberal democracies. Even the influence of common law traditions of legal integrity may have had stronger tendencies toward ideological illusion in the past than in our own times, when civil disobedience has become more open and more challenging on some outstanding issues, and reform of the law has strong internal pressures for change.

The concept of ideology is a useful one to explain certain clusters of illusory beliefs which may persist unnoticed in collective thinking among large sections of society. Shorn of polemics, the mystique of repeated linguistic forms and proselytizing distractions, in expressions that are necessarily external appraisals of *others'* ideologies (since adherents are themselves unaware that they are living certain illusions), ideologies do alert us to the *possibility* that in our habitual ways of looking on the social world we may have been harbouring illusions. For that very reason they are to be taken seriously. Social justice demands action to remove any misconceptions that may frustrate or delay it in practice, as in providing educational opportunity for all.

With a backward glance at the philosophers of the previous chapter, we are reminded that there may never have been an occasion in history when citizens have not felt some unease about the power they have entrusted to rulers, much less that which rulers have seized or arbitrarily usurped. The Hobbes-Locke-Nozick concerns, and to some extent those of Rawls, and of Humboldt and Mill as well, express a widespread apprehension in every society at state power over the individual. The English, American and French Revolutions did not lead to constitutional governments which gave people the comfort that *their* interests and the interests of society as a whole, were in good hands; and more recently the Russian, Chinese and Cuban revolutions – though liberating in one sense in casting off the injustices of former regimes – have been achieved at substantial cost to some of the basic liberties. In this chapter we have compounded the philosophers' concern at the power of the state by showing that illusions militating against social justice may be promoted both ideologically and by non-ideological political deception. In the final chapter we keep in mind both philosophical and practical perspectives as we attempt to bring social justice into sharper focus, with special attention to one of its major problems in equality of educational opportunity.

As we move out of the ideological context we shall have to amend the ideologically-biased expression 'liberal democracies' (as well as 'marxist' and 'socialist'), for we have already used 'liberal' ambiguously: first, in Chapter I to refer to a liberal education; second in Chapter 6 as well as in this, to refer to a philosophical tradition of liberalism carried forward by Rawls from Locke and Mill; third, in this chapter to 'liberal democracies'. In the first and second we have used 'liberal' to refer to fundamental ideas, the first to refer to an educational tradition of enlargement of the mind with knowledge and understanding, but with attitudes of open-mindedness which contrast sharply with ideological total commitment to a point of view; the second to refer to fundamental ideas of liberty in relations between the individual and the state. To dispel any continuing ambiguity in the use of 'liberal', it is important to observe that a set of fundamental ideas of liberty may be held in common by citizens of socialist and of capitalist states, while between the two there may be strikingly different substantive interpretations. The formal notion of liberty as conveyed in a philosophical tradition of liberalism crosses all political and ideological boundaries. 'Liberal democracies' must now be abandoned simply because it is a substantive label – used differently by those of conflicting political and ideological persuasions. From the socialist or marxist perspective 'liberal democracies' is pejorative, implying that capitalist liberalism is in fact illiberal, or that the belief in freedom and equality is illusory. From the capitalist perspective the expression applies authentically to the capitalist state only, supposedly contrasting with illiberalism in socialist states. Similar remarks are relevant to 'marxist' and 'socialist' in the context of liberalism. From this point we shall therefore use 'class-structured' and 'classless' to refer to capitalist and socialist states respectively, despite an inherent simplification in each. (It is difficult to dismiss *totally* the notion of classes in socialist states, as it is difficult to dismiss *totally* the notion of capitalist tendencies in certain socialist states. But the broad distinction is sufficient for our purposes.) The terminological amendments will be in keeping also with our concern in the next chapter with philosophical principles or formal notions, but as we turn our backs on ideological slogans as conveyed by the fixation of ideological labels we must keep in mind the practical usefulness of our examination of ideologies to our deliberations and judgements, serving a similar purpose to our study of dispositions in Chapter 4. From a philosophical stance also we shall have an opportunity to attain a degree of impartiality or objectivity in our discussion, disagreeing with the radical view that all impartiality or objectivity is an illusion. It is not true – as we have noted – that in our practical deliberations, decisions or judgements we are invariably swayed in contra-rational directions by our dispositions, and unlike certain radical formulations we shall not be using our subjective ethical stance as both justification and licence for extreme speculativeness. In short, as we move out of the ideological context and face the final statement of our views on social justice, we make an avowal of our respect for reason and for philosophical modes and traditions, however short we may fall of ideals in each.

8 Social Justice Reflections and Conclusion

We shall return first to the formal notions of justice, morality and education as a means of showing that the principle of equality of educational opportunity is related to all three, and that with this composite moral foundation it points unequivocally to social justice. Then we shall reflect finally on the main emphases we have made, using 'reflect' first in a literal or review sense, second in a contemplative sense.

FORMAL NOTIONS

Each of the formal notions has been directional throughout the discussions, charged with sufficient meaning to avoid the emptiness of formal statements of the kind that permit opposites to be accommodated equally within them. A practical consideration of others' interests cannot admit a complete egoism of *no* consideration at all of others' interests. Justice as fairness in the treatment of persons cannot admit treatment of other human beings that is categorically unfair, or fails to respect them as persons. As a moral notion, justice in its formal sense cannot admit any treatment of persons in conflict with morality, such as treating another solely as a means to one's own ends, thereby again considering one's own interests entirely. Education as the developing of individual potentialities consistent with social values excludes first, any practices which do not contribute to the developing of individual potentialities, such as developing a sun-tan or a distaste for physical exercise, or more seriously – in the classroom situation – drill that becomes an end in itself. The same formal notion excludes – in its social values qualification – activities of developing potentialities without any concern at all for learners' *interests* as prospective or actual members of society, proceeding in ways which are clearly identifiable as contrary to social values – those values which first, are recognizable even in pluralistic societies as dominant, and which in children's interests, in particular, *ought* to be instilled; and which second, are not contrary themselves to the primary moral principle.

Morality

To avoid ambiguity we have used 'morality' to refer to its fundamental or formal idea, not to a system of moral thought such as might be conveyed in 'a personal morality'. For the latter we use 'ethical standpoint', or 'ethical system'. Morality as a practical consideration of others' interests conveys the notion of a completion of moral thought. Moral thoughts, ideas, values or intentions are not enough to indicate that a person is living morally in his social relations. What characterizes morality in the formally complete sense is represented in the standard moral action schema, where moral judgement, decision or conclusion is shown to lead to action, or to a moral act. The act or action is the validation of the thought.

What is meant by a *practical* consideration of others' interests is now clear, with the notion of complete morality leading to a moral act. It is true that there may be moral *thoughts* that have an authentically practical orientation, and in that limited sense too there is a 'practical' consideration of others' interests. But at that stage it is not possible to adjudicate on which such considerations will bear fruit in action or in moral acts. Therefore the formal notion of morality embraces the completion of the moral cycle, which is normally closed with action or with the moral act.

Thus in practical morality the action-schema itself refers to *action* (or act or deed). 'Action' is used to contrast with *inaction* – the kind of inaction or inactivity where the moral thought, idea, intention, deliberation, decision or conclusion ends as a mental event. A distinction may still be needed between 'act' and 'action'. Good intention may terminate with an act of benevolence, such as making a donation to charity; and this is distinct from an action or activity of distributing food and clothing voluntarily to the needy. Both the act and the action are carrying into action the good intention (or decision, conclusion, etc.). There is justification therefore in referring to *action* as the final stage of the action schema in practical morality, but it must be taken as including moral *acts*.

In practical affairs the *moral* action schema contrasts with others o
a non-moral nature, such as the administrative action schema prop
osed earlier. Where the motives or goals are administrative o
non-moral, the most appropriate decision in some situations may be
not to act. But in moral situations where the motives or intentions, as
well as the rational-dispositional deliberations are all *moral* in nature
the standard pattern is the moral action schema where moral though
is carried into appropriate action. Certain complex situations o
dilemmas constitute exceptions to be justified with reasons. Ever
then, in most circumstances some action is morally superior to no
action: supporting a dependant mother rather than enlisting in war
for instance. Where motives or intentions are malevolent rather than
benevolent, such as in situations dominated by revenge, an immoral
situation may be converted by deliberation to a moral situation, and
the appropriate moral decision may be *not* to act. Such instances do
not fall under the standard action schema. In other exceptional
situations, moral motives or intentions followed by deliberation may
lead to a conclusion that the interests of others are best served by no
acting, as in wishing to help the terminally ill with alleviative surgery
thereby prolonging eventual suffering.

The formal notion of morality as a practical consideration o
others' interests is based on a respect for others as persons, mainly
from a simple understanding that desires and emotions, motives and
goals, attitudes and values, deliberations, decisions and action are
universal human experiences. With that insight the dominant fact to
emerge is that others have *interests*, and if we make the effort to
assume another's standpoint, as well as we can, we lose something o
our egocentricity and begin to respect others as persons. Certainly
another effort is required to *live* morally with others in our society
that is, the effort to give up something of our self-interest, to do more
than *understand* that others have interests, but as well to acknowledge those interests in a practical way, to extend our sympathy o
benevolence by a practical reduction of our egoism. Perceiving
another in his own stream of experience, his own action continuity, is
to respect him as a person in his concreteness. In some circumstances
and to some extent this visualizing of another's concreteness is
imaginary and constructive, inasmuch as we do not know enough
about the person to perceive fully the uniqueness of his individuality
So we project something of ourselves and something of others whom
we *do* know in their individualities, so that the person is still
respected as like ourselves and like other persons in these respects

He too is actively desiring and forming motives and goals, deliberating on how to fulfil his aspirations, suffering setbacks in his plans but re-formulating, making judgements and reaching conclusions. We see him in his human potentialities in such an action-continuity, but not as Kant tended to see him, in terms of the abstraction of a Rational Will. Considering others' interests thus expresses interests that are both common human interests and unique individual interests, and it is the particularity of these that gives greater respect for persons than respect based merely on reason.

A related reason for taking as the formal notion of morality a practical consideration of others' interests is that some of another person's interests are his *rights*, and these in every contemporary society – regardless of political and economic organization – are properly assuming increasing moral relevance. Every individual is seen as possessing general Human Rights which are related to treating him with justice as a person. These interests have to be respected by others, for to have rights is to imply that others have obligations to him, and that they may not be overridden by other persons or by any power, without good reason. The attribution of rights confirms the concreteness of individuality, and adds to respect for person. To assert one's rights is not merely to assert self-interest, or to take a non-moral stance of precluding relationships with others. It is rather, in appropriate circumstances, to demonstrate to others that these are vital interests that have to be considered by them, not neglected, ignored, regarded contemptuously, or overpowered. In conjunction with the secondary moral principle pointing to possible legitimate interests of our own, we are able to declare some of our interests in the form of rights, and at appropriate times this does nothing to detract from respecting person: on the contrary it is an assertion of one's own personhood. Again the irreducible notion of morality is a practical consideration of others' interests, for to declare one's own interests is to draw others' attention to them, to make of oneself another person from their point of view.

Morality itself needs no extrinsic justification, but a third reason for deciding on a practical consideration of others' interests as the irreducible notion of morality is that, from a social perspective, its purpose is to promote conflict reduction. A morality based on consistent conflict would be contradictory, though some societies have been based on a preferred social value of aggression: there would be no point of a morality which aimed at society's destruction, for the very concept of society implies rules for regulating interpersonal relations toward the very practicability of human beings living together. Even obedience to such rules is a limited way of considering others' interests, and rule-following is at least the beginnings of a morality.

From the subjective view of morality as based on personal convictions, or the attitudes and values that give rise to them, and on the assumption that in this respect our convictions are not merely idiosyncratic, the interests of sentient animals cannot be excluded by limiting morality arbitrarily to the traditional sphere of human association. The formal notion of a practical consideration of others' interests therefore includes the interests of all beings capable of *having* interests, of being able to experience, as a minimum condition, the difference between suffering and enjoyment. This distinction in experience such things as trees and the environment do not make, but sentient animals *do*. Sentient animals have interests to be considered particularly inasmuch as they can *experience* pain, sometimes as acutely as man, and as well for their capacity for a pleasurable emotional life – for enjoyments such as caring for their young, playing, and freedom of movement as opposed to confinement. Rights are not among their interests, and their interests are indeed very limited, but that they do have some interests to be considered by us is evident, and these interests are not dependent upon an ability to have rights correlative to our moral obligations to them. With obligations or duties, as we have seen, that is not an uncommon situation, even with respect to ourselves, as in cases of *gratitude* and *Good Samaritanism*. Since we base our notion of morality on others' interests, we are not able to defend its formal notion in terms of a practical consideration of others' *well-being*, for that would include insentient plant life and other forms of life incapable of having interests.

Justice

Much of the justification for the formal notion of justice is related to morality as a practical consideration of others' interests, for justice is a *moral* notion, applying to all situations where some individuals exert power or influence over others and so are in a position to 'treat' them in a particular way: that is, to make decisions and to execute them in a way that affects others' interests or well-being. Two value words have been included – 'fairness' and 'persons' – to give the ιotion sufficient possible direction to be used as a stable reference, though each is capable of a variety of substantive variations. It is thus escued from the emptiness of a formal notion that is no notion, one hat might contradictorily admit opposites, in the moral and the ιon-moral. The second reason is that 'fairness' is sufficiently wide-weeping to be filled with content of different kinds that would need ο be separately justified on moral grounds. In particular it is nclusive of the idea of consistency in the application of rules, equity η the sense of establishing a balance or proportion among different ndividuals, with equality of treatment in relevant respects. 'Persons' οο is a value word, whose substantive import is not established in the vord itself, but does imply the possibility of moral agency and moral ɔbligations beyond those suggested by the anonymity and moral ɛmptiness of 'individuals'. Other reasons are more fundamental nasmuch as they relate to morality, and similar explanations apply as ο a practical consideration of others' interests. Fairness in the reatment of persons is dictated by the recognition of others' *interests*, ncluding their *rights*. Again, the clearest perception of their person-ιood which demands such fair treatment by others is in the concrete-ιess of individuality as it is observed in experience, or assumed as a ɔrojection from experience, each as much a living embodiment of lispositions and reason as ourselves. The notion of justice as the equal treatment of persons in the same category' is sufficient to ɛstablish consistency and equity (as balance or proportion) without norality. 'Fairness' removes this deficiency: the possibility of the reatment being harsh, cruel, even bestial, though still consistent and ɛven in its inhumanity, is avoided. Justice is a moral concept: that is ɔo say, justice as fairness in the treatment of persons is one aspect of norality as a practical consideration of others' interests. Legal justice ιs not necessarily justice at all. It is a technical expression to refer to Jeterminations of the courts, according to the law as it stands. If settlements of cases happen to be consistent with justice as fairness in treatment of persons, then legal justice and moral justice to that ɛxtent coincide. If legal justice is an application of unjust laws which do not consider others' interests, legal justice and moral justice remain distinct, and legal justice refers simply to a positivist reference to cases settled in accordance with the law as it happens to be. It would be both inaccurate and unfair to contend that the conjunction of legal justice and moral justice, whenever it does occur in practice, is merely fortuitous. That would be to deny the long tradition of law in some countries (especially common law with judges free of

obligations merely to interpret statutes) where fairness in the treatment of individual persons has been an obvious principle. Even in the
interpretation of statutes, opportunities have been available for
judges to be influenced by their personal moral attitudes and values

To this point we have had no reason to challenge the formal notion
of justice as fairness in the treatment of persons. This has been partly
dictated by the order of the chapters, beginning with education and
justice, and the observation of certain relationships between them
which – because of the nature of education – are necessarily human
relationships. Then when we moved in the third chapter to morality
and in the fourth to rights, we widened our sphere of morality to
include sentient animals. In the last two chapters we focussed on
social or distributive justice which is concerned with the equitable
distribution of social goods, including education, to members of
society. Thus we have led again to a conjunction of justice and
education, in exclusively human relationships, with respect to educational opportunity.

Now, rather than earlier, seems to be the appropriate time to
reflect further on the formal notion of justice, partly to answer
possible objections and to consider an alternative. Would it not be
more appropriate to speak of this formal notion as fairness in the
treatment of *others*, asking whether the 'others' should not be
extended – as in the case of morality – to include *sentient* animals (at
least)? For example, we may reflect on instances in various countries
of wild animals suspected of having taken children, followed by
ferocious and indiscriminate killing of as many of the species as can
be located, when subsequently it is discovered that the children have
in fact perished from other causes. Is it appropriate to speak of this
precipitate and retributive reaction as injustice in the treatment of
animals, since people have harboured suspicions without the firm
supportive evidence that we would require in the case of murder? If
our morality is widened to include sentient animals, and if justice is
part of morality, does it not follow that justice too should be widened
to include them? Is it not logically possible then, for justice to apply
to *sentient* animals (at least)? Formally we should keep in mind that
the converse of the following universal affirmative proposition does
not hold: all instances of justice are instances of morality. From this
we may not infer that all instances of morality are instances of justice:
there may be instances of morality which refer to our relations with
sentient animals, for example, which are not instances of justice. Yet
there are obvious instances in our relations with family pets or

domesticated farm animals where it seems appropriate to speak of fairness in our treatment of them, because our perceptions tend to be anthropomorphic as we regard them as members of an extended family. Thus the underlying notion of equity and non-discrimination in establishing a proper balance or proportion among them seems to apply; we feel it is unfair, that is, to have favourites, or to deny to all what we offer to some by way of food, shelter, kindness, and so forth.

For various reasons, nonetheless, the tendency to extend justice to animals (even to sentient animals only) leads to complications. First, we become selective and discriminatory even when our impulse is to be otherwise. That is, we apply justice to *some* animals – even some *sentient* animals only – those with which we have established some kind of relationship in a domestic setting. We exclude others with which we have no such relationship – pumas in the Andes, tigers in Burma and China, and so forth. Thus our anthropomorphism is not generalized: we do not think of justice as applying to all sentient animals. Second, the inconsistency in our anthropomorphism is compounded by the presumption of our deistic powers as we face the world of living things. That is, we elevate our human situation to one with God's-eye impartiality, responsible not only for justice in human relationships, but also for justice in relationships between ourselves and all other life on earth. Third, if we presume to have this role as the only rational beings on earth, we presume to have as well a perfect, God-like capacity for practical judgement which exceeds our actual human powers. Since we are human, our rationality is necessarily influenced by our dispositions, and we must expect it to be biased, at least on some occasions, in our favour. Fourth, if justice is allowed as applying to fairness in the treatment of animals (even selected, domesticated animals), and if we presume to have, as uniquely rational beings a responsibility to treat animals with justice, what grounds have we for excluding any other living things from our parameters of justice? Are we willing to include earth-worms, leeches, jelly fish and so forth, or indeed any of the plants that struggle for survival: weeds in our gardens, unwanted plants in our orchards and pastures, burs in our lawns? Strict fairness in the treatment of all living things implies total non-discrimination with respect to all species of plant and animal life alike. Then the formal notion of justice quickly gets out of hand as we presume again to have powers which are in excess of our human capabilities and which fail to acknowledge imperfections in our rationality. We cannot defend the presumption of a God's-eye view on all living things, since we cannot

transcend our human limitations or totally surrender our own com
petitive situation.

Our moral attitudes and values are sufficient to explain and t
justify our human relationship with sentient animals in terms of th
interests which they have. Our non-moral attitudes and values help t
explain and to justify our human relationships with non-sentier
animals and with all other living things. The formal notion of justic
as fairness in the treatment of *others* – with the 'others' applying to a
living things on earth – leads to inconsistencies, presumptions an
impracticalities. It is difficult enough for us – sometimes eve
impossible for us – to be just in the treatment of *persons*. In thi
formal notion of justice we are considering persons as rational: tha
is, there is implied a capacity for a mutual rational understanding b
both giver and receiver. While it is true that our formal notion c
morality as considering the interests of others, including sentier
animals, implies a non-reciprocal relationship between man an
sentient animals, there is no such implication in the case of the forma
notion of justice, for in that the receiver of the just treatment has
capacity for rational understanding of the way he has been treatec
This does not require reciprocal treatment of the giver of the justice
if A treats B justly, there is no requirement in the formal notion c
justice that B should return the favour before the act of justice i
completed. Infants, immature children, imbeciles, sentient animals
all fall outside the area of justice: we have moral obligations to ther
as non-reciprocating beings, but since they are not rational, we do nc
speak of fairness in the treatment of them, as we do with rationa
beings. One of our moral obligations may be, in certain circumst
ances, to be non-discriminatory to them, but such apparent fairnes
cannot be perceived by them. The requirement of rational capacitie
in the receiver of the justice does not imply a necessary *acceptance* b
him of the treatment that he has received: rational as he is, he ma
not agree – at least immediately – that justice has been done, largel
because of dispositional influences. Thus a capacity for rationa
responses does not imply that in all circumstances justice will b
perceived for what it is. Further, in some circumstances what i
justice in the treatment of persons may not be unambiguously clear
and some treatment of others may carry with it an element of doub
as to whether justice has in fact been done. In being *fair* in th
treatment of persons we are implying a community of rational being
to which both giver and receiver of justice belong, and one as we
with a perceptible commonality of interests. Justice as fairness in th

treatment of persons is thus more than mathematically commutative or rectificatory: it has a *moral* core of human understanding. Justice is an exclusively human experience, and conferring it is an exclusively human act.

Education

The formal notion of education, like the formal notion of justice, appears at first to err on the side of substantiveness, and we shall need to show first why this is not so, and second why the expression is needed to rescue the formal notion from the possibility of internal contradiction. Education as the developing of potentialities falls into a similar error as in stating the formal notion of justice as 'equal treatment of persons in the same category'. Education as a developing of potentialities is open to the error of all attempts to define education as the unfolding of human nature. Man has propensities for many things which are not in our general interest to unfold or develop: aggression, hostility, murder, anti-intellectualism, worship of power or brute force. 'Developing of potentialities' in the becoming sense, or the Aristotelian sense of possibilities, allows for education as moral or non-moral, whatever education is conceived to be. In the recent Cultural Revolution in China many of the *means* whereby individuals might develop potentialities – especially intellectually – were destroyed. Indeed the history of mankind shows ample evidence of potentiality for exploitation, destruction and even self-destruction. It is necessary therefore to see education in a moral context, as with justice, to recognize it – as the Greeks and Kant recognized it – as a moral activity, not the development of intellect alone. Like justice, education refers to human beings only, not to animals. In the case of the formal notion of justice we found it necessary to use the expression 'person'; in the case of education this is inappropriate, since some of its activities relate to very young children whose personhood, in our sense, is not yet reached.

With respect to social values, the formal notion leaves it open as to how society of a particular time and place will interpret morality, but at least education will not be unmindful of the interests of learners – particularly children – with respect to social membership. That is not an admission of cultural relativism. In a subjective approach to morality the onus is on every society to defend its values with reason, and in some cases individuals may feel a moral obligation to deviate from some of the values widely espoused. But under a common rational review of social values – including moral values which are our main concern – the measure of disagreement in contemporary societies can easily be exaggerated. The formal notion of education recognizes its purposeful moral character: to be consistent with social values is also to be consistent with the formal notion of morality as a practical consideration of others' interests. We have noted even a minimum of morality presupposed by the notion of society itself – of persons making adjustments to live in association with others – in so far as such adjustments are voluntary and at least partly out of thoughtfulness for others.

Distinctions between the formal notions of justice, morality and education are more striking than their similarities, and help us to understand something of the nature of each. We may sum up our perspective by noting that while justice and morality may be aimed at and realized in specific judgements or acts, education may not. That is, education does not inhere, as justice and morality may do, in specific judgements or acts. Education is a notion of becoming without anything, in a sense, to become. We may become senile, but we never become educated in any literal sense. Like *improvement*, with which it has a close affinity, education is always becoming, never reaching an end. No one can conceptualize education in itself, or say what it would be like to have it, or to experience it at any particular time. What we aim at are so-called educational activities and ends that are *learning* ends, especially in knowledge, attitudes and values, and skills. Learners can experience the satisfaction of improvement in learning achievements, such as in speech or reading skills, but no one can experience education as some kind of satisfying state – distinct, that is, from this improvement in aspects of learning. The reason we do not experience *education* as such as something inhering in the improving process is that in one sense it *is* that process, but only in so far as it contributes to the developing of particular individuals in particular ways, so that in a second sense it is more than the process of improvement: it is as well a *judgement* of that process, a recognition that the developmental purpose which we have for education is being fulfilled.

In the formal notion of education it is implied that a developing of an individual's potentialities is observable from an external stance according to criteria consistent with social values, and only *after* some improvement has occurred. Thus in the formal notion we imply a double conceptual shift from concrete experiences of learning achievements: first, we abstract the idea of improvement; second, we abstract further from the idea of improvement to the idea of a developing of individual potentialities. In the second, the perspective shifts from the activity itself which shows some degree of improvement, to the partial fulfilment of a purpose: that is, to the effect of the improvement on an individual. Education is not only, then, an improving notion; it is also a judgemental notion. The second perspective does not necessarily merge with the first. There may be many instances of improvement in specific learning achievements which in themselves are not perceptible as contributing to improving individual potentialities, such as learning a spelling rule applying to 'receive' and 'believe', or the function of indices in algebraic multiplication. But it is misleading to speak of the formal notion of education as referring to a perception of individual potentialities in particular acts of learning achievement. Education as a becoming is recognized from a more detached perspective which comprehends a span of achievements. It is seen as a developing of potentialities from a general and judgemental, rather than a specific, fragmentary stance.

Education is unique among the three formal notions in the misleading tendency to reify it as we confuse it with learning or with the making of the liberal mind. In the first instance such a tendency leads to education being considered in terms of what an individual has learned – particularly a stock of acquired knowledge: a tendency which is aggravated by connections with cognate expresions such as 'educated man'. In the second instance education is not a peculiarly intellectual thing – usually described as a liberal mind. The liberal mind is an intellectual ideal, certainly variable in degree of attainment but always imperfect, as Newman unwittingly demonstrated in his personal remarks on a university education. What is unique about the formal notion of education is that we have to rescue it from the status of a literal no-thing by standing off from so-called educational activities and considering them in relation to an individual's development of potentialities – chiefly intellectual, moral and physical – interested (as Aristotle was) in the satisfaction that comes from a measure of personal fulfilment in certain learning pursuits. The formal notion of education is something of a technical notion: its reference is not what it appears to be in ordinary language. We quickly reach contradictions and uncertainties when we attempt to have education refer to things that are learnt, for we can never agree on what particular knowledge, attitudes and values, and skills are necessary to it. We quickly realise that the liberal mind is not to be identified with education, for it too is impossible to specify definitively, and certainly, in some of its formulations, impracticable for anyone to live up to consistently. Education as a developing of potentialities consistent with social values is not an ideal. It is sustained as a formal notion only by its in-built qualification.

As a final reflection on the formal notions we may ask what their value is, now that we have had an opportunity to consider them against a background of substantive matters in education, justice and morality. We have to recognize first that it is not in all circumstances that we are in a position to penetrate substantive moral values relating to justice or to education, and to go straight to the underlying formal notion of each. A just act may be interpreted in different substantive ways, even though there is fairness in the treatment of persons, since 'fairness' is itself a value word, as 'persons' is. A different kind of question is to ask whether we may be said to have an instance of practical morality whenever there is a practical consideration of others' interests. Then an affirmative answer necessarily follows. What then is the value of the formal notion as a constant reference in our discussions? It is simply this. Without the presence of these ideas in discussions we may say categorically that the discussions are not in the respective areas of morality, justice and education at all. That is, without the idea of a practical consideration of others' interests (since all live in social groups of some kind) morality is not under discussion. Without the idea of fairness in the treatment of persons, the discussion is not positively in the area of justice at all, whatever the substantive variations that may be allowed. And without the idea of a developing of individual potentialities, consistent with social values, activities are not educational activities. They may refer, like air-raid training or fire drill, to a distinctly different area, but they do not refer to the becoming that is education. Each of the fundamental references we have used as formal notions of justice, morality and education holds with the constancy which we sought at the outset. Further, some situations of injustice have an immediate referability to them, and when contact is made, the reaction may be instantaneous, as in cases of inequalities of educational opportunity. The three formal notions may be said to represent reason or intellect, transcending, and contrasting with, the many substantive versions of each which are influenced to some degree by personal dispositions. Each is as abstract as we can allow it to be while retaining practical significance. As statements of the intellect, the formal notions have a universality of reference.

But if each of the formal notions is necesary for corresponding acts or activities – of practical morality, justice or education – is it also sufficient? That does *not* follow: the reasons are to be found in the deliberative phase of the action schema. The formal notion is no more than the underlying, formal *idea*. When it is engaged in the rational–dispositional deliberation the interpretation of each is subjective, and is always to some extent a substantive variation of the formal notion. Although we have used expressions such as 'morality as a practical consideration of others' interests' and 'justice as fairness in the treatment of persons', in all such cases we have been referring to no more than the underlying idea of each, *not* to an objectification of the formal idea as though this itself constituted a uniform element of every practical morality, or every act of justice. It would be false and in contradiction of our views on a subjective morality to claim that the formal notions constitute even a part of an objective morality. In an instance of political repression, or denial of civil liberties, rulers and their critics may each agree on the idea, or formal notion, of justice as fairness in the treatment of persons, but disagree on whether the instance is or is not a denial of justice. There is no constant objective core to be discovered in every instance of justice. The interpretation of the formal notion is a subjective interpretation. On the other hand all persons can agree, whatever their substantive views of justice or morality, for instance, that in some situations the formal notion is not invoked at all. It is not invoked in the case of a person being punished for an offence which he didn't commit, where there is neither an accident nor a mistake, nor any other conceivable excusing condition. Then the idea of justice or of morality is not present to anyone, so that we may say that the formal notion is *necessary* for any discussion of justice or of morality in particular cases. But there is no sense of *sufficient* condition, suggesting that if we have the formal notion, some element of justice or of morality will invariably follow when translated into action. Callous persons may punish merely out of cruelty, or for reprisals, or for deterrence, while still accepting the idea or formal notion of justice or of morality. Nozick's interpretation of the formal notion of morality as a practical consideration of others' interests is as true to it as Kant's. Apartheid theorists are as true to the formal notion of social justice as Rawls. Thus there are possibilities of extreme variations from the formal notion in the respective substantive interpretations. That does not imply that all interpretations are equally justifiable. Each is to be supported with reasons, and it is by the quality of the reasons that it is judged by others.

We have used formal notions which are rescued from the sterile structure of the kind into which opposites could be fitted – education and non-education, justice and injustice, morality and immorality – by giving them a minimum of meaning to stand both as constant and directional. Otherwise they could not be used – as Perelman's formal notion of justice cannot be used – as stable references throughout the discussion. They have most application to simple cases of violations of the primary principles, when we can say unequivocally that a certain act or activity is not moral, just, or an activity of education, inasmuch as it lacks the necessary underlying idea of each. In more complex cases of substantive value variations reference may still be needed to them as the fundamental immovable corner stones of the discussion.

The formal notions have a rational foundation. Their formulation has been largely on that basis after exploring a variety of other possibilities including others' judgements. Yet there is an inherent circularity in returning to them in what appears as a self-justifying way, with a pragmatic reference to the way they stand up in a variety of contexts. But the way they survive rationally is the strongest case in their defence, without moving to a transcendental justification of reason itself. Their rejection can only be made by others with stronger reasons to support alternative sets of fundamental ideas. Given their practical orientation and the rejection of an inert formalism that can have no meaningful relationship with *activities* of justice, morality or education, they retain our support.

With the formal notions now reconsidered, we shall attempt to consolidate our views on distributive justice as a framework for the problem of equality of educational opportunity.

DISTRIBUTIVE JUSTICE

Need Criterion

One of the principles of distributive justice which we have proposed after considering Rawls' formulation is that each person has an equal right to basic social goods according to need. Then, early in the last chapter we arrived at the following principle of equality of education-al opportunity: each person has an equal right to education according to need, regardless of whether he is fortunate or unfortunate in natural endowments or in the social conditions of his upbringing.

We shall now seek to justify the *need* criterion of distributive justice, regarding education as one of the social goods to be distributed. It is clear that from our formal notion of education there is nothing for the state to distribute except possibilities: there is no package of education; and classrooms, teachers and books are not education. There is no more than a facilitation of the becoming, different with respect to every individual according to his intellectual, moral and physical potentialities. But the distribution may still be even or equitable, or it may be biased in favour of some individuals and against other individuals. Again what the needs are for each child, adolescent or adult being educated is not a codified prescrip-tion to suit age levels, ability levels or achievement levels as measured by assessment procedures, but a set for each individual that is as unique as his individuality. It is chiefly economic considerations that indicate needs according to classified levels, and this constitutes the first constraint on any ideal fulfilment of the equality of educa-tional opportunity objective. There are conspicuous individual needs such as of the physically and intellectually handicapped, and much less conspicuous needs of children in the classroom associated with particular learning difficulties. So in this less than ideal sense distributive justice with respect to educational facilitation will be approached, but never completely realised, when the specific needs of individuals in the widest possible sense, needs related to their unique development of individualities in intellectual, moral and physical respects, are promoted by teaching, counselling and other resources supplied by the state or by independent bodies. The facilitation resources would satisfy the equality of educational oppor-tunity conditions when *individual* needs are expertly diagnosed and expertly ministered to, with total non-discriminatoriness on any grounds whatsoever, and with special consideration given to environ-mental limitations, which either create additional needs or impede proper attention to them by individuals being educated, or by those facilitating the process.

In contemporary societies, and because of the great expansion of knowledge and skills of many kinds, the non-finiteness of education is much more readily recognized than it was in the renaissance, for instance, when Comenius believed it possible for one man to comprehend all that was known and therefore to become educated in the complete sense. Correspondingly the educational *needs* of individual learners are now more positively appreciated; in particular it is acknowledged that though the formal notion of education may make it theoretically possible to do without schools and teachers, or even books, substantively such a notion is at odds with the world as we know it. Those becoming educated do *need* all three, and would make little progress in general without them. So one of the basic needs in education is for facilitating resources, school buildings and suitable classrooms, books and other resources such as films or tapes, and in some cases equipment such as microscopes; and especially for human facilitators such as teachers and counsellors, librarians and their various assistants. Since such needs fulfil purposes, these are needs which are instrumental to their learning, to their becoming educated in the non-finite sense. They are *needs* in our society inasmuch as immature learners in particular can make only limited progress, in most situations, without them, and to do without them would be to seriously impair their life prospects, even for a year or two. Therefore the formal and demeaning sense of teachers as facilitators is converted substantively to professionally trained teachers who become learners' indispensable needs, and it has become as wasteful to do without them, in most cases, as it is wasteful and dangerous to do without medical services in coping with physiological ailments. Similarly wasteful is to do without counselling services in schools, offered collectively by headmasters or principals, teachers and professionally-trained counsellors, for there are needs here too of those developing their potentialities: for a sense of individual achievement according to individual standards, for instance, rather than a sense of failure or doubt by reference to hypothetical and artificial group standards. The school thus satisfies a general need, as well as special individual needs, through professional diagnosis of obstructions to learning and psychological support for continued motivation. If it fails to satisfy the general needs of some individuals, assuming adequate professional competence, the source of the obstructions and motivational deficiency may be in deep-seated social conditions, and referral of the problem of inequality of educational opportunity must be to those in government and to the public conscience.

Desert Criterion

Thus from an educational standpoint, and considering education as one of society's goods, *needs* provide the most appropriate criterion of distributive justice. One of the reasons is clearly the immaturity of those whose potentialities are being developed during the years of formal schooling. The question now is whether educational provision in adulthood should still be on the basis of need, or whether another criterion such as *desert* should be used.

Justinian's claim that justice is giving each man his due, and the philosopher Mill's notion of an impartial system of justice in which innocent and guilty receive their deserts (*Utilitarianism*, p.318)[1], each raise the question of how desert is to be evaluated. It might even be claimed that a man deserves to receive from society exactly what he *needs*, and in that interpretation 'desert' and 'need' are identified. Mill saw as equally just, on the criterion of desert, the principle that whoever does his best deserves equally well with others – from an individual perspective; and the principle – from a social perspective – that the efficient worker who contributes more to society than the relatively inefficient deserves more *from* society. The highest standard of social and distributive justice was then expressed in the principle that we should strive to treat equally well those who are equally deserving of us, and society should similarly treat equally well those who are equally deserving of it (p.335). Above this was a supreme principle, that everyone has an equal claim to happiness, including all the *means* to happiness (p.336–7). To that extent his utilitarianism inclined toward equality of educational opportunity, on the assumption that education considered intrinsically is one of the means to happiness or satisfaction; but as we have seen, Mill gave no support to the notion of a general education, so did not himself make this assumption. His separate individual and social perspectives provide some basis for assessment of desert: first, using a criterion of working to the best of one's ability; and second, using a criterion of individual achievement according to efficiency. From the first perspective social goods would be distributed according to optimum individual effort, regardless of quantity or quality of individual production; but from the second perspective a differential principle is introduced of reward for efficiency. The relevance of these notions to education is problematic, even when we distinguish between the educational needs of immature learners during the years of formal schooling, and those of adult learners in post-school years. From the standpoint of immature learners, those who are not doing their best reach this condition in a variety of possible ways, and the task of the educator is to diagnose the problem and to remedy it if at all possible. From the standpoint of adult learners, who are voluntary recipients of educational assistance as one of the social goods being distributed to them, on first thoughts it is difficult to justify withdrawing or limiting this assistance for the reason that they are not doing their best in their educational activities; or more significantly, for the reason that they are not doing their best in the work which is their contribution to society. Even adults have needs for further developing their potentialities by means of education, and on the assumption that their work is affected partly by their attitudes, the further they are developed the more likely it is that their social contribution will improve as satisfaction with their personal condition improves. In other words, if a further developing of potentialities increases individual well-being it would appear not to be a subject for prohibitions or penalties, but rather for encouragement in the interests of individuals and of society alike. To reach this judgement is not necessarily to be committed to utilitarianism, but it is a consequentialist point of view, and the grounds are clearly pragmatic rather than moral. If it is agreed that education should be equally available according to need, is a similar argument justifiable with respect to other social goods, regardless of individual effort, or of whether the person is in fact 'doing his best', in Mill's expression? From the standpoints of the recipient and of other contributing social members alike, this is questionable. Justice as fairness in the treatment of persons appears to be violated when a person works consistently below ability and capacity, and expects to receive equally with others from society's distribution of goods. Such a person is indifferent to the demands of practical morality on our assumptions, possibly even holding other persons in contempt. Other contributing members would also have their sense of justice violated if society were to treat him equally with others: the fairness of consistency and equity would be in question. Therefore on grounds of morality and justice we are able to concede that further education might be regarded as an exception to the general principle of distributive justice that resources be distributed according to need. The need criterion will apply only on condition that individuals have done their best as contributing social members. Those who receive must also give: fairness cuts both ways. Those who give less than they are able to give deserve less of all social goods, including education. We must therefore judge adult learners already in the work force differently from immature learners for whom the need criterion is entirely appropriate for educational provisions by the state.

An increasing social problem in the present technological revolution is that of unemployment, applying both to the initial transition from school to work, and to redundancies and retrenchments and the question of re-training for different occupations to meet the demands of rapid changes in the techniques of production. In neither of these cases is the question of desert relevant. There is a third case of the person dismissed for consistently working below capacity. Here the problem is complicated by *desert*: it is largely a question of a diagnosis of each individual case and subsequent administrative judgement on a suitable area for re-training, as well as counselling on social obligations. Our main concern is with the first two cases. In the first school-leavers have had no opportunity to demonstrate their work capacity; in the second, loss of work is incurred through no moral lapse, through no personal responsibility of any kind. The potential worker and the worker have no debt to pay to society: the obligation – and there is one – is the other way. On the morality of considering others' interests, and the justice of fairness in the treatment of persons, society has an obligation to distribute educational resources according to need, ensuring as well as it is able, that occupational training and re-training are likely to end in work placements, but recognizing that in the world of technology re-training may become increasingly necessary. Since work is assumed to be one of the conditions of human well-being, we assert as a principle of social justice that *each person has an equal right to work according to his abilities and capacities.*[2] In the fulfilment of its obligations under this principle, society has an opportunity to provide continuing education, relevant both to occupational mobility and to development of individual potentialities.

Before considering Mill's second point of distributive justice, on reward for efficiency, we need to distinguish between certain senses of 'need', in particular between basic human needs which are related to Human Rights and common to all members of society, and needs which are idiosyncratic, or even specious. Education refers to the first sense of need, however much it requires to be specified to meet individual cases. In contrast with this, those who assert a need on the basis of a positive want, are expressing desire, and sometimes motive. There can be no justification for distribution of social goods on such a demand basis, because desire translated to demand, such as a demand for tertiary education when ability and capacity are unsuit able, may be no more than an expression of an unrealistic and irrational inclination or ambition, wasteful of society's resources Such personal demands are by their nature unrelated to the needs o other social members, if not indifferent to them. Desires in the guise of needs pressed against society for distribution of its goods to individuals are simply specious rights claims, in contrast with al authentic expressions of human needs which it is proper for society to attend to as common to all members, or to significant groups o members.

Reward for efficiency in the distribution of social goods links deser with effort and quality of achievement, and through them with natural endowments. The extent to which effort contributes to efficiency is indeterminate, for at least part of the achievemen regarded by society as an efficient contribution to its welfare i related to natural endowments. The person who achieves most i assisted by ability and capacity, including physical and mental health He may also be assisted by social advantage, or at least not inhibited by unfavourable attitudes and values with their source in serious social disadvantage. What is needed to evaluate efficiency as warrant ing desert is a measure of the proportional combined contribution o natural endowment and social conditions to efficient effort – an empirical problem of almost insuperable difficulty. Social values o most contemporary societies have swung sharply from elitism and privilege so that while both natural endowments and social advantage have a significant bearing on individual success, there is wide agreement in principle that neither constitutes a suitable basis for moral desert. Further, since desert is itself indeterminate it is not on its own an appropriate criterion for the distribution of social goods. From the standpoint of morality and of justice a principle of need is superior to a principle of desert which may be itself influenced favourably by privilege, or unfavourably by underprivilege and its associated attitudes, as well as, in either way, by natural endow ments. But the particularization of need, as in education and health services, requires to be impartially and expertly evaluated, and can never be supported by linking desire and motive with need, or by linking such ephemeral and idiosyncratic needs with claim rights which cannot be rationally or empirically justified in relation to the needs of other members of society.

To this point we have noted that our general principle that each person has an equal right to basic social goods according to need, has application to education as one of the social goods, both for immature learners and adult learners, but a distinction needs to be made between these two, since adults who are not doing their best as contributors to society cannot expect equal treatment with others in receipt of social goods. That would be a violation of justice as fairness in the treatment of persons. The principle we then deduce is this: *In so far as each person has worked to the best of his ability, he has an equal right to basic social goods according to need.* In other words – in fact in Marx's words – from each according to his ability, to each according to his needs, which comes close to expressing a universal ideal of distributive justice. In some societies there are situations of underprivilege in social conditions which *prevent* a person working according to his ability: effort, achievement, efficiency are all impaired by unfavourable social attitudes and values. When this is the case the principle is nullified: it can become operative only when the sources of the unfavourable attitudes and values are diagnosed and removed. A general condition for the successful operation of the principle is removal of extremes of social disadvantage, so that *whatever* the worker's effort, he will not feel that it is likely to be futile in removing the generational reproduction of social disadvantage. The Marxist principle is therefore not strictly relevant to all societies, but only to societies where initially there is equality of social conditions for all workers. To make it relevant to class-structured as well as to classless states we would need to add a proviso, such as 'other things equal', for all things are in fact *not* equal, especially in relation to social conditions and their effects on work attitudes and values, and on the quality of work itself. The proviso implies that in particular social circumstances a person may have a right to basic social goods according to need, even though his effort and efficiency both fail to match his ability.

Distribution of Talent

Rawls and others hold the view that talent is a national asset to be distributed by society. The view is widely accepted in classless states, which regard the interests of the individual as subordinate to those of the state, so that there is no discrimination against the talented or against any other specific group of persons. The argument generally used is that the talented do not deserve their talent any more than the intellectually limited deserve their disability. It is a matter of good fortune or of bad. On this there can be little disagreement, but objections are sometimes raised when the next step is taken: that is, to regard the talented as public property to be used for the benefit of everyone in society, much as the mining of diamonds by the state might have distributive benefits for all members. From Nozick's standpoint what a man has he is entitled to, including his intellectual gifts, for these have not been gained in any way by harming others. In Locke's language, the state must protect the individual's *estate*, including all his possessions, of which his personal talents are a part. The question of having done nothing to earn such natural good fortune is, in this view, irrelevant to the talented person's natural right to keep what he has, and not make of himself a continually disposable commodity. This liberal idea of the individual free to make his own way in life, from whatever start fortune has given him, and within minimum constraints imposed by the state, is in conflict with any view of the talented as a distributable asset. It would be doubly offensive to the liberal idea if the state were to recognize the talents of a person who had, as an exception to the social reproduction tendency, emerged successfully from seriously underprivileged social conditions, only then to be seized and used by the state for its own purposes by manpower direction. Such a seizure of talent could be justified, according to the liberal idea, only in national emergency. This view we support from the liberty principle of distributive justice: each person has an equal right to basic liberties provided that he does not infringe the liberties of others. The notion of the state seizing an individual and turning him to its own purposes – which are the purposes of the person or persons in power – violates also the principle of equality of vocational opportunity. Social justice requires that each be free to make his own life-plans, and be given an equal right with others to selection, on relevant grounds, to a vocation of his choice. In those instances where the state recognizes talent in childhood or adolescence, and channels it in special institutions with the aid of extrinsically motivating devices, the direction is given before rational vocational choices can be exercised. This is a violation of morality, justice and education: of education inasmuch as an individual's potentialities are apt to be developed narrowly toward service to the state. Education is a developing of potentialities, consistent with social values, and necessarily selective to a degree, but state manipulation of children and direction of their talent is a fundamental deprivation of basic liberty, unfair in the treatment of developing persons, and contrary to morality in an overriding of their interests – unless, fortuitously, the interests of the individual and of the state happen to coincide.

Reward and Distributive Justice

Since the talented are often, on grounds of natural endowments alone, conspicuous achievers, it is sometimes held that they should be rewarded by the state for their contributions to society. We shall consider the case of the talented first in this context, then the problem of reward generally for effort, achievement, efficiency, or volume of production.

Our notion of education, in conjunction with morality and justice, requires that the talented be treated no differently from others: that their potentialities be recognized and facilities provided to develop them selectively in their own individual interests; that in the transition from school to work they be given the same vocational opportunities as anyone else. This non-discriminatory approach we now adopt with the question of reward, reasoning that the talented should be treated according to the same principles as apply to all others in society. As soon as we acknowledge that natural endowment is no more a ground for desert of any kind than is social advantage or privilege, we face the problem already encountered of separating the products of undeserved advantages – such as these – from products that attract desert. A person's achievements and his efficiency in whatever he achieves – however evaluated – are a complex of effort, ability, skill, capacity for work, interest in work and work satisfaction; together with dispositional factors (in our special sense of 'dispositional'), especially motives and goals, attitudes and values, and in particular the relationship between work and self-esteem or the extent to which the individual relates his work to the way he wants others to see him. One person may be said to deserve social recognition more than another, to the extent that his work is an authentic social contribution *exceeding* a performance which is the result of natural ability and all its various consequences in interest, persistence, and skill. In social desert we are not concerned with the self-regarding man or the naturally fortunate man, but with the altruistic man. The family doctor, the social worker, the teacher, may all exceed the theoretical minimum which is unique for each as we consider his ability, motives and goals, attitudes and values, work capacity, and so forth. Their desert in terms of social recognition is similar to supererogation, but it is not so much a matter of exceeding formal duty or social expectations as of voluntarily making sacrifices for the common good. In principle the question of talent is irrelevant, for regardless of ability it is not work considered either quantitatively or qualitatively that is taken into account, but work and achievement that exceed what might be expected from natural endowments and a variety of factors associated with it, and that exceed as well what might be attributable to pursuit of personal satisfaction in various ways. It is work and achievement that must be for others because it exceeds what might be theoretically perceived as for the self, and it is work and achievement that go beyond what might be theoretically perceived as the consequences of natural endowment. In other words, it is motivated by concern for others above all normal work expectations, involving sacrifice of the self in terms of time, energy, or loss of recreation, though not – for obvious reasons – physical and mental health. Such a notion of desert, warranting reward of some kind in terms of social recognition, is simply not measurable on a social scale. If the altruistic excess involving personal sacrifice were to be considered assessable for particular individuals, by complicated techniques of measurement and validation, it would be a socially impracticable task. It is also beyond the powers of external judgement because of its very complexity, and therefore the notion of social desert, or of reward in terms of social recognition, must be shelved as a principle, beyond implementation. It is not that none are deserving; the problem is that there is no reliable means of determining who is and who is not, and the admission of undeserving members to the category of deserving is to treat unfairly those who are authentically deserving. Justice as fairness in the treatment of persons is not observed, or observable, in these circumstances.

Fundamentally the notion of reward as a form of distributive justice conflicts with the principle of distribution according to need, given that each is contributing to the best of his ability. No person deserves to receive more of society's goods in return for contributions, however talented he is and whatever the quality or quantity of his contributions. No society has yet reached the stage of having an excess of total resources in relation to individual needs, so that justice and morality both suggest that if one worker is able to produce more or better than another, his product should become part of the common resources of society to be distributed, without any expectation of recompense or bonus. Even the use of public honours is morally questionable, both on grounds of the impracticability of evaluating desert with sufficient reliability, and on grounds of respect for persons through artificial discriminations. In the last resort merit, like virtue, is its own reward. We conclude that the principle of *need*, rather than *desert*, best fits our notions of morality and of justice in the distribution of social goods, although in some circumstances desert provides a necessary qualification to the general principle of distributive justice.

Principles and Practice of Distributive Justice

Practical Considerations

We shall now state certain practical considerations sometimes raised in discussions of distributive justice before we re-state our various principles. The administration of social justice, like other aspects of the administration of human affairs, involves an eternal contradiction between principles and pragmatism. It is self-evident that our principles must take account of what society can afford, of what in fact it *has* to distribute; and also that there are many different needs in society to be met by distributing limited resources, so the focus on particular needs – as in our repeated references to those seriously disadvantaged socially, and to the influence of their attitudes and values in restricting educational opportunity – must be seen in relation to the whole. These administrative concerns do not affect the justification of the principles of justice and morality, or our notion of what constitutes education. All the principles stand unchanged by practical administrative preoccupations with the limits of social resources. To that extent our proposals for distributive justice, like Rawls' theory of social justice, constitute ideal theory.

One of the recurring social issues of class-structured states is that of the distribution of social resources to independent or non-government schools. We shall not re-state the comprehensive range of arguments on this complex issue, but simply draw attention to the problem of distributive justice when resources are not distributed according to need but are subject to political biases and pressures. There are two classes in this situation who demand equal treatment as equals: first children in the schools; second their parents. From the perspective of the first, resources require to be distributed according to need; from the second, parents as tax-payers require to be treated alike, not expected to contribute, through the fees they pay, to the resources of the non-government schools which their children attend. In the first instance it is unjust for society to endow some schools more liberally than others, regardless of need; in the second instance it is unjust to ask some taxpayers to contribute to education at a higher rate than others. The more serious problem of distributive justice in this context relates to a conflict of equities. While it is equitable for the state to be non-discriminatory in its allocation of resources, providing evenly for non-government as well as for government schools, it is also equitable for children of government schools to have resources equal to those of non-government schools. When the distribution of resources to each ignores the *need* principle, the situation may be encountered of non-government schools being better endowed than government schools, and of offering educational facilities at a higher standard as well. Then a third type of inequity arises: those children who are fortunate in the social positions of their parents are offered an education of better quality than children whose parents are unable to pay the fees. Inequality of educational opportunity is then generated, with its source in the differential incomes and social statuses of parents – a situation which Nozick would condone, but which to some others is seen to be morally questionable. The principle of equality of educational opportunity according to need requires that all children should have an equal opportunity for education, and such inequalities cannot be justified on grounds of morality or of justice. Inequalities in educational opportunity become linked with inequalities in vocational opportunities, and thus the problem of social injustice is compounded.

The practical consideration that only *some* children from privileged non-government schools take advantage of the opportunities offered them is another irrelevance. While it is true that children of advantaged families may be educationally disadvantaged just as may children of underprivileged families, with in each instance the possibility of unsupportiveness of parents resulting in children's unfavourable attitudes and values, and restricted opportunities from formal education, the problem is not *characteristic* of those socially advantaged but is characteristic of the underprivileged. The fortuitous circumstance of educational disadvantage among the socially fortunate tends to be a diversionary observation, though certainly one requiring educational attention.

Another recurring practical consideration relates to opportunities for further education, particularly for those whose educational needs were not satisfied in formal schooling. Every adult may be said to need continuing education according to the notion of education as a developing of potentialities, for there is no limit to the potentialities which may be extended by education as long as human powers endure. The problem of distributive justice in this respect is primarily one of equality of educational opportunity and equality of vocational opportunity. The provision of further education has various forms and we shall confine ourselves to one only: that which attempts to compensate for opportunities missed in childhood and adolescence. Then it becomes a form of recycling of social goods already once distributed, but either distributed unequally, or distributed to some who for reasons such as social disadvantage were unable to take optimum advantage of them in the first instance. In either of these cases the recycling, though necessary because of previous inadequacies, is compensatory in terms of both morality and justice, but in important respects the compensation is too late, for too much has been lost educationally in life-prospects by the time the recycling begins, both intrinsically and instrumentally, especially in vocational opportunities. Prevention by social reform, if necessary, is more consistent with morality and justice than such recycling opportunities to give a second chance, but they in turn have some justice and morality on their side, while doing nothing would have none. Some who need a second chance have suffered from illness or disabilities in their schooling years, or have migrated and have had to cope with a new language in adolescence.

We shall now re-state the two fundamental principles of social or distributive justice, followed by the three that are presupposed by them, relating respectively to educational opportunity, vocational opportunity and the right to work. We shall not distinguish between 'social justice' and 'distributive justice'. It is largely a verbal argument as to whether liberties constitute part of distributive justice. In one sense they may be distributed by those in power, preferentially to groups or classes – and so unjustly; or more broadly and generally in fairness to all. Even in the case of constitutional government, with liberties of the people documented for rulers and subjects alike, it is still open to rulers to give their own substantive interpretations to formal statements of liberties in written constitutions or specific enactments of liberties, and in that sense also to distribute liberties to the people. Liberties of the people may in fact become an ideological illusion, at least some people in either class-structured or classless states living the illusion – as we have seen – that they have the liberties as their constitutions state them.

Principles of Social or Distributive Justice

FUNDAMENTAL

1. Each person has an equal right to basic liberties provided that he does not infringe the liberties of others.
2. In so far as each person has worked to the best of his ability, he has an equal right to basic social goods according to need.

SUBORDINATE

(a) Each person has an equal right to education according to need, regardless of whether he is fortunate or unfortunate in natural endowments or in the social conditions of his upbringing.
(b) Each person has an equal right to a vocation of his choice, with selection on relevant grounds.
(c) Each person has an equal right to work according to his abilities and capacities.

Each of these fundamental principles of social justice is consistent with *morality* as a practical consideration of others' interests, and with *justice* as fairness in the treatment of persons. It is worth observing that these principles go back directly to the foundations of morality and of justice as they are stated in their formal notions and in their corresponding primary principles. That applies to some particular substantive considerations as well, such as the manipulation and direction of talented children in the interests of the state, for there too the stable references of the formal notions evoke an immediate response – negatively toward a violation of each.

The first of the fundamental principles of social justice is a general principle of liberty, consistent with the views of Locke and of his antecedents such as Hooker, the principles espoused in the American and French revolutions, and the views of liberal philosophers such as Mill. The basic liberties are freedom of speech and assembly, freedom of thought and belief, freedom of the person. They are liberties claimable both against other persons, and against the state. The second is a marxist principle, to be qualified in class-structured states to take account of inhibiting social conditions. The principle of equality of educational opportunity is a corollary of the second fundamental principle of distributive justice. Applied to immature learners the desert qualification that is prefixed to the second fundamental principle is not relevant, but it does have relevance to the distribution of education to adults. Obvious unfairness would follow if some adults were allowed to contribute little or nothing to the social well-being, receiving benefits of continuing education without making a work contribution to the best of their ability. Such an objection applies to those who have already joined the work force (and on the assumption that resources to be distributed are limited). For those who have not joined the work force a just society would not distribute its goods, such as in education, without careful scrutiny of its grounds, and the fairness of its distributions, taking all other members of society into account. This matter has been raised in Chapter 5. Both the principle of vocational opportunity, and the principle stating the right to work, assume that work itself is an individual good as well as a social good; from a moral standpoint it is considering others' interests to ensure that work is offered which matches, as far as possible, the abilities and capacities of workers; and from the standpoint of justice, whenever selection is necessary, it is to be made on relevant grounds. In many circumstances discriminatory selection practices persist, such as when sex, colour and race are clearly irrelevant to the occupation. In a just society where there is consistency in the application of rules and equity in establishing a proper balance or proportion among persons, privilege or social advantage would not enhance educational and vocational opportunities, nor would substantial social disadvantage inhibit them. Distributive justice depends on everyone making a work contribution to the best of his ability, so that no one *avoids* work through the advantages of inheritance for instance, yet continues to receive a share of social goods with no contribution of his own.

One of the illusions of a liberal ideology to which we have referred in the last chapter is that educational opportunity is equal when the state provides equal schooling opportunities, with the implication that educational inefficiency is largely responsible when the educational attainments of some have not matched their abilities and capacities. The system of education – with teachers, principals and administrators – is then held responsible for social injustices, including those that become apparent in the transition from school to work, and in subsequent instances of occupational misfits. It has been undoubtedly the case that unskilled and poorly motivated teaching has impaired the life prospects of many students, and to that extent a just society would ensure, by any means possible, that the teaching service is such that students can generally realize their vocational and other aspirations given suitable ability and capacity. But the argument from educational inefficiency may be no more than a convenient rationalization. It is primarily not the educational system that makes second chances necessary for the victims of social or environmental disadvantages. Distributive justice in some societies is dependent partly on an efficient educational system, but largely on the removal of excesses of wealth and poverty as the source of perceived injustice: the conditions that make an extraordinarily good start in life for some, and for others an extraordinarily bad start. We have rejected Rawls' difference principle which asserts that social goods must be distributed equally unless an unequal distribution favours the least advantaged, and his views on the better endowed that they should gain from their good fortune only if, in the allocation of resources, the situation of the less well-endowed is improved. Justice as fairness in the treatment of persons, and morality as a practical consideration of others' interests, require us to distribute resources equitably in the sense that the disadvantaged and the advantaged, the mediocre and the talented all have opportunities to have their potentialities selectively realized. There is to be no taking from the talented, and giving to the untalented or ordinary, no withdrawal of resources from those socially advantaged and transferring them to the disadvantaged. The one fundamental criterion is *need*, and all needs are to be satisfied, provided that, in adulthood, there is adequate return to society in work contribution. In the area of justice and morality both Aristotle and Bentham proposed arithmetical solutions which were each demonstrations of unworkability except in the simplest of cases.

When we put our formal notions of justice, morality and education into the context of a political organization, and include as well our principles and subordinate principles of distributive justice, we face at once the possibility of conflicting substantive interpretations. In classless states the principles of equality of educational opportunity and of vocational opportunity are recognized, along with the right to work, but *choice* of vocation is frequently the choice of the state. Where the talented are segregated and admitted to special schools so that competitiveness and specialized training might produce optimum development, incentives may be used to facilitate ready acceptance. 'Choice' in such circumstances is apt to be euphemistic, even when students are highly motivated and well satisfied with their achievements. From a moral standpoint, the interests of others are seen to be considered by the state: the interests of the talented, and the interests of all others in society who will be beneficiaries of their talents. It is not difficult to explain that such a system fulfils our formal expectations of both justice and morality. There are no marked advantages or disadvantages at the beginning of school life, and at the end, all are treated consistently and with equity in their vocational placements. But liberties are substantially lost, especially liberty of person which enables an individual to plan and make his own way in life. And that implies also a reduction in the appreciation of personhood, both by the self and by others. There is not the same opportunity for the individual to declare his moral values as a human being, to claim natural justice, either against another or against the state, and to that extent each loses self-respect as a person. From others' perspectives, the individual is not respected as one with desires and emotions, motives and goals, attitudes and values, deliberations, decisions and actions, all of which convey a measure of autonomy. The justice of this socialist transition, as it is believed to be, thus has insecure foundations as we penetrate the substantive claims to the foundations of morality and justice as stated in our formal notion of each.

From the perspectives of the socialist who gives his own substantiveness to the formal notions of justice and morality, class-structured states are inconsistent and inequitable in their distributions of resources, morally indifferent in their failure to consider the interests of the underprivileged or socially disadvantaged, and even to tolerate a system which allows social inequities to exist largely unchecked so that 'opportunities' and 'equalities' are at best ideological illusions, at worst conscious rationalizations. Political perspective is able to influence our substantive notions of justice and morality then, as are the social values under which we live. But whatever the perspective, it is impossible to justify, from the formal notion of justice as fairness in the treatment of persons, with a basis of morality which considers others' interests, situations which in our society amount to inequality of educational and vocational opportunity and their consequential inequities. Fairness in the distribution of social goods according to need can only be just with a just beginning. The liberal model of the good fortune of those who make their way from adversity can only be justified if *all* have a reasonable chance to succeed, and even then only in part; there is little equity in a social system which calls on only *some* to make prodigious efforts to succeed, with variable handicaps at the beginning of the race, and some without the burden of a handicap at all. If we follow the procedure of penetrating substantive claims and differences to reach the underlying formal notions of morality and of justice, again our responses are direct and unequivocal.

FURTHER REFLECTIONS

Moral Subjectivism

We shall not dwell further on the formal notions of justice, morality and education, except to note that all three notions become increasingly more complex as they are extended substantively; and with respect to the first two in particular, have been perplexing since Greek philosophy. In other contexts we have held that our particular notion of morality is based on our own personal convictions, and have indicated that of the various moralities that are possible, each must be capable of rational justification even though reason is imperfect, and cannot be an ultimate or transcendental court of appeal in defence of all judgements we make. It is a fundamental flaw in the arguments of those who oppose subjective moralities such as ours, that on a subjective basis anyone may have any morality he likes and that the measure of social harmony achieved is indication enough that the subjective claim is false. While it is true that anyone may make his morality, and *must* so do if he is to be an active moral agent making judgements of his own rather than conforming to prescribed rules of conduct, every morality so constructed or chosen requires that it be tested against reason. On this basis some moralities can be readily rejected, as ours should be if reason did not support it. Despite common tendencies toward benevolence and a wider social diffusion of education, with opportunities for individuals to acquire improved self-understanding and understanding of others, as well as the impact of social values through education, there is some evidence to indicate that most persons develop as rule followers, or as seekers of social approval – especially the approval of those in a relatively cohesive group or community – and only some go on to work out a morality of their own. In the last event, few are radically different in their moralities from others. Our degree of social harmony is not attributable to objective moral values held in common, but to values which we accept as others do, subjectively, sometimes only half-committed to them and in that respect only half functioning as moral agents. When we go further and work out a morality suitable for ourselves in relation with others, we do not search for absolutes or for anything objective in the world outside ourselves, but for principles and rules which we can justify as those *we* ought to have, and extending our normative outlook, those we are convinced *others* ought to have too. We make no attempt to impose them on persons equally rational, but rather seek opportunities unpresumptuously to explain them to others in discussion which is formal, in the sense that it has conditions placed on it which make it a rational and potentially fruitful rather than a potentially competitive, conflict-producing and therefore ineffectual exercise. No morality is justifiable we claim, which does not accept as a starting point the irreducible minimum of a practical consideration of others' interests.

In the mutual appraisal of moral points of view it is the very agreement among us as we point to weaknesses of argument, or reasons that are biased with prejudice or preconceptions, or that stand clearly to us as rationalizations, that gives us confidence in reason itself: that our agreement is a *rational* agreement, not a value agreement, except to the extent that rationality is itself a value. Complications arise when we realise that however much we may be committed to the rational way, we have *other* values apart from rationality and that sometimes value conflict is unavoidable. Thus rational discourse in formal groups is achieved with effort, and prized all the more for it.

Since we have urged that our subjective judgements of social justice require to be supported with the best reasons we can adduce, and that it is by the quality of their reasons that such judgements will be evaluated by others, we now sketch a rational approach to weighing general categories of social justice such as equality of educational opportunity. The common rational criteria which may be applied to such categories are drawn from our preceding argument and therefore will not be elaborated. Each serves as a foundational reason in the evaluation of particular instances whenever relevant, to be supplemented with additional reasons peculiar to each situation. The various criteria are impartiality, respect for persons, truth-telling, liberty, need, and reciprocity.

Impartiality has been shown to have frequent relevance to discriminatory practices which contradict the fundamental notions of morality and of justice. As with other criteria, exceptions are to be argued for. Respect for persons in the special sense which we have developed is related to it, in its association with each individual's well-being in the present and the future. It would be contradictory to refer to plans of social justice which benefited some but not others, or to acts of fairness which – all things equal – favoured some over others. Truth-telling is necessary to social justice in relations between state and individuals, and in relations among citizens. Practices of political deception contradict the formal notions of morality and of justice. Liberty and need are each derived from the fundamental principles of social justice; if there is to be justice and morality it is contradictory to deny anyone these formal liberties. Need has emerged as a more rationally defensible criterion than any other for distributive justice, clearly evident in the case of education as a social good. Again the criterion relates to respect for persons, and to each of the other criteria. Reciprocity is a criterion of moral obligation, offsetting any tendency toward over-compensation or positive discrimination. It implies that whenever relevant, fairness involves giving as well as receiving: that in distributive justice – all things equal – it is unjust to receive without contributing fairly in return. It implies mutuality of respect for persons, as well as integrity of interpersonal relationships. Mutuality implies voluntariness, and so is related as well to the criterion of liberty. A society which invited its own moral and material demise by bestowing goods freely and without conditions, disregarding the fairness of individual contributions, would be acting contrary to reason. The six criteria are interrelated in their rational connections.

The application of rational criteria is no more than a start in defending our subjective morality including our judgements of social justice. One factor influencing the strength of our case when in contention with other judgements is disagreement in the interpretation and application of the criteria themselves, as well as differences in attitudes and values. Those of conflicting viewpoints frequently attest their faith in reason, when in fact it is more clearly their values that they are calling to our attention.

Another possible challenge to our moral subjectivism is that it disregards a morality based on personal belief.[3] This objection too is unfounded, except to the extent that we disagree on the supposed objectivity of our moral values so derived. There are many different sources of the attitudes and values which give us our moral bearings, or our moral convictions of right and wrong, many ways in which our moral attitudes and values may be learned; indoctrination in the home or outside the home, for instance; traumatic experiences such as personal tragedy; fortuitous recurrences of similar experiences over a period of time, such as experiences of authoritarianism, or of meanness or generosity, or of charismatic leadership, or of peer-group affinity in discussions; or rational reflections on contemporary experiences or on human history.

Moral Complexity

We would like everything we do in our moral lives, including all the moral judgements or conclusions we reach, to be governed by reason. But we find that they are not, and that they cannot be. Therefore we have to take account of this simple fact in our understanding of morality: we have to *begin* by asking what is the case, without then leaping to an unwarranted inference that what is, indicates what ought to be. Respect for others, we have stressed, is based on an understanding of our common ground, but also on something that extends beyond an observation of our common humanity to the concreteness of individuality as we attempt to empathize, to assume others' standpoints as persons in action, not as abstractions. Morality is a constant tension between our benevolence and our egoism when we assume a perspective on ourselves and on others. When we assume a perspective on others, attempting to take their standpoint as they face the world, and only then relate ourselves to them, our practical morality is as well a tension between a clear understanding of *their* needs and a considering of *our* interests in relation to them. Then if we are rational we will consider our own interests along with theirs, and our decisions will not necessarily be in their favour. A degree of egoism will still incline us toward our own interests, even when *rationally* we ought to concede to theirs, and in every circumstance our practical judgements on what we ought to do will be dispositionally influenced, usually either toward reason and impartiality, or against it. We make the assumption that to *understand* our dispositions and those of others is an important basis for practical morality, as important as it is to learn to reason clearly. The injunction that we *ought* to use our reason in our moral relations with others is not enough on its own. Behind the moral ought to consider others' interests is a practical ought, an enabling ought, to understand ourselves and others as well as we can. This must become part of our normative outlook, as it was Francis Bacon's.

We shall not repeat the psychological possibilities in this mutual understanding as outlined in Chapter 4. The association of attitudes and values is significant in constituting a formidable influence on reason in moral deliberations, normally either supporting or opposing it, as is its durability and resistance to change, especially when its defence is a defence of the self as well. Complexity occurs not only in the relationship of dispositional components, especially motives or intentions, attitudes and values, but also in the relationship between dispositions and reason. Strong moral convictions expressing moral attitudes and values are the strongest dispositional influences we have to support reason, the closest, indeed, to Kant's notion of moral imperatives, but even then there may be conflict, with reason facing a moral dilemma. Some moral problems are of such complexity that reason, with all the directional support possible from attitudes and values, does not point positively and unequivocally to the best possible solution.

The complexity of practical morality is increased through human imperfection, both rationally and dispositionally. Our moral relations with others are polychromatic, with many kinds of rational and non-rational influences interacting, with attitudes and values that may appear uncharacteristic of us – unprejudiced and dispassionate toward some objects, toward others quite the contrary. Our moral oughts are always then directed toward individual effort, toward improvement, not toward unattainable ideals, or absolutes. There would be no classical literature at all, certainly no Shakespearean tragedy and no *War and Peace*, if a high-minded self-mastery of reason was always in command; and a monochrome of reason would be so uncharacteristic of humanity in Shakespeare's comedies as to make them merely mechanical and dull.[4] Morality, like literature, is for human imperfection, and the greater the imperfection usually the more unpredictable and the more complex the moral relationship. Moral purpose becomes stronger, not weaker, and more pertinent to our lives, as we acknowledge that the moral life is necessarily one of constant striving and adjustment, continually – as in education – setting fresh improvement goals as some gains are made, but foreseeing no point of eventual moral arrival, as we foresee no ultimate arrival for education. Morality, like education, is a becoming, a search for possibilities. In this imperfection-based complexity of our moral lives the vulnerability of reason is also a vulnerability of morality, no better illustrated than in the control of reason by passions in time of war, on a vast national and international scale, after which individual imperceptions of enemies may take an entire generation to erase. These are not grounds for either moral or rational scepticism, but for increasing moral effort supported by more extensive moral education toward independent attitude and value formation, especially in adolescence. In morality, as in justice and education, reason remains by far the most beneficial influence, but it is most effective with the support and direction of moral attitudes and values, rather than in situations of contention with them.

Different Moralities

By various substantive elaborations quite different moralities may be shown to be presupposed by, or dependent upon, the formal principle of considering others' interests. Marxism considers others' interests, and when some argue that it considers the interests of the state first, or considers the interests of others only in ways which suit the communist ideology, such criticism in no way detracts from the claim that it is, formally, a morality. Similarly liberalism in one of its various forms is not formally destroyed as a morality by the criticism that it considers the interests of the well-to-do first, and makes only token gestures to the welfare of the underprivileged, or that it trades on popular illusions, such as that educational opportunities are equal for all through equal or common schooling provisions. That we disagree with either classless or class-based liberalism is simply to take a substantive point of view on morality. If, indeed, any one morality could be established beyond doubt as true in its *values* (and others false in theirs), that would be sufficient justification for its common acceptance; it would be simply irrational to prefer a morality based on false values. But values are not susceptible to such truth determinations. If we argue that one morality is a better morality, on rational grounds, than another, reasons have to be set forth for appraisal by others, and the arguments may be convincing or otherwise. Those who prefer to have morality confined to human relations, and to exclude sentient animals, have to furnish reasons in support of their position, showing in some way that our moral attitudes and values relating to animal suffering are not really moral attitudes and values at all. Without supporting grounds, any stipulative definition of the boundaries of morality collapses as merely arbitrary. One of the strong convictions held by some who work hard for their possessions – work hard perhaps with a clear goal of *acquiring* possessions – is that others they know who receive welfare payments have been relatively indolent and therefore do not *deserve* such provisions. This they believe is *not* natural justice: it is unfair to those who have made the effort, often without much work satisfaction. Locke (and our contemporary Nozick), as well as Humboldt Mill and Herbert Spencer, all have accepted a morality of considering the interests of those who have made sacrifices for their own ends who have exercised initiative and effort and the will to succeed. A substantive antithesis is the morality of those who believe that the state ought to care for its citizens according to *need*, regardless of any presumed source in lack of diligence and conscientiousness. This is based on different values: it is a different substantive morality, or part of one, held by some individuals. Again, it does not, by virtue of its antithetical position, rule out the other as a morality in the formal sense.

Rights and Duties

Human Rights have been given impetus by the passions of war: by a realisation of a need, especially in the last few decades, to safeguard the interests of individual men, women and children, to regard them morally as persons with rights to be respected, not manipulable objects of political ambition. Although Human Rights, like Natural Rights, relate to the formal notion of morality, neither qualify as moral rights according to the formal conditions proposed for them in Chapter 3. Further, they are always open to abuse as instruments of political deception, if not eventually of ideological illusion.

'Obligations may exists without rights', noted Bentham in his Pannomial Fragments;[5] 'rights cannot exist without obligations'. It is this observation that moral rights and duties do not have an invariable correlativity that supports his moral resentment at the infliction of suffering on animals, as it does ours. We have regarded sentient animals as objects of our moral obligations since they have interests, but not rights. When our attitudes and values are extended from sentient animals to insentient living things such as trees, or beyond them even to the environment of inanimate objects, the concern we may feel – though equally strong emotionally and cognitively – is much less obviously a *moral* concern, since it is difficult to attribute interests to such things devoid of thought or emotion. It is rather the people and sentient animals whose well-being is intimately involved with other living things in the environment who may be objects of our *moral* attitudes. Thus the pygmies of equatorial Africa are threatened with the destruction of their unique way of life, and with eventual extinction as a race, through the logging of the forests in which they live and to which they are culturally bound. Our obligations to them, and to sentient animals which also inhabit the forests and suffer from their destruction, are moral obligations, and the people – but not the sentient animals – have moral rights claimable against those depriving them of the means of their subsistence, or attempting to substitute an alien means in an alien culture, which is itself the source of human suffering. Similarly the suffering of indigenous populations from mining in some underdeveloped countries, with the pollution of the rivers, the destruction of a stable culture and the attempt to implant an unwanted substitute, is the object of our moral attitudes and values: the industrial exploiters have moral obligations to the indigenous people, who have moral rights claimable against them. Our attitudes and values toward objects such as rivers, valleys and forested landscapes are, in themselves, non-moral. The question of our obligations to *future generations* is controversial: attempts have been made to defend our moral obligations to them as well. Disregarding the possible interests of generations extending into the future, we can still focus cautiously on the interests of the very young whom we know and whose interests in the future we can more confidently extrapolate from current social and individual interests. For they have interests in a quality of life that will be a perceptible continuation of our own, even given some modifications. To consider our interests solely in the use of the earth's resources in a way which will affect their quality of life is to act without moral concern for them. In this sense we have moral obligations to them, without correlative rights held by them because of their immaturity.

Individual Interests and State Power

In the tension between individual interests and state power the moral obligations of individuals are as significant as those of governments. When governments act prudently and politically rather than on principle, individual electors are powerless to rectify the situation before possible harm is done to their interests. When the people also act prudently and politically in *their* interests as fragmented pressure-groups, holding the common community interest in contempt, the credibility of distributive justice is impaired as it loses its moral stability. Thus the social complexity of contemporary societies has brought problems of morality and distributive justice into greater prominence, emphasizing the need for an extensive *moral education* formal, non-ideological and a-political in character, and based on common individual needs and rights.

The power of the state is not always within the capacity of individuals to control, and some moral issues affecting individual interests appear to be beyond the capacity of some governments to control or to rectify: the volume of defence expenditure to sustain an uneasy balance of power; the economic domination of some multi-national corporations, with their ability to control market prices in a way that seriously affects the underprivileged (as in commodities needed urgently by some for subsistence farming); the strategic siting of nuclear weapons, with the threat of incalculable human suffering as well as suffering to sentient animals. Thus the expansion of state powers increasingly challenges the interests of the *individual*. We return to the paradox of our permitting an enlargement of the responsibilities of the state and of its bureaucratic instrumentalities when we are, at the same time, concerned that some of our vital individual interests are not being safeguarded.

As societies become more complex, so do many of the problems of social justice, and correspondingly the capacity of individuals to continue as moral watch-dogs over governments and bureaucracies diminishes. To illustrate, while in *The Republic* Plato foresaw the possibility of a permanent matching of occupations to individual abilities and aptitudes, in contemporary societies there are the wide-sweeping implications of the technological revolution whose demands for re-training contrast sharply with Platonic immobility. Now the increasing educational responsibility, if equal opportunities are to be offered to all, is to ensure that a worker is suited to various occupations, that he is sufficiently educated for each, and that justice as fairness will be met by occupational mobility, if and when it arrives, which is evenly distributed, with respect to both its goods and its burdens. Plato's constant desire was for a changeless, stable society – even when he wrote *The Laws* with substantial amendments to his earlier social ideal.[6]

A principle of egoism is evident when individual interests are asserted against the state, without conceding that the state requires resources to distribute. In the Locke-Nozick type of defence of the individual against state power there is discernible a staunch property minded individualism.

One of the concerns in class-structured states is that the moral relationship between state and individuals is sometimes broken by factitious needs claims as the state is misperceived as an inexhaustible fountain of benefaction. Then the fundamentally self-interested who have been coerced into acceptance of redistributive schemes are given stronger grounds to support their egoism. The remoteness of bureaucracies is sometimes an invitation to such individual deception when moral attitudes and values are ill-formed. There is some evidence to believe that the welfare state to which contemporary industrialized societies are tending, regardless of political organization, depends upon a moral basis which is not strong enough, at present, to support it. There can be little doubt that citizens require firm moral values if the state is to remain the provider.

Rousseau's notion of a civil society, formed out of a state of nature with new-found moral opportunities, is fanciful when contrasted with the complexity of the contemporary state. The general will has usually become a fragmented pluralistic will of competing sections exerting their own pressures for their own ends. It is this situation that places increased moral demands on governments and citizens alike. The observation of suspicion and egoism in state-individual relations is a reflection of two-sided moral inadequacy.

Conclusion: Equality of Educational Opportunity

The class-structured state can be very visible in its distribution of some social goods such as medical services and welfare, and misleadingly visible in its distribution of education by focussing on schooling, with provisions made available equally for all. What such a welfare state conceals is its failure to dispense equality of educational opportunity; what it continues to tolerate is the size of the handicap for some at the start of formal education and the fact that the handicap, being based on social conditions, is not shaken off during schooling but becomes continually compounded. It is compounded to such an extent that vocational opportunities are likely to be handicapped too, not merely initially in the transition from school to work, but also for some, at least, through the continuing influences of habitual attitudes while in employment – attitudes, that is, that remain socially unfavourable. Perhaps the most pressing social need is for moral attitudes and values, combined with clear reasoning and both social and personal knowledge. Then possible ideological illusions and political deception might be effectively unmasked.

The major themes of legal, social and political philosophy do not refer to the moral problem of inequality of educational opportunity. The reason has now become clear. It is necessary to bring a multi-perspective to bear on the problem. What has been conspicuously missing is the *educational* perspective, the fundamental understanding of education as a developing of *individual* potentialities (consistent with social values). Only when we combine the three perspectives of *justice, morality and education* do we grasp the full dimensions of the problem of inequality of educational opportunity, one that has passed unnoticed by most – for all its obviousness in some societies – in our professions of legal justice and moral justice. The principles of social justice which we have deduced show something of the complexity of the relationships between justice, morality and education. Each has both fundamental and far-reaching connections with morality and education – only some of which have been explored in this general study. To bring them all together in relation to the elemental notion of justice in a final perspective is to attain a deeper understanding of some of the ethical bases of social philosophy, one of whose conspicuous applications is inequity in educational opportunity.

Social justice closes the traverse of this book: its major problems return us directly to the formal notions with which we began. Equality of educational opportunity may be a complex social problem in its many effects on the individual, and in some social and political systems may be complex and difficult too in its opportunities for ready practical solutions. But *ethically* and intellectually, the problem is simple. It violates, without qualification, the fundamental, irreducible, formal notions of justice, morality and education with which we began. Take the ethical problem to them separately, or better, in combination, and it sparks instant understanding. Dostoyevsky remarked that 'poverty is not a crime'.[7] More relevantly, *in their wide moral and educational ramifications*, underprivileged social conditions are simply and fundamentally not justice.

When the intellect or reason is in command – as it may be when we reflect on serious inequalities in educational opportunity – the formal notions of justice, morality and education become the ultimate criteria or reference points for social justice. Thus just as the punishment of innocent persons is plainly not justice when wittingly performed,[8] on the intellectual criterion of the formal notion, so serious inequalities in educational opportunity affecting the life prospects of the young are plainly not social justice. Whatever substantive views people may hold on justice, there is no room for rational disagreement on these matters, since in each case there would be internal contradiction. In our perceptions of social justice, if we are to combine an ideal of reason with an awareness of dispositional influences, our aim will be to hold fast to the three formal notions as ultimate intellectual criteria, while still retaining an awareness of the possible dispositional influences on reason.[9]

As distinct from the ideological traditions outlined in the previous chapter, the broad philosophical traditions on which we have set most store in this book stem first from Plato, with the high value he placed on reason; second from Aristotle, with the respect for observation which he added to Plato's vision; and third from David Hume, with his psychological insights into reason's limitations as we make our practical judgements on what we ought to do.

Notes

CHAPTER 1   EDUCATION AND JUSTICE

1 .The Constitution of the People's Republic of China, with Article 46 which refers to the 'all-round development – moral, intellectual and physical – of young people and children', is published in *Beijing Review*, vol. 25, no.52, 27 Dec. 1982.
2. References to the *Politics* are from the translation by Benjamin Jowett.
3. References to Aristotle's *Nicomachean Ethics* are from the translation by W. D. Ross.
4. 'Metaphysics' (and 'metaphysical') are used in the limited sense of 'beyond the physical', without any connection with a theory of positivism which rejects as factual anything that cannot be observed.
5. .Mill's *Inaugural Address*, delivered in assuming office as rector of St. Andrews, was published by Longman, Green, Reader and Dyer in a People's edition, London, 1867. References are to this edition.
6. J. H. Newman's *Discourses on University Education* was published by James Duffy, Dublin, in 1852. References are to this edition. In some statements Newman was little short of paraphrasing Aristotle's *Nicomachean Ethics* on contemplation, acknowledging him as the 'great Philosopher'. He had a vested interest in the establishment of a Catholic University in Dublin, as its proposed rector. See particularly Discourse VIII, p.286 for his advocacy of a liberal education. Beyond the conventional claims in producing a cultivated intellect, Newman ironically gave way to extravagance in claiming a variety of other benefits from a University education: its ability to equip a person to 'fill any post with credit', for instance, and to be 'at home in any society'. For his rejection of utility as an aim of education, and his argument against professional or scientific knowledge as the sufficient end of a University education, see pp.253, 256. For the liberal ideal of knowledge as its own end, see Discourse VI, p.170.
7. An extension of the Greek notion of a liberal education is illustrated in The Report of the Harvard Committee, entitled *General Education in a Free Society*, Oxford University Press, London, 1946. For an apt criticism, see P. H. Hirst, 'Liberal Education and the Nature of Knowledge', in *Education and the Development of Reason*, ed. R. F. Dearden *et al.*, Routledge & Kegan Paul, London, 1972 (Published earlier in R. D. Archambault, ed. *Philosophical Analysis and Education*, Routledge & Kegan Paul, 1965.)
8. Reference to *The Republic* are from the Everyman edition, J. M. Dent, London, 1935. The translation is by A. D. Lindsay.

9. Rousseau's *Emile* is available in various editions, such as Everyman's, John Dent, London, 1911. It was first published in 1780.

10. Wilhelm von Humboldt's *Sphere and Duties of Government* from which Mill quoted in his essay *On Liberty* (p.57) was written in 1791–92, with the first English translation in 1854, which Mill used. The educationist who gave most prominence to the same views of Humboldt which had attracted Mill was T. P. Nunn in his *Education: Its Data and First Principles*, ch.1, Edward Arnold, London, 1920, 1930, 1945. Ch. 1.

    Humboldt's work has been republished by the Cambridge University Press, 1969, edited by J. W. Burrow, with the title *The Limits of State Action*. 'The highest ideal ... of the co-existence of human beings' Humboldt wrote, 'seems to me to consist in a union in which each strives to develop himself from his inmost nature, and for his own sake' (p.19).

11. It has been observed that the Greek word for 'equality' (*to ison* or *isotes*) expresses the meaning of justice better than does the word which is often translated as justice (*dikaiosyne*). See G. Vlastos, 'Justice and Equality', in A. I. Melden (ed.) *Human Rights*, Wadsworth, Belmont, California, 1970, p.76.

12. This sense of justice as an approximation, and the picturesque analogy, are borrowed from D. Lloyd, *The Idea of Law*, Penguin Books, Harmondsworth, 1964, p.132. In fact the dual administration of law and equity was changed in England with the introduction of the Judicature system in 1876. It is important to note that equity courts were not always without precedent to guide them. Indeed a body of rules called *equity* (as distinct from the rules of common law) developed readily when it was found that so many of the cases reaching the equity courts were of a similar nature.

13. See Kant's *Preface to the Metaphysical Elements of Ethics*, pp.291, 293; *Introduction to the Metaphysic of Morals*, p.282; *Fundamental Principles of the Metaphysic of Morals*, pp.59.72: from Kant's *Critique of Practical Reason and Other Works on the Theory of Ethics*, trans. T.K. Abbott, 6th edn., Longmans, London, 1909.

14. References to David Hume's *A Treatise of Human Nature* are from the Oxford edition, 1888, edited by L. A. Selby-Bigge.

15. References to *Utilitarianism* are from Mill's *Ethical Writings*, ed. J. B. Schneewind, Collier-Macmillan, London, and Collier Books, New York, 1965. See particularly Section 5, pp.315–318.

16. Jeremy Bentham's *An Introduction to the Principles of Morals and Legislation*, in which he stated his principle of utility, is in various editions. It was first published in 1789, with a new edition in 1823. References here are from his *Works*, published by William Tait, Edinburgh, 1843, under the superintendence of Bentham's executor, John Bowring, (vol. 1).

17. See T. N. Carver, *Essays in Social Justice*, Harvard University Press, Cambridge, Mass., 1915, p.9.

18. For the views of contemporary jurists on questions such as equality of opportunity, and rights, see E. Kamenka and A. E-S. Tay (eds) *Justice*, Edward Arnold, London, 1979. Specifically on equality of opportunity, see B. Barry, 'Justice as Reciprocity' in this collection, p.73ff.

19. On the view that judgements of justice may involve a 'creative leap' see Julius Stone, *Law and the Social Sciences in the Second Half Century*, Minneapolis, 1966; and E. Kamenka, 'What is Justice'? in *Justice*, op.cit., p.91.
20. Ch. Perelman: *The Idea of Justice and the Problem of Argument*, Introduction by H. A. L. Hart, translated from the French by J. Petrie, Routledge & Kegan Paul, London, 1963, p.40.

    The notion that justice is 'the principle of treating all under the same rules' is from F. A. Hayek, *Law, Legislation and Liberty*, vol.2, Routledge & Kegan Paul, London, 1976, p.39. A similar inadequacy appears in Morris Ginsberg's statement that 'justice in the broadest sense consists in the ordering of human relations in accordance with general principles impartially applied', for there is no suggestion in this of the quality of the principles: *On Justice in Society*, Heinemann, London, 1965, p.56.

CHAPTER 2   MORALITY

1 .This broad interpretation of 'person' is in keeping with our contemporary concern for rights such as privacy, and the demand for respect for persons which is associated with it. See, for example, Stanley I. Benn, 'Privacy, Freedom, and Respect for Persons' in R. Wasserstrom, ed. *Today's Moral Problems*, Macmillan, New York, 1975, p.7.
2. See Act II of *Pygmalion* in which Eliza reacts sharply to Higgins' mischievous taunt that she had no feelings 'that we need bother about'. The reaction of those conscious of their personhood is a common theme in literature, as in a poem by Shu Ting, 'My Light is Still On', published in *Chinese Literature*, Feb. 1981, p.63, from which this stanza is taken, expressing the feelings of people whose personhood was misperceived by feudal and colonial overlords:

    > The Light is on –
    > With dignity and pride
    > It glares at all oppression
    > Open or veiled.

    From Phillip II's Spanish Inquisition to the 'protection' of blacks in compounds, on reserves, on the outskirts of towns or in segregated communal villages, the failure to acknowledge personhood in others is both historical and contemporary. It inheres in all instances of oppression.
3. References to David Hume's *A Treatise of Human Nature* are again to the Oxford edition, edited by L. A. Selby-Bigge, Clarendon Press, Oxford, 1888.
4. Having stated that 'words and criticism are not so properly objects of the understanding as of taste and sentiment', Hume went on to denounce any books which do not contain 'any abstract reasoning concerning quantity or number', or 'any experimental reasoning concerning matter of fact and existence'. From D. Hume, *Essays and Treatises on Several*

Subjects, T. Cadell, London, 1777. 'An Enquiry Concerning Human Understanding' is contained in Volume II of this work.

5 .The reference to Thomas Hobbes' *Leviathan*, first published in 1651, is to the Penguin edition, Harmondsworth, 1968.

6. Shaftesbury's 'An Essay on the Freedom of Wit and Humour' was published in 1709, included in his *Characteristics of Men, Manners, Opinions, Times*, etc. The page reference is to a recent edition published by Peter Smith, Gloucester, Mass. 1963. John M. Robertson, ed. In this edition see pp. 216–217 for his notion of 'a wrong and a right taste' as in the nature of things. In 'An Enquiry Concerning Virtue or Merit', Part III, Section 1, p.258 he refers to a 'natural and just sense of right and wrong'.

   F. Hutcheson's views on the same subject are found in his *Inquiry into the Original of our Ideas of Beauty and Virtue*, 1725, Section III, iii, available in various collections such as D. H. Munro (ed.) *A Guide to the British Moralists*, Collins, London, 1972, p.149. Shortly before his election to the Chair of Moral Philosophy at Glasgow he published *An Essay on the Nature and Conduct of the Passions and Affections, with Illustrations on the Moral Sense*. (1728).

7. Joseph Butler's support of conscience is from his *Fifteen Sermons*, 1726. The references are to his *Works*, with preface by S. Halifax, Oxford, 1850, vol. II. The reference to benevolence as 'a natural principle' is to Sermon 1, p.4. See also his note *b* on pp. 4–6, where he explains that the natural benevolence in man cannot be found by reason, but is to be discovered by appealing to external senses and inner perceptions. Sermon II, iii contains his reference to the power of conscience which 'magisterially exerts itself', and also to the 'natural disposition to kindness and compassion.'

8. John Gay is included for his psychological insight and as the forerunner of Hartley in his theory of associationism. The page reference is to E. A. Burtt (ed.) *The English Philosophers from Bacon to Mill*, The Modern Library, Random House, New York, 1939, which includes the whole of Gay's short work.

9. The reference is to the 6th edition, published by Thomas Tegg, London, 1834, Part II, ch. III, Section VI. David Hartley was an early utilitarian who learned from Gay of the possibility of deducing pleasures and pains from association. He believed that benevolence could be increased by forming pleasant associations, noting the beneficial consequences of relating one's individual happiness to that of others. Among benevolent persons there is observable, he held, 'a peculiar harmony, love, esteem, and mutual cooperation.'

10. All references to Kant are from *Kant's Critique of Practical Reason and Other Works on The Theory of Ethics*, translated by T. K. Abbott, 6th edn, Longmans, London, 1909.

11. H. Sidgwick, *The Methods of Ethics*, 3rd edn, Macmillan, London, 1884, Book III, ch. IV, p.260.

12. *Principia Ethica* was published by Cambridge University Press in 1903. This reference is to p.10 of the 1962 edition. Moore's viewpoint was influential, his justification not so well received, especially his argument

that 'yellow' like 'good' is a unique property inasmuch as it is irreducible and therefore indefinable. The argument from irreducibility was based on a restricted explanation of definition, referring to natural objects such as horses and tables which are definable to the extent that they can be broken down into parts.

See also p.6 for his dogma that 'good is good, and that is the end of the matter'; that good is indefinable, 'and that is all I have to say about it'.

13. 'Descriptiveness' has been applied to the use of 'good' and 'right' in this sense, describing characteristics of activities as though they were themselves objective qualities to be found in all acts of a particular class, such as all cooperative activities.

One philosopher who reacted strongly to Moore's assumptions about good as a unique property was J. Anderson. See his *Studies in Empirical Philosophy*, Angus & Robertson, Sydney and London, 1962: a collection of papers published 1926–53, pp. 239, 241 and 265.

14. The reference is to Thomas Hobbes' *De Cive* (1642). Hobbes' translation of the Latin was entitled *Philosophical Rudiments Concerning Government and Society*, published in 1651. Chapter 1, to which the views refer, was entitled 'Of the State of Man without Civil Society'. See *The English Works of Thomas Hobbes*, edited by Sir William Molesworth, John Bohn, London, 1841, vol. II, ch.1, 6, p.8: when many have an appetite to the same thing, he says, 'very often they can neither enjoy in common, nor yet divide it; whence it follows that the strongest must have it ...'.

15. For a socialist interpretation of egoism see the *Beijing Review*, no.17, 27 Apr. 1981, p.28 (from *Beijing Ribao*, 9 Jan. 1981).

16. Page references are to *Works*, William Tait, Edinburgh, 1843, vol. I. (See also ch. 1, note 7.) Bentham's 'political arithmetic', as he called it, is explained both in *Principles of Morals and Legislation (Works*, vol. 1, ch. IV, IV, p.16) and in amplified form in his *Codification Proposal (Works*, vol.IV, Part 1, Section 3, p.540.) In the latter he explains: 'Political arithmetic ... is an application ... of arithmetic and its calculation, to happiness and its element'. He illustrated by reference to *intensity*: 'supposing its intensity represented by a certain number of degree, you multiply that number by a number expressive of the moments or atoms of time contained in its duration'.

17. J. S. Mill, *Utilitarianism*, 2. Page references are to *Mill's Ethical Writings*, ed. J. B. Schneewind, Collier-Macmillan London, 1965, which includes the complete text. Mill agreed with Bentham that the 'Truths of arithmetic are applicable to the valuation of happiness, as of all measurable quantities' (p.336 note).

18. The problem of 'is – ought' which Hume raised has become the subject of wide discussion in philosophy, and is much more complex than the way in which we have presented it. Some philosophers have argued that 'ought' can be derived from 'is'. For a variety of points of view on this question see W. D. Hudson ed. *The 'Is/Ought Question*, Macmillan, London, 1969.

The comments of G. E. M. Anscombe in 'Modern Moral Philosophy', pp.175, 194 of this book, on the relationship between psychology and philosophy, have some relevance to our approach to morality.

19. This observation is made in the conclusion to Henry Sidgwick's *The Methods of Ethics*, the 7th edition of which was published in 1907 (Macmillan, London.).

CHAPTER 3   RIGHTS AND DUTIES

1. See W. N. Hohfeld, *Fundamental Legal Conceptions Applied in Judicial Reasoning*, Yale University Press, New Haven and London, 1964.
2. The translation of the *Nicomachean Ethics* is again that by W. D. Ross.
3. See H. A. L. Hart, *The Concept of Law*, Clarendon Press, Oxford, 1961, p.156.
4. In *The Morality of Law*, L. L. Fuller conveys the idea of irrationality as well as of arbitrariness: 'Certainly there can be no rational ground for asserting that a man can have a moral obligation to obey a legal rule that does not exist, or is kept secret from him, or that came into existence only after he had acted, or was unintelligible, or was contradicted by another rule of the same system, or commanded the impossible, or changed every minute.' Revised edition, Yale University Press, New Haven and London, 1969, p.39.
5. See Paul Jackson, *Natural Justice*, 2nd edition, Sweet & Maxwell, London, 1979, p.8. When natural justice has been applied to the requirements of a fair hearing, it has been considered to be redundant by some judges and jurists: a fair hearing is implied by 'justice'.
6. See ibid, p.213. The observations on natural justice in England, with conclusions on indeterminacies, are made from documented cases.
7. See ch.3 of *Introduction to Jurisprudence* by Lord Lloyd, 4th edn, with M. D. A. Freeman, co-editor, Stevens & Sons, London, 1979.
8. In *The Concept of Law,* op cit. pp.189–95, H. A. L. Hart proposes this analysis of human society. There is no suggestion that it is any kind of higher law, but simply part of moral law for the continuance of social life. Lloyd criticises these five points as intuitive rather than based on sociological observation: *Introduction to Jurisprudence, op. cit.,* p.91. They are, moreover, vague at some points, and call for much further analysis to show how they could be useful in law. Equality, for instance, raises questions of impartiality and equality of treatment, and these raise further questions. (Hart appears to have been influenced here by Hume and other moral philosophers interested in the nature of man)
9. See Paul Jackson, *Natural Justice, op. cit.,* p. 29.
10. These expressions are taken from cases cited by Paul Jackson, *Natural Justice, op. cit.,* pp. 11, 24.
11. A criterion of respect for persons is used also by Stanley I. Benn in 'Human rights – for whom and for what?' in E. Kamenka and A. Erh-Soon-Tay, eds *Human Rights*, Edward Arnold (Australia), 1978. Benn refers to non-interference, equal consideration, denial of a capacity for legal rights, and protection of privacy in certain respects as 'rules of procedure in justificatory discourse, not as themselves rights. A common instance of breaching privacy as a violation of individual

integrity is the use of a particular identity or personality against his own interests, either through the collection of personal information about him which gives another person power over him, or through unsolicited or uncontracted use of his name, physical features or reputation, as in advertising.

The threat to privacy comes from electronic surveillance, telephone tapping, the increasing use of computers to store and retrieve personal information, interception of correspondence, searches, private detectives, the press, publicity, snooping, eavesdropping, etc. (See R. Wacks, *The Protection of Privacy*, Sweet & Maxwell, London, 1980, p.166). Much of the concern at the threats to privacy posed by the cybernetic revolution, so-called, is in its growing use in Health Services, Employment Offices, Banking, Credit Organizations, the Census and Social Sciences Research (See R. Wacks, *op. cit.,* ch.4).

12. The Constitution of the People's Republic of China, states that 'the personal dignity of citizens ... is inviolable' (Article 38), that 'the home of citizens ... is inviolable', that unlawful search of, or intrusion into, a citizen's home is prohibited (Article 39); and that 'the freedom and privacy of correspondence of citizens ... are protected by law' (Article 40), *Beijing Review*, 27 Dec. 1982, p.16 (The new constitution was adopted by the NPC on Dec. 4, 1982). Similarly the Constitution of the USSR proclaims the inviolability of the person (Article 54), of the home (Article 55), and protects the privacy of citizens, including their correspondence, telephone conversations and telegraphic communications (Article 56). For a discussion on Human Rights in USSR see K. U. Chernenko, *The CPSU Society Human Rights*, Novosti Press Agency Publishing House, Moscow, 1981, pp.89–91; for comment from an external standpoint see L. Henkin, *The Rights of Man To-day*, Stevens & Sons, London, 1979, ch.2.

13. The Constitution of the People's Republic of China states that citizens 'have the right and obligation to work' but this goes on, in Article 42, to assert that 'work is a glorious duty of every able-bodied citizen' and to describe facilities and opportunities provided by the state, *Beijing Review*, 27 Dec. 1982, p.17. In the USSR Constitution, Article 40 expresses a similar right to work. For comment on this right see K. V. Chernenko, in *op.cit.*, pp.113–124. The Cuban Constitution asserts the right to work in Article 44.

14. The politicization of Human Rights, beyond such abstractions as liberty and equality, is evident in assertions of Human Rights violations by 'hegemonism, imperialism, colonialism, and autocracy', and criticism of claims to property by the bourgeoisie. See, for example, Shen Baoxiang (and others) 'On the Question of Human Rights in the International Realm', *Beijing Review*, no. 30, 26 July, 1982, pp. 13–17.

15. The Virginia Declaration of Rights, on 12 June, 1776, declared in Article 1: 'That all men are by nature equally free and independent, and have certain inherent rights ... namely, the enjoyment of life and liberty, with the means of acquiring and possessing property, and pursuing and obtaining happiness and safety'. The Declaration of 4 July 1776 (of the thirteen united States of America) declared 'Life, Liberty and the pursuit

of Happiness' as inalienable rights. The French National Assembly in 1789 issued its Declaration of the Rights of Man and of Citizens in which it asserted as 'natural, imprescriptible, and inalienable rights', 'liberty, property, security, and resistance to oppression' (Article 11), having stated in Article 1 that 'men are born, and always continue, free and equal in respect of their rights.'

16. Diplomatic efforts have been insufficient to establish any effectively assertable or claimable rights. Various UN covenants and conventions have been concerned with such matters as Prevention and Punishment of the Crime of Genocide (1951), Political Rights of Women (1952), Elimination of All Forms of Racial Discrimination (1963, 1969), Economic, Social and Cultural Rights (1966), Civil and Political Rights (1966), Protection of Human Rights and Fundamental Freedoms (1953). Some declarations have related specifically to the Rights of the Child and to the Rights of Mentally Retarded Persons.

The Helsinki Agreement (1975), while re-asserting principles of respect for human rights and fundamental freedoms, and the self-determination of peoples, emphatically asserted that 'participating States will refrain from any intervention' in the domestic affairs of another participating State.

17. The reference to Mill's essay *On Liberty* (1859) is from the Penguin edition, Harmondsworth, 1974.

18. For these views see H. A. L. Hart in his article 'The Ascription of Responsibility and Rights' in *Essays on Logic and Language*, First Series, edited by Antony Flew, Blackwell, Oxford, 1960, ch. VIII.

19. F. H. Bradley first published *Ethical Studies* in 1876, with a second edition in 1927. The reference is to the Oxford Paperback edition, 1962. His explanation of rights and duties is given in a note to Essay V, pp. 207–13.

20. J. Bentham, *Works*, William Tait, Edinburgh, 1843, vol. 1. Bentham urged that 'the day *may* come when the rest of the animal creation may acquire rights' which only the tyranny of man has denied them. He went on: '... the question is not, Can they *reason*: nor, Can they *talk*? But, Can they *suffer*?'

Similarly in *Principles of Penal Law*, Part III, ch. XVII, he attacked cruel sports of hunting and killing animals 'since they produce the most acute sufferings to sensible beings ...'. He then asked: 'Why should the law refuse its protection to any sensitive being? The time will come, when humanity will extend its mantle over every thing that breathes' *Works*, *op. cit.*, vol. 1, p.562.

21. The attention of some philosophers has been drawn to vivisection with its many abuses from the standpoint of purposelessness or futility, and large-scale duplication; cruelty inflicted on some animals in trivial testing, such as for cosmetics; suffering in long transportation by road or sea; severe restrictions on freedom of movement on some animal farms. For documentation and discussion see P. Singer, *Animal Liberation*, Paladin Books, Granada Publishing, London, 1977, especially p.50 ff, and pp. 105–57. Various views on animals in relation to man have been collected by T. Regan and P. Singer in *Animal Rights and Human*

Obligations, Prentice-Hall, Englewood Cliffs, 1976.

22. Kant held that our duties towards animals are 'merely indirect duties towards humanity. Animal nature has analogies to human nature, and by doing our duties to animals in respect of manifestations which correspond to manifestations of human nature, we indirectly do our duty towards humanity.' *Lectures on Ethics*, trans. L. Infield, Methuen, London, 1930, p.239.

23. As with Human Rights, Human Duties are not always clearly moral, but are often expressions of social and political purposes which make it difficult to think of them as involving a respect for persons. Rather, in some of their expressions, they refer to the generality of people, or to mankind. The ascription of Human Duties can be made from a variety of standpoints. For a collection of essays on Human or Fundamental Duties, see *Fundamental Duties*, ed. D. Lasok *et al.*, Pergamon Press, Oxford, 1980.

24. 'Of the Bad Principle in Human Nature', p.335, fn. The reference is to *Kant's Critique of Practical Reason and Other Works on the Theory of Ethics*, ed. T. H. Abbott, 6th edn, Longmans, London, 1909. A 'propensity' is said to be a predisposition to the desire of the enjoyment: after experiencing the enjoyment there is 'inclination'. Between propensity and inclination there is 'instinct'. After inclination there are 'passions', which are inclinations that exclude self-control.

25. Ross, W. D. *The Right and the Good*, Oxford, 1930

26. The reference is to Stephen Toulmin, *Reason in Ethics*, Cambridge University Press, 1960.

27. In his *Review of the Principal Questions in Morals*, 1758, Richard Price declared that morality is 'eternal and immutable', like a triangle or circle. It is reason or 'understanding' within us that gives us the power to perceive right and wrong, moral obligation or duty. These ideas come from our intuition of truth, or the discernment of the nature of things by the understanding. See ch. 1: Of the Origin of our Ideas of Right and Wrong, Section 1 and Section III, and fn 12. From 3rd ed., 1787. (From D. H. Monro ed. *A Guide to the British Moralists*, Collins, London, 1972, pp. 325–45.).

CHAPTER 4   PRACTICAL DELIBERATIONS

1. *Akrasia* is used in the *Nicomachean Ethics*. It is translated by W. D. Ross as 'incontinence', and the translation is followed by us, despite the varied connotation of akrasia given by Aristotle and some disagreement among translators and philosophers as to its full import.

2. The reference is again to L. A. Selby-Bigge's edition, Oxford, 1888, as are other references to Hume's *Treatise* in this chapter.

3. G. E. M. Anscombe, *Intention*, 2nd ed, Basil Blackwell, Oxford, 1979. References are to this edition.

4. Our notion of a *dispositional complex* with strong action orientation is similar to psychological explanations of attitude, such as G. W.

Allport's: 'An attitude is a mental and neural state of readiness, organized through experience, exerting a directive or dynamic influence upon the individual's response to all objects and situations with which it is related.' ('Attitudes', in Murchison, ed. *Handbook of Social Psychology*, Clark University Press, 1935, p.810.)

5. This formed part of John Dewey's democratic ideal in *Democracy and Education*, Macmillan, New York, 1916 (Free Press edition, 1966). Although Dewey rejected the notion of ultimate ends, he clearly had a social ideal as an end-in-view. The elaboration of the specific valuation theory is given in his *Theory of Valuation*, University of Chicago, 1939. Dewey made the theory fit his social ideal, which involved an intelligent appraisal of the likely consequences of acts as a means to the improvement of individual experience, and an assumption that life was constituted of a succession of problems or obstructions to be overcome by the intellect, or reason. Another assumption was that valuation occurs only in the presence of some 'need, lack, or privation'; that is, 'when something is the matter' (*Theory of Valuation*, p.34). However his social ideal did *not* include a belief in absolute standards or a universal end-in-view toward which all persons would strive (p.56).

6. Lapses in the reasoning of the first three syllogisms are concealed in part by the form in which they are cast. Syllogisms which are expressed formally indicate three terms only: the two premisses assert a relationship between each of the conclusion's terms and a common third term. A term which changes its meaning in the syllogism leads to equivocation. Thus in Case 1 the second term of the first premiss is not used exactly in the same sense as the second term of the second premiss: 'freedom' is vague in each, but there is a perceptible shift in its meaning from the first to the second premiss. The final syllogism is formally accurate and it leads to a true conclusion, but it is not a true conclusion *because* the syllogism is formally accurate. This is illustrated in the following syllogism which has a false conclusion even though the reasoning is formally valid. A conclusion is true only on the assumption that the premisses are true:

All birds are winged creatures (True)
All winged creatures are flyers (False)
Therefore all birds are flyers (False)

It is to be noted that syllogisms of this kind, called 'categorical' since they refer to reasoning about classes or categories of things, have other formal requirements which are explained in texts on elementary logic.

7. In the quotations from the *Politics*, Benjamin Jowett's translation is again used.

8. Reference to J. S. Mill's essay *On Liberty* (1859) is to the Penguin edition, Harmondsworth, 1974.

9. Illusions as part of ideologies are discussed in Chapter 7.

10. 'Discourse on Method', Part one, from *Descartes. Philosophical Writings*, selected and edited by E. Anscombe and P. T. Geach, Nelson's

University Paperbacks, London, rev. ed, 1970, p.7 (from the French text published in 1637).

CHAPTER 5   PRACTICAL APPLICATIONS

1. The reference to J. S. Mill's *On Liberty* (1859) is to the Penguin edition, Harmondsworth, 1974.
2. One of the strongest claims that 'freedom works' was made by A. S. Neill in *Summerhill* (1962) which has value chiefly in its statement of possibilities, and the implied relation between freedom and practical morality. On its successful 'working' no generalizations are possible because of variables of teacher personality, including attitudes and values; selectivity of children in the school population; numbers of children in the school; residential character, and so forth. While there is no doubt that some of the 'free' schools have made extravagant claims, some of the more guarded claims leave little doubt on the effects of freedom on the moral development of some individuals. Penguin Books, 1968 (first published, 1926).
3. See Ch. II, p.16 of *The Limits of State Action*, J. W. Burrow, ed., Cambridge University Press, 1969.
4. References to law, unless otherwise specified, are to *statute law*, which is the law enacted by a legislative body. Historically, *common law* was a law derived from custom and tradition as it was interpreted by judges in national courts, and regarded as *common to* the whole country. 'Common law' is now used in different senses. It applies sometimes to the English system of law as it has been adopted (with modifications) by a number of English-speaking countries including the USA (See ch.7 on common law tradition.) Sometimes it applies to rules of law which the courts rather than legislatures create. Sometimes it is used to refer to the historical common law courts of England, as distinct from the equity courts that developed later (ref. ch.1). Because statutes (usually expressed briefly and formally) need to be interpreted by judges, such interpretations in cases before the courts are a source of judge-made law, as it is built up from *cases* that have been decided and so may be cited.
5. When a person sues another for damages to compensate him financially for loss incurred in a motor accident, for instance, or in other circumstances where there is no criminal offence, the civil action is one referred to as one in *tort*, meaning literally 'wrong' (Cf. ch.1: Aristotle's notion of corrective justice.)
6. Presumption in law is taken as assuming that something is true until it is proved otherwise. The age below which there is no criminal responsibility varies between approximately 7 years and 10 years or more. The age above which there is total criminal responsibility varies also, between approximately 14 years and 16 years.
   In indicating the conflicts that occur between law, morality and justice, and between law, morality and education, we are referring to matters well-known to jurists: most countries now have active law reform

societies which make recommendations to fill in the gaps in the law, where the complexities of modern life are not adequately covered by statutes, but as well to remove many anomalies that have been carried forward from the past, such as in common law. But our discussion of arbitrariness in the law is not intended for practical purposes of legal reform. The drafting of legislation, without favour or privilege, is in many circumstances a complex and difficult task.

7. For general observations on the situation in England, see C. Sachs, 'The Duty to the Child', in D. Lasok *et al.*, eds *Fundamental Duties*, Pergamon, Oxford, 1980, pp.179–85. A study of cases and reports suggests that the welfare of the child is seen as the fundamental duty of the law. In some countries special bodies are set up which make the welfare of the child the primary consideration, as far as possible without formal court proceedings.

8. See note 12 below.

9. In some instances in England courts have decided against schools which have imposed penalties for failure to perform prescribed homework: on this and other matters reflecting changing social attitudes and values.

10. This is a complex question: conflict avoidance in the home is not to be taken lightly, since that too has an important bearing on the adolescent's development. As a matter of principle, the liberty of the adolescent with sufficient intellectual maturity to make up his own mind on matters of personal belief must have precedence over pragmatic considerations, supported wherever possible by counselling of both the adolescent and his parents.

11. The notions of 'due process' and 'equal protection' are derived from the Fourteenth Amendment to the Constitution. By procedural due process, action directed at depriving a person of 'life, liberty, or property' requires that the person be notified of the impending action, be given an opportunity to be heard, and be given a fair hearing. One judgement has stated that due process of law 'requires an evaluation based on a disinterested inquiry pursued in the spirit of science, on a balanced order of facts exactly and fairly stated, on the detached consideration of conflicting claims, ... on a judgement not ad hoc and episodic but duly mindful of reconciling the needs both of continuity and of change in a progressive society'. (Rochin v California 342 US 165, 96L ed. 183, 1951. Quoted in Lord Lloyd, *Introduction to Jurisprudence*, Stevens & Sons, London, 1979, p.129). Some United States jurists have been critical of 'due process' for its vagueness. See, for example, J. K. Feibleman, 'Philosophical Perspectives on Justice', in T. Taylor *et al.*, *Perspectives on Justice*, Northwestern University Press, Evanston, Illinois, 1975, p.85. See R. B. Kimbrough and M. Y. Nunnery, *Educational Adminis-tration*, Macmillan, New York, 1976, p.210, for the reversal in 1968 of an Arkansas State statute prohibiting the teaching of the evolution of man 'from a lower order of animals', and the upholding of the right of a teacher, in out of school hours, to publicly criticize the school adminis-trators.

12. In the USA it has proved very difficult to uphold Accountability Laws, under which claims have been made that an education of an appropriate

standard has not been given. The many variables in the situation include the attitude of the child himself, his abilities and capacities, his support in the home, and the influence of his peers, quite apart from the variability in professional skills and attitudes of teachers. Some judicial opinion holds that despite recent failures before the courts, there is a growing awareness of a need for the law to recognize cases of negligence with respect to the duty to *teach* children. It is the direct object of 'teach' however, which is the crux of the entire problem.

13. Controversial cases of negligence have referred to adequacy of playground supervision before and after school, injuries in the vicinity of the school or in travelling to school, or on excursions.

14. Most of the cases appearing before the courts under the Law of Tort refer to cases of negligence. In England and some other countries the parent of a child injured on school premises may claim negligence against those responsible for proper and safe maintenance of the premises. The Occupiers' Liability Act of 1957 applies to schools in England as well as to other occupied premises. See D. H. Hadjihambis, 'The Moral Duty in the Law of Tort', in D. Lasok *et al.*, eds *Fundamental Duties*, op.cit., p.265.

15. The concept of *in loco parentis* was initially an authority to the teacher to act on the parents' behalf in controlling the child by punishment if considered necessary. In some countries such as England and the USA the courts have found *in loco parentis* valueless: the expectations and standards of parents differ widely, as do the judgements of teachers on what they consider 'reasonable' behaviour.

The courts have generally been cautiously conservative in their approach to corporal punishment in schools. One legal judgement in England saw the schools as special societies where penalties were needed for domestic discipline. For recent cases in England and USA see Paul Jackson, *Natural Justice*, Sweet & Maxwell, London, pp.158–9.

16. This and other references to Thomas Hobbes' views on punishment are from his *Leviathan* (1651), Penguin, Harmondsworth, 1968, ch. xxviii, pp.353–7. For comparison, see A. Flew, 'The Justification of Punishment' in H. B. Acton (ed.) *The Philosophy of Punishment*, Macmillan, London, 1969, p.83 ff.

17. F. H. Bradley's views are in *Ethical Studies*, 1876, 1927, Oxford University Press, 1962, p.26ff. Bradley quotes at length from Kant's *Werke*, vol. vi, pp.331–2, and p.333, to give the views to which we have previously referred: see fn.p.28.

18. W. D. Ross, *The Right and the Good*, Clarendon Press, Oxford, 1930, pp.63–64. We have noted Ross's sense of *prima facie* in the previous chapter: prima facie duties *tend to be* our duty. See p.18n, and pp.28–9. A duty in the full sense 'belongs to an act in virtue of its whole nature and of nothing less than this', while a *prima facie* duty 'belongs to an act in virtue of some one component in its nature' (p.28).

19. G. W. F. Hegel's *The Philosophy of Right* was published in 1821. The page reference is from the Oxford edition, 1942, translated by T. M. Knox.

20. This is a view of J. Feinberg, on *Doing and Deserving*, Princeton University Press, 1970, p.118.
21. The reference is to *A Theory of Justice*, Oxford University Press, 1972, 1973. For his views on social stability and punishment, see pp.314–15. Criminal punishments, he believes, 'are not simply a scheme of taxes and burdens designed to put a price on certain forms of conduct ...'.
22. *As You Like It* from which Jaques' words are quoted (II,VII, 145–7) was probably first produced in 1598. Montaigne's *Essays* were published earlier. The reference is to the translation by William Hazlitt in 1865, C. Templeman, London. Montaigne criticised 'the practice of the pedants, who, instead of tempting and alluring children to letters, present nothing before them but rods and ferrules, horror and cruelty ... nothing more dulls and degenerates a well-born nature' (p.69). John Aubrey's observations on education were not published until toward the end of the Seventeenth Century, though referring to the position as he saw it over the last quarter of the century. (See *Aubrey on Education*, ed. J.E. Stephens, Routledge & Kegan Paul, London, 1972, pp.17–18).
23. A 'taw' was a development of the strap with multiple tails – three, five or seven. For the questioning of corporal punishment in England, see for example the *Report of the Committee of Council on Education for 1845*, vol.2, pp.164–6. This is cited in P. Gosden, ed. *How They Were Taught*, Basil Blackwell, Oxford, 1969, p.19. John Brinsley's *Ludus Literarius or the Grammar Schoole* was republished by the University of Liverpool Press, ed. E. T. Campagnac, Constable, London, 1917. This follows the text of the second edition of 1627. Though Brinsley saw that harsh punishment had an adverse effect and it was preferable to instil a love of learning (ch.XXVI), he still found punishment necessary. See especially ch. XXIX for his advice on corporal punishment with a birch or a small red willow. A stubborn or unbroken boy was to be held fast, 'as in shoeing or taming an unbroken colt' (p.228).
24. Hume believed that usually an observer can infer our actions from our motives and character, and in those circumstances where he cannot, he simply lacks sufficient information about us. If he had everything available to him about 'our situation and temper, and the most secret springs of our complexion and disposition' he would understand that our actions of the will have causes which make our behaviour predictable (*A Treatise of Human Nature*, ed. L.A. Selby-Bigge, Oxford, 1888, Book II, Part III, Section II, pp.408–9). Similarly Mill held that if we knew 'all the inducements which are acting upon him' we could foretell an individual's conduct 'with as much certainty as we can predict any physical event' (J. S. Mill, *A System of Logic*, Book VI, ch.II, Section 2. See *Collected Works*, University of Toronto Press, 1974, and Routledge & Kegan Paul, London, pp.836–7.) Mill acknowledged that 'we are not compelled, as by a magical spell, to obey any particular motive' (p.838).
25. The reference is to the essay 'The Dilemma of Determinism' in *Essays on Faith and Morals*, Peter Smith, Gloucester, Mass., 1943 (Originally published by Longmans, Green, London.)
26. These expressions are used by Hume in *A Treatise of Human Nature*,

op.cit., Book II, Section II, p. 407, as terms used 'in the schools'.

27. One with very strong convictions on this question was C. Darrow. See his *Attorney for the Damned*, Simon & Schuster, New York, 1957, p.95.

28. Mills' views on punishment are given in ch. xxvi, 'On the Freedom of the Will', from his *Examination of Sir William Hamilton's Philosophy* included in *Ethical Writings*, J. B. Schneewind, ed., Collier-Macmillan, London, 1965, p.244.

29. In the United States, corporal punishment is permitted legally in certain states but not in others. Where a teacher or principal inflicts corporal punishment in a state where it is not permitted he is, of course, at once in breach of the state laws; but in a state where it is permitted, he may be sued for improper punishment according to the 'due process' provisions of the Fourteenth Amendment. A parent may sue in any state with respect to other forms of punishment, such as detention. In some other countries, where there are no statutes on school punishment, guidance may be given by common law, but cases before the courts have been concerned especially with severe corporal punishment leading to physical injury.

30. Again the translation used is that by W. D. Ross. The force of habit in the formation of *right* habit was given memorable expression by the psychologist William James. To him it was of overriding importance that children while 'in the plastic state' of 'mere walking bundles of habits' should be taught virtuous ones: 'Every smallest stroke of virtue or of vice leaves its never so little scar' (*Principles of Psychology*, Henry Holt, New York, 1890, p.127).

31. Benjamin Jowett's translation of the *Politics* is again used.

32. Some of the terms used in theories of moral education are derivatives of the Greek word *nomos* meaning *law*. Thus 'anomy' is literally 'without law' (Gk. anomos). 'Heteronomy' contrasts with 'autonomy' by reason of their prefixes: 'heteros' ('other') and 'autos' ('self'). It is to be noted that Kant used 'heteronomy' differently from the meaning given to it by contemporary theorists in moral education, using it for the influence of impulse or inclination on behaviour. It belonged to the world of sense in contrast with the 'autonomy' of pure reason whose fundamental law was the moral law (*The Analytic of Pure Practical Reason* in *Kant's Critique of Practical Reason and Other Works on the Theory of Ethics*, 6th edn, trans. T.K. Abbott, Longmans, London, pp.131–2). In some studies of moral education a hybrid term has been introduced, 'socionomy', to refer to law or morality derived from society: that is, to a concern for social reputation, or social praise or blame.

33. Free Press edition, New York, 1965. Piaget drew his inferences from observations of small groups of children at play, up to the age of 13 years. He found heteronomy dominant to the age of 7 or 8 years; autonomy be found at about 11 or 12 years, in the last stage of intellectual development, with reciprocity based on mutual respect.

34. For an account of his research see L. Kohlberg, 'The Child as a Moral Philosopher' in *Psychology Today*, Sept. 1968, pp.25–30. Reprinted in B. I. Chazan and J. F. Soltis, *Moral Education*, Teachers College Press, Columbia University, New York, 1973, p.136. Kohlberg's original study

was of 75 United States boys aged 10, 13 and 16, whose moral development was recorded at 3-year intervals for 12 years He sought responses to simulated situations posing moral dilemmas. At Stage 5 he claimed to find a respect for others' rights and for standards of conduct which are not merely conventional, but which have been subjected to critical scrutiny within society, and are always socially changeable by rational discussion. Stage 6 he claimed to represent the final growth of the individual toward autonomy.

35. See, for example, J. Feinberg, 'The Idea of a Free Man' in J. F. Doyle, ed. *Educational Judgements*, Routledge & Kegan Paul, London, 1973, p.160. 'If we strip our conception of the governing self of all its standards and values, leaving only a bare impersonal Reason imprisoned in its own royal palace, the notion of autonomy becomes empty and incoherent'. Feinberg refers to an 'inner core self' comprising 'convictions, ideals and purposes'. These constitute 'materials for Reason to work with'.

36. Mill published *The Subjection of Women* in 1869 (after *On Liberty*, 1859, and *Representative Government*, 1861). Although his last published work, it was written in 1861, and fits partly into the context of the extension of the franchise with which he was concerned in that year. Yet he found the legal subordination of one sex to the other 'wrong in itself, and ... one of the chief hindrances to human improvement'. The above three essays were published together by Oxford University Press, 1912. The reference is to p.427.

37. For instances of factory farming and of animal suffering see P. Singer, *Animal Liberation*, Paladin Books, Granada Publishing, London, 1977, pp.105–57. Singer refers to the cruelty inflicted on rabbits when cosmetics and other preparations are tested for effects on eyes and skin; the inducement of 'psychological death' on young monkeys by isolation over long periods; the subjection of dogs to excessive heat (p.50 ff). 'How can these things happen?' he asks (p.75). In these circumstances, we might add, how can anyone confine his morality to relations among human beings, without moral concern for the interests of sentient animals?

38. Friedrich Nietzsche (1844–1900) gave prominence to the strength of will and the passion of strong men that drove them to positions of power, convinced that a morality of equality, cooperation and conventional virtues merely inhibited the strong. The means of their ascendancy was unimportant: even envy, greed, violence, war, might be necessary. 'The noble type of man' creates his own values and does not need approval (*Between Good and Evil*, trans. Walter Kaufmann, Vintage Books, New York, 1966, 260, p.205.). He 'accepts the fact of his egoism without question mark' (265, p.215).

39. *Essays*, ch.XII 'Apology for Raimond Sebond', in *The Works of Michael de Montaigne*, trans. William Hazlitt, C. Templeman, London, 1865, p.20.

40. See also note 12. Accountability in the United States has legal status. A Board of Education or a State Legislature may demand reports on students' achievements in independently conducted tests, and at the same time relate these to the total financial cost of achieving the results. The teacher may be held legally accountable for students' achievements.

In general the complexity of the problem has been realised more clearly by the Courts than by the legislative bodies.

41. Machiavelli (1469–1527), like Nietzsche, should be read to avoid misunderstanding in short quotations. Though in *The Prince* he was forthright in his advice to those who sought power, he favoured republican government with recognized liberties for citizens. See *The Prince: Selections from the Discourses and other Writings*, edited by John Plamenatz, Fontana, Collins, 1972.

CHAPTER 6   PHILOSOPHICAL PERSPECTIVES

1. References are to the Penguin edition, Harmondworth, 1968. (The book was published in London in 1651, while Hobbes was living in Paris to which he had fled in 1640, fearing for his life in the conflict between Charles I and the Commons.)

2. The first three editions of the *Two Treatises* were published in 1689–90, 1694 and 1698. The third edition had many corrections made by Locke, which were included in the 6th edition of 1764. Our references are to the corrected edition of 1823, published by Tegg, London, in *Works*, vol.5. (We have not referred to Locke's First Treatise of Government, which was a criticism of the views of Sir Robert Filmer.) A recent edition based on that of 1764, has been published by Hacket, Indianapolis, 1980, ed. C. B. Macpherson.

3. *An Essay Concerning Human Understanding* was first published in 1690. It has been re-published in a number of editions, some of which are abridged, such as A. D. Woozley's abridgement of the 5th edn in 1964 (Collins, Fontana Library). The references here are to the complete edition in *Works*, Tegg, London, 1823, vols.1–4.

4. *Some Thoughts Concerning Education* was published in 1693. Various editions have been published such as that by R. H. Quick, which was based on the first edition of Locke's *Works*, 1714. Quick's edition was published by Cambridge University Press in 1898, from which the page reference is taken.

5. Robert Nozick's *Anarchy, State and Utopia* is published by Basil Blackwell, Oxford, 1974; page references are to this edition. (Also published by Basic Books, New York.)

6. The individualism which is the main theme in Nozick's book was one of the major currents of thought in both the 18th and 19th centuries. In *Social Statics* Herbert Spencer referred to government as a 'mutual safety confederation' (John Chapman, London, 1851, ch.xix, 1, p.206). In *The Man v the State* (1884) Spencer expressed his conviction that state measures to relieve the plight of the poor may be misguided: 'benefit may result, not from multiplication of artificial appliances to mitigate distress, but, contrariwise, from diminution of them' ('The Coming Slavery', p.22). The function of Liberalism in the past, he explained, was to limit the powers of kings. In the future it will be to put a limit to the powers of parliament (p.88) (Watts & Co., London, 1909).

7. See especially *The Man v the State*, op.cit. The Poor Laws disturbed Spencer. Limited benevolence was conveyed in his forthright opposition to self-sacrificing efforts on behalf of others (p.22), and his protection of personal resources in his attribution of slavery to any condition that required a man to give up, 'for other benefit than his own', some of the fruits of his personal labours' (p.33).

8. The translation is that by A. D. Lindsay in the Everyman edition of *The Republic*, J. M. Dent, London, 1935.

9. *The Social Contract* was published in 1762. References given here are to the Penguin edition, translated and with an introduction by Maurice Cranston, Penguin Books, Harmondsworth, 1968.

10. From *Kant's Critique of Practical Reason and Other Works on The Theory of Ethics*. trans. T.K. Abbott, 6th edn, Longmans, Green, London, 1909. (The heading of this section follows Abbott's translation, not Rawls' *The Foundation of the Metaphysics of Morals*.)

11. See, for example, Sir David Ross, *Kant's Ethical Theory*, Oxford, 1954, pp.75–85.

12. Rawls' reference to these is in *A Theory of Justice*, Oxford University Press, 1972, p.11n. The edition used in this study is the Oxford University Paperback, 1973.

13. For criticisms of Rawls from a variety of perspectives, see for example: J. L. Mackie, *Ethics*, Penguin, Harmondsworth, 1977, pp.95–6. R. Dworkin, *Taking Rights Seriously*, Duckworth, London, 1977, ch.6; Lord Lloyd, *Introduction to Jurisprudence*, 4th edn, Stevens, London, 1979, pp.96–9, W. Lang, 'Marxism, Liberalism and Justice', in E. Kamenka and A. Tay, *Justice*, Edward Arnold, London, 1979, ch.6, pp.138–48 and B. Barry, 'Justice as Reciprocity', in ibid., ch.3.

14. Rawls' political assumptions are evident at a number of points, of which these are examples: p.73 assumption of a class-structured society; p.102 reference to unequal starting-points in society, and assumption of social inequalities as part of the social order; pp.17–21 and elsewhere in his references to the original position, assuming that the economic system of society does not have a bearing on principles of justice.

15. Humboldt's work was published posthumously in 1852. It was written in 1791–1792, and portions of the work were published then. The first English translation was in 1854. For a recent English edition see *The Limits of State Action*, J.W. Burrow (ed.), Cambridge University Press, 1969.

16. References are to the Penguin edition of *On Liberty*, Harmondsworth, 1974. Mill prefaced the essay with a quotation in which Humboldt referred to 'the absolute and essential importance of human development in its richest diversity'. This appears in ch.v, p.51 of *The Limits of State Action*, op. cit.

17. Here Mill denounced an education that was in the hands of a centralized authority, 'directed to the perpetuation of the same type'. See *Utilitarianism, Liberty, Representative Government*, ed. H. B. Acton, Everyman edition, J. M. Dent, London, 1972, p.403. Here selections from *Auguste Comte and Positivism* are given in an appendix. The sequence of publications was *On Liberty*, 1859, *Utilitarianism* (in Fraser's Magazine)

1861, *Representative Government* 1861, *Utilitarianism* (in book form) 1863, *Auguste Comte and Positivism*, 1865.
18. *Inaugural Address*, People's edition, Longman, Green, Reader, and Dyer, London, 1867. Although *The Subjection of Women* was published two years after the Inaugural Address, it was in fact written in 1861.

CHAPTER 7   PRACTICAL PERSPECTIVES

1. Research shows that the socially underprivileged child is at a marked disadvantage generally when he begins school. Some researchers investigating the years of early childhood have been so impressed by the influence of the family environment as to make long-range predictions of its intellectual effects. See B. S. Bloom, *Stability and Change in Human Characteristics*, John Wiley, New York, 1964, where it is inferred that by the time the child is ready for school – at about five years of age – the keel is already laid for his intellectual achievement in adulthood; or in research terms, by that age most of the variance in adult intellectual achievement is already accounted for.

   Other significant points of view by researchers are presented in J. S. Coleman, *Equality of Educational Opportunity*, US Dept. of Health, Education and Welfare, Office of Education, Washington, D.C.; H.J. Eysenck, *The Inequality of Man*, Temple Smith, London, 1973; F. Mosteller and D. P. Moynihan, *On Equality of Educational Opportunity*, Vintage Books, New York, 1972; J.S. Bruner 'Poverty and Childhood', in *Oxford Review of Education*, vol. 1, No.1, 1975 (see also Bruner's bibliography, pp.47–50).

2. Early uses of ideology are given in M. Seliger, *Ideology and Politics*, Allen & Unwin, London, 1976, and D. J. Manning, ed., *The Form of Ideology*, Allen & Unwin, London, 1980. De Tracy used 'ideology' to refer to a science of ideas which studied how ideas came to the mind from sense experience. Napoleon supported 'ideology' when it suited his purposes of social reform, but the 'liberal ideology' which seemed to be working in his favour was discredited by him as soon as it threatened his power: 'ideologues' were then branded as 'utopian'.

3. For an example of his derogatory use of 'ideology' see *The Class Struggles in France*, Lawrence & Wishart, London, 1936, p.35, where he wrote contemptuously of 'so-called men of talent' as the ideological representatives and spokesmen of certain classes.

4. Karl Marx and Frederick Engels collaborated in writing *The German Ideology*. For his condemnation of ideology as an inversion of reality, with the upside down image of a *camera obscura*, see vol.1, 'The Essence of the Materialist Conception of History. Social Being and Social Consciousness', in Karl Marx and Frederick Engels, *Collected Works*, Lawrence & Wishart, London, 1976, vol.5, p.36 (Progress Publishers, Moscow, 1976, 3rd revised edition, p.42). Marx wrote dogmatically of the 'ideological nonsense' among the democrats and the French Socialists in one of his later political writings. See *Critique of the Gotha Programme*, Martin Lawrence, London, 1933, p.32. For the explanation

of ruling ideas associated with ruling classes, see *The German Ideology*, Lawrence & Wishart edition, op. cit, pp.60–2 (Progress Publishers, pp.67–9). Marx and Engels gave this explanation to show how the Hegelian notion of the domination of the spirit in history arose. For their later criticism of equality and a feeling of 'natural affinity', see Lawrence and Wishart edition, p.479 (Progress Publishers, p.506).

5. For the various viewpoints on alienation and its connection with ideology, see *The German Ideology*, Lawrence & Wishart edition, vol.1, pp.47–8, p.51, pp.77–8, pp.78–9 (Progress Publishers, pp.53–4, p.59; p.85; pp.86–7).

Marx makes his most explicit statement of alienation in his early writings, especially in the *Economic and Philosophical Manuscripts* written in 1844. He describes the relationship of the worker to the product of his labour as 'an alien activity not belonging to him'. The relationship to natural objects is also one of an alien and hostile world opposed to him. The alienation of man from man is a consequence of his alienation from the product of his work. (Marx and Engels, *Collected Works*, vol.3, Lawrence & Wishart, London, p.275).

6. See *Capital,* vol.1, Part IV, Ch.XIV, Section 5 – 'The Capitalist Character of Manufacture'. Trans. S. Moore and P. Aveling, ed. F. Engels, Allen & Unwin, London, 1946, pp.355, 356–7 (Progress Publishers, 1954, p.342). Here Marx notes Adam Smith's recommendation, in *Wealth of Nations*, that there should be education of the people by the state; and the reply by G. Garnier, his French translator and commentator, who protested that education of the masses would violate the first law of the division of labour. As society becomes more prosperous, the division between those who work with their hands and those who work with their heads becomes more pronounced; and the division of labour is itself a cause of future progress.

7. *Capital,* vol.II, Part VI, ch.XIX – 'The Transformation of the Value' (and Respectively the Price) of Labour – Power into Wages, Allen & Unwin edition, *op.cit.* p.552 (Progress Publishers, p.507).

8. See *The German Ideology*, op.cit., 'The Essence of the Materialist Conception of History. Social Being and Social Consciousness', Lawrence & Wishart edition, p.36 (Progress Publishers, pp.42–3). Marx held, as he stated in the original manuscript, that men produce their own ideas, conditioned by the mode of production, material intercourse with others, and 'its further development in the social and political structure'. Lawrence & Wishart edition, p.36 n. (Progress Publishers, p.42 n). For the materialist connection between men, determined by their needs and their mode of production (which, as he says, is constantly assuming new forms), see Lawrence & Wishart edition, p.43 (Progress Publishers, p.49). The expression 'dialectical materialism' was not used by Marx. It was Engels who, particularly in his later writings, developed Marx's materialism. On man's consciousness, see Marx's preface to *A Contribution to the Critique of Political Economy* : 'It is not the consciousness of men that determines their existence, but, on the contrary, their social existence that determines their consciousness', Kerr, Chicago, 1913, trans. N.I. Stone, Preface, pp.11–22.

9. See *The New Organon* (1620). References here are to The Library of Liberal Arts edition, Bobbs-Merrill, New York, 1960. Apart from Idols of the Cave (Aphorism, Book 1, XLII, pp.48–9) in which what enters the mind is refracted by qualities peculiar to it as well as by external influences from education and contact with others; and Idols of the Market Place (Aphorism, XLIII, p.49) which come from human communication and interaction; there are Idols of the Theatre (Aphorisms, XLIV, p.49) referring to systems of thought from dogmas of philosophy and elsewhere, which enter the mind like 'so many stage plays, representing worlds of their own creation after an unreal and scenic fashion'.

10. See Karl Mannheim, *Ideology and Utopia*. Routledge & Kegan Paul, London, 1936, pp.67–74, 86. Apart from failing to take account of elements peculiar to a social situation (and so not merely repetitions of Nineteenth Century social situations), Mannheim saw ideology attempting to conceal these new elements 'by thinking of them in categories which are inappropriate' (p.86).

11. References are to the Verso edition, London, 1979, trans. B. R, Brewster (first published as *Pour Marx* by François Maspero, 1965).

12. These views are contained in the essay, 'Ideology and Ideological State Apparatuses' in L. Althusser, *Lenin and Philosophy and Other Essays*, Monthly Review Press, New York and London, 1971, trans. B. Brewster. (First published in *La Pensée, 1970*). Under feudalism, says Althusser, the dominant state apparatus was the Church. Marx considers reproduction from a variety of aspects in vol.II of *Capital*: eg. ch. XX on simple reproduction, and ch.XXI on accumulation and reproduction on an extended scale.

13. John Dewey was one of the educationists and philosophers who espoused and propagated the liberal ideology of equality of educational opportunity. See especially *Democracy and Education* (1916), Free Press, New York, 1966. He saw a political and economic emancipation of the 'masses' by the development of a free public school system for all (p.257).

    For a broad interpretation of the liberal ideology in the United States, see W. Feinberg, *Reason and Rhetoric: the Intellectual Foundations of Twentieth Century Liberal Educational Policy*, John Wiley, New York, 1975.

14. For examples of relevant research into equality of educational opportunity see: S. Bowles and H. Gintis, 'I.Q. in the U.S. Class Structure', in J. Karabel and A. H. Halsey, *Power and Ideology in Education*, op cit., pp.221–2; originally published in *Social Policy*, 3, Nov.–Dec. 1972, and Jan.–Feb. 1973, pp.65–9. See also S. Bowles, 'Unequal Education and the Reproduction of the Social Division of Labor', *Review of Radical Political Economics*, 3, Fall, 1971a; and S. Bowles and H. Gintis, *Schooling in Capitalist America: Educational Reform and the Contradictions of Economic Life*, Basic Books, New York, 1976.

    For criticism of this research, see J. Karabel and A. H. Halsey, 'Educational Research: a Review and an Interpretation', in *Power and Ideology in Education*, op. cit. At times, among such researchers the interpretations exceed the evidence from sophisticated statistical techniques, and at times the same empirical data is interpreted differently by different persons. One of the implications is of the pressure of preconceptions, even among researchers. Karabel and Halsey (p.38n) refer to the theory of Bowles and Gintis of class reproduction (following Marx and Engels) and of the nature of the relationship between what is taught in the school and what is useful in the production process, as 'highly provocative', but still subject to empirical investigation; and of the identification of hierarchy in school and work as 'a vast oversimplification' (p.39). Among the findings of most relevance to our explanation of the liberal ideology is that economic success which tends to run in families is almost completely independent of genetic inheritance expressed as I.Q. One of the strong preconceptions in Christopher Jencks' *Inequality* was that educational reform measures fail to produce educational equality and that schooling is not a major factor in adult success. See C. Jencks, *Inequality*, Penguin Books, Harmondsworth; Basic Books, New York, 1972. Again the findings have been criticised on methodological grounds. (See Karabel and Halsey, op. cit., p.24.) F. Mosteller and D.P. Moynihan (eds) *On Equality of Educational Opportunity*, Vintage Books, New York, 1972, comprises papers from Harvard University on the Coleman Report of 1966, checking its findings by independent studies. See, for example, D. J. Armor, 'School and Family Effects on Black and White Achievement': 'Black students start disadvantaged and the schools are apparently unable to close the gap' (p.223). One Coleman finding was that blacks appear to have facilities as adequate as whites in most parts of the USA. Coleman argued that it is a function of the school to make academic achievement independent of a pupil's social background. For a survey of viewpoints on educational opportunity in USA, see E. W. Gordon, 'Toward Defining Equality of Educational Opportunity', in Mosteller and Moynihan, op. cit., ch.10.

15. The report by James Coleman entitled *Equality of Educational Opportunity*, for the US Office of Education, was a response to the Civil Rights Act of 1964 whereby the Commissioner was to report to the President and Congress on 'the lack of availability of equal educational opportunities for individuals by reason of race, colour, religion, or national origin in public educational institutions at all levels ...'. The report found (in 1966) that the gap between black and white schools in provision of educational facilities was not large.

16. Unsupportiveness of parents is not always rooted in social deprivation. Some children of affluent families are given little or no support by parents, and delinquency among them is not uncommon. The incidence of drug and alcohol addiction is another factor militating against fulfilment of educational opportunities, and this is related to affluence at least as much as it is to social poverty.

17. These refer especially to USSR, China and Cuba.

18. See, for example, K. U. Chernenko, *The CPSU: Society, Human Rights*, Novosti Press Agency Publishing House, Moscow, 1981, pp.174–5.

19. China's inability to establish equality of educational opportunity is fully recognized: it is not expected that universal primary education will be achieved until 1990, and the difficulties with respect to China's vast rural

areas are officially acknowledged. Freedom and equality remain nonetheless part of the ruling ideology: all are equal members of a proletariat in a society of one class only. See Hu Yaobang's 'Report to the 12th National Congress of The Communist Party of China', 1 Sept. 1982. *Beijing Review*, vol.25, no.37, 13 Sept. 1982. On China's criticism of Party members accused of corruption, including privilege-seeking, see *Beijing Review*, vol.24, no.50, 14 Dec. 1981, p.3. Education is a right and a duty. (Article 46 of the ratified Constitution, *Beijing Review*, vol.25, no.52, 27 Dec. 1982)

20. The problems of censorship of literature in USSR need no elaboration: censorship frustrates the intellectual challenge to viewpoints, theories, policies or practices. *Chinese Literature* expresses a relationship between literature and socialist ideology. (The stigma of 'immaturity' has been applied in editorial comment if the socialist point of view is not expressed wherever an opportunity exists to express it.) One novelist, Liu Shaotang, claims to have become mature under the guidance of Mao Zedong's 'Yanan Talks', which explained that literary and artistic works are the product of social life, *Beijing Review*, vol.25, no.21, 24 May, 1982, p.27.

21. The question of a written constitution for Britain has had its strong supporters, who have contended that a Bill of Rights is needed to protect individual rights, especially against the persuasiveness of the state. The Report of the Lords Select Committee on a Bill of Rights (1978) expressed the view that a Bill of Rights can have only a minor role in protecting human rights. Much more important 'is a country's political climate and traditions'.

22. In the Declar. on the Elimin. of All Forms of Racial Discrimin. (1963), Article 9 declared 'all states shall take immediate and positive measures, including legislative and other measures, to prosecute and/or outlaw organizations which promote or incite to racial discrimination, or incite to or use violence for purposes of discrimination based on race, colour or ethnic origin'.

23. In the Covenant on Civil and Political Rights, Articles 18, 22 and 26 on basic liberties have also shown how powerless and unwilling is the international community to curb the violations of rights that continue in some countries. *The American Convention on Human Rights* (1969), established the Inter-American Commission on Human Rights and the Inter-American Court of Human Rights, to ensure that the rights which were agreed to were protected. (Article 33.) The Commission was to represent all member countries of the Organization of American States.

24. The American Declaration of the Rights and Duties of Man was adopted in Colombia, in 1948. See particularly Article XII. In the various international declarations of rights, a reference to equality of educational opportunity is very rare.

25. *The German Ideology*, Lawrence & Wishart edition, pp.90, 91 (Progress Publishers, pp.99–100).

26. *Manifesto of the Communist Party*, Progress Publishers, Moscow, pp.59–60.

27. F. Engels, *Anti-Dühring*, Foreign Languages Publishing House, Moscow, 1954, pp.389, 394 (Lawrence & Wishart, London, 1955).

28. V. I. Lenin, *The State and Revolution*, Progress Publishers, Moscow, pp.85–90.
29. See Lord Lloyd, *Introduction to Jurisprudence*, op.cit., pp.792–6, for an excerpt from 'The Significance of General Definitions in the Study of Problems of Law and Socialist Legality', by O. S. Ioffe and M. D. Shargorodskii.
30. The parental and educative role of the law in the Soviet Union is elaborated by H. J. Berman in *Justice in Russia: an Interpretation of Soviet Law*, Harvard University Press, Cambridge, Mass., 1950. Berman's observations were that the legislator, administrator or judge plays the part of a parent or guardian or teacher. The individual before the courts is 'treated as a child or youth to be guided and trained and made to behave' p.3 (Introduction), and p.288.
31. In China too the ruling party sees the law as fundamentally educative, and reform or re-education in communist theory is frequently prescribed for influences which challenge the integrity of the state. For the work of lawyers in contemporary China see *Beijing Review*, vol.25, no.23, 7 Jan. 1982, pp.14–17. In both USSR and China, for example, lawyers are needed for civil suits, to defend the accused in criminal cases, and to act as advisers in various ways.
32. Bentham's *View of a Complete Code of Laws*, together with his *Pannomial Fragments* are from his *Works*, vol.3, William Tait, Edinburgh, 1843. Comte attempted to create a science of 'sociology' as he called it, which would explain man's entire social activities as they are determined by scientific method.
33. In *Observations of Man* (1749) Hartley had asserted that it is for the public good, and for the sake of peace, order and harmony, that 'every member of a state should submit to the governing power, whatever that be ... We ought to reverence all persons in authority ... to make candid allowances on account of the difficulties of government, the bad education of princes, and persons of high birth'. 6th edn, Thomas Tegg, London, 1834, pp.506, 507.
34. J. Austin, *The Province of Jurisprudence Determined*, ed. H. A. L. Hart, Weidenfeld & Nicolson, London, 1954 p.126 (first published in 1832). See Introduction by Hart, p.x, on Austin's purpose to distinguish positive law from the confusion of Natural Law theorists who introduced precepts of religion and morality. Austin's chief notions were first, of a *command* by a person with certain power to enforce his desire by inflicting a *sanction*, or an evil imposed if his desire is disregarded; second, of a *habit of obedience* to a superior, who is a person or persons who have the power to compel others to obey. A *sovereign* is such a superior who is not in a habit of obedience, but receives habitual obedience from the majority of a given society.
35. On this point see R. M. Dworkin, 'Is Law a System of Rules?' in R. M. Dworkin (ed.) *The Philosophy of Law*, ch. 11. The observation on rejecting law when courts consider it inappropriate to the case before them is also made by Dworkin, in ibid., p.57. For one positivist account, see H. A. L. Hart, 'Positivism and the Separation of Law and Morals' in ibid., pp.17–37. From the broad view of positivism which we have presented there are many substantive variations.

36. In *The Concept of Law*, H. A. L. Hart asserts the position of Legal Positivism to mean 'the simple contention that it is in no sense a necessary truth that laws reproduce or satisfy certain demands of morality, though in fact they have often done so', Oxford University Press, 1961, pp.181–2.

37. H. Kelsen, *The Pure Theory of Law*, University of California Press, Berkeley and Los Angeles, 1967, trans. M. Knight.

38. H. Kelsen, *General Theory of Law and State*, Harvard University Press, 1946, p.18.

39. For a critique of Kelsen see Lord Lloyd, *Introduction to Jurisprudence*, op. cit., p.281 ff.

40. For criticism, see for example H. A. L. Hart, *The Concept of Law*, op. cit., ch.111. The coercive theory held that sanctions are necessary for the *breach* of a law. Coercion is still associated as it was by Austin, with threat, but this seems to be at odds with the way some persons do in fact conform to the law.

41. R. Pound, *Introduction to the Philosophy of Law*, Yale University Press, New Haven, 1925, pp.89, 99.

42. R. Pound, *Social Control Through Law*, Yale University Press, 1942, pp.64–5. Apart from conveying this function of the law in exercising social control, both Pound and Llewellyn were influenced by the development of the social sciences. Pound noted a trend from the old 'legal justice' to the new 'social justice', and Llewellyn contended that the law should study the way persons and institutions are organized in society and their relationship with the law. See *Essays in Jurisprudence from the Columbia Law Review*, Columbia University Press, New York and London, 1963, pp.217–79, and pp.149–83.

43. The references are to *A Theory of Justice*, 1972, Oxford University Press Paperback edition, 1973, pp.364, 386, 391.

44. L. Lloyd, *The Idea of Law*, Penguin, Harmondsworth, 1964, 1979 (with revisions), p.129.

45. Montaigne observed in his time 'double laws, those of honour and those of justice, in many things positively opposite to one another'. *Essays*, p.45. From *The Works of Michael de Montaigne*, translated by William Hazlitt, C. Templeman, London, 1865.

46. Llewellyn, K. *The Common Law Tradition*, Little, Brown, Boston, 1960. For comment on Llewellyn's point of view on common law see Lord Lloyd, *Introduction to Jurisprudence*, 4th edn, Stevens & Sons, London, pp.460–5. One of Llewellyn's main difficulties is that the common decision which he claims is achievable among experienced judges, in similar situations, assumes a series of social situations where there is no likelihood of a conflict of values among them. Reason they may have in common, but not necessarily all values relevant to different social situations. In *Karl Llewellyn and the Realist Movement*, Weidenfeld & Nicolson, London, 1973, W. Twining suggests that Llewellyn's evidence for the spread of the Grand Style is partly speculative (p.251). In England he suggests that the recent emphasis on judicial law-making may sometimes be 'a form of conservative politics masquerading as radical jurisprudence' (p.381).

47. F. E. Dowrick, *Justice According to the English Common Lawyers*, Butterworth, London, 1961 p.217. The comment refers to the English legal system.

48. Thomas Paine had himself become involved in the French Revolution. His *Rights of Man* was published in England in 1791. References here are to the Citadel Press edition, New Jersey, 1974. The articles of the French Declaration are quoted on pp.118–19, followed by Paine's comments on pp.119–21. As a basis of human liberty Paine considered that the Declaration of Rights 'is of more value to the world, and will do more good, than all the laws and statutes that have yet been promulgated' (p.120).

49. This observation was made in 1843 in a review article of Bruno Bauer's *On The Jewish Question*, Marx and Engels, *Collected Works*, vol.3, Lawrence & Wishart, London, p.165. It is worth noting that the liberal principles to which Thomas Paine referred are formally accepted by socialist governments. See *Beijing Review*, vol.25, no.52, 27 Dec. 1982 for the new Constitution of the People's Republic of China, ch.2, The Fundamental Rights and Duties of Citizens, Articles 33–56; and K. U. Chernenko, *The CPSU, Society, Human Rights*, op cit., pp.87–93, 113–51; 165–189.

50. This is the culmination of Russell's analysis of power in *Power*, Unwin Books, London, 1938, p.206.

51. For a frank discussion of ministerial relationships with the civil service see Edward Boyle and Anthony Crosland, with Maurice Kogan: *The Politics of Education*, Penguin, Harmondsworth, 1971. In some cases, partly because of short incumbencies and the time needed to grasp the fundamental background of educational issues, permanent heads of departments of education may be trusted to make decisions for the ministers (p.183). For the determination to fight for more equal opportunity, see p.129.

52. A similar suggestion is made by A. H. Halsey in *Educational Priority*: EPA Problems and Policies, vol.1, HMSO, London 1972, p.8.

CHAPTER 8   SOCIAL JUSTICE REFLECTIONS AND CONCLUSION

1. J.S. Mill, *Utilitarianism*, Section 5. From *Mill's Ethical Writings*, ed. J.B. Schneewind, Collier Books, New York, Collier-Macmillan, London. Page references are to this edition.

2. The right to work is included in the constitutions of classless (socialist) states. It is still controversial in some class-structured states.

3. Moral values supported by religious beliefs are thus included in our moral subjectivism. On the other hand religion is not *necessary* for a morality of considering others' interests, or for the substantive moral principles which we have proposed. For obvious reasons also, evident in both historical and contemporary social circumstances, attitudes and values learned from religious teaching are not *sufficient* for practical morality.

4. The expression 'The controlled monochrome of reason' is used by the

novelist Patrick White in his autobiographical *Flaws in the Glass*, Jonathan Cape, London, 1981, p.38.

5. Jeremy Bentham, *Works*, vol. iii, William Tait, Edinburgh, 1843, p.217. (See also ch.1., note 7.)

6. Because of the contrast between Plato's outlook in *The Republic* and then, much later, in *The Laws*, some commentators have suggested that in *The Republic* Plato's purpose was to shock a complacent society. This interpretation seems to be a concession to Plato's own idea of changelessness, but the more usual interpretation of Plato modifying his attitudes and values – including his ideas and beliefs – from wider experience and reflection seems the more likely. (It is still *possible* that Plato was aware that his ideal state in *The Republic* was unattainable, that he was proposing a model toward which the state might aspire, in order to demonstrate the difference between that and the actual state of social dissension.)

In Book 7, 797 of *The Laws*, Plato stressed the dangers of educational innovation. Adults will live peaceably together as long as they are not subjected to the disturbing effects of change, just as children do who become accustomed to playing the same games under the same rules and conditions, and to playing with the same toys. The person who in Plato's time seemed always to be making children restless by attracting them with something new, was stigmatized as the greatest threat to the state, because he was insidiously changing their character, turning them away from old things which they ought to be valuing, to a superficial valuing of anything novel.

7. Fyodor Dostoyevsky, *Crime and Punishment*, Penguin Books, Harmondsworth, 1951, Part ii, p.119, trans. D. Magarshack.

8. The case of very young children, unable to reason or to understand reasons, is not to be taken as an exception, since they are not *persons* in our sense.

9. Although we are capable of a measure of objectivity in the sense of impartiality, the objectification of values by reason – accepted by Kant – is never complete because of the very dispositional influences which he excluded and discredited. Neither 'rational agreement' nor 'intellectual criteria' conveys an objectivity of moral values.

Select Bibliography

Note: Where various editions or translations are available, those cited are the ones used in the text.

Acton, H. B. (ed.), *The Philosophy of Punishment*, London: Macmillan, 1969.

Althusser, L. *For Marx*, trans. B. Brewster, London: New Left Books, 1977. *Lenin and Philosophy and Other Essays*, trans. B. Brewster, London and New York: Monthly Review Press, 1971.

Anscombe, G. E. M., *Intention*, 2nd ed, Oxford: Blackwell, 1979.

Aristotle, *Nicomachean Ethics*, trans. W. D. Ross, various editions. *Politics*, trans. B. Jowett, various editions.

Austin, J., *The Province of Jurisprudence Determined*, London: Weidenfeld & Nicolson, 1954.

Bacon, F., *The New Organon* (1620), New York: Bobbs-Merrill, 1960.

Bentham, J., *Works*, Edinburgh: William Tait, 1843.

Berman, H. J., *Justice in Russia: an Interpretation of Soviet Law*, Cambridge, Mass.: Harvard University Press, 1950.

Bradley, F. H., *Ethical Studies* (1876), Oxford University Press, 1962.

Chernenko, K. U., *The CPSU: Society, Human Rights*, Moscow: Novosti Press Agency, 1981.

Descartes, R. *Philosophical Writings*, E. Anscombe and P.T. Geach (eds), rev. edn, London: Nelson, 1970.

Dowrick, F. E., *Justice According to the English Common Lawyers*, London: Butterworths, 1961.

Doyle, J. F. (ed.), *Educational Judgements*, London: Routledge & Kegan Paul, 1973.

Dworkin, R. *Taking Rights Seriously*, London: Duckworth, 1977. (ed.), *The Philosophy of Law*, Oxford University Press, 1977.

Engels, F., *Anti-Dühring*, London: Lawrence & Wishart, 1955; Moscow: Foreign Languages Publishing House, 1954.

Feinberg, J., *Doing and Deserving*, Princeton University Press, 1970.

Flew, A. (ed.), *Essays on Logic and Language*, First Series, Oxford: Blackwell, 1960.

Fuller, L. L. *The Morality of Law*, rev. edn, New Haven and London: Yale University Press, 1969.

Hart, H. A. L., *The Concept of Law*, Oxford: Clarendon Press, 1961.

Hegel, G. W. F., *The Philosophy of Right* (1821) trans. T. M. Knox, Oxford: University Press, 1942.

Henkin, L., *The Rights of Man Today*, London: Stevens & Sons, 1979.

Hobbes, T., *Leviathan*, Harmondsworth: Penguin, 1968. *Works*, W. Molesworth (ed.), London: John Bohn, 1841.

Hudson, W. D. (ed.), *The Is/Ought Question*, London: Macmillan, 1969.
Humboldt, W., *The Limits of State Action*, J. W. Burrow, ed., Cambridge University Press, 1969.
Hume, D., *A Treatise of Human Nature*, L. A. Selby-Bigge (ed.), Oxford University Press, 1888.
   Essays and Treatises on Several Subjects, London: T. Cadell, 1777.
Jackson, P., *Natural Justice*, London: Sweet & Maxwell, 1979.
Kamenka, E. and Tay A.E-S (eds.), *Human Rights*, Melbourne: Edward Arnold (Aust.), 1978.
   Law and Society, Melbourne: Edward Arnold (Aust.), 1978.
   Justice, London: Edward Arnold, 1979.
Kant, I., *Critique of Practical Reason and Other Works in Ethics*, trans. T. K. Abbott, 6th edn, London: Longmans, 1909.
   Lectures on Ethics, trans. L. Infield, London: Methuen, 1930.
Kelsen, H., *General Theory of Law and State*, Cambridge, Mass.: Harvard University Press, 1946.
   The Pure Theory of Law, Berkeley and Los Angeles: University of California Press, 1967.
Lasok, D. *et al.*, (eds), *Fundamental Duties*, Oxford: Pergamon, 1980.
Llewellyn, K., *The Common Law Tradition*, Boston, Mass.: Little, Brown, 1960.
Lloyd, D., *The Idea of Law*, Harmondsworth: Penguin, 1964.
——,*Introduction to Jurisprudence*, 4th edn, London: Stevens & Sons, 1979.
Locke, J., *Works*, London: Tegg, 1823.
——,*Some Thoughts Concerning Education*, R. H. Quick (ed.), Cambridge University Press, 1898.
Machiavelli, *The Prince, Selections from the Discourses and other Writings*, J. Plamenatz (ed.), London: Collins, 1972.
Mackie, J. *Ethics*, Harmondsworth: Penguin, 1977.
Mannheim, K., *Ideology and Utopia*, London: Routledge & Kegan Paul, 1936.
Marx, K., *Capital*, trans. S. Moore and E. Aveling, London: Allen & Unwin, 1946.
Marx, K. and Engels, F., *Collected Works*, London: Lawrence & Wishart, 1976. (Especially for *The German Ideology* and *Economic and Philosophical Manuscripts*.)
Melden, A. I. (ed.), *Human Rights*, Belmont: Wadsworth Publishing, 1970.
Mill, J. S., *Ethical Writings*, J. B. Schneewind (ed.), London: Collier-Macmillan, 1965.
——, *Inaugural Address*, London: Longman, Green, Reader & Dyer, 1867.
——, *On Liberty*, Harmondsworth: Penguin, 1974.
——, *Utilitarianism, Liberty Representative Government*, H. B. Acton (ed.), London: J. M. Dent, 1972.
——, *Collected Works*, Toronto University Press, 1974.
Montaigne, M., *Works*, trans. W. Hazlitt, London: C. Templeman, 1865.
Moore, G. E., *Principia Ethica*, Cambridge University Press, 1903.
Munro, D. H. (ed.), *A Guide to the British Moralists*, London: Collins, 1972.
Newman, J. H., *Discourses on University Education*, Dublin: James Duffy, 1852.

Nozick, R. *Anarchy, State and Utopia*, Oxford: Blackwell, 1974; New York: Basic Books, 1974.

Paine, T., *Rights of Man* (1791) Secaucus: Citadel Press, 1974.

Perelman, Ch., *The Idea of Justice and the Problem of Argument*, trans. J. Petrie, London: Routledge & Kegan Paul, 1963.

Plato, *The Republic*, various editions, trans. A. D. Lindsay, London: J. M. Dent, 1935.

———, *The Laws*, various editions, trans. J. Saunders. Harmondsworth: Penguin, 1970.

Pound, R., *Introduction to the Philosophy of Law*, New Haven: Yale University Press, 1925.

———, *Social Control Through Law*, New Haven Conn.: Yale University Press, 1942.

Rawls, J., *A Theory of Justice*, Oxford University Press, 1972.

Regan, T. and Singer, P., *Animal Rights and Human Obligations*, Englewood Cliffs: Prentice-Hall, 1976.

Ross, W. D., *The Right and the Good*, Oxford University Press, 1930.

———, *Kant's Ethical Theory*, Oxford University Press, 1954.

Rousseau, J.-J., *Émile*, trans. B. Foxley, London: J. M. Dent, 1911.

———, *The Social Contract*, trans. M. Cranston, Harmondsworth: Penguin, 1968.

Seliger, M., *Ideology and Politics*, London: Allen & Unwin, 1976.

Sidgwick, H., *The Methods of Ethics*, 3rd edn, London: Macmillan, 1884; 7th edn 1907.

Singer, P., *Animal Liberation*, London: Granada, 1977.

Spencer, H., *The Man v the State* (1884), London: Watts & Co., 1909.

Toulmin, S., *Reason in Ethics*, Cambridge University Press, 1960.

Williams, B., *Morality*, Cambridge University Press, 1972.

Subject Index

Author Index